War, Politics and the Irish of Leinster, 1156–1606

War, Politics and the Irish of Leinster, 1156–1606

EMMETT O'BYRNE

FOUR COURTS PRESS

Set in 10.5 pt on 12 pt Bembo by
Carrigboy Typesetting Services, County Cork for
FOUR COURTS PRESS LTD
7 Malpas Street, Dublin 8, Ireland
e-mail: info@four-courts-press.ie
and in North America for
FOUR COURTS PRESS
c/o ISBS, 920 N.E. 58th Avenue, Suite 300, OR 97213.

A catalogue record for this title is available
from the British Library.

ISBN 1–85182–690–4

Printed in England by
MPG Books, Bodmin, Cornwall

Contents

Illustrations

Acknowledgements

This book originated in my long-held interest in the Leinster Irish – particularly the O'Byrnes of East Leinster and the sixteenth-century Fiach O'Byrne. In school I benefited immensely from the diligence of my teachers both at primary level in Glenealy and at secondary level – particularly those who taught me history and classics. I take this occasion to express my gratitude to Mr Karl Carney and Brother John Kavanagh of De La Salle College, Wicklow, and Mr Brian Doyle and Mr Gerry Haugh of St Peter's College, Wexford. In 1992–5 I read archaeology, classics and history at University College Dublin and then moved from Belfield to Trinity to study for an MPhil. At that stage my interests were mainly focused upon the history of Ireland and Europe during the sixteenth and seventeenth centuries. My proposed thesis was to be a study of Fiach O'Byrne. This was to prove harder than I had expected, as I found it increasingly difficult to explain his career without extensive research on his predecessors. The end result was my MPhil thesis of 1996 – 'The origins of the Uí Bhroin and their lordship to 1434'. In late 1996, I called a temporary halt to my studies by going to live in Israel, where I spent much of my time on Kibbutz Ga'aton near the Lebanese border. Due to the security problems along the Lebanese border and the reminder of nearby ruined crusader castle of Yehiam, I gradually became aware of what it was like to live in a frontier society – experience that stood to me in my research on the cultural interfaces that existed on medieval marches of Leinster. I returned to Ireland in late 1997 to begin my PhD thesis, which was completed in early 2001.

Now that the book is published there are many to be thanked. I take this occasion to express my gratitude to all those people who have helped me. Firstly, I would like to express my thanks to Dr Katharine Simms, the supervisor of my PhD thesis, and Dr Seán Duffy for their help. I also wish to thank the Grace Lawless Lee Fund for funding to aid the production of this book. I am also deeply grateful for the support and encouragement of my employer Mr James Maguire, managing editor of the Dictionary of Irish Biography. The contribution of the other staff and students of the Department of Medieval History at Trinity also deserves recognition. Further I extend my gratitude to Professor James Lydon, Professor A.P. Smyth and Professor Robin Frame, who so generously gave of their time to read the original manuscript. They offered sage advice that was gratefully accepted and was acted upon.

I also wish to thank Mr Mark Candon and his staff at St Laurence O'Toole's National School, Seville Place, Dublin. In August 2001, when I needed a job, Mark gave me the post of teacher to 5th Class at 'Larriers'. This school is part of the Department of Education's 'Breaking the Cycle Scheme', serving the youth of Sherrif Street and surrounding areas. I have to say that my nine months teaching in 'Larriers' was a complete eye-opener. There, I saw at first hand the tremendous difficulties that face teachers and students in the inner city. Although 'Larriers' is far from the hallowed halls of academics, my work there was an experience that I will always be grateful for. Those who teach there are the true stars of the Irish education system.

I now take this opportunity to give my thanks to the staffs of the libraries of the Trinity College Dublin, Royal Irish Academy, University Dublin College, the National Library, the National Archives, the Scottish National Library and the British Library. Also I would also like to acknowledge the aid of the former dean of graduate studies at Trinity, J.A.N. Parnell and his staff. I am grateful to many other people, including Michael Adams, Anthony Tierney and Martin Fanning of Four Courts Press, Dr William Nolan of University College Dublin, Dr Ruth Johnston, Steve and Patrica Minton, Eoin Keehan, Ian Cantwell, Darren McGettigan, Dr Ailbe MacShamhráin, Colonel Donal O'Carroll and Neville O'Byrne, my uncle. Also, I extend my gratitude to all the friends I have made through history and the law, as well as those at home in Wicklow. I would like to pay tribute to my parents, and my family including my new nephew, Daniel John Furlong, for their support during these years.

Above all others, I owe the greatest debt to Dr Conor O'Brien of Annacurra, Co. Wicklow, a scholar of note. Throughout this period, he has been my greatest supporter, proof-reader and adviser. At this point, I wish to acknowledge that the contribution of Conor to this book has been immense and dedicate this book to him.

Abbreviations

AFM *Annala ríoghachta Éireann: Annals of the kingdom of Ireland by the Four Masters, from the earliest period to the year 1616.* Ed. J. O'Donovan. 7 vols. Dublin, 1990.

ALC *The annals of Loch Cé: a chronicle of Irish affairs, 1014–1590.* Ed. W.M. Hennessy. 2 vols. London, 1891.

AU *Annala Uladh: Annals of Ulster … 431 to 1541.* Ed. W.M. Hennessy [and B. MacCarthy]. 4 vols. Dublin, 1887–1901.

Account roll of Holy Trinity, Dublin *Account roll of the priory of the Holy Trinity, Dublin, 1337–1346.* Ed. J. Mills. Dublin, 1891.

Alen's Reg. *Calendar of Archbishop Alen's register, c.1172–1534; prepared and edited from the original in the registry of the united dioceses of Dublin and Glendalough and Kildare.* Ed. C. McNeill; index by L. Price. RSAI, Dublin, 1950.

Anal. Hib. *Analecta Hibernica, including the reports of the Irish Manuscripts Commission.* Dublin 1930–.

AClon *The annals of Clonmacnoise, being annals of Ireland from the earliest period A.D. 1408.* Trans. Connell Mageoghagan. Ed. D. Murphy. Dublin, 1896.

AConn *Annala Connacht: the Annals of Connacht, A.D. 1224–1544.* Ed. A.M. Freeman. Dublin, 1944.

AI *The Annals of Inisfallen.* Ed. S. MacAirt. Dublin, 1951.

ATig *The Annals of Tigernach.* Ed. W. Stokes. 2 vols. (Felinfach, 1993).

BL *The Book of Leinster, formerly Lebar na Nuachongbala.* Ed. R.I. Best, O. Bergin, M.A. O'Brien, and A. O'Sullivan. 6 vols. Dublin Institute for Advanced Studies, 1954–83.

Butler Soc. Jn. *Journal of the Butler Society.* Kilkenny, 1968–.

Cal. Carew MSS *Calendar of the Carew manuscripts preserved in the archiepiscopal library at Lambeth.* Ed. J.S. Brewer and W. Bullen. 6 vols. London, 1867–73.

Cal. Gormanston Reg.	*Calendar of the Gormanston Register circa 1175–1397.* Ed. J. Mills and M.J. McEnery. Dublin, 1916.
COD	*Calendar of Ormond deeds, 1172–1603.* Ed. E. Curtis. 6 vols. Dublin, 1932–43.
Cal. papal letters	*Calendar of entries in the papal registers relating to Great Britain and Ireland.* London, 1893–.
Cal. pat. rolls Ire., Hen VIII–Eliz.	*Calendar of the patent and close rolls of chancery in Ireland, Henry VIII to 18th Elizabeth.* Ed. J. Morrin. Dublin, 1863.
Cal. pat rolls Ire., Jas I	*Irish patent rolls of James I: facsimile of the Irish record commissioners' calendar prepared prior to 1830,* with foreword by M.C. Griffith. Dublin, 1966.
CCR	*Calendar of the close rolls … 1272–[1509].* 47 vols. London, 1909–74.
CDI	*Calendar of documents relating to Ireland … , 1171–[1307].* Ed. H.S. Sweetman and G.F. Handcock. 5 vols. London, 1875–76.
CGH	*Corpus Genealogiarum Hiberniae.* Ed. M.A. O'Brien (Dublin, 1962).
Chartul. St Mary's	*Chartularies of St Mary's abbey, Dublin; with the register of its house at Dunbrody, and annals of Ireland.* Ed. J.T. Gilbert. 2 vols. London, 1884.
CS	*Chronicum Scotorum: a chronicle of Irish affairs … to 1135, and supplement … 1141–1150.* Ed. J.T. Gilbert. 2 vols. 1884–6.
CJR	*Calendar of the justiciary rolls … of Ireland.* Ed. James Mills. 2 vols. Dublin, 1905–14. Ed. Herbert Wood and A.E. Langan; revised by M.C. Griffith. Dublin, [1956].
Clyn, *Annals*	*The annals of Ireland by Friar John Clyn and Thady Dowling, together with the annals of Ross.* Ed. Richard Butler. Dublin, 1849.
Civil Survey	*The Civil Survey, A.D. 1654–56.* Ed. R.C. Simington. Dublin, 10 vols. Dublin, 1931–61.
CSPI, 1509–73 (etc.)	*Calendar of the state papers relating to Ireland, 1509–73 (etc.).* (24 vols, London, 1860–1911).
Curtis & McDowell, *Ir. hist. docs*	Edmund Curtis and R.B. McDowell (ed.), *Irish historical documents, 1172–1922.* London, 1968.
Dept. Agric. Jn.	*Eire, Department of Agriculture Journal.* Dublin, 1938.
Dinnseanchas	*Dinnseanchas: journal of An Cumann Logainmneacha.* Dublin, 1964–.
Dowling, *Annals*	*The annals of Ireland by Friar John Clyn and Thady Dowling, together with the annals of Ross.* Ed. Richard Butler. Dublin, 1849.

DKR	*The Deputy Keepers' Rolls*
EHR	*English Historical Review.* London, 1886–.
Expugnatio	Giraldus Cambrensis. *Expugnatio Hibernica: the conquest of Ireland.* Ed. A.B. Scott and F.X. Martin. Dublin, 1978.
Grace	Grace, Jacobus. *Annales Hiberniae.* Ed. R. Butler. Dublin, 1842.
Hist. & mun. doc. Ire.	*Historic and municipal documents of Ireland, 1172–1320.* Ed. J.T. Gilbert. London, 1970.
Hore, *Wexford town*	P.H. Hore, *History of the town and county of Wexford.* 6 vols. London, 1900–11.
Ir. Geneal.	*The Irish Genealogist: official organ of the Irish Genealogical Research Society.* London, 1937–.
Ir. Jurist	*The Irish Jurist, new series.* Dublin, 1966–.
Ir. Sword	*The Irish Sword: the journal of the Military Historical Society of Ireland.* Dublin, 1949.
JRSAI	*Journal of Royal Society of Antiquaries of Ireland.* Dublin, 1892–.
Kildare Arch. Soc. Jn.	*Journal of the County Kildare Archaeological Society.* Dublin, 1891–.
L. & P. Rich III & Hen VII	*Letters and papers illustrative of the reigns of Richard III and Henry VII.* Ed. J. Gairdner, 2 vols. London, 1861–3.
L. & P. Hen VIII	*Letters and papers, foreign and domestic, Henry VIII.* 21 vols. London, 1862–1932.
Louth Arch. Soc. Jn.	*Journal of the County Louth Archaeological Society.* Dundalk, 1904–.
MA	*Miscellaneous Irish annals.* Ed. S. Ó hÍnnse (Dublin, 1947).
Med. relig. houses	A. Gwynn & R.N. Hadcock, *Medieval religious houses Ireland.* London, 1970.
NHI	*A new history of Ireland.* Oxford, 1976–.
NLI	National Library of Ireland.
N. Munster Antiq. Jn.	*North Munster Antiquarian Journal.* Limerick, 1936–.
Peritia	*Peritia: journal of the Medieval Academy of Ireland.* Cork, 1982–.
PRIA	*Proceedings of the Royal Irish Academy.* Dublin, 1836–.
Red Bk Kildare	*The red book of the earls of Kildare.* Ed. G. MacNiocaill. Dublin, 1964.
Red Bk Ormond	*The Red Book of Ormond.* Ed. N.B. White. Dublin, 1932.
Reg. Swayne	*The register of John Swayne.* Ed. D.A. Chart. Belfast, 1935.

Rev. Celt.	*Revue Celtique.* Paris and London, 1870–1921, 41 vols.
RI A	Royal Irish Academy
Riocht na Midhe	*Riocht na Midhe: records of the Meath Archaeological and Historical Society.* Drogheda, 1955–.
Rot. pat. Hib.	*Rotulorum patentium et clausorum cancellarie Hiberniae calendarium.* Ed. E. Tresham. Dublin, 1828.
S.P.Hen. VIII	*State Papers, Henry VIII* (11 vols, London, 1830–32).
Sheedy, *Pontifica Hib.*	M.P. Sheedy (ed.), *Pontifica Hibernica: medieval chancery documents concerning Ireland, 640–1261.* 2 vols. Dublin, 1962–3.
Song of Dermot	*The song of Dermot and the earl.* Ed. G.H. Orpen. Oxford, 1892
Stat. Ire., John-Henry V	*Statutes and ordinances and acts of the parliament of Ireland: King John to Henry V.* Ed. H.F. Berry. Dublin, 1907.
Stat. Ire., Hen VI	*Statutes rolls of the parliament of Ireland, reign of King Henry IV.* Ed. H.F. Berry. Dublin, 1907.
Stat. Ire., 1–12 Edw. IV	*Statutes rolls of the parliament of Ireland, 1st to 12th year of the reign of King Edward IV.* Ed. H.F. Berry. Dublin, 1910.
Stat. Ire., 12–22 Edw. IV	*Statutes rolls of the parliament of Ireland, 12th and 13th to the 21st and 22nd years of the reign of King Henry IV.* Ed. H.F. Berry. Dublin, 1914.
Studia Hib.	*Studia Hibernica.* Dublin, 1961–.

Introduction

War and politics in Leinster have played a defining role in the history of Ireland, but until now there has been no linear political narrative of the Irish of Leinster between 1156 and 1606, partly due to the absence of a specific history of Gaelic Ireland. Students and historians have had to view this period through published histories that focus on how successive English governments sought to extend their authority throughout Ireland. Through the medium of a political and military narrative, this book attempts to trace the history of the Leinster Irish from the death of Toirdhealbhach O'Connor in 1156 to the shiring of Wicklow in 1606.

The neglect of the Leinster Irish originates in a failure to objectively analyze their society; that failure can be traced back to Gerald of Wales' remarkable account of the arrival of English in Ireland during the 1170s. The original English conquerors of Leinster were actively recruited by its deposed and refugee king, Diarmait MacMurrough. Diarmait – ever resourceful – had fled Leinster to Bristol in August 1166 and thence to France in search of Henry II. With Henry's approval, he returned to Bristol to recruit knights to help him reclaim his kingdom. His decision to seek foreign help was a logical and a natural one, and it changed the course of Irish history. Within a few brief years, Diarmait and his mercenaries had, arguably, prevented the emergence of a centralized kingdom of Ireland under the high-kingship of Ruaidhrí O'Connor. With Leinster secure in his grasp, Diarmait dreamt of taking the high-kingship with the help of his English allies. This was not to be, as he died at his capital of Ferns in May 1171 before putting his plans into action. F.J. Byrne has argued that if Diarmait had 'been successful, the name of Diarmait na nGall might yet be revered as that of the true founder of the national monarchy'.[1] But Diarmait's premature death and what followed it has, somewhat unfairly, earned him the vilest place in the history of this land.

It must be said, however, that the English conquest of Leinster also formed part of the great expansionary movement of western European nobles of Frankish descent between the tenth and thirteenth centuries, a period that saw Latin Europe push its frontiers outward, with Frankish aristocrats cutting out

---

1 Byrne, *Irish kings*, p. 274.

lordships and even kingdoms for themselves from Poland to Palestine, across the Iberian peninsula and on to Britain and Ireland. To these new lands, they brought with more than chain mail, charters and coins: they carried with them a world-view that was confident, vibrant and convinced of its cultural supe-riority. The men who landed on the Leinster coast between 1167 and 1171 were representative of their breed, living for conquest, glory and domination. Their superior military technology proved to be as devastating in Ireland as it had earlier been in Wales.[2]

Gerald of Wales, who provided the intellectual justification for the English conquests of Leinster, makes it quite clear that the world the English found there was radically different to their previous experience. In Leinster, to his mind, Latin Europe came face to face with the barbarian. The picture he painted – that of uncivilized society – provided an apologia for their actions. Gerald ascribed barbaric tendencies not only to the ordinary people but to the highest of the Leinster nobility; he describes, for example, how Diarmait MacMurrough allegedly gnawed at the severed head of one of his MacGillapatrick enemies after a battle in Ossory. Such images and the English behaviour that they attempted to absolve contributed to the growth in later middle ages of what Robert Bartlett has termed 'a new biological racism'.[3] Racial prejudice was not, of course, the preserve of the newcomer, as the Irish were well able to express their own intolerance – often in savage reprisals. But Gerald's failure in the twelfth century to comprehend the warrior-dominated society of the Leinster Irish has survived into our time. We find Cyril Falls, for example, describing the sixteenth-century Fiach O'Byrne as little more than 'a simple-minded savage'.[4]

Many of the misconceptions about the Leinstermen arose because of where they dwelt – in mountainous and densely forested regions that have been characterized as the angry world of the Celtic fringe. Usually, our only glimpses of this society in its natural habitat come from accounts of government campaigns; rarely do we get a cogent picture of the world of the Celtic fringe at peace, but there is a nice story from the fourteenth century that tells of how Henry Crystede, an Englishman, was captured by Brin Costerec (probably an O'Byrne warlord),[5] who, instead of treating him harshly, took him to his fortified residence in the Wicklow mountains, where he kept him for seven years, eventually giving him a daughter in marriage; after his eventual release Crystede and his family went to live near Bristol (because of his knowledge of Irish ways, he was appointed by Richard II in 1395 to liaise with the Irish provincial kings during their stay in Dublin). However, reports evidencing this sort of mutual toleration are rare; much more often we are presented with images of conflict such as Shakespeare's 'rough rug-haired kerns, which live like venom, where no venom else' (*Richard II*): witness, for example, the impressive

---

2 Davies, *Domination and conquest*, p. 27.   3 Bartlett, *The making of Europe*, p. 237.   4 Falls, *Elizabeth's Irish wars*, p. 199.   5 *Froissart's chronicles*, pp 409–16. Brin is usually a corruption of Braen, the traditional O'Byrne forename. Costerec seems to be a corruption of 'the victorious'.

and hostile figure of Art Mór MacMurrough, who parleyed with Richard II's army in summer 1399.[6]

Great advances have been made over the past thirty years in the study of Gaelic Ireland through the work of such scholars as Kenneth Nicholls, Katherine Simms and A.P. Smyth. Dr Simms' unpublished doctoral thesis 'Gaelic lordships in Ulster in the middle ages' (1976) remains the only major study focusing upon the Irish in the latter medieval and early modern periods; with regard to Leinster, we know now more about the province and its kings before 1156 than we do for the middle ages or the early modern period, thanks largely to the work of A.P. Smyth, F.J. Byrne, Donnchadh Ó Corrain, Ailbhe MacShamhráin and Colman Etchingham.

My study of the Leinster Irish between 1156 and 1606 encountered the problems involved in any study of Gaelic Ireland, the greatest single one being the fragmented nature of the sources. As Katharine Simms points out, the staple diet of any student of Gaelic Ireland are the annals.[7] To the uninitiated eye, these sources are a jumble of births, deaths, plagues, battles and marriages. But if viewed from regional and dynastic perspectives, they are laden with continuities, allowing the historian to track the activities of a dynasty and its leading figures over long periods of time. That exercise reveals things not previously noted. For example, the annals are the best indicators of political alliances in Gaelic Ireland, for they are full of references to marriage, gossiprid and fosterage; by following a line through time, one is able to see who were the natural allies and rivals of a particular dynasty.

The major problem confronting the historian of the Irish of Leinster is the absence of a set of annals devoted to the politics of Leinster as such. Consequently, we are forced to rely upon fragments from annals compiled in distant Irish territories for information relating to Leinster lordships and their nobles. The annals, together with genealogical studies of particular Leinster dynasties, English chronicles and government accounts, combine to tell us quite a lot about the political dynamics of the Leinstermen; individual dynastic case studies help us to see how a dynasty interacted with its Irish neighbours within a particular region and to construct a political narrative. Moreover, a very helpful way to track the pattern of war and politics in Leinster is to adopt the geopolitical approach used by Professor A.P. Smyth in his pioneering book *Celtic Leinster*.[8] The over-kingdom of Leinster, he shows, consisted of two regions, which reflected its traditional division between the royal Leinster dynasties of the Uí Dúnlainge and the Uí Cheinnselaig. These regions were known as Laigin Tuathgabhair (North Leinster) and Laigin Desgabhair (South Leinster).[9] With the arrival of the English and the subsequent reconfiguration of the area after 1171, it makes more sense to distinguish two regions – which we will call East and West Leinster.

6 Webb, 'The deposition of King Richard II', 39–43.   7 Simms, *From kings to warlords*, p. 3.
8 Smyth, *Celtic Leinster*, pp 3, 17.   9 Byrne, *Irish kings*, p. 130.

East Leinster was a well-defined political and territorial unit, reflecting the over-kingship of the kings of Uí Cheinnselaig and their MacMurrough descendants. It stretched through the modern counties of Wexford, Carlow and Wicklow to Dublin. In the middle ages, its border with West Leinster was formed by the strategic Barrow valley. (It can be argued that the imposition of English settlement along that vital artery actually preserved and accentuated the division between West Leinster and East Leinster.) East Leinster was bounded on one side by the Irish Sea; it could be argued that, because of its geographical location, it was somewhat isolated from the rest of Ireland, having more in common with parts of Wales than with Connacht or Ulster. This point has been made by Dr Seán Duffy in his 1993 doctoral thesis 'Ireland and the Irish Sea region', which identifies many social connections between Wales and Leinster, in particular the troubles in both lands during 1282 and 1295.

West Leinster formed part of the wider region of the midlands, a hotly disputed region regularly subject to the ambitions of those seeking to impose themselves upon the island.[10] A.P. Smyth in *Celtic Leinster* placed considerable emphasis upon the midland landscape and its passes;[11] using literature, historical accounts and maps, he illustrated that the physical features of the midlands changed little until the seventeenth century.[12] His work demolished the perception that this region was just wilderness. Of great importance was his identification of what he termed the 'midland corridor', lying on the eastern bank of the middle Shannon basin, running north-south from modern Westmeath for about twenty miles to Birr on the fringes of Munster.[13] Smyth's identification of the significance of this corridor and of the region's passes was not disputed by Nicholls in his review article, 'Land of the Leinstermen'.[14] And Smyth's thesis was further complemented by George Cunningham's 1987 book, *The Anglo-Norman advance into the south-west midlands of Ireland, 1185–1221*.[15] In a sense, this region with its interconnecting passes and routeways helped to facilitate warfare throughout the island, making Leinster one of the most contested regions in Western Europe between 1156 and 1606.

10 Ibid., pp 133–4, 144–5.   11 Smyth, *Celtic Leinster*, pp 69, 70, 75, 86.   12 Ibid., p. 76. 13 Ibid., p. 86.   14 Nicholls, 'Land of the Leinstermen'.   15 Cunningham, *The Anglo-Norman advance*, pp 39–47, 170–3.

CHAPTER I

The kings of Leinster in an age of
conflict and change, 1156–80

The death in May 1156 of Toirdhealbhach O'Connor, king of Connacht and
high-king of Ireland, was a decisive turning point in the history of Leinster.
Throughout his career, Toirdhealbhach sought to forge a kingdom of Ireland
under his suzerainty. In this endeavour, he modelled his view of Ireland on the
careers of previous high-kings; and he must have learned much from those of
Toirdhealbhach O'Brien and Muircheartach O'Brien of Thomond, his maternal
grandfather and uncle, for he cannot but have observed how they built their
successive high-kingships upon control of Leinster and its kings. The advance of
the O'Briens of Thomond from Munster into Leinster resulted from the
weakness of the Uí Dúnlainge and Uí Cheinnselaig – its two competing royal
dynasties; and it was especially facilitated by the victory in 1072 of Conchobhar
O'Melaghlin, king of Meath, over Diarmait mac Máel na mBó, the Uí
Cheinnselaig king of Leinster from whose son Murchadh the MacMurroughs
took their name. The defeat of Diarmait left the province disorientated and
defenceless and removed its kings from the race for the high-kingship, reducing
Leinster to the level of a client state. The rising power of the O'Connors of
Connacht along the Shannon and its hinterland had resulted in a series of wars
with the O'Briens in the 1080s and the 1090s (the importance placed by the
O'Briens on their suzerainty over Leinster – particularly the part of it lying in
the midlands – was evidenced by the severity of their response to threats to their
dominance there). The present chapter, focusing on events between 1156 and
1180, shows how Toirdhealbhach O'Connor's son Ruaidhrí attempted to build a
centralized kingdom of Ireland, and the part played by Diarmait MacMurrough's
Leinster in this process. It also discusses the early days of the English in Leinster,
and charts the course of Leinster's political and military history, with special
reference to the settlers' relationships with the local nobility.

Toirdhealbhach O'Connor's death meant that war was unavoidable between
Connacht and his rival Muircheartach O'Loughlin – king of the northern Uí Neill
since 1136 (with one interval between 1143 and 1145). On, learning of Toirdhealbhach's death, O'Loughlin seized the initiative and marched into Leinster, took
hostages from Diarmait MacMurrough,[1] subdued the MacGillapatrick king of

---

1 Ó Corrain, *Ireland before the Normans*, pp 163–4.

Ossory and burnt Durrow. The first clash between Connacht and O'Loughlin came in Meath, where the old enmity between MacMurrough and Tigernán O'Rourke of Bréifne surfaced, with the Leinsterman emerging victorious.[2]

Like Toirdhealbhach and earlier high-kings, Muircheartach O'Loughlin saw West Leinster as a critical battleground; there, he and Ruaidhrí O'Connor would each strive to impose his own clients and topple his opponent's. This intrusion of O'Loughlin influence into central Ireland forced Ruaidhrí to respond. In 1157 O'Loughlin was back in the midlands to depose and raise kings throughout Meath, Leinster and Munster (it was Ruaidhrí's clients who felt the full brunt of this, as evidenced by the flight of rulers of Laois and Ossory to Connacht).[3] O'Loughlin completed his circuit by taking the pledges of Munster and dividing it between Conchobhar O'Brien of Thomond and Diarmait MacCarthy of Desmond. Secure by now as king of Connacht, Ruaidhrí consolidated his foothold in west Meath before attacking Tyrone. Then, moving with the speed that characterized his campaigns, he swept into Munster to reverse O'Loughlin's work.[4] He was to prove himself a skilful intriguer: in 1158 he briefly reimposed his midland suzerainty by marching as far east as Leighlin in Uí Cheinnselaig, exacting hostages from Ossory, and carrying Macraith O'More of Laois over the Shannon to captivity; as a parting shot, he encouraged the successful deposition of Donnchadh O'Melaghlin of Meath by the O'Kearys of Carbury and the Tethbae, and oversaw the installation of Diarmait O'Melaghlin before burning O'Loughlin's northern coast.[5]

The following year, 1159, Ruaidhrí attempted to follow up his success; drawing support from the O'Briens of Thomond and Tigernán O'Rourke of Bréifne, he challenged O'Loughlin to battle at Ardee in Louth, but O'Loughlin inflicted a crushing defeat on him, forcing him back over the Shannon.[6] With the aid of Diarmuit MacMurrough, O'Loughlin then wreaked vengeance on supporters of Ruaidhrí in West Leinster, deposing several O'Connor clients – including the king of Uí Fáeláin (who seems to have been Fáelán, the half-brother of Domhnall MacFháeláin, Toirdhealbhach O'Connor's puppet king of Leinster in the late 1120s).[7] As a reward for his service, O'Loughlin invested MacMurrough with Uí Fáeláin and confirmed his provincial kingship. He proceeded to invade Connacht, burning several fortresses. Faced by this onslaught, Ruaidhrí proved how formidable he could be when, fighting on home ground, he forced O'Loughlin to retire disappointed.[8]

In Ruaidhrí O'Connor's attempts to reassert the power of Connacht in the midlands and West Leinster, two purposes stand out: he was concerned to counter the turmoil caused by O'Loughlin's manoeuvring on Connacht's troubled eastern frontier, and he plainly sought to consummate his father's old policy of fusing Connacht and the midlands into one geopolitical region.[9] He

---

2 ATig, AFM, 1156.   3 ATig, AFM, 1157.   4 AFM, 1157.   5 AFM, AClon, 1158.   6 ATig, AFM, 1159.   7 AU, ALC, 1127; O'Byrne, 'The Uí Bhroin of Co. Wicklow', pp 23–4, 95; ATig, AFM, 1159; CGH, p. 13.   8 AFM, ATig, 1159.   9 AU, 1129.

emulated his father by improving existing fortifications, building new chains of Irish castles stretching from the western seaboard of Connacht to the Shannon, and throwing new bridges over that artery. In 1161 he crossed again into the midlands seeking to detach the Uí Dúnlainge kingdoms of West Leinster from MacMurrough's provincial kingdom.[10] Aiding him were many Leinster exiles, including Fáelán MacFháeláin of Uí Fáeláin and Máelsechlainn O'Connor Faly of Offaly. After a successful campaign through Meath, Ruaidhrí took hostages from Offaly and Uí Fáeláin. In spite of this success, O'Loughlin was able to force Ruaidhrí to do him homage in Tethbae.[11] Still, Ruaidhrí's Leinster campaign paid off, for both Máelsechlainn and Fáelán were left as rulers of their kingdoms – which suggests that Ruaidhrí and O'Loughlin reached agreement on this. As the price of their restoration, these princes, even though they were O'Connor clients, recognized MacMurrough's overlordship. O'Loughlin's acknowledgment of the advance of Connacht into the midlands forced MacMurrough to adapt. This he did by focusing his attention on Uí Fáeláin and by taking Fáelán's son hostage. Moreover, he also seemingly maintained the Mac Con Lothair dynasty as a check upon the Uí Fáeláin king.[12] In Offaly, evidence suggests that MacMurrough tried to contain Ruaidhrí's client Máelsechlainn O'Connor Faly by using the O'Dempseys against him; and, to the south of Offaly, he used the Uí Chremthannain of Dunamase to check their O'More overlords and replaced the neighbouring rulers of Uí Buidhe with his own protégés. Moreover, while in Ossory, he tried to intrude his foster family, the O'Keallys, at the expense of the MacGillapatricks.[13]

The events of 1161 really created two distinct political zones in Leinster. The midlands and West Leinster, despite MacMurrough's nominal suzerainty, were increasingly under the sway of Connacht, while in eastern Meath and East Leinster the O'Loughlin/MacMurrough axis remained firmly embedded. Far from settling down, provincial politics ebbed and flowed as each side struggled for the upper hand. The year 1162 opened with O'Loughlin and MacMurrough consolidating their hold on East Leinster and Ostman Dublin. To the west, Ruaidhrí engaged in a similar enterprise, forcing Diarmait O'Melaghlin of Meath to give five score ounces of gold in tribute for west Meath.[14] This sparring resulted in constant friction between these two spheres, a process at times resembling a political game of musical chairs. For instance, in 1163, the Meathmen deposed Diarmait O'Melaghlin and did homage to Muircheartach O'Loughlin, but Ruaidhrí forcibly reinstalled him two years later.[15] The annalistic evidence of these years shows Ruaidhrí eroding O'Loughlin's power in the southern half of Ireland – twice subduing Munster between 1164 and 1165, burning as far as Dublin in 1164, and razing Meath and neighbouring Carbury in 1165.[16]

10 Ó Cléirigh, 'The impact of the Anglo-Normans in Laois', p. 164.　11 ATig, AFM, AU, 1161.　12 Nicholls, 'Mediaeval Irish dynasties', pp 414–15.　13 Ó Cléirigh, 'The impact of the Anglo-Normans in Laois', p. 164.　14 AFM, 1162.　15 ATig, 1163, 1165.　16 ATig, AFM, 1165; MA, 1164.

Diarmait MacMurrough watched Ruaidhrí's rise with apprehension. In 1166 the storm broke out, unleashed by O'Loughlin's blinding of Eochaidh MacDunleavy of Ulaid, the foster-son of Donnchadh O'Carroll of Oriel (O'Loughlin's leading vassal). This started a chain of events that demolished MacMurrough's kingship of Leinster. An indignant O'Carroll repaired to Connacht, where he gave his allegiance to Ruaidhrí. Realizing his time had come, Ruaidhrí marched on Dublin and was acknowledged as high-king. Deep inside O'Loughlin's sphere at Drogheda, Ruaidhrí took O'Carroll's submission, but instead of moving to attack O'Loughlin, he first dealt with MacMurrough, drumming up support among the Uí Dúnlainge of West Leinster, where he took the homage of Fáelán MacFháeláin of Uí Fáeláin and the O'Connor Falys of Offaly – MacMurrough's natural enemies. This signalled the rebellion of West Leinster against MacMurrough and an invasion of Uí Cheinnselaig. Caught up in the sheer momentum of events, MacMurrough set his capital, Ferns, aflame and took to the field, but in the face of overwhelming odds, he had to submit to Ruaidhrí. Having corralled MacMurrough, Ruaidhrí's army marched to Donegal to ensure that its lords did not go to the aid of O'Loughlin. Thereafter the collapse of O'Loughlin's power base in Ulster was rapid; Ruaidhrí's allies closed for the kill, hunting down and killing O'Loughlin in Tyrone.

In Ruaidhrí's absence, MacMurrough attempted to reassert himself by arranging the killing of MacGiollamocholmóc, the recalcitrant lord of the Wicklow/Dublin territory of Uí Briúin Chualann. This act, along with O'Loughlin's demise, weakened still further MacMurrough's grip on Leinster as did the second Uí Dúnlainge revolt. The O'Connor Falys and Fáelán, perhaps nervous of MacMurrough's revival, gave pledges to Ruaidhrí's lieutenant, Diarmait O'Melaghlin of Meath, and, along with the Dublin Ostmen and O'Rourke, they marched into Uí Cheinnselaig. In response, MacMurrough executed his hostage, the son of Fáelán, as well as hostages that Domhnall MacGillapatrick of North Ossory had given him earlier.[17] At this critical point MacMurrough's brother, Murchadh MacMurrough, along with the second Uí Fáeláin lord, Murchadh O'Byrne, deserted him. The almost contemporary chanson de geste known commonly as *The song of Dermot and the earl* recounts how a desperate MacMurrough disguised as an Augustinian pleaded with O'Byrne to aid him, but O'Byrne ejected him from his house, breaking decisively with him.[18] Abandoned and betrayed, MacMurrough fled in search of Henry II of England (1166). The Uí Dúnlainge revolt appeared to have paid off: Uí Cheinnselaig was divided between Murchadh MacMurrough and one of the two MacGillapatrick kings of Ossory.[19] Before the close of the year, Ruaidhrí at Athlone rewarded all those of his clients who had played decisive roles in his

17 ATig, AFM, AI, 1166.   18 *Song of Dermot*, pp 12–17, 46–7, 158–9; Butler and Bernard, 'The charters of the abbey of Duiske', p. 5; Nicholls, 'Crioch Branach', p. 10; AFM, 1166.   19 ATig, 1166. For the MacGillapatrick kings of Ossory, see Carrigan, *History and antiquities of the diocese of Ossory*, i, pp 57-68.

capture of the high-kingship; these included Fáelán, who was given a stipend of twelve score cows, and the MacGillapatrick kings of North and South Ossory.[20]

Like every high-king before him, Ruaidhrí had to contend with the ambitions of the provincial kings, particularly the O'Loughlins. He was determined to rule these disparate kingdoms by campaigning throughout Ireland. In 1167 he took further steps towards the achievement of effective royal government by presiding over a quasi-national synod at Athboy in Meath, a secular and ecclesiastical convention attended by princes and churchmen, including the Leinsterman Donnchadh MacFhéaláin and 2,000 followers.[21] Later that year, with a bevy of sub-kings including Uí Dúnlainge princes, Ruaidhrí destroyed O'Loughlin resistance, forcing them to share Tyrone with the O'Neills. But Ruaidhrí's ambitions for his kingship were now to be thwarted by the reappearance of Diarmait MacMurrough. In August 1167, MacMurrough eventually returned from aboard, bringing English troops; he quickly re-established himself by reconquering Uí Cheinnselaig and deposing his estranged brother, Murchadh.[22] Ruaidhrí and Diarmait O'Melaghlin of Meath, probably with the aid of the Uí Dúnlainge, reacted quickly by invading Uí Cheinnselaig and forcing MacMurrough to submit. Ruaidhrí seemed confident that he could restrain MacMurrough; he clearly felt secure: witness his celebration of the fair of Tailtiu in 1168, an act proclaiming his dominance throughout the island.[23]

Meanwhile, in the kingdoms lying on the fringes of Connacht, a rash of succession disputes broke out. In Thomond, Muircheartach O'Brien, the Connacht-sponsored ruler and Ruaidhrí's half-brother, was assassinated; he was succeeded by his brothers, Domhnall O'Brien of Thomond and Brian O'Brien of Ormond. Domhnall (a son-in-law of MacMurrough, no less) then blinded Brian and went onto annex Ormond.[24] Even more alarming for Ruaidhrí O'Connor was a political crisis developing in Meath, where Diarmait O'Melaghlin publicly disobeyed him by executing a dissident who was under O'Connor protection. Even though O'Melaghlin gave Ruaidhrí the man's honour price, the trouble did not stop there, for, angered at O'Melaghlin's payment of the fine, the Meathmen deposed him; and Ruaidhrí's troops sent to restore him were routed by Art O'Melaghlin. At the close of 1168, though, Ruaidhrí still dominated the country: witness the attendance at his convention at Athlone. From there he travelled into Munster (dividing it between Domhnall O'Brien of Thomond and Diarmait MacCarthy of Desmond), accepted compensation for the death of Muircheartach O'Brien and took the submission of the kings of Tyrone.[25]

In May 1169 Diarmait MacMurrough's long-expected second wave of English troops landed, and he began his challenge to Ruaidhrí's high-kingship by taking Ostman Wexford. This began a chain of events in Meath and West

20 ATig, 1166. **21** AFM, 1167. **22** AI, 1167. **23** ATig, 1168. The same apparent lack of concern is inscribed in the pages of the virtual O'Connor court chronicle, 'wealth and abundance of every good thing bestowed by God on the kingship of Ruaidhrí O'Connor'. **24** AI, 1168. **25** AFM, AU, 1168.

Leinster. In Meath, Ruaidhrí's lieutenant, Diarmait O'Melaghlin, was cut down by his nephew, Domhnall O'Melaghlin of Bregia, who proceeded to establish himself as king of eastern Meath.[26] To prevent further deterioration of equilibrium there, Ruaidhrí then expelled Domhnall O'Melaghlin, kept west Meath for himself, and gave the east to Tigernán O'Rourke.[27] But as Ruaidhrí plugged one leak, others appeared. MacMurrough, well aware of the strategic importance of West Leinster, attacked Ruaidhrí's clients, particularly his deadly enemies, the MacGillapatrick kings of North and South Ossory. He had, of course, scores to settle with Domhnall son of Donnchadh MacGillapatrick of North Ossory, who had blinded his son Enna MacMurrough.[28] MacMurrough and the English tore into Ossory. The MacGillapatrick kingdom of South Ossory apparently collapsed, but once the chase reached the more defensible landscape of North Ossory, MacGillapatrick resistance stiffened considerably and the fighting proved harder and bloodier than anticipated. Here for the first time the contrasting styles of Irish warfare and that of Latin Europe clashed in a major confrontation. Bested in Ossory's forested hills by the tactics and traps of MacGillapatrick, the English cavalry then feigned flight and drew the Irish out into the plains, slaughtering them.[29] In that instant, warfare changed forever in Ireland.

MacMurrough then turned north and began his revenge upon the rebellious Uí Dúnlainge. In a horrifically brutal campaign, he pulverized his enemies. The kingdoms of Uí Fáeláin and Uí Muiredaig, headed up by Fáelán MacFháeláin and Giolla Chomghaill O'Toole respectively, were devastated.[30] After this, Dublin meekly submitted. Not content with this success, MacMurrough then ministered another dose to Domhnall MacGillapatrick of North Ossory. This provoked the high-king into action; but after some sparring away in the forests of Uí Cheinnselaig, Ruaidhrí's confidence melted. Avoiding a trial of arms, he dispatched clerics to treat with the Leinster king. They found him receptive and struck a deal which confirmed MacMurrough as king of Leinster in return for his recognition of Ruaidhrí's high-kingship; the English were to be sent home; MacMurrough's last legitimate son, Conchobhar, was taken by Ruaidhrí as a hostage and to him was promised one of Ruaidhrí's daughters.[31] Satisfied with these arrangements, Ruaidhrí departed.

MacMurrough had no intention of keeping his word. With a further supply of English troops (*c.*May 1170), he again harassed Ruaidhrí's supporters in the midlands. Ossory was ravaged, and there were upheavals in Meath – probably evidence of MacMurrough involvement. Before the summer of 1170, MacMurrough dispatched English troops to aid Domhnall O'Brien of Thomond (his son-in-law), further distracting Ruaidhrí's attention from Leinster. Ruaidhrí marched into Thomond, but O'Brien and the English forced him out and eastwards over the

26 AU, 1169. Among the accomplices of this Domhnall of Bregia was the O'Kelly dynast, Donnchadh Ceinnselach, who was fostered in Uí Cheinnselaig. 27 AFM, 1169. 28 ATig, 1168; MA, 1167. 29 ATig, 1169; *Expugnatio*, pp 36–7. 30 *Song of Dermot*, pp 66–9. 31 Martin, 'Allies and an overlord, 1169–72', pp 69–7; ATig, AFM, 1169; MA, 1167.

Shannon.[32] Undeterred, he then wasted Ormond (O'Brien territory) and split the O'Brien over-kingdom by knocking down Killaloe bridge.[33]

By late August 1170, MacMurrough's campaign was boosted by the arrival of two English fleets. Richard fitzGilbert de Clare, earl of Pembroke and Strigul, better known as Strongbow, landed on 23 August 1170; Waterford fell to the English and MacMurrough two days later and, amidst the ruins, Strongbow married MacMurrough's daughter Aoife before setting out for Dublin. Hasculf MacTurkill, the Ostman king of Dublin, appealed to the high-king, who hastened to his aid.[34] Spies informed MacMurrough of Ruaidhrí's plans; moreover, he had a plan of his own: he led his army northward into the Wicklow wilderness, bypassing Ruaidhrí's at Clondalkin by cutting through the mountains to reach Dublin. The Ostman king, judging that MacMurrough had bested Ruaidhrí, entered into secret negotiations with MacMurrough (in doing so, he played into MacMurrough's hands, falling for his game of divide and rule). Aware of this double-cross, Ruaidhrí prudently withdrew his army from the hinterland of the city. While MacMurrough and the Ostmen continued their negotiations for the submission of Dublin, Raymond le Gros and Miles de Cogan with a force of impetuous knights repaid the Ostmen in their own treacherous coin by seizing the city on 21 September 1170; MacTurkill escaped to the Western Isles, to fight another day.[35]

Ruaidhrí's withdrawal left MacMurrough in control of virtually all East Leinster; it also removed the screen that protected his clients in West Leinster. There MacMurrough struck at the nerve centre of Ruaidhrí's high-kingship. The impact of English cavalry forced Fáelán MacFháeláin and Domhnall MacGillapatrick of North Ossory to flee to Connacht.[36] MacMurrough and Strongbow then proceeded to flay Meath, where they were joined by the rebel Domhnall O'Melaghlin of Bregia, who submitted to them. O'Rourke's kingdom of Bréifne and neighbouring Oriel were also devastated. Even Ruaidhrí's hold on west Meath was endangered, for Art O'Melaghlin, Domhnall of Bregia's half-brother, declared himself king.[37] Control of the midlands was the cornerstone of any high-king's authority, as Ruaidhrí was all too well aware; now, with MacMurrough rampant and the high-kingship in crisis, this fact was graphically illustrated when Ruaidhrí was forced to execute the son and grandson of MacMurrough (hostages in his keeping), his father-in-law O'Rourke having made this a condition of continued fealty. Ruaidhrí and the Irish kings in general were now so alarmed that they dispatched a delegation to Henry II of England seeking his protection from Strongbow.

Despite the scale of MacMurrough's and Strongbow's inroads, Ruaidhrí recovered, but he and his vassals were unable to take full advantage of the turning tide. For example, in early 1171, Diarmait MacCarthy of Desmond

---

32 Ibid., p. 72.   **33** ATig, 1170.   **34** Martin, 'Allies and an overlord, 1169–72', p. 77.
35 AFM, 1170; *Expugnatio*, p. 67.   **36** ATig, AFM, 1170.   **37** ATig, 1170.

inflicted a series of defeats upon the newcomers, penning them in Waterford; Ruaidhrí, who was keen to march to support MacCarthy, was prevented by the continuing O'Brien rebellion. However, on the Shannon, the high-king was still supreme, and he used his naval superiority to force O'Brien's submission by mid-year.

In May 1171, Diarmait MacMurrough suddenly died. Sometime that summer, MacTurkill returned from the Western Isles, bringing a fleet with him; after a brave fight he was routed and executed.[38] On top of this, MacMurrough's successors were confronted by a Leinster rebellion led by his disgruntled brother, Murchadh MacMurrough, Archbishop Lorcán O'Toole and the Uí Dúnlainge, including Fáelán MacFháeláin, Murchadh O'Byrne and the O'Tooles. These regained control over much of East Leinster; forcing Domhnall MacMurrough-Kavanagh of Uí Cheinnselaig to flee to Strongbow at Dublin. (Domhnall's succession to the Uí Cheinnselaig kingship had been opposed by Murchadh MacMurrough, who claimed it under Irish law; Murchadh also refused to acknowledge Strongbow as Diarmait MacMurrough's successor in Leinster.) With Leinster up in arms, Ruaidhrí now struck at Strongbow. Through August and September 1171, he besieged Dublin and reduced it to desperate straits. With success within his grasp, he dictated terms of a peace: Strongbow could retain the Ostman towns of Dublin, Wexford and Waterford, but nothing more.

Ruaidhrí's confidence was such that he now divided his army. According to the Irish annals, he left a large contingent at Castleknock to contain the English at Dublin city, and moved off to rendezvous with his Leinster allies, who were maintaining the blockade south of the city. He also led an expedition inland to punish those still sympathetic to the family of Diarmait MacMurrough and their English allies, while he dispatched the calvary of Bréifne and Oriel to burn the cornfields of the English near Dublin. The weakening of the Irish vice around Dublin proved to be Strongbow's opportunity and Ruaidhrí's undoing. With conditions now desperate within the city, Strongbow, rather than accept Ruaidhrí's terms, ordered Miles de Cogan and Raymond le Gros to join him in an attack upon the O'Connor army at Castleknock. Twilight was falling as English knights descended on the unprepared Irish camp, slaughtering them in their hundreds and breaking the siege. Ruaidhrí's presence at the rout is disputed. The Irish sources say that he was still away campaigning in Leinster, while *The song* makes no specific reference to his presence at the camp during the attack. Only Gerald of Wales states that Ruaidhrí was there; he claims that Ruaidhrí was having a bath when Strongbow's riders thundered into his camp, and that he escaped through the slaughter in his pelt.[39] Be that as it may, Ruaidhrí's high-kingship of Ireland had suffered an irreversible setback.

The English conquest had regained the upper hand; still, subduing those Leinster nobles opposed to Strongbow proved a bloody business. Even Gerald of

38 ATig, 1171; *Expugnatio*, pp 76–9.   **39** ATig, AFM, 1171; *Expugnatio*, p. 83.

Wales baulked at the loss of life that followed, remarking about 'new and blood-stained acquisition of land, secured at the cost of great bloodshed and the slaughter of a Christian people. But it is common knowledge that this last-mentioned failing has been shared by almost all our soldiers in Ireland from their first arrival there to the present day – which makes it all the more amazing and all the more deplorable'. Crucial to the subjection of Leinster was Strongbow's cultivation of his image as the conqueror: witness the English devastation of Uí Fáeláin and their widepread plundering of ecclesiastical foundations on the Leinster plains.[40] As Bartlett and Davies point out, this sort of strategy demanded acts of brutality designed to create a psychology of inferiority and dependence among those resisting conquest. In Leinster, examples were made of Irish leaders who resisted: in early 1172 Murchadh MacMurrough (the brother of Diarmait MacMurrough and king of Uí Cheinnselaig) was killed by the troops of Henry II, but Strongbow reserved his worst for Murchadh O'Byrne – Diarmait MacMurrough's deadly enemy. After capturing O'Byrne and his son in 1172, Strongbow conveyed them to the MacMurrough capital of Ferns for public execution and, in a carefully calculated act, fed their bodies to his hounds, sending a brutally effective message to the Leinster nobility.[41] This did not end the war, for Murchadh MacMurrough's son, Muircheartach, burnt Ferns; but, according to *The song*, Strongbow and Muircheartach later agreed a settlement whereby Strongbow recognized him as king of Uí Cheinnselaig, while Domhnall MacMurrough-Kavanagh, the other claimant to the title, was appointed seneschal of the Irish of Leinster.[42] Bereft of Ruaidhrí's protection, many of the Uí Dúnlainge, acknowledging the political reality, welcomed the arrival in Ireland of Henry II in autumn 1171. Because Henry II was eager to brake the ambitions of Strongbow, a throng of Irish princes scrambled to avail themselves of his protection – notably Fáelán MacFháeláin and the O'Tooles. However, the political pragmatism of these figures didn't save them, for Henry confirmed Leinster to Strongbow after his submission and granted its sub-kingdoms to English adventurers.[43]

From 1172 onwards, the English consolidated their hold on East Leinster, establishing working relationships with Irish leaders in the more inaccessible parts of that region. By encouraging these leaders to acknowledge a loose framework of obedience, the English began to draw them steadily into the feudal net. Outside East Leinster, the traditional heartland of the MacMurrough provincial kingship, a desperate struggle was emerging. One reason for this was that the English conquest of the eastern midlands threatened the *Lebensraum* of the Irish provincial kings. In these vital midland passes that led deeper into the O'Connor, MacCarthy and O'Brien kingdoms, the real battle for countrywide dominance was to be fought. By withdrawing to a highly defensible landscape

---

40 *Expugnatio*, pp 156–7; AFM, 1171.   **41** Bartlett, *The making of Europe*, pp 85–6; Davies, *Domination and conquest*, p. 51; AU, 1172; *Song of Dermot*, pp 158.   **42** *Expugnatio*, pp 170–3; *Song of Dermot*, p. 161.   **43** Ibid., pp 94–5; Flanagan, 'Henry II and the kingdom of Uí Fáeláin', p. 233.

of dense forest and mountain, Irish kings were enabled to attack English armies in terrain that rendered their heavy cavalry useless. An instance of this landscape-driven warfare in Leinster is Strongbow's offensive against the Irish of Offaly during 1172: after being mauled by Cú Aifne O'Connor Faly in Offaly's interior, Strongbow ordered a withdrawal to Kildare; this became a messy affair, for Diarmait O'Dempsey of Clanmaliere used the topography to savage the English rearguard as it passed through a valley. Another incident from 1171–2 shows the Leinster Irish attempting unsuccessfully to trap Strongbow in the pass of Idrone.[44]

Despite the success of English attacks on the O'Farrells of Annaly in 1172, the inhospitable character of midland topography was certainly an obstacle to colonization. One way they managed to stabilize their foothold in the midlands was by exploiting rivalries within Irish dynasties; this usually resulted in an Irish leader acknowledging English overlordship – a sort of political subjection that could stabilize and formalize the position of the Irish leader through the protection it conferred. Intermarriage, another element in the strategy of subjection, it could bring benefits to both the Irish and English parties.

Because heavy cavalry could not always master the rigours of the land; the English resorted to their favourite instrument of conquest – the castle. Castles positioned in strategic passes and river valleys proved the most potent weapon to prevent the interaction of Irish of different regions. From the late 1170s the feudal noose began to tighten around the necks of Irish midland kings, dispelling any myth of co-existence. This policy involved the expropriation by the English of Irish land, causing powerful feelings of anger and racial antagonism. The Irish quickly began to see English settlers as disturbers of the natural order of regional polity; this led to the most destructive element of Irish warfare – settlement eradication.

Strongbow's grip on Leinster remained tenuous. Dissent was rising among the provincial nobility, especially those of Uí Cheinnselaig. During Henry II's visit to Ireland of 1171–2, Domhnall MacMurrough-Kavanagh and the Leinster nobility submitted before him at Dublin. According to the Annals of Tigernach, Henry II then assumed the kingship of Leinster (this may have offended Domhnall MacMurrough-Kavanagh).[45] Muircheartach MacMurrough, king of Uí Cheinnselaig, showed his satisfaction with Strongbow's settlement of the MacMurrough succession by visiting Winchester with the burgesses of Wexford at Henry II's expense between 1172 and 1173.[46] Early in 1173, both Domhnall MacMurrough-Kavanagh and Muircheartach campaigned with Strongbow in

---

44 O'Conor, *The archaeology of medieval rural settlement in Ireland*, pp 98–9; *Song of Dermot*, pp 202–5. On another occasion, the compiler of the *Song of Dermot* captures English discomfort at their inability to bring their cavalry to bear upon the nimble Irish. See ibid., pp 50–1: 'Lords barons all, Let us pass through this valley promptly so that we may be on the hill on the hard field and in open ground.' See also *Expugnatio*, pp 86–7.   **45** ATig, 1171; For the submission of Domhnall and the Leinstermen, see MA, 1172.   **46** *CDI, 1171–1251*, no. 39, p. 7.

Meath; but *The song* describes these men as the earl's 'enemies of Leinster'; so that tension still lingered.[47] Roughly around the same time, Domhnall O'Brien of Thomond and Ruaidhrí O'Connor invaded nearby Ossory, throwing the English there into chaos. Upon the approach of O'Brien and Ruaidhrí, the townsmen of Kilkenny and their ally Domhnall MacGillapatrick of North Ossory fled to Waterford. The turmoil in Ossory and the sack of Kilkenny probably encouraged Domhnall MacMurrough-Kavanagh to use this moment of colonist chaos to force Strongbow to grant him better terms than those of 1172; this resulted in a major clash in Uí Cheinnselaig between his supporters and Strongbow;[48] the Irish annals record that Domhnall MacMurrough-Kavanagh emerged the victor and went on to defeat Strongbow's troops in a series of later skirmishes.

This was only a foretaste of the storm to befall the colony in 1174. In 1173, Strongbow held a hosting in Meath which demonstrated his grip upon Leinster. In addition to the MacMurroughs, most of the Leinstermen (including Fáelán MacFháeláin, O'Dempsey of Offaly and O'More of Laois) were in attendance;[49] yet, as subsequent events displayed, many of these were biding their time. Central to their grievances was loss of land. Despite Fáelán MacFháeláin's submission to Henry II, a private peace with Strongbow and performance of feudal service, Fáelán was deprived of his kingdom, which was then divided into three cantreds which were granted by the king in 1171–2 to Maurice Fitzgerald, Robert Fitzstephen and Meyler Fitzhenry.[50] After 1173, Henry reversed this decision, ceding the cantreds to Strongbow along with the towns of Wicklow and Wexford. Fáelán's discontent at the subinfeudation of Uí Faeláin was palpable. In summer 1174, he got the opportunity to overthrow Strongbow's settlement of Leinster.

In July 1174, Domhnall O'Brien and Conchobhar Maenmhaighe, Ruaidhrí's most able son, annihilated a large English army at Thurles. Flushed with success, Ruaidhrí himself crossed the Shannon into Meath,[51] seeking to follow up this victory and exploit the absence of Hugh de Lacy, lord of Meath, in Normandy. For the Uí Dúnlainge, the allure of their old master was too much and they rode to his banner. Much of Meath, including Trim castle, was burnt; and Ruaidhrí even penetrated to Dublin, but he failed to deliver a fatal blow.[52] He then pulled back to the Shannon, exposing his Leinster clients to the English backlash: witness the killing of Máelruanaidh O'Keary of Carbury by the English. The repercussions continued into 1175. Meath was wasted from Drogheda to Athlone, and Maghnus O'Melaghlin was hanged by the English at Trim[53] (the scale of this English onslaught forced many of Ruaidhrí's midland supporters to flee to Connacht). The rest of Leinster took longer to quell. Domhnall MacMurrough-Kavanagh may well have again taken up arms against Strongbow, as he is described as king of Leinster that year.[54] But with his death shortly afterwards, East Leinster became significantly more peaceful.

47 *Song of Dermot*, pp 232–3.   **48** ATig, 1173; MA, 1174.   **49** *Song of Dermot*, pp 234–5.
50 Flanagan, 'Henry II and the kingdom of Uí Fáeláin', p. 233; O'Byrne, 'The rise of the Gabhal Raghnaill', pp 49–50.   **51** ATig, AI, AU, 1174; MA, 1175; *Song of Dermot*, p. 235–45.
52 *Expugnatio*, pp 140–1.   **53** ATig, AU, 1175.   **54** AFM, ATig, 1175; *Expugnatio*, n. 32, p. 294.

Perhaps the most notable result of all this warfare was its effect on Ruaidhrí. After 1174, he clearly lost confidence in his ability either to drive out or to subdue the English,[55] for, instead of prolonging hostilities, he came to accept the English as part of an evolving political landscape. In 1175 he actually used them to check a rebellion by Domhnall O'Brien, king of Thomond, replacing him temporarily with a son of Murchadh O'Brien.[56] On 6 October 1175, through emissaries, Ruaidhrí submitted to Henry II, acknowledging him as his lord. By the terms of this treaty of Windsor, he undertook not to interfere in Leinster, and to compel the refugees from Meath and Leinster in Connacht to return home;[57] furthermore, he agreed to cede his overlordship of Leinster, and abandoned his claims to islandwide dominance. In return, Henry II promised not to dispute Ruaidhrí's overlordship in Connacht as long as he fulfilled his obligations as liegeman.

Although Ruaidhrí agreed not to interfere in Leinster, it was a promise he could not keep: the treaty of Windsor really bisected Leinster; because Ruaidhrí could not defeat the English militarily, he had to recognize their primacy over the *East* part; but the *West* was a different matter. Over the previous century, successive O'Connor kings expended considerable resources on locking West Leinster and the midlands into Connacht's sphere of influence. And in the western parts of Meath, Offaly, and Tipperary, a vibrant Irish web of social interaction woven together by alliance and kinship continued to survive under Ruaidhrí's protection. Clonmacnoise was still such an integral part of Connacht that it housed a O'Connor royal mint which continued to coin money into the 1170s.[58] O'Connor involvement in Clonmacnoise is further illustrated by the fact that it remained the burial place of Connacht princes. This O'Connor patronage of Clonmacnoise ensured that the surrounding Irish kingdoms benefitted from O'Connor protection.

The major casualties of Ruaidhrí's political expediency were the Uí Dúnlainge. With Ruaidhrí pinned back on the Shannon, the second phase of the subinfeudation of Leinster began. It opened with the expulsion of the more troublesome Irish ruling classes often from fertile to less fertile lands. Right across eastern Ireland, mottes, manors and peasant settlement came to take the places of the dispossessed. The Uí Dúnlainge kingdoms are a good example of this process. As constituted by Strongbow, the medieval county of Kildare was a stitching together of parts of three kingdoms (the O'Toole kingdom of Uí Muiredaig, Uí Fáeláin and O'Connor Faly's Offaly); the (separate) cantred of Wicklow lying against the Leinster coast where some O'Byrnes lived formed the final piece of the Kildare jigsaw.[59] Deprived of Ruaidhrí's protection, lords like Fáelán MacFháeláin now sought to cooperate with the newcomers. In 1177

---

55 Perros, 'Crossing the Shannon frontier', p. 119. **56** ATig, 1175. **57** Curtis & McDowell, *Ir. hist. docs*, pp 22–4. **58** Perros, 'Crossing the Shannon frontier', p. 117. **59** Otway-Ruthven, 'The medieval county of Kildare', pp 182–3. Kildare's borders were marked in the north-west by the modern baronies of east and west Offaly and in the south by the Laois baronies of east and west Maryborough, Strabally and Cullenagh.

Máelmorda MacFháeláin, perhaps Fáelán's son, was killed by the O'Tooles of Uí Muiredaig. His death coincided with the introduction of a second wave of settlers into Leinster from the de Clare lands in Wales and England, and the enforcement of Strongbow's earlier grant of Uí Muiredaig to Walter de Riddlesford, so that the MacFháeláins were either forced southward into Uí Muiredaig by colonist pressure or else had become auxiliaries in English service.[60]

The defeat of the O'Tooles in 1177–8 led to the active colonization of Kildare. To hammer down his prize of Uí Muiredaig, Walter de Riddlesford planted castles and colonists to control the more belligerent O'Tooles before pushing into Imaal in Wicklow to complete the conquest. As a result of his subsequent victory and the killing of Dúnlaing O'Toole in 1178, some of the O'Tooles fled to the lands of the bishopric of Glendalough; there, Archbishop Lorcán (Laurence) O'Toole of Dublin, Dúnlaing's brother, seems to have created a sanctuary on church lands for his kinsmen by a grant of land around Glenmalure to the local priory of the Desert of St Coemgen.[61] In Uí Fáeláin, the colonization followed a similar path. English mottes and villages were grafted onto both secular and ecclesiastical centres at Naas, Clane and Cloncurry. The density of the English settlement in Kildare is evidenced by the fact that the majority of smaller moated sites, perhaps farmsteads, known to us are in southern Kildare. A later programme of castle building under Hugh de Lacy sought to tighten the English grip on southern Kildare (1180 and 1181). Inevitably, the pressure for land was to the disadvantage of the Irish and led to racial segregation, as evidenced by the fourteenth-century Irishtowns south of Mullaghmast and near Moone.[62]

As the English pushed further into the interior, their problems increased, for the midland topography impeded a full conquest.[63] In Offaly despite the conversion of the O'Connor Faly centres of Lea and Rathangan into Fitzgerald manorial hubs, English settlement never reached the same intensity as in East Leinster.[64] Similar problems were encountered in much of west Meath and Laois, forcing the engine of conquest to stutter. However, the English offset the protection that the region's physical features afforded the Irish princes by patronizing their rivals. A case is point is Diarmait O'Dempsey of the Offaly subkingdom of Clanmaliere. Despite initial opposition Diarmait (described as lord and defender of Offaly in 1172) seemingly allied himself to the English from about 1173 onwards. This elevated him beyond his traditional vassal status to superiority over his former O'Connor Faly overlord. Other facts confirm the probability as he, a hitherto unknown, was able to found a Cistercian house at Monasterevin in 1178. Diarmait's political eclipse of the O'Connor Falys was such that he was lauded as lord of Offaly at his death in 1193.

---

60 ATig, 1177; Eager, 'The Cambro-Normans and the lordship of Leinster', p. 201. **61** *Expugnatio*, II. 113, p. 305; *COD*, i, no. 8, p. 4; *CDI, 1171–1251*, no. 1757, p. 262; *Song of Dermot*, pp 67–9; ATig, 1178; *Alen's Reg*, p. 8; Price, *Placenames*, p. xl.   **62** *CJR, 1295–1303*, p. 191; *CJR, 1305–1307*, p. 29.   **63** Ó Cléirigh, 'The problems of defence: a regional case-study', p. 29.

Similarities can be found in the experiences of the O'Mores of Laois. Throughout MacMurrough's difficulties in the 1160s, the O'Mores remained loyal to him.[65] Despite this and their later service with Strongbow in 1174, they were at war with the English as the 1170s closed. Their hostility to the English was probably linked to the struggle between their overlord Domhnall MacMurrough-Kavanagh and Strongbow (1173–5). The circumstances of Domhnall MacMurrough-Kavanagh's death may throw some light on the conflict in Laois. In 1175 he was killed in an incident surrounded by considerable confusion; according to the Four Masters, his killers were the O'Nolans of Forth, but the Annals of Tigernach record that he was cut down by the Uí Nialláin, who lived on the borderlands of Offaly and Laois. Possibly during his term as seneschal of the Irish of Leinster, the chronicler describes him as king of Leinster – perhaps indicating a resurgence of his hostility to Strongbow.[66] In contrast, Domhnall's cousin, Muircheartach, had become close to Strongbow – joining him on campaign to Limerick in 1175.[67] Significantly Domhnall MacGillapatrick of North Ossory, the enemy of Diarmait MacMurrough and Domhnall MacMurrough-Kavanagh, also joined this hosting, which suggests that Muircheartach and the Ossory king allied themselves with the English to protect themselves from Domhnall MacMurrough-Kavanagh. If Domhnall MacMurrough-Kavanagh was killed in the midlands by the Uí Nialláin, he may have been drumming up support for his war among his vassals such as O'More. If so, it would be unsurprising, given his activities in the aftermath of O'Brien and Ruaidhrí's offensive of 1173.

According to Gerald of Wales, between 1181 and 1182 Laois was given to Meyler Fitzhenry. Gerald stressed the enormity of the task facing Fitzhenry, describing Laois as a difficult, hostile and wooded land.[68] Fitzhenry's subsequent partial conquest of Laois must be studied in the context of the drive of the English of Meath into Ruaidhrí's sphere. In 1176 the de Lacys, along with Art O'Melaghlin and some of the O'Rourkes, plundered Carbury and Meath. Meath provided an launch pad for the English advance to Connacht: but the southern Irish kingdoms of Ulster were exposed also. Faced by a threat similar to that experienced by Ruaidhrí, Máelsechlainn O'Loughlin of Ulster razed much of northern Meath including Slane castle. Although the English advance had contravened the terms of Windsor, it secured Henry II's nod in 1177; in that year an English probe into west Meath failed; as did an attempted invasion of Connacht by Miles de Cogan.[69]

The pressure on Connacht grew in 1178, when Ruaidhrí's cherished Clonmacnoise and the neighbouring kingdom of Fearceall were attacked by Hugh de Lacy, lord of Meath. Ruaidhrí did drive him out, but English threat remained. Drawing on the support of Art O'Melaghlin and the O'Connor Falys,

64 Idem, 'John fitzThomas pp 25–6.   **65** Martin, 'Allies and an overlord, 1169–72', p. 71.
66 AFM, ATig, 1175; *Expugnatio*, n. 32, p. 294.   **67** BL, i, p. 186; *Song of Dermot*, p. 161;
Expugnatio, n. 264, p. 326; AI, 1176.   **68** *Expugnatio*, p. 195.   **69** ATig, AU, 1176; ATig, 1177.
See also *Expugnatio*, pp 182–3.

they returned and routed Máelsechlainn Beag O'Melaghlin and the Tethbae, Ruaidhrí's clients. This gradual weakening of Ruaidhrí's authority in the region led to chaos. The annals for 1178 reveal an ever-changing political landscape littered with broken diplomatic and military ties and dotted with new ones. Clearly a new political pattern had emerged. The turmoil between the competing spheres of Ruaidhrí and the colonists created a political void. An example of these fractious and sometimes confusing political patterns is the English defeat in 1178 by the O'Connor Falys, their recent allies.[70]

The O'Connor Faly volte-face prompted the formation of a wider Leinster confederation in 1179. Ruaidhrí may gave given his covert encouragement; if he did so, it must have been in the hope that the Leinstermen could tie down the English, deflecting their focus from Connacht. Although these Leinstermen did temporarily relieve the pressure on Connacht by their rout of English at Tochar Cluana Eidhneach and Fiodh Mór in Laois in 1179, they were essentially pursuing their own agenda.[71] Their successes may have been what forced lords like Meyler Fitzhenry to acknowledge the rights of the Irish. Ironically, the English seemed to have adopted the age-old midland policy of the high-kings – the creation of a ring of clients to stabilize their zone against the more hostile Irish. Within this English strategy, political arrangements were flexible. Those who resisted, risked annihilation. Other local rulers, although curtailed, were often left in place. In reality they merely had switched masters, exchanging Ruaidhrí's overlordship for a English one, but the evidence tends to suggest that some midland lords thrived in these conditions (after the English arrival in Leinster, Diarmait O'Dempsey was still rich enough to found a Cistercian house, and to the south of his kingdom, Cú Críoche O'More of Laois established the abbey of Abbeyleix for the Cistercians in 1183). However, alliance with the English also had untoward effects: in 1196 Domhnall O'More was killed while defending the colonists from the O'Connors of Connacht, and an O'Connor Faly dynast fell during a English expedition to Ulster.[72] These new regional alignments and the setting up of these native sentinels to watch over the English colony may not have been to the liking of Ruaidhrí. Thus, perhaps to redress the midland equilibrium, he now shifted for himself, by giving the hand of Rose, his daughter, to Hugh de Lacy shortly after 1180 – an indication that Ruaidhí had now truly acknowledged that English Leinster was the new reality.

---

70 ATig, 1178. **71** MA, 1179. See also Cunningham, *The Norman advance*, p. 29. That the English were defeated in Laois indicates the involvement of the O'Mores with the O'Connor Falys. Cluana Eidhneach was the royal monastery of the O'More kings of Laois: see Smyth, *Celtic Leinster*, p. 84. **72** Carrigan, *History … Ossory*, ii, p. 116; AFM, ALC, 1196. With regard to Diarmait O'Dempsey, his father Cú Brogha was killed by Ruaidhrí's client, Máelsechlainn O'Connor Faly, in 1162. See AFM, 1162.

CHAPTER 2

The reaction of the Irish nobility of East Leinster, 1180–1265

The rise of an anglicized native elite in East Leinster has always been neglected feature of Irish history. In the past, nationalist historians tended to paint the effect of the English upon the Irish in apocalyptic terms, but, in fact, the reactions of the Irish dynasties to English dominance were quite mixed. Long before the English arrival, the Irish had adopted some Viking forenames – heralding the later common Irish usage of English appellations. This shift in native naming practices indicates a desire to assimilate. In East Leinster, the O'Tooles adopted 'Walter', the forename of their de Riddlesford overlords, while several O'Byrnes were named Gerald after their thirteenth-century masters, the Fitzgeralds. (After 1177, settlers from de Clare lands in Wales, England and France flooded Leinster.) Significantly, in West Leinster where the settlers were not so thickly planted, the Irish adoption of English names occurs less frequently.[1] The budding colony's need for security preserved some of the Leinstermen's power. Some Irish dynasts were employed as overseers of their followers or as guardians of the marches. There is also evidence to suggest the growth of a hybrid society in Leinster, and indeed in parts of Connacht, particularly in the decades following the English arrival.[2] Some settlers in Connacht quickly assimilated themselves into Irish society, adopting nicknames or assuming Irish variants of their surnames; for example, Gilbert de Angulo, who was in service to Cathal Cróibhdhearg O'Connor in 1195, became Mac Oisdealbaig and subsequently his descendants were known as MacCostellos.

MeicGiollamocholmóc of Uí Briúin Chualann

In East Leinster the MeicGiollamocholmóc dynasty of the Wicklow terri-tory of Uí Briúin Chualann quickly spanned the ethnic divide. Domhnall MacGiollamocholmóc, lord of that territory, was married to Diarmait

---

1 Ó Cuiv, 'Personal names as an indicator of relations between native Irish and settlers in the Viking period', p. 86; Bartlett, 'Colonial aristocracies', pp 27–8; Eagar, 'The Cambro-Normans and the lordship of Leinster', p. 201; *Red Bk Ormond*, p. 20; Pender, O'Clery, para. 1749, p. 130, para 1767, pp 131–2, para. 1768, p. 132. 2 Duffy, 'The problem of degeneracy', p. 103; O'Byrne, 'The Uí Bhroin of Co. Wicklow', pp 29–33; Walton, 'The English in Connacht', p. 197.

MacMurrough's daughter, Derbforghaill, and had aided his father-in-law and his English allies.[3] After MacMurrough's death in May 1171, he grew ambiguous in his support for the English. When the deposed Ostman king of Dublin, Hasculf MacTurkill, attempted to retake the city, Domhnall held aloof until the struggle turned against MacTurkill. Later he joined the Leinster princes and Ruaidhrí O'Connor to besiege Dublin;[4] but, after the breaking of the high-king's siege in autumn 1171, he wisely accepted Strongbow's overlordship. His salvation was ensured by the fact that he was brother-in-law to both Strongbow and Domhnall MacMurrough-Kavanagh, and that two of his sons were Diarmait MacMurrough's grandsons.[5] In winter 1171–2 Domhnall joined the throng to submit to Henry II. By the terms of his submission he was to hold his lands directly of the king, an act that ensured his dynasty's survival as major landowners for a further century and a half. However, his lands at Santry, Raheny and Clontarf in north Dublin were granted to the newcomers.

Domhnall's family were to acquire and emulate the trappings of the new order. They became anglicized, adapted their forenames to the Latin norm and changed their surname to Fitzdermot.[6] The cultural leap of Domhnall's dynasty may not have been such a drastic change. For centuries the MeicGiolla-mocholmóc had lived in the shadow of Dublin with its high stone walls and densely packed streets, and the city was always a transmitter of new ways that influenced its hinterland and in turn Ireland. Its importance had long been realized by those with aspirations to the high-kingship. Before the English arrival, Domhnall had lived in an world of church synods, Latin, imported wine, coin and charters. Indeed, his dynasty in the early twelfth century played a role in the foundation of the Cistercian abbey of St Mary at Dublin.[7] He saw his innovative father-in-law, MacMurrough, raise up new foundations for the white-robed Cistercians at Baltinglass and Killenny, and for the Augustinians at Ferns and All Hallows in Dublin. MacMurrough enthusiasm for the Continental model percolated down to lesser members of the Leinster nobility such as Diarmait O'Ryan of Idrone, who, with MacMurrough assent, collaborated in the foundation of Killenny.[8] Before the English arrival, a form of castle was already a feature in the Leinster landscape. MacMurrough himself dwelt in his stone house of Ferns, and it has been suggested he encouraged the construction of the castle of Machenlodher (Mac Con Lothair) in Uí Faeláin to check its restless lords.[9] Without doubt, this relative sophistication eased Domhnall's transition from Irish king to nobleman.

Domhnall's quick assimilation is evident from his witnessing Strongbow's charter confirming Glendalough's lands in 1172; and a document from the reign

---

3 Simpson, 'Anglo-Norman settlement in Uí Briúin Chualann', p. 193, pp 195–6, 202, 210, 214. **4** *Expugnatio*, p. 85. **5** *Chartul. St Mary's*, i, p. 32. **6** Byrne, *Irish kings*, p. 151. **7** *Chartul. St Mary's*, i, p. xv. **8** Ibid., ii, p. 231; Orpen, *Normans*, iii, p. 57; Butler & Bernard, 'The charters of the abbey of Duiske', pp 56–7. **9** ATig, 1166; *COD*, i, no. 37, p. 19; Nicholls, 'Medieval Irish dynasties', p. 415; for Cristin McLothyr in 1304 see *Red Bk Ormond*, p. 33.

of Archbishop Luke of Dublin (1228–55) tells us more about Domhnall's commitment to the new way: during Archbishop John Comyn's reign (1181–1212)
'Gilleholmoc and other good men' enclosed a common of turbary and pasture
on the mountain called Slestoll (later Archbishop Luke granted it to the
'burgesses of Radcull').[10] In the early years after the English arrival, Domhnall's
charters featured Ostmen, Leinster aristocrats and Englishmen. By the late
twelfth century, however, a clear shift was under way; we find Diarmait, Domhnall's
son, granting lands to newcomers such as Richard de Felde in charters in which
the names of English witnesses predominate.[11]

It was during the lifetime of Diarmait that the pace of feudalization and
anglicization of the MacGiollamocholmóc dynasty gathered momentum.
Indicative of this was the change of the MacGiollamocholmóc surname to
Fitzdermot. Diarmait described himself as Dermod filius Gillemolmoc and
received lands as Dermot Mac Gilmeholmoc in 1207.[12] In turn, his son John was
known as Johannes [Gillemo] Holmoc but his widow referred to him as
Johannis filius Dermicii in a charter after 1230. Testimony to the ever-deepening
incorporation of this Irish dynasty within the Plantagenet nexus was the fact that
John was specifically named in a summons of 1227 to perform military service
for Henry III. Further evidence is the change of the forenames of the family
over the generations from Diarmait to Ralph.[13] The family also eased their
passage into the colonial aristocracy through marriage: John son of Diarmait was
to marry Claricia, daughter of Gilbert Fitzgriffin of Knocktopher, Co. Kilkenny;
and John's grandson, Ralph, married another woman of the colony named
Joan.[14] The transformation brought about by their ethnic revolution was so
complete that, were there not earlier evidence of their Irish lineage, the
Fitzdermots would have been indistinguishable from the settler aristocracy. The
only documented trouble that did arise was either in late twelfth or early
thirteenth centuries when a Donohoe MacGiollamocholmóc killed Roger
fitzGilbert, an Englishman.[15]

---

10 *Alen's Reg*, pp 2, 84.   **11** *Chartul. St Mary's*, i, pp 31–6; J. Gilbert (ed.), pp 149–50 (*Reg. St Thomas*). Mills, 'The Norman settlement in Leinster – the cantreds near Dublin', p. 172.
12 Simpson, 'Anglo-Norman settlement in Uí Briúin Chualann', pp 193, 195–6, 202, 210, 214; *CDI, 1171–1251*, no. 356, p. 53; *Chartul. St Mary's*, i, nos 6–7, pp 31–3. It seems Domhnall had more than one heir. In these charters there is a John mentioned alongside Domhnall and his wife, Dervogilla MacMurrough. Before Diarmait mac Domhnaill always seemed to have been his father's sole heir; *CDI, 1171–1251*, no. 569, p. 88. There is a John Deremot called nephew and heir of Gillehom. The lands associated with him are within the Newcastle Lyons region. Does this indicate an east/west division of the MeicGiollamocholmóc lands between Domhnall's line and the sons of a brother named Diarmait?   **13** *Chartul. St Mary's*, i, p. 5; Gilbert, *A history of the city of Dublin*, i, p. 233; Bartlett, 'Colonial aristocracies', p. 28. John had a son, known as John fitzJohn. In turn he had at least two sons, both bore English names, Ralph and Robert. Indeed, Robert's own son was known as William fitzRobert. It seems either John fitzJohn or his son Ralph fitzJohn assumed the Fitzdermot surname. See Nicholls, 'Anglo-French Ireland', pp 381–2.   **14** *COD*, i, p. 35.   **15** Nicholls, 'Anglo-French Ireland', p. 381; *Alen's Reg*, p. 110.

The benevolence of the English to the MacGiollamocholmóc dynasty greatly facilitated the bedding-down of the feudal settlement south of Dublin. There the colony prospered, living cheek by jowl with the traditional lordship of the Fitzdermots over Uí Briúin Chualann. Land tenure among the thirteenth-century tenantry of Uí Briúin Chualann, the O'Kelly and O'Tire families, displays a strong strand of continuity with pre-English times.[16] In Uí Briúin Chualann itself, the Fitzdermots held at least eight carucates, while in 1207 Diarmait MacGiollamocholmóc is recorded as holding another fifteen carucates in the Vale of Dublin for the service of one knight and two otterskins.[17] Until 1215, at least, their lands stretched to Glencullen and included Newcastle Lyons; grants of lands to Glendalough and St Mary's Abbey further display the extent of their holdings. South of Uí Briúin Chualann, the Fitzdermots seemingly also gained additional lands at the expense of both Ostman and Irish dynasties, particularly the MacTurkills dwelling within Uí Briúin Chualann and the former O'Farrell rulers of Uí Garrchon (east Wicklow). In Uí Garrchon, the Fitzdermots held lands at Newcastle and at Ballinagran into the fourteenth century.[18] (Thus the O'Farrells and probably the Uí Fiachrach of Uí Enechglaiss of southeast Wicklow were seemingly largely dispossessed by the English, but that is not to say they were not still living upon ancestral lands.)[19] The Fitzdermots also held estates well outside their traditional ambit: through his mother Clarissa Fitzgriffin, John fitzJohn held lands in Carlow at Fynnore and Kellistown, enfeoffing William de Dene with a third of them before 1260.[20]

Links between the Fitzdermots and their MacMurrough cousins persisted well into the thirteenth century. Two charters from the early English period highlight this continuing closeness. Henne MacMurchade (probably Énna MacMurrough) witnessed an undated grant by Derbforghaill MacMurrough, wife of Domhnall MacGiollamocholmóc, to St Mary's abbey at Dublin.[21] Domhnall's own charter also bears a MacMurrough witness, Maurico. Between

16 *CDI, 1285–92*, no. 149, p. 60, no. 180, p. 85 , p. 150, 153, no. 1148, p. 502; Nicholls, 'Medieval Irish dynasties', p. 412; Simpson, 'Anglo-Norman settlement in Uí Briúin Chualann', pp 195, 202, 224–5; *Red Bk Ormond*, p. 24. **17** *CDI, 1171–1251*, no. 356, p. 53; *DKR*, xxxviii, p. 78. **18** *Alen's Reg*, p. 21; *Chartul. St Mary's*, i, pp 31–7; Simpson, 'Anglo-Norman settlement in Uí Briúin Chualann', pp 193, 195–6, 202, 210, 214, 218; Long, 'Three settlements of the Gaelic Wicklow 1169–1600', p. 256; *DKR*, xxxviii, p. 96. **19** *Grace*, p. 53; This is strengthened if Klymanach mentioned in 1301 with Rathdown is Kilnamanagh near Glenealy, see *DKR*, xxxviii, p. 78. The possibility of the Fitzdermots holding lands further down the coast is strong. The pedigree of Domhnall records a victory of an ancestor over the Uí Enechglaiss, mentioning that they were forced over the river Dee close to Arklow. See Gilbert, *The history of the city of Dublin*, i, p. 405; Significantly included within the modern townland of Ballinagran is Ballyderborgeyle. This Derbforghaill was possibly the MacMurrough wife of Domhnall MacGiollamocholmóc, strengthening the Fitzdermot connection with this area. Price, *Placenames*, p. 440. This is a local tradition in the Glenealy valley in Wicklow. **20** *COD*, i, pp 35, 60, 136. John fitzJohn is mentioned as a witness to Avice de la Cornere's grant to Lord Theobald Butler; E. St John Brooks (ed.), *Knights' fees*, (Dublin, 1950), pp 64–5. **21** *Chartul. St Mary's*, i, pp 31–2; Flanagan, *Irish society*, n. 67, p. 101.

1240 and 1254, Luke MacMurrough witnessed Clarissa Fitzgriffin's confirmation of an earlier grant of the church of Kellistown in Forth, Co. Carlow, to the priory of Kells in Granard.[22] However, by the last decades of the thirteenth century the Fitzdermots' influence with the Irish of east Wicklow had all but disappeared. By 1276–7, when Ralph fitzJohn was paid for defending the Vale of Dublin from the Irish, their transformation to marcher lord was complete. It was crowned by Edward I's rubber stamping of Ralph fitzJohn's status by knighting him in 1282.

By 1291 Sir Ralph was dead; his widow married Albert de Kenley in 1292, and during the minority of John fitzRalph, Sir Ralph's son, the Fitzdermot estates was given into de Kenley's custody.[23] The Fitzdermot decline within the region was confirmed by the Irish burning of east Wicklow and Rathdown in 1301. By 1305 the Fitzdermots had sold their remaining lands in Uí Briúin Chualann to Nigel le Brun, while their lands in the Glencapp and Glencree uplands were under pressure, as evidenced by the killing of John Shilgry, the king's serjeant of Glencry (probably Glencree), by the Harolds that year. This ebbing social capital was evident also in 1311 when a Robert fitzRalph (perhaps John fitzRalph's brother) and a Robert fitzJohn were noted as small holders in the now Butler manor of Bray.[24] Fitzdermot lands near Tallaght were also contracting, as John fitzRalph in 1306–7 granted away a carucate at Kilnamanagh.[25] Still, members of the family conspired to maintain their access to the common law and their social status within the English lordship. In 1379 Brother Richard Dermot, an Augustinian monk, described as an Anglicus, was famously murdered at the Augustinian friary of the Holy Trinity.[26] Remarkably, other Fitzdermots managed to preserve themselves as landowners: an unpublished pipe roll of Henry IV records a John, son of Dermod, behind in his rent for Rathdown in 1408. Moreover, some Fitzdermots were to hold land in north Dublin at Lusk until the middle of the sixteenth century, demonstrating this family's remarkable capacity for survival and adaptation.[27]

22 Nicholls, 'Anglo-French Ireland', p. 382; for another example of Irish accommodation within the feudal settlement, see *Red Bk Kildare*, no. 51, p. 48; Price, *Placenames*, pp 296–7, Luke MacMurrough's son, Maurice, held lands in freehold from the archbishop of Dublin at Stagonnell among the Fitzdermot uplands, now within the Powerscourt Demesne. And much later in 1286–7, William MacMurrough was Ralph fitzJohn's pledge for good behaviour. See *CDI, 1285–92*, no. 309, p. 137.   23 *CDI, 1252–84*, no. 1496, p. 285. He was also part of a jury which determined the extent of Henry Marshal's lands in Newcastle Lyons, see ibid., no. 2003, p. 458, nos 1122–3, p. 493. For the knighting of Ralph, see also *CDI, 1285–94*, no. 2344, p. 562. 24 Dowling, *Annals*, p. 17; *Chartul. St Mary's*, ii, p. 330; Simpson, 'Anglo-Norman settlement in Uí Briúin Chualann', p. 218; *CJR, 1305–7*, p. 480; *Red Bk Ormond*, p. 25.   25 *Alen's Reg*, p. 161.   26 Martin, 'Murder in a monastery, 1379', pp 468–98.   27 Gilbert, *A history of the city of Dublin*, i, p. 235; Burry, p. 37; see M. Griffith (ed.), *Cal. of Inquisitions* (Dublin, 1991), Hen VIII 7/6 (c), p. 4. Walter Dermot of Swords was part of the jury determining the lands of the archbishopric of Dublin in January 1552. See also Jas I (109) n. 2, p. 391. Thomas Dermot was part of a jury at Dublin in 1612, see Jas I (154), p. 407.

The Ostmen

Others, however, were neither so lucky nor so prudent. Following the beheading of Hasculf MacTurkill in summer 1171, Walter de Riddlesford I, hero of the English victory, was rewarded with the MacTurkill lands around modern Bray.[28] As a further punishment Strongbow also confiscated the properties of Sigerith and Torphin MacTurkill, granting them to the abbey of St Mary. The cost of defeat didn't end there, as the dynasty also lost their extensive lands at Portrane, Malahide, Portmarnock and Kilbarrack. Their disfavour was temporary, however: about 1174, Hamund MacTurkill's title to his lands of Kinsealy was confirmed, as were those of his brothers. Although considerably reduced in status, the MacTurkills, as is apparent from their surviving charters to the abbey of St Mary, remained reasonably important (we find references to them in King John's grant of 1202 to Holy Trinity).[29] This enduring English favour towards the Ostman community was evident by the incorporation of the Ostmen at a higher social level than most Irish, as evidenced by thirty-six identifiable Ostman rents for lands within the Vale of Dublin.[30] Other prominent Ostman families in Uí Briúin Chualann and the barony of Wicklow were the Harolds and perhaps the Archbolds. The Harolds were incorporated within the feudal settlement early on, particularly on the archbishop's lands.[31]

The O'Tooles of Uí Muiredaig

The same pattern is to be seen in the neighbouring Fitzgerald barony of Wicklow. Unlike the MeicGiollamocholmóc, the O'Tooles of Uí Muiredaig were hostile to the English in the 1170s. They were gradually subjugated between 1176 and 1180, and some of them fled to lands of the bishopric of Glendalough, where, as we saw, Archbishop Lorcán O'Toole of Dublin granted lands around Glenmalure to the priory of the Desert of St Coemgen, probably to protect them.[32] The dynasty seems to have split into two families, one based in Kildare and the other in the Wicklow mountains. Like most of the Irish nobility of East Leinster, both families gradually adopted a more conciliatory attitude to the English and sought to carve a place within the new order.

Although the O'Tooles lost most of Uí Muiredaig, they were not evicted entirely. Those remaining in Kildare seem to have been accommodated easily into the English settlement. When, in 1199, King John granted Milo le Bret twelve carucates at Loug in fee of Othothel (probably somewhere in southern Kildare), it was achieved with the minimum of disturbance – a testimony to the

28 *Song of Dermot*, p. 181; *CDI, 1171–1251*, no. 355, p. 53.   **29** *Chartul. St Mary's Abbey*, ii, no. 61, pp 83–4, no. 244, p. 477, no. 269, pp 504–5 and nos 216–17, pp 233–4; *Alen's Reg*, pp 28–9; Burry, p. 37; Duffy, 'Ireland and the Irish Sea region', p. 61; for John McTorkoill see *CJR 1308–14*, p. 285.   **30** Simpson, 'Anglo-Norman settlement in Uí Briúin Chualann', p. 203.   **31** Nicholls, 'Crioch Branach', p. 17; *Alen's Reg*, p. 31; *CJR, 1295–1303*, p. 306; *CJR, 1305–7*, pp 476; *CJR, 1308–14*, p. 285; NA, RC 7/13 (iv), pp 22–4; *CDI, 1252–84*, p. 313; *Chartul. St Mary's*, ii, p. 349.   **32** *Song of Dermot*, pp 66–9; ATig, 1178; *Alen's Reg*, p. 8; Price, *Placenames*, p. xl.

good relations between native and newcomer; in the same year, Murchadh and Alexander O'Toole, and several English, including Milo le Bret, appear as witnesses to a charter of Domhnall MacGiollamocholmóc – a further indication of good relations.[33] The O'Tooles adopted forenames such as Meyler, Agatha, David, Richard and Walter, and in 1209 Giollapádraig O'Toole was enfranchized with the law by William Marshal, lord of Leinster, and hung on to ancestral lands. Interestingly, a probable O'Toole named Gilkogil of Johnstown was admitted to the Dublin merchant guild roll between 1235 and 1236. Furthermore, the obit of Féilim O'Toole for 1259 describes him as lord of Uí Muireadhaigh, which suggests the survival of a much reduced O'Toole lordship in medieval Kildare.[34]

Giollapádraig O'Toole's great-grandson Walter is a good example of this accommodation. He was a man of some importance, who had access to the law through the charter granted to Giollapádraig. Walter's ancestor was probably enfranchized because of his status as a free tenant rather than by way of receiving a specific grant. An extent of the Kildare barony of Kilkea in 1311 reveals that Walter held seven carucates of land there. During the late thirteenth and early fourteenth centuries, Walter accounted rents for one fifteenth of Kildare.[35] Furthermore, earlier in 1298, this Walter with other landowners in Kildare pledged 100s. for the release of the rapist John Waas. In this incident Walter's rival, Fáelán mac Giolla Chaomghin O'Toole of Imaal, also displayed access to the law – pledging 40s. for Waas' bail. However, racial tension could still arise between anglicized Irish lords and the English due to prejudice and land disputes. In 1299 Walter took legal action against the le Jordan brothers. Before Justiciar John Wogan, he claimed that they disseized him of a freehold at Corbaly Otothill near Tancardeston in the barony of Kilkea. The le Jordans replied that they did not have to answer an Irishman – which prompted Walter to produce Giollápadraig's charter enfranchizing him with rights to common law. Walter's importance among the O'Tooles of the mountains was also evident in the fact that he was the only O'Toole included on the jury to investigate the state of the archdeaconry of Glendalough in 1299.[36]

Walter's cousins living in the Leinster mountains were also especially favoured – particularly by the archbishops of Dublin. They retained their tenure of the abbacy of Glendalough; Thomas and Tadeus O'Toole were abbots between 1170

33 *CDI, 1171–1251*, no. 100, p. 15; *Chartul. St Mary's*, i, p. 32. **34** *CJR, 1295–1303*, p. 271; Becker, 'Dublin Guild Merchant Roll, p. 112; AFM, 1259. **35** Nicholls, 'Anglo-French Ireland', p. 376; *CJR, 1295–1303*, p. 271; *Red Bk Ormond*, p. 15; *CDI, 1293–1301*, no. 549, p. 246, no. 586, p. 278, no. 612, p. 291; *CDI, 1301–7*, no. 563, p. 163. **36** *CJR, 1295–1303*, pp 206, 270-1. Between 1300 and 1301 Walter sat on an inquisition at Castledermot with Maurice MacMurrough and with the de la Hides gave 40s. for John de la Roche's release in 1306. See *CJR, 1305–7*, p. 497. And later in 1328, the Adam Duff O'Toole, son of Walter Duff, burnt for heresy was probably his son. See *Grace*, pp 107–8; Dowling, *Annals*, p. 22; Adam is described in this entry as being the son of Walter Duff O'Toole of Leinster; Frame, *Ireland and Britain, 1170–1450*, fn. 12, p. 251. In 1315–16, Eglantina O'Toole brought a case before the Dublin bench.

and 1228.[37] Another confirmation of their favour in the eyes of the archbishops was the presence of a Lorcán O'Toole on the campaign of Justiciar Archbishop Henry de Londres in 1214 against Máelsechlainn Óg O'Melaghlin and O'Connor Faly – a decision which cost him his life in the wilds of west Meath.[38] Meyler O'Toole, probably Lorcán's son, did homage to Archbishop Luke of Dublin for his father's lands between 1228 and 1255 (the archbishop's grant may have been meant to seal over an illegitimacy, rather than confirm a doubtful inheritance).[39] Other O'Tooles held lands in the archbishop's western manor of Ballymore and at Glenealy and Kilfee in east Wicklow before 1272, while two others served on an inquisition in 1264 at Castlekevin, and Elias O'Toole was serjeant of Archbishop Fulk de Sandford's lands.[40] Other O'Toole lands were located within the Glen of Imaal. Of particular interest are those held by various members of the O'Toole family of Cnoclorkan in Imaal;[41] this family's holdings were better defined in the extent of Imaal of 1311, according to which six O'Tooles, some known malefactors, held sizeable upland holdings of the Butlers.[42] The scattered nature of their lands can be seen from the fact that Richard McKyoghy O'Toole (one of the Cnoclorkan family) in 1296 also held part of Ballycolgan in east Wicklow, while his brother Henry was recognized as one of the bishop of Ferns' betaghs in 1299.[43] An earlier O'Toole lord, Moriertagh (Muircheartach), also held land in Imaal from the Welsh settler Philip Fitzrhyss before 1256.[44]

The MacMurroughs

The most interesting Irish reaction to the English was that of the MacMurroughs. After the killing of Domhnall MacMurrough-Kavanagh and subsequent temporary eclipse of the political significance of his sons and grandsons after 1175, the tension among Diarmait MacMurrough's successors lessened. Much of MacMurrough's Uí Cheinnselaig overlordship became the administrative units of Wexford and Carlow and fell now to Strongbow (as lord of Leinster) and his Marshal successors. The union of Strongbow and Aoife, Diarmait MacMurrough's daughter, was not the only marriage between the MacMurroughs and the English.

---

37 In 1219 the men of the archbishop mentioned living in the royal forests in the former see of Glendalough were probably O'Tooles. See *CDI, 1171–1251*, no. 892, p. 133. Sometime between 1228 and 1255 Abbot Tadeus of Glendalough granted Killmacbyrn to Archbishop Luke, while Alexander and Richard O'Toole, probably Abbot Thomas's son and grandson, witnessed charters confirming lands to the abbeys of St Thomas and St Mary. See *Alen's Reg*, p. 76; MacShamhráin, p. 164.　　**38** AClon, 1214. This Lorcán may be the Laurentio filo Alexandri who witnesses the grants of Domhnall MacGiollamochmolóc and his grandson, John. Abbot Thomas of Glendalough had a son named Alexander and Laurence/Lorcán is a traditional O'Toole forename; see *Chartul. St Mary's*, i, p. 32.　　**39** *Alen's Reg*, pp 81–2; Nicholls, 'Anglo-French Ireland', p. 382.　　**40** Ibid., pp 110–11, 121, 136; later O'Tooles held church lands in freehold from the archbishops at Glenealy and Kilfee in east Wicklow. Maghnus O'Toole, the father of one of them, was granted his Glenealy lands by John de Sandford before 1272. Price, *Placenames*, p. 1; *CDI, 1252–84*, no. 1577, p. 314.　　**41** *CJR, 1308–14*, p. 173.　　**42** *Red Bk Ormond*, p. 20.　　**43** *CDI, 1293–1301*, no. 329, p. 153; *CJR, 1295–1303*, p. 254.　　**44** *Alen's Reg*, p. 141.

Even Diarmait MacMurrough's rebellious brother, Murchadh MacMurrough, apparently married one of the de Barrys before his death in 1172. These marriages and the fact that Strongbow and the settlers did not encroach too forcefully on the northwest of Uí Cheinnselaig made Muircheartach MacMurrough's co-operation much easier. (These marriages laid the foundations of an alliance between English Leinster and the MacMurroughs that was to last for almost a century.) Strongbow's favour is possibly demonstrated in Muircheartach's epithet 'na Maor', meaning 'of the stewards or rent collectors'; he may have inherited, with Strongbow's approval, Domhnall MacMurrough-Kavanagh's position as seneschal of the Irish of Leinster.[45] Upon Muircheartach's death in 1193, he was recorded as king of Uí Cheinnselaig, and seemingly he used Ferns as an official residence.[46] Furthermore, another MacMurrough described as the son of MacMurrough, grandson of Máel na mBó, fell alongside an O'Connor Faly and O'Phelan of the Déise during Ruaidhrí MacDunleavy's unsuccessful campaign with English help against the Irish of Tyrone in 1196.[47]

As one of the five bloods enfranchized about 1219 with a grant of common law by Henry III, the later MacMurroughs are found participating widely within the new order. For example, Aoife MacMurrough's children by Strongbow held vast estates either side of the Irish Sea through the legacies of Strongbow and MacMurrough.[48] MacMurrough's granddaughter and ward of Henry II, Isabella de Clare, married William Marshal, the earl marshal of England in 1189. (Probably in the following year she set about building the town of New Ross;[49] That the town was not walled until 1265 is significant; even then, the walling took place because of fear of attack, not from Irish, but from feuding English. The MacMurroughs actually received an annual payment of 10 marks from the burghers of the town.)[50] This union of bloods was symbolically depicted in a cenotaph of Isabella set up in New Ross within sight of the lands of her MacMurrough cousins. Later, in 1225, four of Isabella's MacMurrough cousins fell during the Connacht campaign of William Marshal II, her son.[51]

This smooth transition of suzerainty in Uí Cheinnselaig is evident on another level. Until 1223 there was an Irish bishop of Ferns, the controversial Albin O'Mulloy – and an Irish abbot of the Cistercian abbey of Baltinglass until 1227.[52] Between 1218 and 1228 a Maurice MacMurrough witnessed a grant to the church of St Mary and St Columba of Inistioge, while a Luke MacMurrough, sometimes known as Luke de Macmorth, bore witness to Richard de la

---

45 Frame, 'Two kings', pp 155–6; Colfer, *Arrogant trepass*, pp 63, 221; AFM, iii, n.f, p. 96; Pender, 'O'Clery', para 1739, p. 129.   46 Orpen, *Normans,* ii, p. 390.   47 Flanagan, *Irish society,* n. 173, p. 226; ALC, AFM, 1196.   48 Otway-Ruthven, 'The native Irish and English law in mediaeval Ireland', p. 6 – the others being the dynasties of O'Neill of Ulster, O'Melaghlin of Meath, O'Connor of Connacht and O'Brien of Munster, cited from BM Cott MS Titus BXI, f.70 – MacMurrough is described as McMourgho de Lagenia; Flanagan, *Irish society,* pp 124–30.   49 Leask, 'A cenotaph of Strongbow's daughter', pp 65–7.   50 Hore, *Wexford town,* i, pp 50–6.   51 Leask, 'A cenotaph of Strongbow's daughter', pp 65–7; AConn, 1225. 52 Orpen, *Normans,* iii, pp 29–31.

Rochelle's grant of lands in Connacht to St Mary's abbey in 1270.[53] Maurice, Luke's son, held lands from Alymer de Valence at the unidentifiable Drumhad, and later with several English landowners of Kildare and Carlow he pledged money for the release of the Cheures brothers from the prison of Dungarvan in 1297.[54]

The brothers Muircheartach and Art MacMurrough enjoyed good relations with their cousin Roger Bigod, lord of Carlow. Bigod, also earl of Norfolk and earl marshal of England, wisely continued the accommodating policies of his Marshal predecessors. Within his liberty of Carlow, the MacMurroughs held a recognized position as heads of the Irish there and were very much his protégés.[55] The account of New Ross records the buying of cloth and furs for the ceremonial gowns of Earl Roger's officers in 1279; Art received a robe with a hood lined with fur to match, implying strongly that he was an officer of Bigod. In early 1280 Earl Roger met the MacMurroughs while visiting his Carlow lands; to Art, he gave a robe, a cap, furs, money and a cask of wine, while Muircheartach received money.[56] That year Roger wrote to Edward I, acknowledging the MacMurroughs as his cousins; and the accounts of his estates in Ireland reveal that they received fees as his officers up to the time of their murders in 1282. In spite of these murders, relations remained good between Bigod and the MacMurroughs, for the earl's forces, including the MacMurroughs, crushed a rising of the O'Byrnes and O'Nolans at some date between 1279 and 1294. The smooth flow of the earl's power was also evident when Thomas MacMurrough was escorted to Dublin without incident to face trial.[57] In 1306, when Earl Roger died, his lands passed to the crown, but a 1307 extent shows Douenald Mcmurwoth holding two of the six carucates of Fynnagh for life.[58]

The MeicDalbaig
The pragmatic political example of the MacMurroughs moulded the attitudes of their vassals. The MacMurrough cousins, the O'Donnells and their offshoot, the MeicDalbaig, were accepted within the feudal system. Density of English settlement in the Uí Cheinnselaig over-kingship reflected pre-English political divisions. Earlier, Diarmait MacMurrough had placated the MeicDalbaig ancestors by marrying his sister to their eponym, Dalbach. In addition he made Dalbach king of Uí Felemeda Tuaid, a region located in north Carlow and south Wicklow.[59] Through this dynastic engineering MacMurrough bound the MeicDalbaig to him and weakened his more inveterate O'Donnell enemies.

---

53 *COD*, i, no. 45, pp 22–3; *CDI, 1293–1301*, no. 550, p. 247; *Chartul. St Mary's*, i, p. 257. 54 Nicholls, 'Anglo-French Ireland', p. 382; *CJR, 1295–1303*, p. 166. In 1298 a Gerald Fitzdavid was fined for not producing Maurice. It seems he survived this case, emerging unscathed for we find him serving on an inquisition at Castledermot in 1300–1. See *CDI, 1293–1301*, no. 550, p. 247, no. 764, p. 356. 55 Nicholls, *Gaelic Ire*, p. 170. 56 Hore, *Wexford town*, i, pp 14–15, 18, 143, 146, 148. 57 Mills, 'Accounts of the earl of Norfolk's estates in Ireland, 1279–1294', pp 55–6. 58 *CJR, 1305–7*, p. 347. 59 Flanagan, 'Mac Dalbaig, a Leinster chieftain', pp 6–7.

During the war of the Leinster princes in summer 1171, the MeicDalbaig leader joined the attack on Dublin, but following its failure he submitted with other Leinstermen to Henry II and joined Strongbow's army in Meath during 1173.[60]

Like the O'Toole kingdom of Uí Muiredaig, the MeicDalbaig patrimony was conquered; it became the manor of Tullowphelim. About 1192 John, then lord of Ireland, granted Theobald Walter (the Butler progenitor) the manor of Tulauth in Ofelymth, and later William Marshal confirmed John's grant. On the whole, the English settlement in Uí Felemeda Tuaid seems to have been quite dense.[61] But it was not just English who acquired holdings there: the favoured Moriertagh O'Toole held land there before 1256, and later two fourteenth-century O'Byrnes also did;[62] and the MeicDalbaig remained there, albeit reduced in status. Before 1303, a Milo MacDalbaig and his sons, Dermot and Malauthin, held lands near Aghowle. In 1311 William son of Philip O'Donnell of Aghowle, his brother John and Robert O'Donnell – all three freeholders at Aghowle – were charged with receiving Robert mac Gerald O'Byrne. In their defence they pleaded that they were powerless to resist, and the court eventually found them innocent, releasing them with a fine.[63]

The O'Byrnes

In comparison with other Irish dynasties of East Leinster, virtually nothing is recorded of the O'Byrnes. The evidence suggests that they became tenants of the Fitzgerald barons of Naas through Strongbow's division of Uí Fáeláin in 1173–4.[64] The Fitzgeralds were granted Naas, Uí Fáeláin's most northern cantred, along with Wicklow cantred which held some of the O'Byrne territories. Fragmentary evidence gives some insight as to the O'Byrnes' status during the first decades of the thirteenth century. Their genealogies reveal a kingly line presiding over a series of closely related families amid a hilly and thickly wooded territory, and the occurrence of Fitzgerald forenames in the family suggests that they were on good terms with the Fitzgeralds for most of the thirteenth century.[65]

Those O'Byrnes living on Earl Roger Bigod's lands in north Carlow were recognized feudal tenants. Between 1279 and 1294 he made a gift of 66s. 8d. to their

60 *Expugnatio*, p. 85 and p. 95; *Song of Dermot*, p. 233. **61** *Red Bk Ormond*, no. 2, pp 90–1; *Knights' fees*, pp 80–1, and p. 258; Nicholls identifies further settlement at Kilcommon near Tinahely. Nicholls, 'Anglo-French Ireland', p. 373. **62** *Alen's Reg*, p. 141; *COD*, i, p. 35. John fitzJohn Fitzdermot was mentioned as a witness to Avice de la Cornere's grant to Lord Theobald Butler between 1261 and 1264, see ibid., no. 136, p. 65; *Knights' fees*, pp 64–5. **63** *Red Bk Ormond*, no. 1, p. 6; *CJR, 1308–14*, pp 233–4; In 1325 a William Odonnelan was captured with some O'Tooles from Imaal, see (*Rot.pat. Hib*) p. 31b; In 1297 Johanna la Botiller cancelled the debts of Maurice fitzGeoffrey for his killing of Dúnlaing MacDalbaig, see *CJR, 1295–1303*, p. 156. Douenald McTalewy, a monk of Baltinglass, was implicated in the murder of William fitzRalph in 1297, and was accused of being in league with rebellious kinsmen in 1299, see ibid., pp 186, 199. Their disaffection continued and Gilledonesagh Otauly was a noted rebel in the liberty of Wexford in 1312; see *CJR, 1308–14*, p. 235. **64** *Expugnatio*, p. 143; *Gormanston Reg*, pp 145–6. **65** Pender 'O'Clery', para.1750, p. 130, para 1760, p. 131.

leader, Maurice. The O'Byrnes were also living on the Kilpipe lands of the bishopric of Ferns near Aughrim in 1299. Bishop Richard de Northhampton of Ferns described Richard O'Byrne and other Irish as his betaghs, meaning tenants.[66] The sons of this Richard O'Byrne also held lands within the Fitzgerald barony of Wicklow; indeed, during the early fourteenth century, Murchadh mac Gerald O'Byrne seemingly was the leading feudal tenant there.[67] This view of incorporation within the feudal structure is supported by further evidence: we find O'Byrnes holding lands of the Butlers at Aghowle near Shillelagh in 1303, and many more of them were recognized tenants of the barony of Wicklow in 1306.[68] Thus, the relatively peaceful acceptance of the English settlement by the MacMurrough clients indicates MacMurrough satisfaction and influence.

THE IRISH OF EAST LEINSTER AND PROVINCIAL POLITICS, 1205–65

East Leinster did not become widely disturbed until several decades after the emergence of unrest in West Leinster. But there were rumblings. In early 1207 the arrival of William Marshal, lord of Leinster, to visit his wife's inheritance ensured a clash with Justiciar Meyler Fitzhenry and the royal government at Dublin, and created a serious crisis in Leinster. Even though Fitzhenry was a vassal of Marshal, he was determined to enforce the writ of King John within the English lordship; and the king, eager to expand royal prerogative and power in Ireland, determined that the English lordship there should conform to the law of England, which meant the expansion of the central authority – even if it broke the power of individual English magnates in Ireland. Accordingly, in 1207 King John encouraged Fitzhenry to seize the barony of Offaly and the neighbouring land of Fearceall – an action that provoked Marshal's outrage. When both Fitzhenry and Marshal were summoned before John late in the year, the Irish of West Leinster and the midlands sought to take advantage of their absence.[69] After his return, the justiciar, with the king's encouragment, made war in Leinster upon Isabella de Clare, Marshal's wife – attacking her town of New Ross. However, Marshal with the de Lacys ejected him from Fearceall and captured him at Thurles, thus forcing the king to revise his tactics. The justiciar was compelled to disgorge Offaly; and John, after meeting Marshal at Bristol during April 1208, confirmed Leinster to him for the service of 100 knights.[70]

The bad blood between Marshal and the king persisted. In late 1208 John's determination to enforce royal jurisdiction in Ireland led him to dispatch one of his most trusted curial clerics, Bishop John Grey of Norwich, to succeed Meyler Fitzhenry as justiciar. Marshal now confirmed his alienation from the king by extending his protection to the rebel William de Braose after the latter landed

---

66 Mills, 'Accounts of the earl of Norfolk's estates in Ireland, 1279–1294', p. 55; *CJR, 1295–1303*, p. 254. **67** NA, RC 7/13 (iv), pp 22–4. **68** *Red Bk Ormond*, pp 2, 6; NA, RC 7/13 (iv), pp 22–4. **69** AClon, 1207. **70** Orpen, *Normans*, ii, pp 210–17. See Martin, 'John, lord of Ireland, 1185–1216', p. 137; *Alen's Reg*, p. 31.

with his family at the port of Wicklow. Grey demanded that Marshal hand the
de Braoses over, but Marshal refused and conveyed them to their de Lacy kinsmen.
As in 1207, the feud between Marshal and the royal administration seems to have
unsettled the Irish. An incident occurred at a festival in Cullenswood in Co.
Dublin in 1209, when many of the citizens of Dublin were surprised by an Irish
force (probably from the Wicklow mountains); a great many people were
reportedly killed.[71] Clearly, Marshal was finding it difficult to control his Irish
vassals; and in fact we find the seneschal of Leinster attacking the MacFháeláins
of Uí Fáelain about 1210. Indeed, it seems Marshal became embroiled for the
next two years in continuous warfare with the Irish of Leinster.[72] The rising
tension within the Marshal lordship of Leinster and the slaughter at Cullenswood
may have reflected ethnic tensions between the Irish and English of Leinster
caused by the growing power of an aggressive royal government at Dublin.
Marshal's grant in 1209 to Giollapádraig O'Toole of a charter enfranchizing him
with recourse to common law may have been an attempt to incorporate the
Irish leader more fully within English Leinster; or it could have been a reward
for Giollapádraig's probable service against his kinsmen of the Leinster
mountains – the most likely perpetrators of the massacre at Cullenswood.

The fraying ethnic edges in Leinster were also reflected in the church. As
throughout Europe, the Irish church became an arena fraught with fierce ethnic
competition. In 1216, the bishopric of Glendalough was amalgamated with the
archbishopric of Dublin; to help Archbishop Henry de Londres finance his
project of fortifications at Castlekevin (between Annamoe and Laragh), Henry
III granted him the manor of Swords.[73] After the death of Bishop Albin
O'Mulloy of Ferns shortly after 1223, an Englishman succeeded him. Similarly,
in Kildare, Ralph of Bristol, another Englishman, succeeded Bishop Cornelius
MacFháeláin upon his demise in 1223.[74] By 1228 there were thirty-four Irish
Cistercian houses in Ireland, ten of which had been founded by the English.
Between 1216 and 1217 the Irish houses of Mellifont and its daughters of
Jerpoint, Kilbeggan, Killenny, Bective and Baltinglass resisted attempts by
delegations sent from France to introduce reforms. In 1227, the mountainous
region around the Cistercian abbey of Baltinglass became disturbed; when the
new English abbot attempted to take office, he was driven away by the
supporters of the deposed Irish abbot; however, he returned with an armed force
and forcibly took up his abbacy. In 1228, Stephen of Lexington, dispatched to
Ireland by the Cistercian general chapter to put a stop to the increasing
xenophobia of the Irish houses, eventually imposed his will and re-introduced
the internationalism of the order. His reforms, however, must have alienated
many of the local Irish.[75] The reaction of the MacMurroughs, the founders of
Baltinglass abbey, is not recorded, but they must have been in considerable

71 *Ancient Irish histories*, ii, pp 370–1.   72 *The Irish pipe roll, 1210–1211*, p. 19; *DNB*, xii, p. 1114.
73 *Alen's Reg*, p. 161.   74 *NHI*, ix, pp 311, 314.   75 Watt, *The church and the two nations*,
pp 93–4; O'Dwyer, *The conspiracy of Mellifont*, pp 16–30.

disarray following the loss in battle of four principal figures during William Marshal II's campaign to Connacht in 1225 (see p. 50).[76] Their recovery took decades. In 1244 Henry III sent letters to several Irish kings to attend upon his forthcoming campaign against the Scots. Significantly, no MacMurrough received a letter, whereas Ross O'Phelan of Déise (Waterford), their neighbour, did.[77]

The rise in Irish discontent in East Leinster was slow and gradual. It was largely due to the gradual extension and tightening of royal jurisdiction throughout the English lordship in Ireland which resulted from a further struggle between the Marshal lords of Leinster and the English monarchy. In autumn 1233 a struggle emerged in South Wales between Henry III and Richard Marshal, lord of Leinster. By February 1234 Marshal was winning. The king was keen to prevent him from landing in Leinster to stir rebellion, but Marshal slipped through the king's naval net, landing on the Leinster coast in early February. Although he had initial success, he was mortally wounded by the Fitzgeralds on the Kildare plains during a parley in April 1234, and died later in Kilkenny.[78] During the struggle, fighting had extended into the Leinster mountains. Walter de Riddlesford II stormed the Marshal vill of Comyn – now modern Blessington in Co. Wicklow. Soon afterwards Gilbert Marshal, Richard's brother and successor, ended the war, but de Riddlesford was determined to retain the vill; this prompted Gilbert to complain to the king in 1235. The extent of the fighting is revealed by the fact that Archbishop Luke was awarded 300 marks for damage to his diocese during the struggle, and it is possible that the neighbouring Fitzgerald barony of Wicklow was also a battleground between the protagonists.[79] However, as yet it is impossible to discern the effect of the upheaval upon the Irish.

Much of the growing Irish discontent in Leinster centred upon the issue of common law. After Henry II took the submissions of the Irish princes in 1171 and made the treaty of Windsor with Ruaidhrí O'Connor in 1175, he and his successors intended that the English lordship in Ireland would be governed by the laws of England. There were, however, considerable differences between the law of England and which applied in English areas of Ireland (ruled as they were by quasi-independent magnates). The extinction of the Marshals after Anslem Marshal's death during 1245 afforded the crown an opportunity to extend English law into the Marshal lordship of Leinster. Traditionally, the partition of the lordship in 1247 is considered to have begun the weakening of seigneurial and English authority in Leinster;[80] but there is no real evidence of this. In a letter of June 1246 the king spelt out his intentions to the seneschal of Leinster: effectively, royal jurisdiction and royal judges were to be installed throughout the courts of the Leinster lordship. In September 1246 Henry III reaffirmed his declaration, ordering that English common law be the observed writ without

---

76 AConn, 1225 and p. 761 (index).   77 *CDI, 1171–1251*, no. 2716, p. 405.   78 Clyn, *Annals*, p. 7.   79 *CDI, 1171–1251*, no. 2139, p. 317, no. 2186, p. 324, nos 2224 and 2227, pp 330–1, no. 2255, pp 335–6.   80 Lydon, 'The expansion and consolidation of the colony, 1215–54', p. 168.

exception in Ireland.[81] The application of the law seems to have varied from court to court, but it overrode the older legal practice previously dominant in the baronial courts and which seems to have lingered in the courts of episcopal lands and liberties. The introduction of English common law in its purest sense radically changed the status of the Irish freeholder for the worse. As elsewhere in contemporary Europe, law increasingly defined ethnicity in Ireland as well as custom and language. English law was not for all; it was settler law, and the Irish had very little access to it. Legal status in the eyes of the law became a distinction into which discrimination was built. Accordingly, the Irish desire for admittance to the benefits of common law was manifest. In 1277 the Irish, excluding those of Ulster, petitioned Justiciar Robert de Ufford for access to the common law. Although Edward I agreed, the grant was never implemented. This sort of discrimination led to a deep sense of alienation and victimization in the Irish mind, as evidenced by the Remonstrance of the Irish to the papacy in 1317.

The emergence of unrest in East Leinster has also been interpreted in the context of a wider series of anti-English wars waged by Irish kings – labelled the Irish Resurgence. A swathe of settlement stretching from eastern Meath to Kilkenny had the effect of insulating both the English and the Irish of East Leinster from the anti-settler feeling found in the west and elsewhere. During the late 1260s the Irish of East Leinster gradually became more restless and aggressive. Moreover, the war that broke in the Leinster mountains in 1269–70 had been brewing since the 1240s. One cause was the deterioration of relations among the English themselves. Between 1244 and 1251 Archbishop Luke of Dublin granted lands in central Wicklow to Theobald Butler;[82] it is uncertain why he took this decision, but there is one clue: in 1243 Henry III ordered Maurice Fitzgerald to desist from interfering within the archbishop's manor of Sancto Bosco (probably Hollywood in west Wicklow); and maybe because of Fitzgerald intrusions, Luke granted these lands to Butler to shore up and bolster his own local position. The Butlers continued to expand into the region during the 1260s.[83] This growth of their influence probably unsettled the O'Tooles of Glenmalure and some of the O'Byrnes near Aughrim, alienating the Fitzgeralds and the archbishops of Dublin.

Luke's policy seems to have been reversed by his successor, Archbishop Fulk de Sandford. Between 1256 and 1271 Fulk granted the lands of Glandeluri (probably Glenmalure) to Moriertagh O'Toole, possibly overseer of his mountain estates. In return, Moriertagh, in an elaborate property exchange, transferred to the archbishop his Imaal lands and those in Uí Felemeda Tuaid.[84] This has been interpreted as an attempt by the archbishop to legitimize the tenurial rights of his O'Toole servants, but it may have been designed to protect his Irish tenants from Butler attentions. It has been suggested that Fulk tried to regularize Moriertagh's position as overseer of the Irish living on the archbishopric's lands

---

81 *CDI, 1252–84*, no. 2836, p. 424, see also no. 2849, p. 426, ibid., no. 2850, p. 426.   82 Price, 'The case of Phelim McFeagh and the lands of Ranelagh', pp 50–1.   83 *Crede mihi*, p. 144. 84 *Alen's Reg*, pp 136, 141.

in Wicklow, but close reading of the Glenmalure grant tells a slightly different story. It reveals that Moriertagh's ancestors had long rendered three marks for these lands to the archbishop's predecessors, so his family may have been long established as the archbishopric's Irish overseers.[85] A strong possibility also exists that Moriertagh was otherwise known as Meyler O'Toole when disguised by a English forename. By February 1264 this Meyler was dead and the wardship of his only recorded legitimate child and heiress, Agatha, was purchased by Adam de Wudeford in April 1264 from Archbishop Fulk.[86] The demise of Meyler/Moriertagh and the absence of a strong heir had profound and far-reaching effects upon Irish populations nestled within these mountains, creating a vacuum at a time when Butler ambition was on the march within the region. This allowed younger and much more hard-line Irish leaders to emerge to challenge Butler advances.

Theobald Butler further annoyed the Fitzgeralds during the English civil war between Simon de Montfort, the barons' leader, and Henry III in 1264. The violence that exploded between these protagonists at Castledermot can be interpreted as constituting part of a wider struggle between Maurice Fitzgerald and Earl Walter Burke of Ulster. On 6 December 1264, the Fitzgeralds prompted countrywide fighting by capturing Burke's allies, including Justiciar Richard de la Rochelle and Earl Walter. This crisis caused Geoffrey de Joinville, the acting justiciar, to provision Dublin against siege and to dispatch further provisions to Butler's castle of Arklow, which faced a threat from the Fitzgeralds of the barony of Wicklow. Further evidence suggests that there were disturbances within the mountainous lands of the archbishopric: in 1265, jurors at an inquisition at Castlekevin replied that the archbishop's tenants never aided the enemies of the king; this may be connected to de Joinville's campaign against the Fitzgeralds early in 1265.[87]

As has been shown, the Irish dynasties of East Leinster were profoundly affected by the arrival of the English. By 1180 the conqueror's hand was evident throughout the province. However, East Leinster was more penetrated by the settlers than was the West. This is reflected in the change of land tenure, in political structures and in naming practices. The evidence suggests the Irish were incorporated within the English settlement, most notably the MacMurroughs, who became the hereditary seneschals of the Irish of Marshal Leinster. As has been shown, a hybrid society of sorts emerged. This mutual toleration promoted mutual indulgence, resulting in a long-lived peace, which was doubly insured by the relative insulation of the Irish dynasties of East Leinster from the rest of Ireland by a strong belt of settlement. But this peace must have come under pressure after the extinction of Diarmait MacMurrough's Marshal successors in 1245, which led to the extension of English common law into Leinster. This, combined with Butler activities in the Wicklow region, must have placed considerable strain upon peaceable co-existence, increasing racial tension and shortening the paths to war for the Irish and English of East Leinster.

---

85 Ibid., pp 136, 141; *Crede mihi*, pp 93–4; Price, *Placenames*, p. xlix.   **86** Ibid., p. 114; Nicholls, 'Anglo-French Ireland', p. 382.   **87** Otway-Ruthven, *Medieval Ireland*, p. 196; Lydon, 'The years of crisis, 1254–1315', fn.6, p. 183; *Hist. & mun. doc. Ire.*, p. liii and pp 150–4.

CHAPTER 3

The reaction of Connacht and
West Leinster, 1180–1270

By 1180, the English had almost pegged back O'Connor power to the Shannon. But Ruaidhrí O'Connor knew that Connacht's fortunes were bound up with those of Meath. The centrality of Meath to Ruaidhrí's earlier plans was borne out in 1169, when he annexed its western part to Connacht. And the danger to Connacht created by Hugh de Lacy's colonization of Meath led to Ruaidhrí's campaign of 1174.[1]

About 1180 Ruaidhrí gave his daughter Rose in marriage to de Lacy, hoping to stall the colonists' advance and remain protector of Clonmacnoise and of the nearby Irish kingdoms. For a while, this policy worked. Befriending Ruaidhrí also bought de Lacy time to tighten his grip on Meath; he also possibly helped to restore Ruaidhrí in Henry II's eyes. A sign of this rapprochement was when one of Ruaidhrí's sons in 1180 accompanied Archbishop Lorcán O'Toole to visit Henry (it may also about this time that Ruaidhrí resumed payment of tribute from Connacht).[2] To his credit, de Lacy tried to accommodate the grievances of the Irish who had fled Meath to Connacht, and thereby encourage their return. He seems to have been tolerant of many of the former O'Melaghlin rulers of Meath and attempted to foster co-existence among all his vassals.[3] But, while de Lacy's alliance with the O'Connors briefly stabilized the region, it was a cause of concern for Henry II.[4]

The O'Connor/de Lacy pact probably contributed to a wider improvement of relations between the Irish and the English in West Leinster. The best display of the pragmatism adopted by a former O'Connor client was that of Fáelán MacFháeláin of Uí Fáeláin. After Fáelán's desertion of the English in 1174 to join

---

1 AFM, 1169; ATig, 1174; *Expugnatio*, p. 139. 2 Perros, 'Crossing the Shannon frontier', p. 122; AFM, 1186. 3 *Expugnatio*, p.191; he provided the example, fathering at least one son with Rose. See Perros, 'Crossing the Shannon frontier', p. 134. Some O'Melaghlins bore traces of de Lacy's favour. In fact, Art O'Melaghlin, Ruaidhrí's enemy, seemed allied to de Lacy throughout the 1170s; see ATig, 1178. In 1184, this alliance appears to have ended as Diarmait O'Brien with English encouragement assassinated Art, see ALC, 1184. Apparently de Lacy had found new O'Melaghlin allies. For example, a member of the dynasty was described as a knight. In turn, this figure was to christen his own son Henry. Henry O'Melaghlin was killed by the English of Meath in 1227, see AClon, 1199, 1226. 4 *Expugnatio*, pp 191, p. 338, n. 351.

Ruaidhrí's unsuccessful campaign, Uí Fáeláin was devastated. This forced Fáelán to modify his attitude and to temporize. And sometime between 1189 and 1203, Fáelán was granted lands at Killarney (identified as being within Carbury, which traditionally lay in Offaly).[5] Before his death in 1203, Fáelán in turn granted Killarney to the priory of Clonard (in 1293 a dispute arose between William de Vescy and other heirs of the Marshals with the prior of Clonard, de Vescy complaining that Fáelán had no right to make the grant; besides, the O'Melaghlins of Meath and O'Kearys of Carbury were long associated with Clonard). Fáelán appears to have been compensated for losses in Uí Fáeláin with lands in Meath and Offaly, and seems to have acted as a guardian of the marches against the O'Connor Falys, O'Kearys and O'Melaghlins. Grants also reveal that the MacFháeláins enjoyed good relations with the de Herefords, who held the Uí Fáeláin cantred of Cloncurry. It has also been suggested that the motte and manor near Cloncurry church was a later MacFháeláin residence. Fáelán died a monk at Meyler Fitzhenry's newly founded abbey of Connell in 1203, while Cornelius MacFháeláin was bishop of Kildare (1206–23).[6] Unlike the O'Tooles, the MacFháeláins never recovered any of their former power in the later thirteenth century, becoming largely an ecclesiastical family. Others of the name clung to fragments of ancestral lands in the manor of Cloncurry, while another, Dowenild OHelyn, held church lands at Kill and was recorded as trading in pottery clay in 1343.[7] The MacFháeláins were the biggest Irish losers in the English settlement of Leinster.

To the south of Uí Fáeláin, Laois was given to de Lacy's son-in-law, Meyler Fitzhenry, to conquer in 1181. After the conquest, Fitzhenry and de Lacy consolidated their advance, constructing Timahoe castle in 1181–2.[8] Later Meyler erected another castle on the rock of Dunamase. (Meyler, like de Lacy, actually had quite good relations with the Irish: Domhnall O'More of Laois defended settlers from the O'Connors of Connacht in 1196 and some of his dynasty adopted forenames such as Henry, Simon and Nigel.)[9] As in Uí Fáeláin, some of the Irish elite of Laois and Ossory possibly copied the English by building mottes at Monally and Srahan in the Slieve Blooms. The pipe roll of 1211–12

5 ATig, AI, AU, 1174; *Song of Dermot*, p. 237; *Expugnatio*, p. 137; *CDI, 1293–1301*, no. 22, pp 16–18; this grant seems to have been made between 1189 and 1203. Flanagan, *Irish society*, p. 124; Nicholls, 'The land of the Leinstermen', p. 552. **6** *Reg. St Thomas*, p. 78 and p. 82; Flanagan, 'Henry II and the kingdom of Uí Fáeláin', pp 235–6; AFM, 1203. **7** In November 1304 two Walters and a Thomas MacFháeláin held lands there of the Butlers. See *Red Bk Ormond*, pp 30, 32. Variants of the surname include Makylan, Makelan, Mckelan, Offelan, Macelan, MacGelan, MacKellan and MacGealan. See *Reg St Thomas*, p. 298; *The Irish pipe roll, 1211–12*, p. 19; *CDI, 1293–1301*, pp 17–18; *Cal. Gormanston Reg*, p. 145; *Account roll of the priory of the Holy Trinity, Dublin*, pp 55, 195. Much later in the census of 1659, the descendants of the MacFháeláins were shown still living in Kildare Offaly, Laois and Ossory and not on their ancestral lands See S. Pender (ed.), *A census of Ireland circa 1659* (Dublin, 1939), pp 399, 404–5, 496, 498, 500–5. Variants of the name include Helan, Felan alias Holan, Felan alias Helan, Hylan, Filan alias Hilan. **8** *Expugnatio*, p. 195. **9** ALC, 1196; *CJR, 1295–1303*, p. 178. Ó Cléirigh, 'The problems of defence: a regional case-study', p. 44.

records that the Irish of Dunamase gave £53 6s. 8d., and after 1245 they were recognized feudal tenants of the Mortimers, holding much of western Laois.[10]

The same English approach can be detected in Offaly. There Diarmait O'Dempsey thrived as lord of Offaly, whilst seemingly recognizing English overlordship. This was at the expense of the O'Connor Falys. The meagre evidence suggests that the O'Connor Falys, too, integrated themselves, serving on an English campaign in Ulster during 1196 and fighting against the O'Connors of Connacht in 1200. It has also been suggested that they acknowledged the lordship of the Fitzgeralds and the Berminghams by rendering an annual tribute.[11] This recognition by the English was achieved at a cost, as many of the O'Connor Faly centres (such as Rathangan and Geashill) became hubs of English manors. Parallels can be found among the MacGillapatricks of North Ossory. Despite suffering the assault of MacMurrough and the English, Domhnall son of Donnchadh MacGillapatrick won over Maurice de Prendergast. And from his recorded actions of 1171–2, Domhnall's power was initially relatively unhindered: he killed Domhnall O'Fogarty of southern Ely, and O'Kaelly.[12] By allying with the English and submitting to Henry II in 1171–2, Domhnall preserved most of his kingdom; and his commitment to the new order is proved by his presence on English campaigns against Domhnall O'Brien of Thomond and Diarmait MacCarthy of Desmond in 1175 and 1176.[13]

Even before Hugh de Lacy's assassination in 1186, there was considerable tension between the English and the Irish of West Leinster and the midlands. Reasons for this gradual deterioration lie in the English advance to the Shannon.[14] The provincial kings and Ruaidhrí O'Connor knew that the outright loss of this region to the English threatened their kingdoms in the long term. As a result, any attempt to plant these territories was strenuously resisted. However, Ruaidhrí was unable to push the English back due to rebellions in Connacht and Donegal during the early 1180s.[15] In 1183 Ruaidhrí briefly resigned in favour of his son, Conchobhar Maenmhaighe, a man who believed he could restore the O'Connor high-kingship,[16] and who was less inclined than his father to temporize with the English (he had a right to be confident, having bested an English army at Thurles in July 1174).

10 McNeill, *Castles in Ireland,* p. 73; O'Conor, *The archaeology of medieval rural settlement in Ireland,* p. 76; idem, 'Norman castles in Co. Laois', p. 198; *The Irish pipe roll, 1211–12,* p. 13; Nicholls, *Gaelic Ire,* p. 174.   11 AFM, 1196; ALC, 1196, 1200; Otway-Ruthven, 'The partition of the De Verdon lands in Ireland in 1332', p. 413; *The Irish pipe roll, 1211–12,* pp 37, 67. This probable situation has parallels with those of the O'Farrells of Annaly, O'Rourkes of Bréifne and the O'Neills of Tyrone.   12 AFM, ATig, 1171; AU, 1172.   13 *Expugnatio,* pp 95, 161–3; AI, 1176. The appearance of MacGillapatrick annalistic obits attest to their continuing importance. ATig, 1176; ALC, 1185, 1193.   14 *Expugnatio,* p. 191.   15 AI, 1181; AU, 1180, 1181, 1188; ALC, 1180, 1181, 1182, 1183; MA, 1180. The major threat to Connacht was Flaithbertach O'Muldory, king of Donegal. He was married to Ruaidhrí's daughter, see *DNB,* xv, p. 852. Earlier Dubhchobhlaigh, Toirdhealbhach O'Connor's daughter, was married to another ruler of Donegal, Flaithbertach O'Canannan. They drowned when their ship was wrecked in 1153. See ATig, 1153.   16 ALC, 1183; MA, 1184; Joynt, 'Echtra Mac Echach

Like his father, Conchobhar Maenmhaighe fully understood how the colonization of West Leinster affected Connacht. Throughout his brief career, he sought
to preserve the O'Connor overlordship east of the Shannon by attempting to
reverse the English imposition of castles astride the passes and fords of West
Leinster. Naturally, the siting of these castles alarmed the Irish, and Conchobhar
Maenmhaighe exploited their fears. The clearest sign of his intentions east of the
Shannon was his linking up with Máelsechlainn Beag O'Melaghlin to raze a
castle belt in west Meath during 1184.[17] What favoured Connacht's kings in this
struggle was the partial English failure to comprehend the strategic importance
of the mid-Shannon basin centred on Clonmacnoise.

The re-emergence of Ruaidhrí in 1184–5 from the monastery of Cong
stalled Conchobhar Maenmhaighe's efforts to push back the English. Matters
were further complicated by the landing of John, lord of Ireland, at Waterford
in April 1185. John brought plans for an offensive into Munster as far as the
Shannon, and built Tibberaghny, Ardfinnan and Lismore castles to protect the
royal lands lying between Waterford/Dungarvan and the Munster Blackwater.[18]
This royal wedge was flanked to the east by the Leinster marches and to the west
by MacCarthy Desmond, while its northern frontier faced Thomond and
Connacht. John's advance into the southern midlands drew forceful responses from
Domhnall O'Brien of Thomond and Diarmait MacCarthy of Desmond. On 24
June 1185, O'Brien attacked Ardfinnan castle and then went on to burn Ossory.
Gerald of Wales, writing during the reign of Conchobhar Maenmhaighe, points
out that O'Brien's offensive into Ossory enjoyed support from other Irish
leaders. His treatise paints a picture of a conquest slowly running out of steam
because of mounting Irish resistance and the inhospitable nature of the terrain.[19]

The writings of Gerald of Wales recognize that the Irish adapted their tactics
in response to the English, with regard to archery and the laying of ambushes.[20]
The basic principle of Irish warfare and its relationship with the landscape can
be discerned from the annals: withdrawal upon the approach of a superior force
into a naturally protecting environment, usually a densely wooded and mountainous territory. (Concentration in this landscape allowed Irish kings to attack
English armies in terrain which rendered heavy cavalry useless; this enabled

Mugmedoin', pp 91–111; see Ó Cuiv, 'A poem composed for Cathal Cróibhdhearg
O'Conchobhair', pp 156–174. In the first year of his kingship, Conchobhar signalled his
intention of rebuilding Connacht's power by crushing Donnchadh O'Connor. See AU, 1184.
17 AFM, 1184. For instance, in 1184 Art O'Melaghlin became disaffected with his English
masters, leading them to procure Diarmait O'Brien of Ormond to assassinate him. See ALC,
AU, 1184. Earlier in 1178 Hugh de Lacy, with Art, attacked Máelsechlainn Beag and the
people of Tethbae. See ATig, 1178. In this attack Muircheartach the son of An Sionnach was
killed. This was to be the reason for de Lacy's assassination in 1186. See *Expugnatio*, pp 235, 353
n. 480. This Máelsechlainn Beag was the half-brother of Art O'Melaghlin (*d.*1184).
18 Orpen, *Normans*, ii, pp 93–5; *Expugnatio*, pp 234–5; Martin, 'John, lord of Ireland,
1185–1216', p. 128. **19** *Expugnatio*, pp 235, 241. In Desmond, the Irish fared worst as
Diarmait MacCarthy was killed at a parley with Theobald Walter and the Ostmen of Cork in
August 1185. **20** Ibid., p. 231.

them to dictate the pace of warfare against the enemy, who now faced Irish horsemen wielding weapons similar to their own.) Improvements had also been made in Irish armour; and the Irish learned English military techniques, modifying their traditional armour with coats of mail.

Like many of his English contemporaries, Gerald acknowledged the immense military strength lying behind the Shannon. To counter Conchobhar Maenmhaighe's push against the castle builders, Gerald proposed that the Shannon become the western frontier of English Ireland. His proposed fortification of the Shannon reflected the circles in which he moved. According to Gerald, the success of this project depended upon improving communications between English outposts by cutting passes through Irish territories.[21]

The year 1186 was disastrous for the English colonization of the midlands. It saw de Lacy assassinated by the Irish during his inspection of Durrow castle. The Annals of Loch Cé and Gerald report that de Lacy's death resulted from the vendetta of An Sionnach O'Kearney, a neighbouring Irish lord.[22] De Lacy's death opened up opportunities for Conchobhar Maenmhaighe, who, having seen off Ruaidhrí's challenge, capitalized upon the mounting anti-settler feeling. Significantly, between 1185 and 1189 Domhnall O'Brien of Thomond, Domhnall MacCarthy of Desmond, Ruaidhrí MacDunleavy of Ulaid, Aodh O'Rourke of Bréifne, and Máelsechlainn Beag O'Melaghlin of Meath pledged their vassalage to him. In 1187 Conchobhar Maenmhaighe with Máelsechlainn Beag O'Melaghlin destroyed Killare castle in west Meath.[23] In spite of continued unrest within his Connacht kingdom, Conchobhar Maenmhaighe partly restored Connacht's fortunes in West Leinster. He tried also to establish personal links with the Irish there, fostering a son in Tethbae.[24] However, the long-term effects of this strategy of positioning his sons as watch-dogs in the midlands emerged only in the early 1200s. The assassination of Conchobhar Maenmhaighe in 1189 and subsequent O'Connor civil wars deflected Connacht's attentions from the midlands.[25] Conchobhar Maenmhaighe's hitherto obscure uncle, Cathal Cróibhdhearg O'Connor, his eventual successor, was aware of the dangers of settlement to Connacht and was determined to preserve his kingdom.[26]

If the English penetration of the midlands made the king of Connacht nervous, it had a similar effect upon other Irish kings, particularly those of Munster.[27] Much of the conflict in the midlands between the Munster kings and the English seems to have been fought out in Ossory, a virtual frontierland

---

21 *Expugnatio*, pp 137, 249, p. 251.   **22** ALC, 1186; *Expugnatio*, p. 235.   **23** AFM, 1187, 1189; Perros, 'Crossing the Shannon frontier', p. 124.   **24** ALC, 1204, 1207; AFM, 1203. Interestingly another Connacht dynast was fostered in Tethbae in about this period. The Four Masters mention the death of Sitric Teptach O'Kelly of Uí Maine in 1203.   **25** AFM, 1189. After Ruaidhrí's return in 1189, O'Muldory invaded Connacht. Since Ruaidhrí was king presumably it was he who opposed the invader. In 1190 Cathal Cróibhdhearg and Cathal Carrach, the eldest son of Conchobhar Maenmhaighe, formed an alliance at Clonfert. This peace seems to have given Cathal Cróibhdhearg the kingship as he is referred to as O'Connor in the next entry.   **26** Perros, 'Crossing the Shannon frontier', pp 127–8.   **27** AFM, 1192.

between Leinster and Munster. Despite considerable initial resistance to the English in the early 1170s, the MacGillapatrick kings of South and North Ossory soon trimmed their sails to suit Strongbow and their own interests. In fact, Domhall son of Cearbhall MacGillapatrick, king of South Ossory, had little choice but to do so: the devastation wrought by Strongbow and MacMurrough during 1169 and 1170 caused the collapse of his kingdom (an area seemingly co-extensive with the territory of Overk in Ossory). This collapse was confirmed by the death of Domhnall son of Cearbhall in 1176 and by Strongbow's grant of Overk before that year to Milo Fitzdavid.[28]

However, the kingdom of North Ossory was an entirely different matter. Its king, Domhnall son of Donnchadh MacGillapatrick, had put up considerable resistance to MacMurrough and Strongbow between 1169 and 1171, but in autumn 1171 he pragmatically submitted to Strongbow and became his vassal.[29] He was allowed to hold North Ossory, gaining the benefits of Strongbow's protection from the threat of Domhnall O'Brien of Thomond. Domhnall, king of North Ossory, was nobody's fool, and he doubly ensured his position by bending his knee before Henry II in winter 1171. In fact, the only part of North Ossory given to the settlers belonged to the O'Keallys, Domhnall's bitter enemies.[30] Domhnall rendered feudal service to Strongbow by campaigning for him in 1173, 1175 and 1176, a service that dovetailed perfectly with Domhnall's agenda. The arrangement proved mutually advantageous to both MacGillapatricks and the English until Domhall's death sometime in 1185.[31] He was succeeded by his son Máelsechlainn MacGillapatrick, who continued to hold North Ossory as a vassal of the heirs of Strongbow. However, he did not have the same relationship with the English as Domhnall had; his position was complicated by John's advance during 1185 into the southern midlands which provoked the O'Briens of Thomond and the MacCarthys of Desmond. On 24 June 1185, the O'Briens sacked Ardfinnan castle and then marched into Ossory. Gerald of Wales wrote that this march drew widespread support from the Irish there – perhaps a sign that the MacGillapatricks had resented John's intrusions.

Ossory was to remain a hotly disputed faultline between the Irish of Munster and English Leinster. In 1189 Domhnall MacCarthy of Desmond displayed an impressive degree of regional mobility by razing castles from Desmond to Ossory, capping this performance with the defeat of an English army at Thurles the next year. This clearly unsettled the MacGillapatricks of North Ossory. The dramatic decline of relations between the English and Maelsechlainn of North Ossory also coincided with the emergence of a new English lord of Leinster. In 1189 (as we know) William Marshal married Isabella de Clare, Strongbow's daughter, and became lord of Leinster. After September 1189, Marshal obtained

---

28 AFM, 1176; Carrigan, *History … Ossory*, i, p. 58. 29 Carrigan, *History … Ossory*, i, p. 65; *Song of Dermot*, p. 233. Domhnall MacGillapatrick of North Ossory is referred to as a vassal of Strongbow on the earl's campaign of 1173 into Meath. 30 *Expugnatio*, p. 95; Carrigan, *History … Ossory*, i, p. 58. 31 AFM, 1185.

seisin of his wife's vast inheritance and dispatched his bailiff to Leinster. As the heir of Strongbow and Diarmait MacMurrough, Marshal was determined to rule Leinster in its entirety. Clearly, the growing MacGillapatrick hostility and the threat from the Munster kings endangered the security of the southern borders of the Marshal lordship of Leinster. About 1191/2 Marshal apparently authorized that the right of his MacGillapatrick vassals to hold North Ossory be declared forfeit and that a sentence of eviction be passed upon them. These actions had immediate effect in Ossory: the stewards of Marshal tightened his hold over central Ossory, building Kilkenny castle in 1192 and beginning the expulsion of the MacGillapatricks to the Slieve Bloom mountains on the borders of Laois. The Irish response was furious. (During the upheaval, Bishop Felix O'Dulany of Ossory complained that his diocese was engulfed in warfare and transferred his capital from Aghaboe to the safety of Kilkenny in the south.)[32] The English of Leinster quickly moved to curtail the threat of Domhnall O'Brien by invading Thomond, only to be stopped in their tracks by Domhnall's army on the plain of Killaloe in east Clare. Domhnall then pushed into the midlands, defeating another English force at Thurles before capitalizing on the turmoil raging in Ossory. What is clear, though, is that the MacGillapatricks had been forced from central Ossory into the Slieve Blooms just before or just after the death in 1194 of Máelsechlainn MacGillapatrick.[33]

The warfare in Ossory and the Irish exploitation of it represent determined attempts by the kings of Munster to maintain their midland ambits. Domhnall O'Brien, however, was a pragmatist. In an act reminiscent of Ruaidhrí O'Connor, he married a daughter to William Burke, his English neighbour.[34] After 1194, Cathal Cróibhdhearg O'Connor showed himself to be the inheritor of Conchobhar Maenmhaighe's policy. Much of this change has to do with the O'Brien/Burke alliance, forging of which was possibly motivated by John's probable grant of Connacht to Burke in 1194.[35] Cathal Cróibhdhearg tried to prevent English expansion into Connacht by creating trouble in Munster and the midlands; and in 1195 he showed that Connacht still packed a considerable punch by crossing the Shannon to campaign in Munster with the MacCarthys – a campaign devoted mainly to the destruction of several castles in Tipperary and the pillaging of Burke's lands near Athassel.[36] There was also renewed O'Connor

---

32 Carrigan, *History … Ossory*, i, pp 70–1.   **33** AFM, 1192; AI, AFM, 1194.   **34** Martin, 'John, lord of Ireland, 1185–1216', p. 129. One of the reasons behind O'Brien's somersault was his fear of the growth of MacCarthy power arising from Domhnall MacCarthy's victories. To doubly guard his position, O'Brien encouraged the erection of an English castle in the Tipperary parish of Clanwilliam to check any further extension of MacCarthy's influence. See AI, 1193. **35** Perros, 'Crossing the Shannon frontier', p. 126. The O'Briens were also probably encouraging the O'Flathertys against the O'Briens. Ruaidhrí O'Flaherty fled West Connacht because of Cathal Cróibhdhearg for the sanctuary of O'Brien's house in 1196 See ALC, 1196. **36** AI, MA, 1195. Perros, 'Crossing the Shannon frontier', p. 128. Once back in Connacht, Cathal Cróibhdhearg opened negotiations with the English. At Athlone he obtained recognition of his kingship from John de Courcy and Walter de Lacy before dispatching a

activity in the midlands as evidenced by the attacks by the sons of Conchobhar Maenmhaighe in 1196 on the O'Mores and the English of Laois.[37] Cathal Cróibhdhearg's hostility to the English served him well until 1199, when serious divisions emerged between him and Conchobhar Maenmhaighe's sons.[38]

By 1199, Connacht was under siege, with an English motte standing symbolically at its doorstep, Athlone. Now, with invasion looming, Cathal Cróibhdhearg again stirred up the midland Irish by extending them military assistance.[39] Interestingly, from this date an eastward drift in countrywide warfare can be detected, with Connacht acting as its engine. In Munster, Cathal Cróibhdhearg was still promoting a war against the settlers, sending forces to attack the English in Limerick in 1199. However, his attention was quickly diverted back to the Shannon frontier with the midlands where the English were on the make. In response he pushed into west Meath[40] and, on his way back to Connacht, his forces were routed by the settlers. The effects of this defeat were compounded by Cathal Cróibhdhearg's feud with Cathal Carrach O'Connor, the leader of Conchobhar Maenmhaighe's sons,[41] who enlisted the support of Burke and the O'Briens and burnt Clonmacnoise before expelling Cathal Cróibhdhearg to Ulster. In his absence Cathal Carrach installed himself as king of Connacht. By February 1200 Cathal Cróibhdhearg had returned to Connacht, establishing his influence in Annaly and raiding Limerick in May; he also attacked the O'Connor Falys of Offaly and burnt English settlements in west Meath. In 1201 Cathal Cróibhdhearg tried again to reclaim his kingship but Cathal Carrach proved too strong.[42] Eventually Cathal Cróibhdhearg was restored to his kingship by John in 1202 but it took him a year to firmly re-establish himself; in 1207 he earned a charter to Connacht.[43] Having come so close to losing all, Cathal Cróibhdhearg was determined to avoid conflict with the English.

In the midlands, the political climate was seething. In the southern midlands, from their refuge among the Slieve Blooms of North Ossory, the MacGillapatricks pursued a deadly war with the English from the early 1200s. The MacGillapatricks were not the only Irish dynasty of the diocese of Ossory under considerable English pressure: the tightening of the English grip was also keenly felt by the O'Brennans, whose problems with the settlers seemingly began after John's midland campaign of 1185 and his grant of their territory to his follower, Alard fitzWilliam. Soon after this, they seem to have been expelled from their ancestral lands to the highland region around Castlecomer in northeast Kilkenny. They too were considerably aggrieved by the loss of their land and status. In 1200 this

second expedition to help Flaithbertach O'Muldory crush a rebellion in Donegal. See ALC, 1195; Orpen, *Normans*, ii, pp 153–6. **37** ALC, 1196. **38** AClon, 1199. **39** Orpen, *Normans*, ii, p. 183; AClon, 1199. This is shown by the presence of the Knight O'Melaghlin amongst Cathal Cróibhdhearg's troops during their attack on Cathal Carrach in 1199. **40** ALC, 1200; Perros, 'Crossing the Shannon frontier', p. 128; Orpen, *Normans*, ii, pp 183–4. **41** Perros, 'Crossing the Shannon frontier', p.129. **42** ALC, 1200, 1201, 1202, 1203; AClon, 1200, 1201, 1202; MA, 1200, 1201. See Orpen, *Normans*, ii, pp 189–90; Martin, 'John, lord of Ireland, 1185–1216', p. 131. **43** Perros, 'Crossing the Shannon frontier', pp 131–2.

anger boiled over, resulting in their sacking of Castlecomer castle and the towns of Leighlinbridge and Wellys (probably Wells in the barony of Idrone West) in Carlow.[44]

Cathal Cróibhdhearg must have been aware of the growing resentment of the midland Irish at the expropriation of their lands. In spite of the turmoil in Connacht between 1200 and 1203, the links between the Connacht kings and the midland Irish remained close. Cathal Cróibhdhearg's diplomacy in the midlands is evidenced by the fact that, the second wife of his son Aodh was Raghnailt O'Farrell of Annaly. The axis between the kings of Meath and Connacht was affirmed by Máelsechlainn Beag O'Melaghlin's erection of an altar at Clonmacnoise in 1205.[45] While both Máelsechlainn Beag and Cathal Cróibhdhearg avoided conflict with the English, discontent was rising among their junior branches. When these lesser lords appealed to their overlords to help against the English, none came. The junior branches of the O'Melaghlins, the O'Briens and the O'Connors now began to co-ordinate their attacks upon the English. Thus, the rowdy frontierland of West Leinster and the midlands was transformed by an explosion of Irish anger. Connacht still provided a focus for the midland Irish, but it was in decline; the anger caused by the attempted English conquest of Connacht destabilized the midlands, where the Irish, aggrieved over issues such as land, race and culture, were opposing the English advance westward. Now the Irish began to make serious inroads right along the frontier of English Leinster, Irish princes who had adapted to the tide of change pushed the English out of partly colonized peripheries. Herein lay the genesis of what has been termed the Irish Resurgence.

The rise of royal government as a force within the region was also an additional catalyst for Irish anger. As Davies has pointed out, King John's reign witnessed a momentous advance in the territorial gains of the English kings in Ireland. John ruthlessly advanced the cause of English crown through the extension and the development of the power of the central authority at Dublin. During the early thirteenth century, royal power in Ireland advanced through a series of custodies and dramatic forfeitures, and the erection of royal castles was sustained and remorseless. This had the effect of placing the feudal noose even more tightly round the necks of both the English and Irish of West Leinster and the midlands. Between 1205 and 1207, after a series of baronial deaths, John obtained direct custody and control over the whole of Tipperary and a considerable part of Limerick. The subsequent disruption within these English lordships may have created unease among the Irish elites which took the form of mounting opposition to royal officals and the settlers, and which was probably the cause of the attacks by the previously pacific O'Carrolls of Ely on the English settlers in 1205.[46]

---

44 Carrigan, *History … Ossory*, i, p. 12; J. Otway-Ruthven (ed.), *Liber Primus Kilkenniensis* (Kilkenny, 1961), p. 127. 45 AClon, 1205. 46 Davies, *Domination and conquest*, p. 71; Otway-Ruthven, *Medieval Ireland*, pp 76–80; AClon, AFM, 1205.

The greatest Irish opposition to the English advance in the midlands was led by Cormac mac Airt O'Melaghlin of west Meath. He and his brothers were not inspired by the plight of an embattled Connacht; they had a history of enmity towards the O'Connors. By 1205, Máelsechlainn Beag O'Melaghlin, their uncle and overlord, had become a spent force; this allowed the brothers emerge as a potent regional force through skilful use of terrain and adoption of English military techniques. From their heartland in the hilly and woody regions of southwest west Meath where the settlers were lightly sprinkled, Cormac mac Airt waged a war of attrition upon the English.[47] Without doubt, the rise of these brothers among the midland Irish had been facilitated by the disintegration of Cathal Cróibhdhearg O'Connor's influence in the midlands and by the advance of English royal jurisdiction. In 1206, Cormac mac Airt O'Melaghlin made his move, attacking the west Meath town of Baleloghoe and defeating Máelsechlainn Beag and the English. He may also have benefitted from the fact that the MacGeoghegans and O'Laeghaghans were at each other's throats in nearby Kineleagh.[48] A major reason for Cormac mac Airt's success was the vulnerability of the settlers along the long external frontier of English Leinster. Having such a long frontier, these settlers (unlike those of East Leinster) were exposed to the effects of threats and influences promoted by resurgent rulers of the still unconquered lands in Connacht, Munster and Ulster.

One aspect of this warfare was the successful Irish use of passes against the settlers. Since ancient times these corridors provided a nexus of communication to the nobilities of Leinster, Connacht and Munster. Despite the turmoil caused by the English advances, this nexus still operated. The great artery of the midland was what A.P. Smyth termed the 'midland corridor', running for about twenty miles from west Meath to Birr on the fringes of the north Munster lordship of Ely. Off it ran several interconnecting passes that drew in other territories. These were the hinges on which this Irish geopolitical region hung. As mentioned earlier, the English did not fully comprehend the necessity of colonizing these vital valleys.[49] Where they did incastellate these arteries, as at Geashill, Leys and along the Barrow valley, Irish regional polity had very limited room for manoeuvre. The failure of English to control the midlands through the plantation of these passes was to be their ultimate undoing.

It was not only the Irish who destabilized the midland colony. King John's feud with William Marshal, lord of Leinster, greatly contributed to the crisis in West Leinster. Intent on extending the perimeters of royal law by breaking the power of the English magnates in Ireland,[50] in 1207 John encouraged Justiciar

---

47 Meenan, 'Deserted mediaeval villages of Co. Westmeath', p. 21; AClon, 1206; AFM, 1209; ALC, 1210. **48** AClon, 1206. Another sign of this trans-Shannon world is the capture of Murchadh O'Kelly in this encounter. AClon, AFM, 1205. **49** Smyth, *Celtic Leinster*, pp 86–9; Ó Cléirigh, 'John fitzThomas', p. 11. For Davies' comments on the midland corridor, see Davies, *Domination and conquest*, p. 41. **50** The repercussions of the collapse of John de Courcy's almost autonomous lordship of Ulster in the opening years of the thirteenth century

Meyler Fitzhenry, Marshal's vassal, to seize the barony of Offaly and seemingly nearby Fearceall, causing uproar among Marshal's allies in Meath and Offaly. The resulting turmoil caused both Marshal and Fitzhenry to be summoned before John late in the year, and it created new opportunities for the Irish. More dangerous for the settlers was the intervention of Muircheartach O'Brien of Ormond, who now inflicted serious damage upon the midland English. Then he burnt Birr and besieged its castle before sacking Ballyroan castle in Laois with the help of O'Connors of Connacht and striking at the castles of Lothra (Lorrha, North Tipperary) and Kinnity in the midland corridor.[51] In the meantime Meyler Fitzhenry's followers attacked the Marshal town of New Ross. However, the Marshals with the de Lacys drove Meyler from Fearceall and captured him at Thurles, forcing John to reverse his tactics; Meyler was ordered to give up Offaly, and in April 1208 John gave Marshal a charter confirming Leinster to him for the service of 100 knights.[52]

By 1210 the midlands were seriously disturbed by the king's struggle with the de Lacys. On 20 June that year John came to Ireland to break the power of Hugh and Walter de Lacy as well as William de Braose. At Ardbraccan in Meath, Cathal Cróibhdhearg O'Connor met the king and joined his expedition to Carrickfergus. By the end of July, the fighting was over. John now held Meath and John de Courcy's lordship of Ulster together with the lordship of Limerick.[53] On 12 August Cathal Cróibhdhearg left the king and returned to Connacht after promising to bring his son, Aodh O'Connor, to the king at Rathwire in west Meath; but after consulting his council and his wife, he decided against doing so; this annoyed John so much that he seized four hostages. This cooling in relations spurred John to order Justiciar John Grey to build castles along the Shannon. The king planned to extend royal jurisdiction into Meath and Ulster. To ensure Connacht's compliance with this matter, Geoffrey de Marisco and Donnchadh Cairbrech O'Brien of Thomond forced Cathal Cróibhdhearg to peace. By the terms of the peace, Grey seemingly granted Connacht to him, a sign of royal recognition that pleased Cathal Cróibhdhearg, who spent Christmas with Grey at Athlone. With Connacht pacified, and Meath and Ulster in the king's hand, Grey attacked the Irish kings bordering Connacht and the midlands.[54]

were still becoming apparent, and the subsequent loosening of the bands of English power in Ulster may have encouraged Irish kings there to become more bold. See Martin, 'John, lord of Ireland, 1185–1216', pp 135–6. **51** AI, 1169. The father of this Muircheartach O'Brien was Brian of Slieve Bloom who was the brother of Domhnall Mór O'Brien (d.1194). This Brian was blinded by his brother in 1169; AClon, 1207. **52** Orpen, *Normans*, ii, pp 210–17. See Martin, 'John, lord of Ireland, 1185–1216', p. 137; *Alen's Reg*, p. 31. **53** Lydon, *Lordship*, p. 65. **54** ALC, 1210; Curtis, *Med. Ire.*, pp 104, 115. The primary targets for colonist expansion were the Irish ruled territories in Ulster. But before these intrusions into Ulster, the Irish of the region were already restless. See Otway-Ruthven, *Medieval Ireland*, p. 82. Earlier during John's royal progress, Aodh Meith O'Neill, king of Tyrone, firstly feigned fealty before making off with much of the royal baggage train. See Duffy, 'King John's expedition to Ireland, 1210: the evidence reconsidered', p. 24; *The Irish pipe roll, 1211–12*, pp 37, 39 63. When the royal emissaries demanded the renewal of O'Neill's pledge of loyalty, his reply captured the

However, the humbling of Connacht and the erection of the castles of Athlone, Clones and Cael Uisce made Cathal Cróibhdhearg and other Irish leaders look weak. By 1211 the pressure of the English vice was evident. While Cathal Cróibhdhearg tried to preserve a kingdom for his son Aodh, John's castle building activity only heightened the dissatisfaction of the junior O'Connor branches, particularly since Cathal Cróibhdhearg's later collaboration in the building of Cael Uisce castle during 1212 displayed that he no longer regarded the Shannon as a defensive frontier.[55] The erection of these castles and the advance of common law provided the English with the launch pads to conquer Connacht and the midlands. And it showed, particularly in the midlands. With no prospect of military aid from their overlords, the junior O'Brien, O'Melaghlin and O'Connor branches took matters into their own hands. At their head was Cormac mac Airt, who had consolidated his position as the most powerful midland lord. In 1211 west Meath exploded when Cormac mac Airt and his brother Máelsechlainn attacked the settlers, forcing Grey to order Donnchadh Cairbrech O'Brien of Thomond and the English of Munster to bring reinforcements. But at Kilnagcrann Ford in Fearceall, Cormac mac Airt defeated Grey before expelling the English from Delvin.[56]

In 1212 Irish attacks upon these castles intensified. With the help of an O'Connor army, Grey strengthened Cael Uisce castle. To the east, the building of Clones castle continued despite attacks from Niall MacMahon and Aodh Meith O'Neill. Then the tide turned in Ulster in favour of the Irish. In an offensive co-ordinated by O'Neill, the English of Ulster were plundered and Cael Uisce and Clones castles were destroyed.[57] Another English force marched into west Meath to crush the Irish – but Cormac mac Airt, the MacCoghlans and the sons of Conchobhar Maenmhaighe annihilated them at Kilnagcrann Ford.[58] One of most surprising aftermaths of Cormac mac Airt's victories was his defeat in that year by his cousin, Domhnall Bregach O'Melaghlin, whose allies, remarkably, included Cuilen O'Dempsey, Muircheartach O'Brien of Ormond and Domhnall Clannach MacGillapatrick of North Ossory.[59] (Cormac mac Airt's intention to extend his power possibly frightened his Irish neighbours, causing them to unite against him. Their alliance against him confirms the survival of a vibrant Irish web of communication stretching from Meath into

---

hardening of Irish attitudes to the colonists 'depart, O' foreigners, I will give no hostages at all this time'. See AI, 1210.   **55** In 1211 the sons of Ruaidhrí and Conchobhar Maenmhaighe rebelled and attacked Connacht. Twice Aodh defeated them and drove them into Ulster and over the Shannon. In the north Domhnall Mór O'Donnell and Aodh Meith O'Neill now laid aside their feud and united to defeat the English assembling at Cael Uisce in 1210. See ALC, 1211; AFM, 1210. ALC, 1212. Perros, 'Crossing the Shannon frontier', p. 132.   **56** AClon, 1211. **57** AClon, 1212; AFM, 1212, 1213; ALC, 1213; AU, 1213.   **58** MA, 1213; these victories produced a reaction throughout the region. See Orpen, Normans, ii, p. 298. Also 'Murechot Offelan', Cormac mac Airt's neighbour, was now warring along the Uí Fáeláin marches. *The Irish pipe roll, 1211–12*, p. 19.   **59** Cunningham, *The Norman advance*, p. 71; AClon, AFM, 1212. For Domhnall Clannach see *Ancient Irish histories,* p. 11.

North Ossory and Ormond. Moreover, the fashioning of this alliance suggests a serious weakening of English power here.) In any event, Domhnall's triumph was short-lived, for Meyler Bermingham killed him shortly afterwards. In spite of his defeat, Cormac mac Airt and the junior O'Connors defeated another English force at Kilnagcrann Ford.[60] Then Muircheartach O'Brien suddenly turned against the English of Ely and Ormond, destroying five of their castles. Such was the intensity of his offensive that it must have been prompted by the success of Cormac mac Airt and the descendants of Conchobhar Maenmhaighe. Drastic action was needed. In autumn 1212, Archbishop Henry de Londres, now justiciar of Ireland, proclaimed a royal service at Roscrea, from where he marched into Offaly, defeating Muircheartach O'Brien and Máelsechlainn O'Connor at Killeigh.[61]

In 1213 English power now concentrated on the destruction of Cormac mac Airt. The English of Ulster, Leinster, Meath and Munster were summoned to west Meath. Cormac mac Airt struck first, attacking Ardnurcher and Kinclare castles. But when these English forces converged, they defeated Cormac mac Airt at the river Brosna, probably forcing him to flee to Connacht.[62] Among the fallen was Ruaidhrí O'Keary; and the later hanging of two O'Dempsey leaders in 1213 at Dublin suggests that they also had fought for Cormac mac Airt.[63] To counter further erosion, the colony's character in West Leinster became essentially defensive. The construction of a chain of castles (these included Clonmacnoise, Birr, Durrow and Kinnity) within the midland corridor attempted through plantation to deny Cormac mac Airt access to the natural routeways to English settlement;[64] but it was the construction of the Clonmacnoise castle that ignited the midlands.[65] Throughout the remainder of the year, Cormac mac Airt concentrated upon the eradication of castles – burning Kinclare, Athboy, Smerhie castles, damaging Birr and forcing Máelsechlainn Beag O'Melaghlin to flee from Delvin.[66] (Cormac mac Airt at this point assumed the lordship of Delvin.) Then Muircheartach O'Brien of Ormond re-entered the fray, but soon after this he was killed by the English.[67] Cormac mac Airt's destructive sweep from Meath to Birr in north Munster illustrated two important points. First, the general Irish determination to destroy castles threatened freedom of regional manoeuvre. Secondly, Cormac mac Airt's clever use of the passes indicates that he utilized the 'midland corridor', which serves to show its importance as a conduit for war.

The emergence of O'Connor Faly hostility seems to have been connected to the war in west Meath. Why they became hostile to the settlers is uncertain, but probably it had to do with the castle-building in Offaly during 1213 and 1214.

---

60 Cunningham, *The Norman advance*, p. 71; AClon, AFM, 1212; ALC, 1213. 61 Otway-Ruthven, *Medieval Ireland*, pp 83–5; AClon, AFM, 1212. 62 AClon, 1213; ALC, 1214. 63 AClon, 1213. Donnchadh and Fionn O'Dempsey were later hanged by Geoffrey de Marisco at Dublin in the year. The proximity of the references and severity of the punishment suggests their involvement in Cormac mac Airt's activities. 64 AClon, AFM, 1213; ALC, 1214. 65 AClon, 1213; ALC, 1214. 66 AFM, AClon, 1213; ALC, 1214. 67 ALC, AU, 1214.

Another reason can be offered: since their arrival, the English had undermined the power of traditional overlords in favour of lesser lords. An example of this was Diarmait O'Dempsey, whose military power overshadowed the O'Connor Falys in the last quarter of the twelfth century. By 1212/13 the English grip on the midlands was shaken. It is clear that the O'Dempseys were attacking the settlers: witness the hanging of two of their leaders at Dublin during 1213. This double body blow to the O'Dempseys perhaps allowed the O'Connors Falys to reassert themselves in Offaly. During 1214, another army was dispatched to west Meath to fight Máelsechlainn Óg O'Melaghlin (Cormac mac Airt's rival) and an unnamed O'Connor Faly lord. In 1215, the resurgent O'Connor Faly killed his traditional client, O'Molloy of Fearceall. The English sought to regain control of the region by hanging Gillekoewgyn O'Kelly at Trim in that year, while Meyler Fitzhenry aided by the O'Molloys reasserted Fitzgerald overlordship in Offaly, killing Máelsechlainn O'Dempsey in 1216.[68]

Despite Cathal Cróibhdhearg's incorporation into the feudal system, he remained apprehensive. On 13 September 1215 John granted him Connacht but made a similar but secret grant that day to Richard Burke (William Burke's son). Faced by such double-dealing, Cathal Cróibhdhearg obtained papal protection for himself, his son Aodh, and their kingdom during 1220–1.[69] From 1218, de Lacy activities in the midlands had caused Cathal Cróibhdhearg concern. After 1219 Cathal Cróibhdhearg's problems magnified, as a result of de Lacy expansion into Bréifne, Cavan and Leitrim.[70] In 1221 the de Lacys, accompanied by Aodh Meith O'Neill, attacked Meath and burnt West Leinster – which probably spurred Cathal Cróibhdhearg to ask Henry III for armed protection.[71] By 1222 Cathal Cróibhdhearg's sensitivity about his eastern frontier caused him to destroy Walter de Lacy's castle of Ath Liag in Annaly. The 1223 burning of Clonmacnoise indicates considerable midland unrest. Later that year de Lacy castle-building in Bréifne brought another Connacht army over the Shannon.[72]

After Cathal Cróibhdhearg's death on 27 May 1224, Aodh O'Connor faced a struggle to preserve his inheritance. Although he had co-operated with his father's temporizing with the English crown, he was alarmed by de Lacy probing

68 AClon, 1215, 1216. 69 Perros, 'Crossing the Shannon frontier', pp 135–8; Lydon, 'The expansion and consolidation of the colony, 1215–54', p. 161; *CDI, 1171–1251*, nos. 653–4, pp 100–1; Sheedy, *Pontifica Hib*, i, p. 234; Byrne, 'The trembling sod', p. 36. 70 ALC, 1219, 1220. Then the English and the O'Farrells of Annaly raided Connacht, resulting in O'Connor retaliation; Curtis, *Med. Ire.*, p. 127. 71 AFM, ALC, 1221; AU, 1222. 72 ALC, 1223; AClon, 1222; The dangers posed by William de Lacy in Bréifne and Conmaicne directly interfered with Connacht's interests. This caused Cathal Cróibhdhearg to specifically spell out Connacht territorial claims east of the Shannon. In 1224 he asked that the lands of Bréifne and Conmaicne, now the counties of Cavan, Leitrim, and Longford, be granted in fee to Aodh. This request was part of a final effort by the old king to obtain a grant of Connacht for Aodh. The regency government did not grant his wish. Thus Cathal Cróibhdhearg died, leaving his greatest wish unfulfilled on 27 May 1224. See Lydon, 'The expansion and consolidation of the colony, 1215–54', p. 161. Cathal Cróibhdhearg 's renewed interest in the midlands is evidenced by his foundation of the Francisan monastery at Athlone in 1223. See AFM, 1224.

of Connacht's Shannon frontier. His position was precarious as a confederation of enemies moved against him. Moreover, Richard Burke, with the support of his uncle, Justiciar Hubert Burke of England, pressed his claims to Connacht.[73] Trouble flared in late 1224, but the intervention of Justiciar William Marshal II soothed Aodh's anger. About this time Aodh confiscated the lands of Donn Óg MacGeraghty. Encouraged by MacGeraghty, the Connacht nobility invited the sons of Ruaidhrí O'Connor to challenge Aodh. Aodh's support crumbled – culminating in Toirdhealbhach mac Ruaidhrí O'Connor's inauguration by Aodh Meith O'Neill of Tyrone. Aodh fled to Marshal at Athlone and gathered an expedition to drive Toirdhealbhach out of Connacht. The support given Aodh by Cormac mac Airt O'Melaghlin and the O'Dempseys shows that Connacht was still influential in West Leinster and the midlands; moreover, Marshal was able to convince the MacMurroughs of East Leinster to join the expedition for Aodh's restoration. After a series of destructive campaigns, Aodh and his allies eventually drove his rivals into Ulster.[74]

This success ironically undermined Aodh's position, for Marshal was replaced as justiciar on 26 June 1226 by Geoffrey de Marisco, and tension between Aodh and de Marisco exploded when Aodh went on in early 1227 to destroy Athlone castle. His actions established a pretext for the grant of Connacht to Burke; by May Burke was granted Connacht and Aodh expelled to Donegal.[75] The invasion of Connacht that ensued created considerable unrest among the midland dynasties, particularly those of Offaly, Laois and west Meath. Between 1226 and 1227, Cuilen O'Dempsey, whose brother was killed fighting for Aodh, twice checked the O'Connor Falys (who were possibly allied to Ruaidhrí O'Connor's sons), while O'More killed O'Molloy of Fearceall in 1227. In west Meath, Cormac mac Airt's rivals engaged the settlers in a series of unsuccessful encounters. Significantly, Clonmacnoise, the emblem of the Connacht kingship, suffered sustained assault. Although the Leinstermen employed by Aodh to protect the monastery, killed Conchobhar O'Sionnach of Tethbae, they were later overrun. Prominent among those attacking Clonmacnoise was the son of Domhnall Bregach O'Melaghlin, the ally of Ruaidhrí's sons, who ravaged Clonmacnoise three times that year. Significantly Cormac mac Airt, Aodh's ally, was captured at Clonmacnoise by the English that same year.[76] These incidents appear to fit into a campaign by the English supporters of the sons of Ruaidhrí to weaken Aodh's allies in Meath and Leinster. After his return from Donegal to Connacht, Aodh was defeated again but this time escaped into Leinster, only to be murdered there in 1228.[77]

73 Lydon, 'The expansion and consolidation of the colony, 1215–54', p. 162.   74 AConn, 1225. The brother of Cúilen O'Dempsey and the four sons of MacMurrough were killed during these campaigns; AFM, 1225. Donnchadh Cairbrech O'Brien and Richard Burke also fought for Aodh in 1225, see Lydon, 'The expansion and consolidation of the colony, 1215–54', p. 162; Orpen, *Normans*, iii, pp 159–63.   75 Lydon, 'The expansion and consolidation of the colony, 1215–54', p. 163.   76 AConn, 1227; AClon, 1226. In 1225 Cowlen O'Dempsey killed Moylemorey O'Connor Faly. Cullen O'Dempsey, most likely the Cowlen of 1225, slew Melaghlen O'Connor Faly; AFM, 1227.   77 AFM, AI, 1228.

Burke's position was strengthened by his succession to the justiciarship on 13 February 1228. With his support, Aodh mac Ruaidhrí O'Connor defeated his elder brother, Toirdhealbhach, to claim the Connacht kingship. In 1230, Aodh mac Ruaidhrí, encouraged by his vassals, challenged Burke's provincial overlordship; Richard Burke then allied with Féilim O'Connor, the murdered Aodh's brother, and exiled Aodh mac Ruaidhrí to Tyrone, paving the way for Féilim's installation as provincial king. By 1231, Féilim had fallen from the favour of Burke and was incarcerated by him in his castle of Meelick. During 1232 Burke now made the repentant Aodh mac Ruaidhrí king in Féilim's place.[78] But before Burke could secure Connacht, his uncle, Hubert, was dismissed on 29 July 1232 by Henry III from the office of justiciar of England.[79] The king then proceeded to dispossess Richard Burke of his Irish lands and ordered him to release Féilim. On 2 September Burke was succeeded as Irish justiciar by Maurice Fitzgerald. Furthermore, Burke was commanded to surrender Connacht but refused; this angered Henry III, who ordered Fitzgerald and then Féilim to take Meelick. Pragmatically, they declined to do so. This series of events proved disastrous for Burke's settlement of Connacht, for Féilim then went on the rampage, levelling more of Burke's castles before going on to defeat Aodh mac Ruaidhrí in early 1233.[80]

Féilim's re-emergence as king of Connacht spelt trouble for the English of an already restless West Leinster. There the MacFháeláins were disillusioned with the Marshals. In 1232, Roger de Hyda, the Marshal seneschal of Leinster, recorded sixty cows taken from 'Morchad Ofelan'.[81] In the next year, the wider region was torn by upheaval among the English: the feud between Earl Richard Marshal and Henry III had spilled over into Ireland, culminating in the fatal stabbing of Marshal in April 1234 by the Fitzgeralds on the Curragh.[82] That year, Féilim, maybe to exploit this unrest, burned Ardnurcher and Baleloghoe in west Meath (it was probably during this attack that Féilim allied himself with Cormac mac Airt O'Melaghlin).[83] However, Richard Burke was now back in favour with the king because of his service against the Marshals in 1234; in summer 1235 he defeated Féilim and Donnchadh Cairbrech O'Brien of Thomond, forcing Féilim into Donegal.[84] Shortly afterwards Féilim submitted before the justiciar, Fitzgerald, obtaining the king's five cantreds in Roscommon – in effect, recognizing the partition of Connacht. But late in the year, tensions between Féilim

---

78 AConn, 1230, 1231, 1232; Waters, 'The Anglo-Irish gentry of Meath', p. 36. Arguably it seems that this belligerence must have been widespread as it is graphically reflected in contemporary obits from various parts of Ireland. The Four Masters describe Aodh Meith O'Neill, king of Tyrone, as the defender of Leth Chuinn against the English of Ireland in 1230. See AFM, AClon, AConn, 1230. **79** Lydon, 'The expansion and consolidation of the colony, 1215–54', p. 164. **80** Orpen, *Normans*, iii, pp 180; AU, AConn, AClon, AFM, 1233. **81** *DKR*, xxxv, p. 133. **82** Clyn, *Annals* p. 7. **83** AClon, 1234. **84** AFM, AConn, AU, 1235 Earlier in 1234, there was trouble between the MacCarthys and the English. At Tralee the English inflicted a heavy defeat on the Irish in which Diarmait the son of Cormac Liathanach MacCarthy was killed. See AI, 1234; Orpen, *Normans*, iii, p. 180, see also fn. 1.

and Burke emerged yet again, leading the Connacht king to take the field and vent his anger by sacking Burke's castle of Meelick. As a result, the justiciar in early 1236 summoned Féilim to parley at Afeoran on the River Suck to discuss the situation. There an unsuccessful attempt was made to capture or kill the king of Connacht – but he and his horsemen eluded their pursuers and fled to the safety of Domhnall Mór O'Donnell of Donegal.[85] With Féilim out of the way, Fitzgerald depossessed him of the cantreds and gave the Connacht kingship back to the family of Ruaidhrí. According to the Four Masters, Féilim was invited back by Connacht lords, including Cormac mac Airt; their description of Cormac as a Connacian again highlights the intricate relations between the midlands and Connacht.[86] This association between Cormac mac Airt and Connacht is confirmed in 1239. In that year he died on the Connacht island of Inisdowginn on the Suck; the fact that he was staying there shows that parts of the midlands were still considered integral parts of Connacht.[87]

Later in 1236 Féilim, returning from Donegal, burned Rinndown in Roscommon and then defeated his cousins.[88] Returning from an absence in England, Burke found Connacht in chaos. He left Fitzgerald to extinguish the struggle between Féilim and his rivals, and proceeded to subdue Mayo and Galway.[89] Féilim established himself in Connacht in late 1236 or early 1237 by making peace with Burke and accepting the lease of the 'king's cantreds'. Essentially, though, Connacht belonged to Burke, who encouraged settlers to cross the Shannon, but that province was not destined to become a little England. In 1240 Féilim, turning to diplomacy, travelled to England to petition Henry III for confirmation of tenure of his reduced inheritance.[90] By 1241, however, he was finding it hard to control his nephews, the sons of Aodh O'Connor, in this he was not helped by a rapid increase of anti-settler feeling among the Irish. Not only was Connacht threatened, but the English were advancing into Donegal, Tyrone, Munster and the midlands. Crucial to comprehension of the phenomenon which has become known as the Irish Resurgence was the emergence of new Irish leaders throughout the island.[91] As during the crisis of 1210–15, many of them were drawn from the junior branches of Irish dynasties or were princes frustrated with the temporizing of their fathers. Now, it was the turn of the provincial kings to be on the receiving end of English aggression. As a result, any further violence to be greatly magnified.

During early 1243 Richard Burke died on Henry III's campaign to Poitou in France and, because his sons were minors, Burke's lands in Connacht and

---

85 AFM, AConn, ALC, AClon, 1236; Orpen, *Normans*, iii, n. 1, p. 183, pp 184–6.   86 AFM, AConn, 1236.   87 AFM, AConn, ALC, AClon, 1239.   88 AFM, AConn, 1236.   89 Orpen, *Normans*, iii, n. 2, p. 187; AFM, AConn, 1236.   90 The best account of this process is pieced together in Orpen, Normans, iii, pp 190–224. Also McNeill, *Castles in Ireland*, pp 130–7; Duffy, *Ireland in the middle ages*, pp 120–1; AFM, AConn, AU, ALC, 1240, 1245; AClon, 1240, 1246. See also *CDI, 1171–1251*, no. 2738, p. 408.   91 Domhnall Mór O'Donnell died and was succeeded by his son, Máelsechlainn. This Máelsechlainn then helped Brian O'Neill to defeat Domhnall O'Loughlin to become king of Tyrone, see AFM, AConn, AU, ALC, 1241. For the hostility of

Munster were taken into the royal hand.[92] Significantly, in 1245, Féilim moved closer to the crown, helping Maurice Fitzgerald, the justiciar, consolidate his grip in northwest Connacht. He and Fitzgerald also brought an army to campaign in Wales for Henry III in October and November 1245.[93] However, Féilim was gradually becoming more isolated in his appeasement of the English. The loss of belief in appeasement by the Irish nobility of Connacht and Donegal was dramatic: witness Máelsechlainn O'Donnell of Donegal's devastation of the English of northwest Connacht at the end of 1245. Fitzgerald sometime in 1246 attacked Donegal, taking hostages from O'Donnell. Although smarting from this reverse, O'Donnell on 1 November 1246 appeared before Sligo and sacked its town; however, he failed to take its castle and was mocked by the defenders, who then defiantly hanged O'Donnell's hostages from its walls in full view of his army.[94] Then the English, perhaps with the support of Féilim, captured his nephews (the sons of the murdered Aodh O'Connor), placing them in Féilim's custody. In autumn, Toirdhealbhach O'Connor, their principal leader, escaped, only to be soon recaptured and handed over to the English, who confined him in the castle at Athlone. By early 1247 a major conflict was unavoidable, as Toirdhealbhach escaped again and began a war against the settlers. The crisis exploded when the de Angulos expelled Cathal MacReynolds from his territory in Leitrim, sparking an inferno of war.[95]

The fact Toirdhealbhach enjoyed a high level of support among the O'Connors indicates that Féilim had lost control of his vassals. By early 1247 Toirdhealbhach had welded together an Irish confederation stretching from Donegal to North Ossory. With Donnchadh MacGillapatrick of North Ossory, he scorched an arc of settlement stretching from Galway town to the Mayo barony of Carra.[96] The annals are unequivocal, stating that Donnchadh and Toirdhealbhach organized the Connacht Irish to fight a war purely against the English. Among his Irish contemporaries, Donnchadh was a legendary figure who believed that Irish resistance to the advancing settlement should cause maximum devastation. He was the architect of a war that brought violence to the doorstep of the English, for he realized that systematic destruction of English settlements facilitated his access to other Irish leaders. Donnchadh's obit illustrates how high the destruction of settlement was on the agenda of many Irish lords; in it, Donnchadh is lauded in titanic terms as having the quality of a good king.[97]

Tadhg O'Connor to the English of eastern Connacht in 1241 see AConn, 1241.   **92** Otway-Ruthven, *Medieval Ireland*, p. 100; AFM, AConn, AClon, 1243.   **93** AFM, AConn, 1245; AClon, MA, 1246.   **94** AFM, 1245, 1246; AConn, ALC, 1246.   **95** AFM, 1246, 1247; AConn, 1246; AU, ALC, 1247. For Cathal MacReynold's previous attachment to Féilim O'Connor in 1237, see AConn, 1237. We can not be certain as to the nature of relations between Toirdhealbhach and Féilim, his uncle. But it is safe to assume that they had become estranged because of Féilim's failure to protect his clients from English aggression. As to Toirdhealbhach's personal ambitions upon Féilim's crown, we are uncertain as to their nature. But it seems there is more to his actions than mere political opportunism.   **96** AFM, AConn, MA, 1247.   **97** AFM, AConn, ALC, AClon, 1249.

War broke in 1247 and lasted three years. While Leinster remained relatively peaceful to begin with, it is unlikely that Donnchadh's troops kept the peace upon their return home from Connacht. What is curious about this passage of events in Connacht is the absence of Féilim. Féilim has traditionally been viewed as an appeaser during these years, but there is no evidence from these years to support this view. Although he seems to have been inactive during this time, many of those who fought for Toirdhealbhach had close links to Féilim, so it is unlikely that he was an appeaser at this time; and there certainly seems to have been a degree of co-ordination between wars in Connacht, the midlands and Desmond during 1249. When the evidence is examined, Féilim comes across as the moving spirit behind the disturbances. Moreover, the possibility of Féilim's orchestrating events behind a screen of dissidents becomes more plausible in 1249. He could not have picked a better time to exploit English weakness in Connacht. In Leinster, the division of the Marshal inheritance was only beginning to take effect, and Walter Burke, the English lord of Connacht, was still a minor.[98]

The terminology applied by the annalists to the Irish participants in these wars is significant, for it indicates considerable change in attitudes. Interestingly, the Irish princes at war in Connacht, Leinster and Munster of 1249 are described as 'sons of kings'.[99] The use of this term to describe these princes suggests that there may have been a considerable unity of purpose among the Irish at this time. The chains of events of 1249 illustrates a clear progression. The trouble began in West Leinster early in that year and spread to Connacht. In a rare reference to Leinster, the Annals of Connacht and the Annals of Loch Cé mention a war between Justiciar John Fitzgeoffrey and unnamed Leinster princes.[100] The term 'Leinster princes' suggests that the Irish of Laois and Offaly were involved, as it is later used to refer to the O'Connor Falys in 1289 and 1311.[101] The Annals of Connacht provide further clues to the identities of the Irish midland leaders. The Connacht chronicler lists the Irish princes who later fell at Athenry in September 1249 as including Cormac mac Airt O'Melaghlin's son, Diarmait Ruadh.[102] Another reference dating from 1248 shows the O'Farrells of Annaly attacking the English of west Meath.[103] The references dealing with the English retribution upon the midland Irish are also revealing. In his obit, Donnchadh MacGillapatrick is mentioned alongside two other great destroyers of English

---

98 Walton, 'The English in Connacht', p. 210; Orpen, *Normans*, iii, pp 211–24. A perusal of the names of Burke's grantees reveals that many families of English Connacht had their origins in English Leinster. Indeed many English of West Leinster after 1236 received lands west of the Shannon. **99** AU, 1247; AI, 1248; AConn, ALC, AFM, 1249. **100** AConn, ALC, 1249. **101** AConn, ALC, AU, 1289, 1311. This reference mentions the killing of two sons of William Liath Burke by the Leinster princes. This the only other time that this phrase is used in the annals. It is clear from the context that this phrase does not apply to the Leinster princes of the eastern Leinster mountains. According to Ó Cléirigh the Irish of Offaly were active around this date. The O'Connor Falys and the O'More dynasties are the most likely the Leinster princes of the annals. If so, it dovetails perfectly with the reference of 1249. See Ó Cléirigh, 'John fitzThomas', p. 194. **102** AFM, AConn, 1249. **103** MA, 1248.

settlement, Conchobhar O'Melaghlin and Conchobhar na gcaisleán MacCoghlan, indicating that these were among the prominent leaders of the midland revolt.[104]

The next phase of the war opened when the MacCarthys of Desmond attacked English of Munster. Following the outbreak of war in Desmond, Féilim O'Connor's son Aodh ambushed Peter Bermingham, who had custody of Richard Burke's lands.[105] Maurice Fitzgerald's subsequent attack on Féilim's lands indicates that he had no doubt of Féilim's complicity in Aodh's actions. The Irish sources are in unison as to Féilim's reaction to Fitzgerald: instead of fleeing to the English, he sent his movable wealth into Bréifne and Ulster. Significantly, his choice of refuge was with Brian O'Neill of Tyrone, who was intimately connected with anti-settler wars of recent years. Justiciar Fitzgeoffrey also combined with Maurice Fitzgerald to devastate the O'Connor territory of Sil Murray in Roscommon; they attacked Bréifne, deposed Féilim and chose Toirdhealbhach O'Connor as provincial king, ordering him to defend Connacht against Féilim.[106] If Féilim was secretly encouraging Toirdhealbhach, this fractured their alliance. Content with his achievements, Fitzgerald returned to Sligo while Fitzgeoffrey went to Meath. Then a remarkable turn-about happened. Instead of consolidating his position, Toirdhealbhach reluctantly agreed to attack the English. Again an O'Connor king called upon the midland Irish for support; it came from the O'Melaghlins and it is likely that Donnchadh MacGillapatrick was involved. Despite some success, Toirdhealbhach was routed outside Athenry in September 1249. Late in 1249, Toirdhealbhach made his peace with the government, but there was no mercy for Donnchadh MacGillapatrick.[107]

In 1250 Féilim finally returned from exile in Tyrone. Fear of Féilim drove Toirdhealbhach to seek English protection (confirmation of their split). Féilim was in the event restored,[108] but his restoration came at a price: by Henry III's wish, the justiciar dispossessed Féilim of the cantred of Omany and made grants of O'Connor lands. Furthermore, Connacht's hostages were blinded by the

104 AI, 1248; AFM, AConn, AClon, 1249.   **105** AFM, AConn, AU, 1249. Piers son of Henry Power was killed in Aodh's ambush. There is some confusion as to the identity of this Piers Power. This entry suggests that Piers Power was one and the same as MacHenry Butler whose castle was burnt by the Clan Muircheartach Muimhnech. If so, this further strengthens the thesis that Féilim and Aodh were lending support to their cousins. For the Butler lords of Umhall, see Orpen, *Normans*, iii, pp 221–2. For Bermingham see ibid., p. 231.   **106** AConn, AFM, ALC, AClon, AU, 1249; Otway-Ruthven in her book says that Féilim fled to the colonists, disowning his son's activities. This interpretation is not supported by the evidence and nor does she supply a reference to buttress this claim. See Otway-Ruthven, *Medieval Ireland*, p. 193.   **107** AFM, AConn, ALC, AClon, AU, 1249. This proved to be the decisive defeat for the Irish, but Connacht was far from pacified. The Irish then turned north and extracted retribution for their defeat upon Peter Bermingham's town of Dunmore. Late in the year, Gofraidh O'Donnell's plundering of northwest Connacht threw the province into further turmoil. See AFM, AConn, 1249; Kelleher, 'Mac Anmchaid Lebroir', p. 56; *Chartul. St Mary's*, ii, p. 315. To the south it was the same story for Finghin mac Diarmait MacCarthy, the arch rebel of Desmond. He suffered the same fate at the hands of his rival Domhnall Got MacCarthy and the de Cogans in 1250. See MA, AI, 1249; AFM, 1250.   **108** AConn, 1250.

English and Toirdhealbhach in Athlone; thus, the sort of treatment reserved for those engaged in rebellion.[109] Clearly the English concluded that Féilim and his son were implicated at least in the events of 1249. Despite the setbacks of 1249–50, desultory fighting continued in Connacht and the midlands.[110] These years saw a continuing hardening in Féilim's attitude towards the settlers. Indeed, his alliance with O'Neill, and his favourable disposition to Aodh's views, sparked Connacht's resurgence. As a result, these years witnessed a shift in the O'Connor political compass away from West Leinster and the midlands towards southern Ulster – a change in policy confirmed by the relative peace in West Leinster and the midlands throughout the 1250s; even the O'Melaghlins and MacGillapatricks remained peaceful.[111] As for the O'Connors, they spied opportunities for conquest in the lands of the O'Reillys, who had the support of Walter Burke. The revived O'Connor expansion across the Shannon led to wars with the O'Rourkes of Bréifne. In 1255 Féilim sent Aodh to confirm his alliance with O'Neill as well as dispatching envoys to the court of Henry III;[112] Aodh's mission paved the way for the recognition of O'Neill's high kingship at Cael Uisce during 1258 by the O'Connors and their cousin Tadhg O'Brien.[113]

Generally speaking, West Leinster and the midlands seemed unaffected by these events. The region's immunity had to do with the change in the 1250s of the geopolitical axis of the O'Connors, although Aodh did bring with him a contingent of O'Melaghlins to Down to fight for O'Neill's high-kingship. Following O'Neill's defeat by the English on 16 May 1260 at Down, the O'Connors again reviewed their strategies.[114] In the 1260s the trend of midland warfare was dictated by events in Connacht. The really striking point about this

---

109 Otway-Ruthven, *Medieval Ireland*, p. 193; Orpen, *Normans*, iii, p. 232; AFM, AConn, ALC, 1250. Further confirmation of Féilim's feud with Toirdhealbhach came after the blinding. Then Féilim expelled his nephew Cathal, Toirdhealbhach's brother, from Connacht, see AFM, AConn, 1250.   **110** AConn, 1250. In 1250 Cairbre O'Melaghlin was killed by David Roche in Fearceall. During the same year Maurice Fitzgerald re-established his grip in the northwest by capturing Diarmait of Luighne and by campaigning into Tyrone for the hostages of Brian O'Neill. In Donegal he deposed Niall O'Canannan, killing him. See AU, AConn, ALC, AFM, 1250. In 1251 Tadhg mac Tuathal O'Connor of the Clan Muircheartach Muimhnech were killed by the English, see AFM, AConn, 1251.   **111** In Ossory Archbishop David MacGillapatrick of Cashel and Donnchadh's successor Sefraidh steered their dynasty along a more peaceable course. Archbishop David MacGillapatrick of Cashel died in 1253, see AConn, AFM, 1253. Sefraid son of Domhnall Clannach MacGillapatrick died in 1269, see AConn, AFM, 1269. The only mention of disturbance among the O'Melaghlin dynasty was in 1254. Then Murchadh O'Melaghlin before his own violent demise killed Piers Risturbard, lord of Síl Mailruain now Ballinlough in west Roscommon, see AFM, 1254.   **112** For the wars against the O'Rourkes and the O'Reilly lords, see Orpen, *Normans*, iii, p. 236; Otway-Ruthven, *Medieval Ireland*, pp 193–4. In 1255 Aodh went to settle an alliance with Brian O'Neill. At the time he was engaged in fighting the O'Reillys. After the conclusion of the alliance with Aodh, O'Neill unsuccessfully attacked the O'Reillys probably as part of the deal, see AConn, 1255. For the defeat of the O'Reillys by Aodh at the battle of Mag Slecht in northwest Cavan in September 1256, see AConn, 1256.   **113** AFM, AConn, ALC, AClon, AU, 1258.   **114** AFM, AConn, AU, ALC, AClon, 1260. A further sign of O'Connor hostility to the

latest O'Connor volte-face was the rapidity with which the midlands descended into warfare. Again west Meath was the cockpit of the struggle. In response to Aodh's successes against the English of Athlone and Meath, the settlers of Annaly in 1262 deposed Giolla na Naomh O'Farrell, replacing him with the son of Murchadh Carrach O'Farrell. Giolla na Naomh returned, banished the usurper and ejected the English.[115] Two years later Aodh O'Connor's wars, and the feud between Earl Walter Burke of Ulster and Maurice fitzMaurice Fitzgerald, possibly spurred Art O'Melaghlin into conflict. His successes were considerable, for he routed the English at the river Brosna and destroyed their settlements throughout west Meath.

The politics of Connacht continued to set the trend. The feud between Burke and the Fitzgeralds exploded on 6 December 1264, when the Fitzgeralds swooped on Castledermot in Kildare, capturing Justiciar Richard de la Rochelle and confining him in Lea and Dunamase castles in Offaly and Laois.[116] After Féilim's death in 1265, Aodh's first raid as king of Connacht was upon Offaly.[117] This offensive weakened the English grip on the region – perhaps encouraging Art O'Melaghlin in 1266 to clash with Burke at Ath Crocha Ford.[118] Moreover, Aodh's continued attacks around Athlone probably contributed to the uprisings of the O'Farrells, MacCoghlans and O'Molloys between 1268 and 1269, setting the scene for the dramatic upheavals within the region during the 1270s.[119]

government was Aodh's marriage in 1259 to the daughter of Dubhghall MacSorley at Derry, gaining him a dowry of galloglass. Otway-Ruthven, *Medieval Ireland*, p. 195; Orpen, *Normans*, iii, p. 239. **115** AFM, AConn, ALC, 1262. **116** Otway-Ruthven, *Medieval Ireland*, p. 196. **117** AFM, AConn, ALC, AClon, 1265. **118** AFM, AConn, ALC, 1266. **119** AFM, AConn, ALC, AClon, 1268. Before Aodh's attack on the Faes of Athlone in 1268, Amlaib O'Farrell was killed by the English. While after it Máelsechlainn MacCoghlan and Ferghal O'Molloy were separately killed by the English. Domhnall O'Farrell was also killed by the English. However, the killings of the O'Farrell dynasts may be connected to a dynastic struggle. This Domhnall's son, Aodh, was also killed in 1269 by his own kin and the English, see AFM, AConn, ALC, AU, 1269.

CHAPTER 4

Leinster, 1265–1320

EAST LEINSTER, 1265–1320

Between 1265 and 1320, the political landscape of East Leinster was utterly transformed. At the start of this period, the peace of Diarmait MacMurrough and Strongbow still held, the two communities living cheek by jowl and their respective economies seemingly interlocked. Tension may have increased between them after the partition of Marshal Leinster two decades earlier, but the outbreak of war could not have been predicted. By 1269, however, the Wicklow mountains echoed the clash of steel in a war that arose independently of other Irish wars in this period – originating in a seismic shift in attitude among the Irish of East Leinster towards the English.

Butler expansion in the Wicklow mountains sharpened ethnic edges, contributing to the explosive situation between Theobald Butler and the Fitzgerald barons of Wicklow in 1265. (Many of the Butler designs were focused upon the lands of the Irish clients of the Fitzgeralds and the archbishopric of Dublin.) The outcome of this clash so profoundly disturbed the *pax Lageniae* that relations between the Wicklow Irish and the English never recovered. Despite the outbreak of widespread Irish hostility in 1269, from his base at Arklow castle Theobald Butler continued to buy lands from the beleaguered settlers. By 1275–80 the church of Disirt Keyvn located in the central Wicklow highlands was included in the deanery of Arklow, and Theobald Butler significantly had custody of the march of Glendelory or Glenmalure in 1277[1] (the boundaries of rural deaneries are regarded as reliable indicators of secular jurisdiction).[2] Later in 1294, Geoffrey Fitzrhyss of Imaal granted his holdings to the Butlers, who also held the cantred of Wicklow of the Fitzgerald heirs from an unknown date in the late thirteenth century.[3] But in the long term, when war broke in 1269, this conflict marked the end of Butler and other English lordships in the mountains.

The spark that ignited the Irish of Wicklow was famine. This, combined with worsening weather and poor English decisions resulting from the probable initial

---

1 *Crede mihi*, p. 144; *CDI, 1252–84*, no. 1496, p. 284; *COD*, i, nos 165–7, pp 71–2.   **2** Empey, 'The cantreds of the medieval county of Kildare', pp 128–34.   **3** *COD*, i, nos 165–67, pp 71–2, no. 426, p. 168, nos 319–21, pp 130–1, no. 490, p. 196. In 1297 Hugh Lawless, a Butler client, was joint serjeant of the manor of Arklow and the Wicklow cantred. Price,

58

insensitivity of Archbishop Fulk de Sandford of Dublin towards the Irish, shattered the long-lived regional co-existence of both races in the region. The disturbance began among the Irish of the archbishopric and spread to the O'Byrnes, and it involved much and widespread violence, as evidenced by the response of the government: no less a figure than the king's nephew, Henry of Almain, son of Richard, duke of Cornwall, was dispatched to Glenmalure to end Irish resistance. He quelled the disturbances, but his campaign failed: by July 1270 the war in the Leinster mountains had reached crisis proportions, leading to a directive from England to Justiciar James de Audley to aid the archbishop against what was termed a 'malicious rebellion'.[4] The slow build-up of this war coincided with a marked decline of the existing Irish dynastic elite, and the appearance of new leaders, particularly among the O'Tooles.[5] Generally neglected in the analysis of this war has been the void created by the death of Muircheartach (Meyler?) O'Toole. The new O'Toole leaders seem to have belonged to the more belligerent lineage of Imaal, who were linking up with Gerald O'Byrne, lord of his name. The absence of Muircheartach's restraining influence and his failure to sire a strong male heir contributed to the swift spread of war throughout the Leinster hills.

Belatedly, Archbishop Fulk realized his blunder and sent John de Sandford as his envoy to the Irish in 1270–1; he did much to restore peace. But Fulk's death in May 1271 complicated matters in a still tense Wicklow. The brief reign of his absentee successor, John of Darlington, resulted in a prolonged archiepiscopal vacancy which led to a disastrous intrusion of royal officials and the extension of royal law into the Wicklow mountains. The hard-edged attitudes of officials towards the Irish destroyed any possibility of a return to the previous status quo. Their insensitivity brought the crisis to fever pitch in 1270. Then a devastating disaster struck the Irish when a combination of heavy snow, plague and rainstorms destroyed their remaining foodstuffs and livestock. Their economic base now destroyed, the Irish burnt English settlements from the mountains to the sea. The identities of the raiders were confirmed by the fact that three O'Tooles, one O'Byrne and one Harold were in custody by summer 1271. Furthermore, a campaign brought to Glendalough by de Audley before June 1272, and a probable expedition to Glenmalure between June 1272 and April 1273 by his successor Maurice fitzMaurice Fitzgerald, failed to achieve their objective, leaving the war to rage on.

There is a hitherto hidden side to the emergence of this war. The Irish of East Leinster were relatively insulated by several layers of settlement from Irish hostility to the English, in Connacht and the midlands, but East Leinster was not so well protected from the drift of anti-English sentiments from across the Irish

---

Placenames, p. lviii.   **4** Frame, 'The Dublin government n. 6, p. 80. For Richard of Cornwall, see Davies, *Europe: a history*, pp 357, 377–8; Lydon, 'Medieval Wicklow', pp 158–9.   **5** *Alen's Reg*, p. 114; *CDI, 1252–84*, no. 1038, p. 178. Interestingly, the name of the O'Toole leader is not mentioned, a fact which may indicate that he was of a different lineage to Meyler/ Muircheartach.   •

Sea from Wales. This is not to say that the Leinster wars of the 1270s contained a genesis of pan-Celticism. Still, it has been argued that there were some connections between the Leinster rebellions of the 1270s and those which erupted some sixty miles away in Wales during the same period. As we have seen, the Irish of East Leinster had many links with Wales before 1169. The Irish annals give post-1270 events in Wales more prominence than earlier events.[6] Moreover, many of the English lords of Leinster, such the Bigods, de Valences, de Bohuns, de Clares and Mortimers, held lands in Wales,[7] and lesser lords such as the Blends, Roches, Fitzrhysses, Lawlesses, de Valles and Pencoits were all Cambro-English in origin. On the Leinster coast there seem to have been Welsh merchants at Arklow and Wicklow.[8] It is easy to see how news of Welsh victories could have filtered into the Irish hinterland surrounding these ports. Interestingly, Welsh forenames do occur roughly about this time among the O'Byrnes.[9] While it is idle to speculate how these names came to be among the O'Byrnes, clearly the Irish close to the Leinster coast had a knowledge of events in Wales.

Although these changes in the political climate were noticed by the MacMurroughs, their initial response was both hesitant and pragmatic. Between 1269 and 1273 Muircheartach MacMurrough, traditional overlord of the O'Byrnes and O'Tooles, remained aloof from the war. At the crux of MacMurrough indecision was their duality. The MacMurrough leaders were fully incorporated within the feudal settlement, but yet they retained their leadership of the Irish of East Leinster. Unlike their Fitzdermot cousins, they had largely preserved their Irish identity despite their affilation to the English, but they must have been aware that the power of other anglicized Irish leaders was being steadily eroded by more militant kinsmen.

---

6 Without doubt in previous centuries the kingdoms scattered along the Leinster coast had political and commercial links with the Welsh. To demonstrate this point, MacShamhráin has shown the occurrence of British names within the early genealogies of the Uí Máil and the Uí Dúnlainge princes. Furthermore, the cult of Coemgen was also exported successfully to the Isle of Man, while Welsh and Cornish saints figure prominently in the hagiography of Glendalough. Moreover, a cadet line of the Welsh ruling dynasty of Gwynedd held lands at Balrothery in North Dublin from the eleventh century to the seventeenth, see Curtis, 'The Fitzrerys, Welsh lords of Cloghran, Co. Dublin', pp 13–15. And earlier the Welsh annals describe the eleventh-century Leinster king, Diarmait mac Máel na mBó, as king of the British. MacShamhráin, pp 68, 124; AI, 1257, 1283, 1295. 7 Duffy, 'Ireland and the Irish Sea region', p. 135. The Welsh rebel, Rhyss ap Maredudd, fled Wales to perhaps the de Clare lands in Kilkenny in 1289, see H. Luard (ed.), *Annales Monastici*, iv (London, 1869), p. 311. In 1289 Edward I ordered the justiciar of North Wales to prevent Rhyss' escape, see *Calendar of various chancery rolls* (London, 1912), p. 323. Another contact between Wales and Kilkenny comes in 1282. A William son of Llewellyn sat on a jury examining the lands of John FitzThomas in Kilkenny during August 1282, see *CDI, 1252–84*, no. 912, p. 425. 8 Becker, 'Dublin Merchant Guild Roll, c.1190–1265', p. 125. 9 A father and son of the Gabhal Siomóin branch of the O'Byrnes bear the Welsh forenames, Ailgeoid (Elias) and Cuug. O'Clery, para. 1751, p. 130. This Cuug's descendants became known as Gabhal Cuug and the modern townland of Ballycooge in the Avoca valley to the north of Arklow seems to contain their eponym's imprint.

The reluctance of Muircheartach MacMurrough to enter the war can be compared with the initial reticence of King Féilim O'Connor of Connacht to openly join the O'Connor dissidents between 1247 and 1249. Muircheartach's entry into the war during 1274 was not because of a deteriorating relationship with his cousin, Roger Bigod, lord of the liberty of Carlow; Muircheartach's main concern had to do with the growth of O'Byrne power. His assumption of the leadership of the war against the English probably represented a combined decision to protect his traditional position and to short-circuit O'Byrne ambition. Significantly, only when he moved to war did East Leinster become widely disturbed. Muircheartach's victory over an English army at Glenmalure that year affirmed his leadership of the Irish of East Leinster.[10] This dramatic rise in the tempo of the war in East Leinster brought a second, but inconclusive, expedition by Justiciar Geoffrey de Joinville to Glenmalure that same year, while de Joinville again failed in 1275 to overcome the Irish. Muircheartach was captured at Norragh by Walter Lenfant that year, but the Leinstermen prospered under Art, his brother, who routed de Joinville in Glenmalure in 1276. The Annals of Clonmacnoise records his defeat, hailing Art as king of Leinster[11] (this suggests that the MacMurroughs were compelled to lead this rebellion because of their heritage of provincial overlordship dating from the time of Diarmait mac Máel na mBó). However, de Joinville's successor as justiciar, Robert de Ufford, successfully ended the war in 1277–8.

Discontent remained. To his credit, Roger Bigod visited the MacMurrough brothers and tried to allay their grievances by giving them gifts and reinstating them as officers of his liberty of Carlow in 1280. On 24 July 1280 Bigod's request that they be given safe conduct to England was approved, but it is uncertain whether they went. By 1281, trouble was brewing again, and perhaps as a precautionary measure Muircheartach was arrested by the government. Later in the year he was brought to Dunamase in Laois to negotiate with the Irish – probably a sign that his kinsmen were plotting with the midland Irish. It may be that some Irish lords in the midlands still acknowledged the MacMurrough provincial kingship. After the breakdown of negotiations, Muircheartach was returned to Dublin but was released by early 1282. Subsequent events, however, adduce his heavy involvement in the unrest among the Leinster Irish – to be seen in his support for Art's raids on the Vale of Dublin.[12] This was clearly the government's view.

Again this latest unrest can be paralleled with events in Wales, where rebellion broke out in March 1282 and three months later Gilbert de Clare, earl of Gloucester and lord of Kilkenny, was routed by the Welsh at Llandeilo fawr. (Among the dead was the son of William de Valence, lord of Wexford.) Moreover, that year it was noted that the Welsh successes greatly encouraged the

10 Flower, 'The Kilkenny chronicle in Cotton MS', p. 332. 11 Lydon, 'Medieval Wicklow', p. 160; *Grace*, p. 39; AClon, 1276. 12 However, their defeat still rankled, as evidenced by the apprehension of Dermitius McMorkada in 1280. See Clyn, *Annals*, p. 9. Lydon, 'Medieval Wicklow', p. 163.

Irish to be more daring. While it is unlikely that the Welsh victory sparked a revolt in Leinster, it must have encouraged the Irish already in the field. Perhaps fearful of the effect of the Welsh victory upon the Leinster Irish, the government decided to act. Justiciar Stephen de Fulbourne decided to eliminate Muircheartach and Art. Five weeks after Llandeilo fawr, in July 1282, the suspected conductors of the orchestra of Irish violence in Leinster were summoned to Arklow. They arrived, under a safe conduct, to embark for England. Before they could board ship, they were murdered by de Fulbourne's assassins.

This crime delayed war for years. Between those murders and Muiris mac Muircheartaigh MacMurrough's appearance on the political scene in 1295, the MacMurroughs remained passive. In the interim they were led by Alexander and Diarmait MacMurrough and by another Art MacMurrough.[13] Their passivity was reflected among the Irish of East Leinster in 1289. Then John de Sandford, archbishop of Dublin and justiciar, summoned them to a conference and accepted their promises to join him on campaign in Offaly.[14] Others, however, were not so inactive. During this period, the O'Byrnes of the Wicklow mountains became more reluctant to accept MacMurrough hegemony. On at least one occasion between 1282 and 1294, they combined with the O'Nolans of Forth to wreak havoc in south Wicklow and north Carlow. The MacMurrough response was instructive; they, with Bigod's forces, crushed the O'Byrnes and their allies.[15] Swift action such as this preserved the MacMurrough provincial kingship.

In spring 1295 Muiris MacMurrough decided to fully reassert his dynasty's leadership of the Irish of East Leinster. His decision to return to war was further influenced by a combination of deteriorating weather, the Fitzgerald/de Vescy feud and the linked successes of An Calbhach O'Connor Faly of Offaly. Significantly, it also coincided with a new Welsh rebellion. By 19 July 1295, the war was over and Muiris knelt before Justiciar Thomas Fitzgerald at Castlekevin, high in the Wicklow mountains. The occasion was Muiris' submission to the justiciar and, as the subsequent terms of the peace reveal, Muiris was the acknowledged leader of the Irish of the Leinster mountains. By the terms of the peace he gave hostages for Murchadh mac Gerald O'Byrne and Fáelán O'Toole, promising to campaign against them if they broke the peace. Thus the agreement clearly shows that the English recognized Muiris as the overlord of O'Byrne and O'Toole, a fact acknowledged by the two vassal lords themselves.[16] In spite of the enforced submission of Muiris and his allies, their war succeeded in achieving some of their aims – costing the Dublin government some £336 to bring it to an end. More significantly there is strong evidence that the Irish had terrorized the English settlers living in the frontier cantred of Shillelagh, forcing some to abandon their lands and flee. We know that Hugh de Sampford and Gilbert de Lyvet, both manor holders in Shillelagh, were compensated in 1296

---

13 *CDI, 1285–92*, no. 270, p. 124, and no. 287, p. 130; *CDI, 1293–1301*, no. 41, p. 27, and no. 550, p. 250.   14 Ibid., no. 559, p. 272.   15 Mills, 'Accounts of the earl of Norfolk's estates in Ireland, 1279–1294', pp 55–6.   16 *CJR, 1295–1303*, p. 61.

by William de Valence, lord of Wexford, for their losses with lands in Forth in southern Wexford.[17]

This resort to war has been termed 'The Irish Resurgence'. This label, which dates from the late nineteenth and early twentieth centuries, is misleading. It was not only against the settlers that the Irish lords of Leinster moved. Several inter-dynastic wars were fought as frontiers expanded and contracted; moreover, many discarded scions of Leinster dynasties enlisted government help against their overlords. By 1300, Muiris MacMurrough was well established as the overlord of the Leinster mountains. On the surface, the future augured well for the young provincial king, but appearances were deceptive. To say that Muiris enjoyed an easy suzerainty over his vassals would be very untrue, for he inherited many of the problems that confronted his father Muircheartach between 1270 and 1282. These were compounded by tensions in the MacMurrough/O'Byrne relationship, some of which may have had their roots in the expulsion of Diarmait MacMurrough from Leinster in 1166, when O'Byrne deserted Diarmait in his hour of direst need. More recently, however, a rift emerged as a result of the ambitions of Gerald O'Byrne.

In the early years of the fourteenth century, events were shifting against the MacMurroughs, the political balance among the Irish of East Leinster moving in favour of the O'Byrnes, thanks to upheavals in the Irish politics of wider Leinster. Although East Leinster was largely geographically isolated from the rest of Gaelic Ireland, the ambits of the Irish of West and East Leinster began to meet in the strategic Barrow valley in the last decades of the thirteenth century. One reason for the emergence of the O'Byrne challenge was the dramatic change in the political situation in the midlands due to the decline of the O'Melaghlins of west Meath from 1290, and the massacre of the O'Connor Faly leadership in 1305 – events that had switched the focus of warfare in the midlands from the northwest region southwards to Laois and Munster (as is seen in the rise of the O'Mores of Laois).[18] In turn, this tipped the fragile political balance in East Leinster in favour of Murchadh O'Byrne, to the detriment of Muiris MacMurrough.

Murchadh probably became leader of his dynasty in the years before 1295. At first he accepted his role as Muiris' vassal. Muiris' rule extended fitfully over the rump of the old kingdom of Leinster stretching from central and north Wexford through Wicklow to the emerging Dublin Pale. To the northwest, his ambition was contained by Co. Kildare, now in the hands of the king, while Roger Bigod's liberty of Carlow with the eastern Butler and the Mortimer lands formed an increasingly porous western frontier with the Irish of the midlands. To the south, the liberty of Wexford checked any MacMurrough advance.

Essentially what drove the O'Byrnes forward was the geographical location of their lordship. For the most part, it was blanketed by mountain, forest and bog,

17 Colfer, *Arrogant trespass*, p. 226. **18** AConn, 1290; AClon, 1305. In 1306 the O'Mores burnt Ballymore, see *Chartul. St Mary's*, ii, p. 333.

and consequently one of their most pressing problems was the fact that much of their cultivable land was poor or marginal, so poor that the area often suffered harvest failures, animal plagues and ultimately famine. Furthermore, the O'Byrnes were surrounded by potential enemies, both English and Irish. If his lordship was to survive, Murchadh O'Byrne had to break this virtual siege and gain the living space required to secure his power. One of the secrets of his success was that he kept a tight rein on his kinsmen. Unlike the MacMurroughs and the O'Tooles, the O'Byrnes led by their ruling family, the Gabhal Dúnlaing, were a fairly homogeneous group. This O'Byrne unity allowed Murchadh to exploit the anger of the Irish of East and West Leinster. He was able to extend an alliance to the O'Mores, and by exploiting divisions among the English and creating new alliances with the O'Tooles of Imaal and some of the Ostmen of north Wicklow, his rise was assured.[19]

Before detailing Murchadh's challenge to the MacMurrough provincial king, his rise must be examined. Despite the movement of the wider politics in his favour, this may not have been immediately obvious to Murchadh, for he did not break finally with Muiris MacMurrough until at least 1308. The 1295 concord with the government held until Lent 1301, when Muiris and Murchadh joined forces. Primarily, Murchadh's objective was to consolidate his hold on eastern Wicklow, particularly the vital Glenealy valley, against the Fitzdermots, O'Tooles and the marcher family of Lawless. That Lent, the O'Byrnes, O'Tooles and the MacMurroughs burnt the settlements bordering the length of the Leinster mountains and ravaged east Wicklow – including the castles of Wicklow and Rathdown. A massive English counterattack was to inflict serious losses upon the Irish in terms of both men and cattle.[20]

In 1305, a train of events was begun that further inflamed the Leinster nobility. Piers Bermingham and John fitzThomas Fitzgerald arranged the murder (at a feast in Bermingham's castle) of the O'Connor Faly leaders in June, and the English slaughter of four prominent MacMurrough leaders at Ferns that same year. At an inquiry held in Duiske, Co. Kilkenny, on 15 November 1305, it emerged that the four MacMurroughs had gone to Ferns under a promise of safe conduct from Justiciar John Wogan. The inquiry (presided over by Wogan) revealed that Englishmen had taken the law into their own hands to settle old scores; so to abate Irish fury, Wogan ordered Gilbert Sutton, seneschal of Wexford, to arrest the murderers. When he dithered, Muiris MacMurrough became convinced that his sympathies lay with the murderers, and he unleashed his followers, who killed Sutton near the town of Hamond Grace before the close of 1305.[21]

These events promoted co-operation between the Irish of both parts of the province, a co-operation that probably increased when the liberty of Carlow was

19 *Chartul. St Mary's*, ii, p. 348; *CJR, 1308–14*, pp 285; *CDI, 1252–84*, no. 1577, p. 313; NA, RC 7/13 (iv), pp 22–4.   20 *The Book of Howth*, p. 126, mentions Irish disturbances in Leinster and their defeat by Lord William Power in this year. *Grace*, p. 47; *Chartul. St Mary's*, ii, p. 330. 21 *CJR, 1305–7*, pp 466–7. The MacMurrough leaders were Henry, Muircheartach Mór,

transferred into royal hands upon the death of Roger Bigod in 1306. May 1306 saw the burning of Ballymore in the western Wicklow mountains by the O'Mores; several sources mention that Justiciar Wogan punished Murchadh O'Byrne for the devastation of Ballymore. Testament to growing co-ordination between the Irish of both parts of Leinster was the Irish victory over Wogan's army at Glenealy in the O'Byrne lordship later in 1306. The Book of Howth, mentioning this victory, records that Irish came from other parts of Ireland to aid the Irish of Leinster.[22] By early 1307, the government was in crisis in Leinster; drastic action was needed. By summer 1307, however, the Irish effort had faltered, partly as a result of the beheading of Murchadh Ballach MacMurrough (described as *princeps Lagenie*), by Lord Edmund Butler and David de Cauntetoun on 1 April 1307.[23] A hosting against the O'Tooles met with little success later in the month;[24] and the most successful official move to defuse the crisis in East Leinster was the offers that Wogan now made to Murchadh O'Byrne.

Wogan realized that Murchadh was prepared to treat with the government in order to pursue his ambitions. In 1307 Murchadh's importance on the political landscape was confirmed when he was among several Irish kings, including David O'Toole of Imaal, asked to join a campaign to Scotland.[25] His pragmatism was evident in his dealings with Lord Edmund Butler and Wogan, both of whom wished to secure their hold upon their eastern Wicklow lands, and prevent Murchadh's growing consolidation of the region. Now they attempted to sow dissension between Murchadh and the O'Tooles by offering to the former the confiscated Glenealy lands of the outlawed Richard O'Toole during 1307 (Hugh Lawless, Lord Edmund Butler's client, received a grant of David McGilnecowil O'Toole's lands at Kilfee).[26] These Murchadh happily accepted, a grant which probably drove some of the O'Tooles into rebellion in early summer 1308. But in June 1308 Murchadh, typically, coolly changed sides, joined the O'Tooles and annihilated Wogan's force at Glenmalure on 8 June, burning Dunlavin eight days later.[27]

Murchadh and Domhnall Óg MacMurrough; *Grace,* p. 49; Dowling, *Annals,* p. 17. **22** Dowling, *Annals,* p. 17; *Chartul. St Mary's,* ii, p. 333. In 1306 Thomas de Suerterby, constable of Castlekevin, executed Macnochi, two of his sons and a strong thief called Lorcán Oboni. This Macnochi seems to be a son of Eochaidh O'Toole, otherwise known as Richard or Yoghy O'Toole; see *CJR, 1305–7,* p. 336; *The Book of Howth,* p. 127; *Grace,* p. 51; *Chartul. St Mary's,* ii, p. 333. **23** Dowling, *Annals,* p. 18. The description of this Murchadh Ballach as *princeps Lagenie* may infer that he was a brother of Muiris, king of Leinster. See also *Chartul. St Mary's,* ii, p. 335; *Grace,* p. 51, see also p. 55 fn.g It seems de Cantetoun was hanged for the murder of Murchadh Ballach at Dublin in 1308; *CJR, 1308–14,* pp 32, 55. These sources are explicit that Edmund Butler killed Murchadh Ballach. It seems most unlikely that David de Cantetoun was hanged for the murder of Murchadh Ballach, also described as a felon. Rather it must have been for his rebellion. **24** Frame, 'The Dublin government', pp 165–9, 171–3; Nigel le Brun received wages for 33 hobelars and 106 foot campaigned the O'Tooles in April 1307. The constable of Castlekevin was provisioned with food as well as 1000 quarrels for crossbows, suggesting an attack was expected, see *CJR 1305–7,* p. 355. **25** *Grace,* fn. g, p. 50. **26** *CJR, 1305–7,* p. 354; O'Byrne, 'The Uí Bhroin of Co. Wicklow', p. 59. **27** *Grace,* p. 53; Dowling, *Annals,* p. 18.

Despite Wogan's reverses, his luck was in. During this period a bitter feud erupted between Muiris MacMurrough and Murchadh O'Byrne. It dominated the Irish polity of East Leinster for years to come, destroying their joint attempts to promote alliances with the Irish of the midlands. The 1308–10 rebellion of the de Cauntetouns against the government again disturbed the region. The O'Byrnes joined the de Cauntetouns, while Muiris MacMurrough gave his support to the government.[28] At the same time Murchadh's attacks chipped away at the grip of the Fitzgeralds upon the barony of Wicklow. In 1308, during a suit before the Dublin bench, Murchadh was among those charged with the seizure, at Wicklow, of rents which had been extracted by George de la Roche, one of the co-heirs of the barony.[29] However, Piers Gaveston with the aid of Henry O'Toole brought Murchadh's activities to a temporary halt by defeating him in 1309.[30]

The evidence also points to a sustained period of O'Byrne expansion south-wards into Carlow and Wexford between 1295 and 1314. The Glenmalure lands of the O'Tooles were Murchadh's target. He must have enjoyed considerable success in this enterprise by 1311. After Murchadh and the O'Tooles burnt Saggart and Rathcoole on 29 June that year, another great army was sent into the mountains to punish the Irish. But at Glenmalure Murchadh with David O'Toole fought him to a standstill, compelling him to retreat.[31] (No mention is made again of the O'Tooles of Glenmalure; this suggests that they were finally absorbed into David O'Toole's Imaal lordship. Certainly, O'Toole lands had contracted substantially in east and central Wicklow during Murchadh's reign. By 1320 the O'Toole heartland was now centred in Imaal with a discontinuous territorial arc stretching to the north of Glendalough.)

Increasingly, after 1309, the MacMurrough territories in the northern Carlow and Wexford suffered O'Byrne enroachments.[32] Faced by the rise of Murchadh O'Byrne on his northern frontier, Muiris MacMurrough considered his options carefully. The O'Byrne offensive began around the time that Muiris stayed, for unknown reasons, at Dublin Castle (before 9 December 1309). Significantly, upon his return from Dublin, Muiris' first response to O'Byrne aggression was to fight – resulting in extensive warfare on the Wexford borders. When MacMurrough discovered that O'Byrne had successfully wooed the O'Nolans to his side, he then turned to the government for support and entered its service[33] – the clearest indication of the mutual interest of the government and the MacMurroughs being Muiris' acceptance of a fee for defending of the Wexford borders from O'Byrne incursions. However, English feuding also

---

28 *CJR, 1308–14*, pp 200, 237; Colfer, *Arrogant trespass*, pp 227–9.   29 NA, RC 7/13 (iv), pp 122–4.   30 *The Book of Howth*, p. 127.   31 Ibid., p. 128; *Chartul. St Mary's*, ii, p. 339.   32 *CJR, 1308–14*, pp 200, 232–3, 237.   33 Blake-Butler, 'The barony of Dunboyne' (October, 1945), p. 68; Richard mac Philip O'Nolan of Fotherd was at war against the settlers in 1311, while a David McEthe was charged with robbing the cattle of John Tallon, Richard Boscher and the wife of Maurice le Clerk and bringing them to the Onolans and Obyrnns of Kynalo, see *CJR, 1308–14*, p. 172. Lydon, 'Medieval Wicklow', pp 169–170; *CJR, 1308–14*, pp 159–63,

helped the O'Byrnes, who cleverly exploited the chaos caused by Maurice de Cauntetoun's rebellion of 1308–10 to advance deeper into the MacMurrough sphere; and the support given by Murchadh O'Byrne's brothers to de Cauntetoun, a sworn enemy of the MacMurroughs, was a direct challenge to Muiris MacMurrough.[34] (During January 1310 Carlow was also wasted by a war between Arnold le Poer and John de Boneville, the two competitors for the seneschalcy of Kildare and Carlow. On 26 January 1310, le Poer, the former seneschal, with the help of the Irish of the Leinster mountains – perhaps the O'Byrnes – even laid siege to Carlow castle, where de Boneville had taken refuge. The struggle climaxed in le Poer's successful assassination of his rival seven days later.)

The government gave Muiris the manor of Courtown in north Wexford as a reward for his capture of an O'Byrne plus a fee of 40 marks. His determination to retain his kingship was evident from his endorsement of the establishment in his ambit of English garrisons at Clonmore, Arklow, Ferns and Wicklow. Competition for the support of the lesser Irish lords was a continual feature of the struggle between the O'Byrnes and the MacMurroughs. (Murchadh was also able to draw considerable support from the Ostman families of Harold, Archbold and MacTurkill.) In Lent 1313 Murchadh suffered a considerable setback when he was routed by Lord Edmund Butler in Glenmalure;[35] however, the O'Byrnes recovered temporarily to become the most powerful Irish family in East Leinster by 1314. Muiris MacMurrough remained in service during that year, earning a fee of £76 for fighting the O'Byrnes, and he probably died in late 1314, to be succeeded by the shadowy Domhnall Riabhach MacMurrough. Although there is virtually nothing known of Domhnall Riabhach, it is clear that he and his dynasty remained at odds with Murchadh O'Byrne.

The campaigns of Edward Bruce between 1315 and 1318, greatly aided Murchadh's expansion. By 1315, his influence was felt west of the Barrow, where he formed an alliance with David O'Toole and Laoiseach O'More. This chance he seized, directing hammer blows at the crumbling Fitzgerald barony of Wicklow. With David O'Toole, he burnt English settlements the length of the Wicklow coast, burning the towns and castles of Arklow, Wicklow, Newcastle McKynegan and Bray before sacking Athy with Laoiseach O'More in late 1315.[36] However, Murchadh's plans were dealt a blow by Lord Edmund Butler's defeat of Laoiseach late in the year.[37] The year 1316 was to prove the high

---

174, 222.   **34** *CJR, 1308–14,* pp 32, 55; Nicholls, 'Crioch Branach', p. 15; the tenants of the prior of Glascarrig were charged with recieving the de Cauntetouns and Dúnlaing O'Byrne in 1312; The MacMurroughs were not in service all of 1311. In 1311 an Ellok Ynymcmurghut (MacMurrough) raided the Raymond de Valle, while Muiris MacMurrough, king of Leinster, stole 27 cows from the abbot of Duiske, see *CJR 1308–14,* pp 174, 237.   **35** NA, RC 7/13 (iv), pp 122–4; see *CJR 1308–14,* p. 285; *Chartul. St Mary's,* ii, p. 341; O'Byrne, 'The Uí Bhroin of Wicklow', p. 60.   **36** Dowling, *Annals,* p. 19; see also Ó Cléirigh, 'The impact of the Anglo-Normans in Laois', pp 177–8; *Chartul. St Mary's,* ii, pp 348–9; *The Book of Howth,* p. 134.   **37** *Grace,* p. 69.

watermark of Murchadh's career. In January and February Lord Edmund Butler inflicted a series of defeats upon the O'Mores, routing them at Castledermot before destroying Laoiseach's main force at Ballylehane on the borders of Laois and Carlow.[38]

Perhaps in response to the defeats of the O'Mores, Murchadh O'Byrne exacted a terrible revenge upon the English of east Wicklow. Before Lent 1316 he linked up with the O'Tooles and the Ostman lineages of Harold and Archbold to completely devastate the remnants of the Fitzgerald barony of Wicklow – culminating in the sack of Wicklow town. The devastation wreaked by the O'Byrnes on the Fitzgerald Wicklow lands was so thorough that no rents could be collected from them that year. From the surviving evidence, it is clear that Murchadh was steadily eradicating the English presence in east Wicklow, forcing their evacuation of lands and farms. This process starkly mirrored the tactics he had employed against the settlers of Shillelagh in 1295–6. Hugh Lawless, leader of the English of east Wicklow, pleaded before Lord Edmund Butler in February 1316 for relief from the O'Byrne onslaught, graphically describing the terrible plight of the Wicklow settlers, caught in 'a confined and narrow part of the country, namely between Newcastle McKynegan and Wicklow, where they have the sea between Wales and Ireland for a wall on one side, and the mountains of Leinster and divers other wooded and desert places on the other where the said Irish felons live'. Lawless did not mince his words: 'by the malice and wantonness of the Irish of the mountains of Leinster, felons of the king, they [the English] have been expelled and removed from their fortresses, manors and houses up to the present, and many of the said faithful subjects of the king have been slain by the said Irish felons'.

Murchadh's luck was to change for the worse as mid-year approached. On 22 May his brother Dúnlaing was killed near Dublin. Worse was to follow: in June, David O'Toole's attack on Tullow was annihilated (with the loss of some 400 fighting men) by the English with probable MacMurrough connivance; this was followed up by another English victory over the Wicklow Irish at Baltinglass. On 8 September, O'Toole narrowly avoided the fate of Dúnlaing when the Dublin citizens led by John Comyn attacked the encampment of his raiding party at Cullenswood.[39] These reverses shattered Murchadh's alliance-building, and as Bruce's threat began to recede during 1316–17, the English took the offensive in Leinster. In September 1317, Lord Lieutenant Roger Mortimer waged a successful campaign against David O'Toole in Imaal before defeating another Irish force on the borders of Uí Cheinnselaig. On his way back to Dublin, Mortimer invaded Murchadh's lordship, forcing battle in Glenealy in east Wicklow, where Mortimer inflicted a heavy defeat upon the O'Byrnes and their Archbold allies; this forced Murchadh to come to peace at Dublin Castle.[40]

---

38 *Chartul. St Mary's*, ii, p. 353; Clyn, *Annals*, p. 12.   39 Clyn, *Annals*, p. 12; *Chartul. St Mary's*, ii, pp 297, 350–1; Grace, p. 75.   40 *Chartul. St Mary's*, ii, pp 356–7; *Grace*, p. 91; Lydon, 'Medieval Wicklow', p. 172; *The Book of Howth*, pp 141–2.

Murchadh's defeat failed to bring peace to the region. The MacMurroughs and the O'Byrnes remained deadly enemies. However, there is some uncertainty as to who was the MacMurrough leader after 1317. For that year the annals mention the death of Domhnall Riabhach, describing him as an 'illustrious king of Leinster'.[41] Moreover, Thomas Fitzgerald, 2nd earl of Kildare, attempted to recover the lost Fitzgerald influence in Wicklow at the expense of a weakened Murchadh. After the submission of Murchadh, Kildare gave security for the Archbolds on 28 October 1317. Later in September 1318, Kildare drove a wedge between Murchadh's O'Toole allies by giving O'Toole land to Aodh Óg O'Toole in return for service against his Imaal kinsmen.[42] But clearly the region remained unsettled, as the O'Tooles and the O'Nolans had raided the Barrow valley earlier in January, killing John de Lyvet. This situation was further complicated by MacMurrough raids on the liberty of Carlow and Co. Kildare, which signalled a return to their previous form, now that their leadership of East Leinster was secure.

WEST LEINSTER, 1270–1320

Apart from the occasional large-scale raids by Aodh O'Connor of Connacht, the Irish of West Leinster were mostly at peace in 1270. Since 1240s the English had encountered little resistance from the Irish kings of this region, the O'Melaghlins being the only major exception. By 1272, however, the region was engulfed in warfare. Various theories have been put foward to explain this upsurge in Irish violence in West Leinster and the province as a whole, ranging from the bad weather conditions in the 1270s to the perceived crisis of lordship caused by the extinction of the Marshal lords of Leinster in 1245.[43]

Under the Marshals, Leinster enjoyed a long-lasting economic boom. After the death of the last Marshal, the lordship of Leinster was painstakingly portioned out among the surviving female heirs, resulting in the emergence of the four liberties of Carlow, Wexford, Kilkenny and Kildare – subdivisions which were then further divided. However, this partition of the lordship of Leinster does not seem to have adversely affected the English of West Leinster. If anything, English Leinster continued to boom, which would indicate generally good relations with the Irish despite the turbulence of the period; but in the longer term, the breakup of the Marshal lordship did create problems: after 1247, many of the new landowners were absentees. In the absence of these landowners, their lands were administered by seneschals. The smooth governance of these lands was affected by the conflicts of interests arising from the dual nature of the office of seneschal. Primarily, a seneschal was an officer of the crown entrusted with the defence of a liberty, but he was also the steward of the absentee liberty-holders

41 ALC, 1317. **42** *Chartul. St Mary's*, ii, p. 357; *Red Bk Kildare*, no. 139, p. 129. **43** Lydon, 'A land of war', pp 256–7, 264; AI, 1271.

and had a duty to collect and maximize rents due to them. When these interests clashed, the seneschals tended to favour the crown. As ever where the crown was involved, this resulted in high-handedness, particularly with the Irish, and this had disastrous consequences for the English settlers.

A key factor contributing to the crisis was the dire weather conditions of the 1270s. Both parts of Leinster suffered heavy snow and famine in the early 1270s, but the reasons why the Irish of both regions revolted are separate. The effect of the harsh weather certainly played a decisive role in East Leinster, creating conditions in 1269 that drove to war the formerly peaceful Irish living on the lands of the archbishop of Dublin; but that war in the Wicklow mountains probably had no repercussions in West Leinster.

In Connacht, Aodh O'Connor continued to harass English settlements along the western bank of the Shannon. During 1270, he destroyed castles throughout Connacht before routing Walter Burke, lord of Connacht and earl of Ulster, at Athankip. There seems to have been a direct connection between the defeat of the Burkes at Athankip and a seemingly unexpected but fierce attack by the O'Connor Falys and other Irish upon the English of Offaly: a fragmentary account records that the English were almost expelled from Offaly, losing many castles – Lea castle being the only major exception.[44] The ferocity and success of the Irish in Offaly suggests that they may have received considerable support from the Connacht king. Over the next two years, Aodh conducted a reign of terror, devastating English fortresses along the Shannon and lending his support to Brian Ruadh O'Brien of Thomond. The barriers penning the O'Connors to west of the Shannon were crumbling, as can be seen from Aodh's devastation in 1272 of the northern midlands and Athlone;[45] but Aodh's death on 3 May 1274 brought this resurgence to a close; thenceforth the O'Connors were plunged into a series of internecine feuds, distracting their attentions from the midlands until the Bruce invasion forty years later.

O'Connor raids and the bad weather may supply two reasons for why war now broke out in West Leinster and the midlands. It is also clear that the anti-English feelings extending all the way from Thomond to Tyrone were affecting the region.[46] Again obits of Irish kings provide clues. In 1274, Aodh O'Connor was described as 'a king who inflicted great defeats on the Galls and pulled down their palaces and castles'.[47] This political undertone is also found in the obits of Conchobhar O'Melaghlin and Art O'Melaghlin of Meath, both of whom are lauded for their destruction of castles and general belligerence towards the English; Art's obit of 1283 notices his destruction of twenty-seven castles.[48]

---

44 AClon, AU, AI, AFM, AConn, 1270; *Cal. Carew MSS Miscellaneous*, p. 323.   45 AConn, AClon, 1272. Another entry records that the son of John de Verdon was killed by Walter Burke, see AU, 1271. This indicates that Burke had considerable influence among the Irish of the northern midlands. Indeed, this was not to be the last time the Burkes would show their influence over the O'Farrells, see below; See also Otway-Ruthven, *Medieval Ireland*, p. 200 Otway-Ruthven also connected Aodh's devastation of Athlone and Meath with the O'Farrell outbreak.   46 Curtis, *Med. Ire*, pp 151–2.   47 AConn, AClon, 1274.   48 AClon, 1283. For

While the wars in the two parts of Leinster began for separate reasons, in the longer term they heralded the re-emergence of the military strength of the MacMurrough provincial kings, who were to return to prominence as the remnants of Connacht's almost two-century grip upon West Leinster slowly receded.

In West Leinster after 1270 the growing prominence of the Irish in both the annals and the English records suggests that momentum for war came from within Irish midland society. Outside Offaly, trouble was also brewing among the Irish in the mountainous borderlands of the liberties of Kildare, Carlow and Kilkenny. It has been suggested that an attack by the MacGillapatricks of North Ossory about 1271 upon the O'Dempseys of Clanmaliere plunged the whole region into chaos.[49] This renewed MacGillapatrick activity coincided with the emergence of a new but unknown leader. In comparison to his predecessor Sefraidh son of Domhnall Clannach MacGillapatrick (he died in 1269), this new leader seems to have had the same ideology as Donnchadh MacGillapatrick did during the 1240s; this unknown leader seems to have been determined to prosecute a war at every opportunity against the settlers and their allies.

In response, the O'Dempseys seemingly appealed for protection from the government. Mindful of MacGillapatrick potential for wreaking havoc upon the English from their Slieve Bloom heartland, the government's reaction was immediate. A force under Sir William de Cadel was dispatched to protect the O'Dempseys. If this war spread, the Shannon defensive line would be exposed to attack from both sides of the river. Spread it did. But not west, east. If the Shannon formed English Leinster's western frontier, the Barrow was the province's internal border between West Leinster and East Leinster. Just as the Shannon and its adjacent passes were communication routes to the English lordships in Thomond and Desmond, the Barrow valley performed the same function, linking Dublin to the southeast and Munster. Thus, the emergence of war in this pass-laced region between the Shannon and the Barrow was potentially disastrous for the English. The risk of Irish expansion along the western bank of the Barrow was increased in 1274 by spread of the war in the Wicklow mountains to the MacMurrough territories close to the Barrow's eastern bank.[50] If the Leinster Irish were to co-ordinate their efforts, there was a strong probability that this portal would be blocked against the English lordship (but this Irish coming together was still some way off). From the outset of the Leinster wars, the government acted quickly to restore the peace. However, Sir William de Cadel's intervention against the MacGillapatricks only served to intensify the conflict and exposed the vulnerability of the English of Offaly to Irish attack. Some of the Irish successes there may also be explained by the vacancy within the Fitzgerald lordship of Offaly since 1268.

Conchobhar mac Domhnaill Breagach O'Melaghlin's obit, see AClon, 1277. And later in 1295 similar praise is heaped upon O'Melaghlin's neighbour and contemporary, Sefraidh O'Farrell of Annaly. AConn, AU, 1295.   **49** Lydon, 'A land of war', p. 264.   **50** Flower, 'The Kilkenny chronicle in Cotton MS', p. 332.

By 1272, the Dublin government was forced to dispatch an expedition led by Justiciar Maurice fitzMaurice Fitzgerald to Offaly. The outbreak of war there marked the start of the English retreat from western Offaly and much of West Leinster and the slow emergence of the Pale. As the English lordships in the midlands contracted under Irish pressure, the Irish inevitably warred among themselves for territory and spoils.[51] All in all, though, the situation by 1275–6 was worsening for the English of the midlands: the MacGillapatricks of North Ossory and perhaps the O'Carrolls of Ely combined to resist the advance into the Slieve Blooms of Thomas de Clare, the brother of Gilbert de Clare, earl of Gloucester and lord of Kilkenny.[52] To the east of these mountains Laois was disturbed, suggesting that the O'Mores were riding with the O'Connor Falys, the O'Carrolls, and the MacGillapatricks. Only O'Dempsey, for his own reasons, sided with the government, and he was duly rewarded with the gift of a horse from the justiciar in 1277.[53] The spread of the war there was confirmed in January 1278, when the situation in Laois became so serious that Roger Mortimer, lord of Dunamase, and his tenants were excused from contribution to a royal subsidy because of huge costs incurred fighting the Irish.[54] The sources point to co-ordinated campaigns being waged by a confederation of the MacGillapatricks, O'Connor Falys and the O'Mores, forcing Justiciar Robert de Ufford to campaign in Laois on two occasions as far as the outpost of the Newtown of Leys between 1279 and 1280. De Ufford's campaigns, combined with strenuous efforts of the seneschals of Kildare, apparently forced a general peace upon the midland Irish. The records show An Calbhach O'Connor Faly and O'Dempsey agreeing to hand over 100 cattle in addition to 100 marks for a grant of peace at a date after 1280.[55]

For the first time in a decade, Leinster was at peace. But this peace did not last, and there is evidence to suggest that the English nightmare of a growing solidarity among the Irish of both parts of Leinster was beginning to manifest itself. Those Irish dynasties pushing for greater co-operation were the MacGillapatricks of North Ossory and the MacMurroughs. For the three years from 1278 to 1281, the MacMurroughs had observed a uneasy peace, but their discontent still rankled, as evidenced by the arrest of a Dermitius McMorkada in 1280. By 1281, war was back on the agenda in Leinster. In the midlands the MacGillapatricks were again in arms, but their leader Hogekyn was killed before the close of the year,[56] while Muircheartach MacMurrough, the provincial king, was arrested by the English – perhaps as a precautionary measure against an outbreak of trouble in the region. Later in the year he was escorted (as we have seen) to Dunamase in Laois to treat with the Irish – which strongly suggests that

---

51 *DKR*, xxxv, p. 24; AClon, 1275. Art mac Cormac O'Melaghlin was wounded by the MacGeoghegans and the O'Molloys of Fearceall.   52 Lydon, 'A land of war', p. 264. 53 There seems to have been a campaign into Slieve Bloom in 1277, see *DKR*, xxxvi, p. 35. *CDI, 1252–84*, no. 1389, p. 258.   54 Lydon, 'A land of war', p. 264.   55 *DKR*, xxxvi, p. 73. 56 Clyn, *Annals*, p. 9; *DKR*, xxxvi, p. 64; There seems to have been trouble in Leys and Slieve Bloom in 1281. That year Maurice fitzMaurice was lent 100 livres for bringing a force from Connacht to campaign in Slieve Bloom.

his kinsmen were intriguing with the Irish of the midlands and that maybe some midland lords still acknowledged him as provincial king. After the collapse of the talks, he was returned to Dublin, but was freed by early 1282. Events after his release suggest that he was heavily involved in the conflict emerging in Leinster; we find his brother Art attacking the English of the Vale of Dublin.

These disturbances in Leinster took place against the background of the outbreak of a serious Welsh rebellion against Edward I in March 1282; the Welsh successes stirred the Munster Irish, but in Ossory their effect was earth-shaking. In June 1282 Gilbert de Clare, earl of Gloucester and lord of Kilkenny, was defeated by the Welsh at Llandeilo fawr. Fearful of the effects of the news of Llandeilo fawr, Justiciar Stephen de Fulbourne sanctioned the murder of the MacMurrough brothers: in July 1282, five weeks after Llandeilo fawr, they arrived, under a safe conduct, at Arklow to embark for England, but were murdered by government assassins.[57]

The strangulation of the probable MacGillapatrick/MacMurrough alliance had the effect of reorienting the political axis from East Leinster to West Leinster. This shift seems to be confirmed by the emergence of an alliance between the O'Connor Falys and the O'Melaghlins by 1282, one of the moving forces behind which was Cairbre mac Airt O'Melaghlin, king of Meath (1283–90). This coincided with the emergence of two brothers, Muircheartach and An Calbhach O'Connor Faly (Muircheartach was head of their dynasty; An Calbhach, a leader of tremendous military ability). Under this triumvirate, the conflict in the midlands dramatically escalated,[58] steadily eroding the revenues accruing to the English from their Offaly lands: in July 1283, a Kildare jury observed that the Offaly territory of Oregan, which belonged to the O'Dunnes, had annually rendered £90 13s. 4d. during peacetime, but was now worth less than half of that sum.

Such was the military strength of this axis that all campaigns to curb the Irish of Offaly and west Meath failed. An impending sense of doom descended upon the English of Offaly when the Fitzgerald manorial hub of Lea fell to the O'Connor Faly/O'Melaghlin alliance in June 1284.[59] The conflict also reignited the O'Mores of Laois who were now threatening the Dunamase lands of Edmund Mortimer.[60] The fall of Lea prompted a co-ordinated counter-offensive into Offaly in 1285, but in a series of clashes the Irish under Cairbre O'Melaghlin proved victorious, routing the incursions of Theobald Butler, Geoffrey de Joinville, lord of the liberty of Meath, and Piers Bermingham. Worse followed. Somewhere in Offaly, the expedition of Gerald fitzMaurice Fitzgerald, 4th lord of Offaly, was destroyed by a highly mobile enemy; Gerald was taken prisoner

57 Duffy, 'Ireland and the Irish Sea region', pp 135–42. There is further evidence linking Ossory and Wales. See *Annales Monastici*, iv, p. 311; *Calendar of various chancery rolls* (London, 1912), p. 323; *CDI, 1252–84*, no. 912; Frame, 'The Justiciar and the murder of the MacMurroughs in 1282', pp 223–31; Dowling, *Annals*, p. 16; *Grace*, p. 39; Clyn, *Annals*, p. 9; AFM, 1282. **58** Ó Cléirigh, 'The impact of the Anglo-Normans in Laois,' p. 172; Dowling, *Annals*, p. 16. **59** AI, 1283; Chartul. St Mary's, ii, p. 319. **60** Ó Cléirigh, 'John fitzThomas', p. 32; *Chartul. St Mary's*, ii, p. 319.

for an unspecified period, while, to the south, MacGillapatrick paid £6 to have the king's peace in 1285–6.[61]

In 1286 the military situation improved for the English, when An Calbhach O'Connor Faly was captured; this forced the O'Connor Falys to peace. A further improvement in English fortunes was the emergence of John fitzThomas Fitzgerald as the 5th lord of Offaly upon the death of the hapless Gerald about July 1287. The region was still volatile: witness the raids of Toirdealbhach O'Brien of Thomond on Limerick and the Butler lands in Ormond;[62] and fitzThomas' inheritance soon fell foul of the endemic political instability and slid back to warfare by summer 1288. Such was the enormity of the threat posed by the midland Irish to the English that Justiciar John de Sandford, who was also archbishop of Dublin, caused the royal service due from Leinster to be proclaimed, and proceeded to attack the Irish of Laois and Offaly. It was an operation of considerable scale, lasting a year and involving the co-ordinated efforts of fitzThomas, de Joinville and Bermingham.[63]

Despite these expeditions, the threat remained; in 1289 two armies had to be dispatched into west Meath and Offaly. In April 1289 de Sandford invaded west Meath from Connacht, with a large force that included Maghnus O'Connor of Connacht and Domhnall O'Kelly, king of Uí Maine. They were confronted by Cairbre O'Melaghlin, the O'Molloys, the MacGeoghegans and O'Sionnach and were heavily defeated. Further south, Bermingham and fitzThomas clashed with An Calbhach O'Connor Faly and 'the rest of the princes of Leinster' after May 1289.[64] It seems the O'Connor Falys, the O'Mores and the O'Melaghlins pounced on fitzThomas' force deep in Offaly. Again the Irish proved too strong; John fitzThomas seemingly was captured, and de Sandford had to organize a rescue mission. In response to this latest setback, de Sandford temporized with the O'Connor Falys, but by autumn 1289 he mounted another expedition against them, being accompanied into Offaly by a large contingent of Irish troops from Wicklow.[65] While the army was assembling, de Sandford still pursued diplomacy. A parley at Aghaboe with the O'Connor Falys and, apparently MacGillapatrick of North Ossory, failed, and in September 1289 de Sandford attacked the Irish of Laois and Offaly, bringing the war to a successful close by 4 October. De Sandford's correspondence suggests that the Irish capitulation was complete.[66]

By the terms of the peace, the Irish of Offaly paid a series of fines through the abbot of Rosglas in late 1289.[67] Later evidence (dating from January 1292) showed that An Calbhach O'Connor Faly gave hostages and promised the

61 AClon, 1285; Clyn, *Annals*, p. 10; *Chartul. St Mary's*, ii, p. 319; *CDI*, *1285–92*, no. 180, p. 87. **62** Lydon, 'A land of war', p. 254. **63** Ó Cléirigh, 'The impact of the Anglo-Normans on Laois', p. 172; *CDI*, *1285–92*, no. 559, p. 265. **64** AConn, AClon, AU, 1289; *CDI*, *1285–92*, no. 559, pp 269–70. **65** *CDI*, *1285–92*, p. 272. **66** Ibid., pp 272–3; The trouble had definitively spread to Tipperary as its sheriff Roger de Penebrok rendered £38. 3s. 4d. for the defence of the land, see ibid., p. 276. However, as Ó Cléirigh points out while this campaign did succeed in forcing the submission of the Irish, it was to be temporary. Ó Cléirigh, 'The problems of defence: a regional case-study', p. 33. **67** *CDI*, *1285–92*, no. 559, p. 277.

payment of 1000 marks for his own release,[68] but in June 1290 he negotiated the lifting of his fine as well as the release of his hostages from Dublin Castle. In return, the government secured the release of Sir John de Fulbourne, who had been a prisoner of the Irish since de Sandford's last campaign into Offaly. An Calbhach's successful manipulation of this delicate situation reveals that much of Offaly lay beyond the land of peace. If he wished, he could at will throw the region again into chaos.

However, the killing of Cairbre O'Melaghlin, king of Meath, by the MacCoghlans proved the major event in Irish midland politics during 1290. O'Melaghlin's demise marked a decisive turning-point in his dynasty's fortunes. His son and successor, Murchadh died of natural causes in 1293.[69] This left the door ajar for the O'Connor Falys to become the great Irish regional power. As has been noted, the Irish of Laois and Offaly returned to war between 1291 and 1292, expanding into Carlow, Kildare and Meath;[70] it was a period that saw an acrimonious dispute between John fitzThomas and Sir William de Vescy, justiciar of Ireland and lord of the liberty of Kildare. De Vescy arrived in Ireland in November 1290 to succeed de Sandford, and immediately mounted a determined campaign to reassert his rights as lord of Kildare. This of course directly impinged on fitzThomas, whose lordship of Offaly he challenged in 1291. To strengthen his position against this threat, fitzThomas seems to have buried his differences with the O'Connor Falys, an apparent rapprochement that was confirmed when Edward I granted him permission to negotiate with the Irish, both within and outside his own lands, in May 1292.[71]

For his part, de Vescy brought hostings into Offaly, harassing the Irish followers of fitzThomas and causing the latter to make vigorous complaints to the king. De Vescy defended his actions to the king, alleging that these Irishmen had raided the liberty of Kildare and that it was his duty as its lord to prosecute them for their misdemeanours. He took the feud a step further by proclaiming a royal muster to take place at Kildare on 24 July 1293. Ostensibly this campaign was to be against the Irish of Offaly; in reality, fitzThomas was the target. Bloodshed was averted (but only postponed) by Edward I's countermanding of de Vescy's decree on 1 July 1293.[72]

During Michaelmas 1293, fitzThomas and others made a series of complaints against de Vescy before the English parliament. On 1 April 1294 in the presence of the Dublin council, de Vescy accused fitzThomas of slandering him to the king. Dramatically, a challenge of arms was made, and both men were summoned before the king. In the meantime de Vescy was removed from his justiciarship by the king on 4 June 1294. On 24 July de Vescy appeared for the

---

68 Ó Cléirigh, 'John fitzThomas', p. 42.   69 AConn, 1290, 1293; AClon, 1290; *Chartul. St Mary's*, ii, p. 320.   70 Ó Cléirigh, 'The impact of the Anglo-Normans in Laois', p. 173. 71 *CDI, 1285–92*, no. 1103, pp 488–9; Dowling, *Annals*, p. 16. This mentions hostility between fitz Thomas and de Vescy in 1292.   72 Lydon, 'The years of crisis, 1254–1315', p. 186; *CDI, 1293–1301*, nos 62–3, p. 37.

duel at Westminster, but fitzThomas failed to show; consequently de Vescy won his case by default. Meanwhile, in Ireland, the feud exploded; according to the evidence given at a general eyre in Kildare between July 1297 and April 1298, the western cantred of Offaly and its neighbour of Leys were aflame – with multiple murders and a considerable degree of fraternization between the Irish and fitzThomas. Broadly speaking, the actions of fitzThomas can be dated between late 1294 and early 1295, and they involved a spree of violence through Clane in Offelan, Reban in Leys and the barony of Dunlost in the cantred of Omurthy.[73] The extent of the violence eventually led to de Vescy's surrender of the Kildare liberty to the crown in 1297.

The situation was further complicated by fitzThomas' power struggle with Earl Richard Burke of Ulster for supremacy in Connacht. In December 1294, the earl was taken prisoner by fitzThomas and held him in Lea castle, not being released (after prolonged negotiations) until 11 March 1295. The Irish must certainly have exploited this great feud of fitzThomas and de Vescy. While there are difficulties in dating the events recorded in the proceedings of the eyre, it is clear that the O'Mores and O'Dempseys were independently preying on the English living on the edges of their territories.[74] More serious was the close collaboration between fitzThomas and An Calbhach O'Connor Faly. John fitzThomas may well have been glad of O'Connor Faly aid, but the Irish were pursuing their own agenda. Most notoriously, fitzThomas and An Calbhach seem to have separately attacked de Vescy's castle of Kildare during late 1294.[75]

This renewed O'Connor Faly activity set the scene for four years of continuous violence, which roughly coincided with the emergence of Muiris MacMurrough's war of 1295, the Welsh rebellion of 1294/5 and a period of prolonged famine between 1294 and 1296.[76] By 1297, the extent of the English collapse in West Leinster was clear: nobody was appointed to succeed Walter Sweyn as coroner of Offaly, while Simon Swedeual was to be serjeant of a much diminished sergeantcy of Offelan. The pleas of the crown of Kildare also reveal endemic feuding among the English of Leys, which caused as much unrest as Irish raids. Even more worrying for the government were reports of fraternization between the Irish and some Englishmen. One instance records the campaign of

---

73 Ó Cléirigh, 'John fitzThomas', p. 73. However, it is impossible to obtain a general picture of Kildare as the proceedings relating to Offelan, Kildare's richest cantred, have not survived; *CJR, 1295–1303*, pp 193, 202. **74** *CJR, 1295–1303*, pp 168, 176. **75** Ó Cléirigh, 'John fitzThomas', pp 73–4; see also Dowling, *Annals*, p. 17. Interestingly, the Irish agenda and their priorities become clearer when An Calbhach burnt the tallies and rolls of the Kildare liberty. *Chartul. St Mary's*, ii, p. 323; *CJR, 1295–1303*, p. 118; *Grace*, p. 43. **76** Frame, 'The Dublin government', p. 92; Duffy, 'Ireland and the Irish Sea region', pp 147–50; *CJR, 1295–1303*, p. 61. Indeed, the hiatus of the O'Connor Faly dynasty at the close of the century exposes patterns of eastward raids from Offaly into the southern Kildare cantreds of Omurethy and Leys. In January 1298, twelve jurors of the cantred of Omurthy said that Calaugh Oconughor and other felons destroyed the country of Kilkolyn and made off with a huge herd of cattle, see ibid., p. 194.

Nigel le Brun against the Irish of Irry in Offaly. Upon le Brun's return to the Newtown of Leys, he was brought to battle by the Irish with their English allies. Robert Braynock, then sergeant of Offelan, only escaped with his life by killing an Englishman named William Balaunce. Depressingly, some of the English of Dunamase were also receiving the Irish and were swearing oaths with them to disturb the peace.[77] To counter such threats, English lords such as Piers Bermingham sought to pacify the O'Connor Falys, playing an elaborate game of diplomatic chess with them. Bermingham and John fitzThomas even stood as godfathers to An Calbhach's sons, John and Maisir. However, whenever conditions were favourable, as they were in 1299, Bermingham campaigned into Irish territories.[78]

Significantly, though, the thrust of Irish expansion was turning southward, focusing particularly on the western side of the Barrow valley. Because of Irish successes, huge stretches of the midland landscape were now outside English control, and it seems these lands were centred around Irry in Offaly, and Clonboyne in Laois.[79] Moreover, Kenagh Óg (Cétach Óg) and Leyssagh (Laoiseach) O'More were extracting blackrents and foodrents from the settlers in parts of Leys.[80] They were making dramatic progress, conquering the highland region of Slemargy to the northwest of the Barrow valley. Clearly, the expansion of the O'Mores was pushing the English back to the Barrow frontier, concentrating their attacks upon the settlements along the highway through the valley, a vital lifeline that connected Munster with the rest of the country. English problems in the Barrow valley area were compounded by the desertion of their O'Dempsey allies for the lucrative business of ambushing travellers and merchants on the highway outside Castledermot.[81]

The most dramatic statement yet of Irish power came in 1297, when the Irish of Slemargy, probably the O'Mores, broke into the Barrow valley and destroyed Leighlinbridge. It was also a time that saw the brief alliance of the MacMurroughs with the O'Connor Falys in 1297.[82] War reared up again in Ossory; in October 1297 Justiciar John Wogan was compelled to campaign against MacGillapatrick near Castlecomer. That year among the crown pleas of Offaly the outlawry of Sefraidh O'Carroll is recorded, indicating that some of the O'Carrolls were also dragged into the war. Meanwhile in the northern midlands, Sefraidh O'Farrell of Annaly had been attacking the settlers of Annaly from at least 1295.[83] From this date onwards, the English would have to thoroughly reconquer Leinster if the midland settlements were to survive.

It would be a mistake to view the ongoing Irish warring as being solely racially motivated. In spite of the strength of the Irish at this time, much of their

77 Ó Cléirigh, 'The impact of the Anglo-Normans in Laois', p. 174. **78** *CJR, 1295–1303*, p. 189; see also Ó Cléirigh, 'The problems of defence: a regional case-study', p. 38; AI, 1305. **79** Ó Cléirigh, 'The impact of the Anglo-Normans in Laois', p. 174. **80** Nicholls notes that Slemargy had formed no part of the pre-invasion territory of the O'Mores, see Nicholls, *Gaelic Ire*, p. 174; *CJR, 1295–1303*, pp 167–9. **81** *CJR, 1295–1303*, p. 189. **82** Ibid., pp 69, 189, 394. **83** CJR, *1305–7*, p. viii; AU, 1295.

success can be put down to deep divisions within settler society. In particular, the feud between the English of Tipperary and Kilkenny after 1300 increased the volatility of the marches.[84] The anti-English feeling that fuelled earlier wars in Connacht and elsewhere does not seem to have been so omnipresent among the Leinster Irish; the expansion of the Leinster Irish seems to have had more to do with opportunism. There was still much social interaction between the Irish and English nobles of this frontier world. For instance, in 1290, Earl Richard Burke of Ulster obtained a small measure of revenge for the murder of his sometime ally Cairbre O'Melaghlin by devastating the lands in Delvin of the murderer, David MacCoghlan. The annals also later record that the earl encouraged the killing of David MacCoghlan by the Berminghams in 1293.[85] Favour was also shown by the earl to Sefraidh O'Farrell of Annaly in the early fourteenth century, by a grant to him of lands and tenements. Also the sight of An Calbhach O'Connor Faly in 1298, prosecuting a case against Robert Typer for theft of cattle during peacetime, seems paradoxical, given his record.[86] Other social contact between the Irish and the English included marriage and spying. In 1297 Nicholas Toan was hanged for spying on Kildare for the Irish and for his participation in their raids.

Intermarriage and fosterage between the Irish and the English of the marches further demonstrates the depth of the complexities of the relationships between both communities. During 1302 Isabella de Cadel and her maid were charged with having part in robberies carried out by the Irish of the Leinster mountains, and with spying out English territories. As it transpired, Isabella was married to Diarmait O'Dempsey, whom she called her lord. From her own account, she had gone at his command to visit and give gifts to his allies in the Leinster mountains. Luckily for her, the court took into account the good service rendered by her father, Sir William de Cadel, the former royal seneschal of Kildare and Carlow. (Links between the de Cadels and the O'Dempseys dated back as far as 1272, when Sir William was sent to protect them from the MacGillapatricks of North Ossory.)[87] In regard to the fosterage of English youths among the households of Irish nobles, Dr Seán Duffy argues that the incorporation of a toponymic epithet into names of Englishmen is an indicator of such practices. He points to the case of Philip Falyagh Keating, a man of English lineage from the marches of south Leinster and Tipperary. The epithet of Falyagh tends to suggest that Philip was fostered among the neighbouring O'Connor Falys of Offaly.[88] There were additional signs of the absence of royal government on the marches: many

---

84 *CJR, 1295–1303*, p. 350. This marks the emergence of serious warfare between the English of Tipperary and Kilkenny in 1300. Between November 1303 and January 1304, there was a government campaign against the MacGillapatricks, see *CJR, 1305–7*, p. xii. In 1305 the English community of Tipperary had to pay for horses lost guarding the Slieve Bloom marches, see *CJR, 1305–7*, pp 85. In 1306 no serjeant could do his duty in the march of Ely, on account of the Irish of Slieve Bloom, see *CJR, 1305–7*, p. 194.   **85** Dowling, *Annals*, p. 16; AConn, 1292.   **86** *CJR, 1295–1303*, p. 197.   **87** Ó Cléirigh, 'The problems of defence: a regional case-study', p. 40.   **88** Duffy, 'The problem of degeneracy', p. 102.

I Detail from a woodcut in John Derricke, *The image of Ireland* (1581) showing an attack by the Irish on English settlers

settlers were forced to treat, without licence, with the Irish for the return of goods and livestock – behaviour that landed them in trouble with the royal justices.[89] We also find that discarded scions of Irish dynasties eagerly served in government armies against their kinsmen; several O'Mores appear performing military service, and a Nigellus O'More was entrusted with Morett castle in Laois by John fitzThomas in 1303.[90]

The opening years of the fourteenth century marked the start of the second epoch of Irish expansion in West Leinster and the province as a whole. In East Leinster, the power of the O'Byrnes of Wicklow was rising, as a result of upheavals in the Irish politics of West Leinster. This put pressure on Muiris MacMurrough, king of Leinster. The Irish dynasties of West Leinster were in close contact with the MacMurroughs; their ambits increasingly met along the strategic Barrow valley during the last decades of the thirteenth century, as evidenced by the growing closeness between the MacMurroughs and the O'Connor Falys of Offaly.[91] The primacy of the latter in the midlands is confirmed by the decline of the O'Melaghlins of Meath. But in June 1305 (as we have seen), Piers Bermingham sanctioned the murders of An Calbhach and Muircheartach O'Connor Faly. This dramatically reshaped the politics of the region. If John fitzThomas Fitzgerald and Piers Bermingham thought that the decapitation of the O'Connor Faly leadership would pacify the region, they were mistaken, for the removal of the brothers profoundly upset the balance of regional Irish polity. Consequently, Diarmait O'Connor Faly, their successor, faced a series of intertwined threats from the English and their Irish allies. Such was the chaotic warfare after the murders that Justiciar John Wogan toured the western marches of Kildare in September 1305, basing himself at the Newtown of Leys; but not even this could not restore order to the frontier. In October 1305, Gilbert de Clare, earl of Gloucester and lord of Kilkenny, led a hosting into MacGillapatrick Slieve Bloom,[92] but it proved fruitless and the midlands remained turbluent.

Of all the attempts to defeat the O'Connor Falys, John fitzThomas' proved the most important. To embark upon the reconquest of Offaly, fitzThomas recruited the O'Dempseys, who had always resented the regional O'Connor Faly supremacy.[93] In response, Diarmait O'Connor Faly formed a rival alliance

89 *CJR, 1295–1303*, pp 368–9. See the case of John de Lyuet, he along with John Tallon was taken prisoner by the Irish of Wicklow in 1301/2. To obtain his release, he had to negotiate terms with them and give hostages. Another case shows a less merciful face of the law. A member of the de Valle family of the Barrow valley married an Isabella Octouthy, who was accused of receiving her brothers, the killers of Geoffrey de Langs. In 1312 after delivering her child, she followed her mother to the gallows. 90 Ó Cléirigh, 'The impact of the Anglo-Normans in Laois', p. 174. Simon son of Domhnall O'More was rewarded in 1312 for service against the Irish of the Leinster mountains, see *CJR, 1308–14*. p. 237. In 1314 Stephen Offlen (MacFháeláin) served with Maurice Howell against the Irish of Leinster mountains and Offaly in 1314, see *CJR, 1308–14*, pp 315–6. In 1314 William Swyft was charged with riding with the O'Tooles against the settlers, see *CJR, 1308–14*, p. 318. 91 *CJR, 1295–1303*, p. 189. 92 *CJR, 1305–7*, pp 84, 124, 135, 467–8. 93 Ó Cléirigh, 'The impact of the Anglo-Normans in Laois',

that included O'Dunnes, MacGillapatricks, MacGeoghegan, and the O'Molloys (the marriage of his daughter to the rising Muircheartach Mór MacGeoghegan may have helped cement the alliance).[94] Diarmait was soon to pressure the O'Dempseys, and late in 1305 Fionnán O'Dempsey petitioned the government for assistance. In January 1306 the Dublin government responded by sending troops and sanctioning fitzThomas to aid the O'Dempseys. Thus fortified, they launched an assault against the O'Connor Falys that drew the latter out of the safety of Offaly, and in early April 1306 the O'Dempseys routed them at John fitzThomas' castle of Geashill, killing their O'Dunne ally.[95] This war was widespread, as Muircheartach Mór MacGeoghegan, who took Diarmait O'Dempsey hostage, forced Fionnán O'Dempsey to negotiate. But the prospect of Fionnán allying with MacGeoghegan to effect the release of Diarmait led fitzThomas and Bermingham to compel him to deliver three hostages into their hands: such were the complexities of regional politics.[96]

Despite the defeat at Geashill, the allies of the O'Connor Falys protected them from the worst of the English and O'Dempsey assault. In June 1306, the O'Melaghlins and Muircheartach Mór MacGeoghegan defeated Bermingham.[97] Further south, the MacGillapatricks widened the extent of their attacks into Tipperary and Laois. And the first mention of a strong march in Ely seems directly linked to these attacks.[98] Because of the proximity of Laois and Offaly to the strategic Barrow valley, this boded ill for a government already under pressure from the Irish of East Leinster. On a general level, co-operation was plainly increasing between the Irish of both parts of Leinster. The Annals of Inisfallen record that the English of both Munster and Leinster were coming under severe Irish pressure as the year closed.[99]

In East Leinster, the situation was particularly violent. The murder of four MacMurrough leaders by Englishmen at Ferns in 1305 echoed Bermingham's slaughter of the O'Connor Falys in June of the same year.[100] And the disturbances in East Leinster continued to match those of West Leinster. Irish co-ordination in Leinster may have been helped by the transfer of the liberty of Carlow into royal hands upon the death of Roger Bigod in 1306. Certainly, Irish envoys were crisscrossing the Barrow frontier, promoting war. For example, the O'Mores in May 1306 burned Ballymore in the western Wicklow mountains.[101] Several sources point to the fact that Justiciar Wogan brought a large army to punish Murchadh O'Byrne's lordship for the devastation of Ballymore – and the Book of Howth records that Irish came from other parts of Ireland to aid O'Byrne. In

p. 175.   **94** *CJR, 1305–7*, p. 151. MacGeoghegan's expansion was already noted by the Dublin government in 1305; the name of MacGeogheghan's O'Connor Faly wife was Joan. She died in 1310 – see AClon, 1310. She is described as Siban in the annals of Connacht, see AConn, 1310.   **95** Ó Cléirigh, 'John fitzThomas', p. 176; *CJR, 1305–7*, p. 270, this records that Fionnán and John fitzThomas received a sum of 40 livres for the beheading of O'Dunne; *Chartul. St Mary's*, ii, p. 333; Dowling, *Annals*, p. 18; *Grace*, p. 49.   **96** *CJR, 1305–7*, p. 271; Ó Cléirigh, 'John fitzThomas', p. 117.   **97** MA, 1306.   **98** *CJR, 1305–7*, p. 194.   **99** AI, 1305.   **100** *CJR, 1305–7*, pp 466–7.   **101** *Chartul. St Mary's*, ii, p. 333; O'Byrne, 'The Uí Bhroin of Co. Wicklow', p. 59

an encounter at Glenfell (probably Glenealy in east Wicklow) the Irish routed Wogan.[102]

By the opening of 1307, the government was in crisis because of the military situation in Leinster. The Barrow frontier was in a state of collapse. The bloody encounter at Glenealy confirmed the English nightmare of Irish confederation and co-operation. Wogan with his deputy, Lord Edmund Butler, now adopted a policy of steel and stealth to meet the Irish challenge. By early summer 1307, they had stopped the Irish gallop in East Leinster, the blow that took the wind out of the MacMurrough sails seemingly being the killing of Murchadh Ballach MacMurrough (see p. 65 above).[103] During the same month, another hosting marched against the O'Tooles of Wicklow, but this met with little success. Having failed militarily, Wogan switched to diplomacy. His success was considerable. In 1307, during the vacancy in the archbishopric of Dublin, he exploited Murchadh O'Byrne's greed for ecclesiastical lands in O'Toole possession. His grant of O'Toole lands to O'Byrne turned the Irish against each other, disarming the potency of the Irish danger in the southeast.[104] Wogan suffered reverses in the next year, but the emerging struggle between Muiris MacMurrough and Murchadh O'Byrne dominated the Irish polity of East Leinster for years to come and meant that they did little to maintain closer relations with the Irish of the midlands. The 1308–10 de Cauntetoun rebellion against the government further inflamed the region as O'Byrnes and MacMurroughs rushed to support the opposing sides.[105]

Wogan now concentrated on the midlands. Although in 1307, Edward II asked the Leinster lords to serve against the Scots, the Irish were in no mood to listen, but Wogan cannot have reckoned with Diarmait O'Connor Faly's next move – a devastating offensive upon the English. With probable O'More support, O'Connor Faly extracted revenge for fitz Thomas' support of the O'Dempseys by burning Geashill and ravaging Leys in July 1307.[106] His siege of the Newtown of Leys forced Wogan to dispatch Butler and his father-in-law, John fitz Thomas Fitzgerald, who forced the O'Connor Falys to retreat. Even so, the fighting continued for another year. Diarmait O'Connor Faly's efforts considerably drained the midland English, but they also exhausted his dynasty. It was the earl of Ulster's campaign against MacGeoghegan, the O'Connor Faly ally, that finally forced a truce.[107] Even so, the condition of the English of Offaly was terminal. With much of west Meath, Offaly, Laois, and North Ossory and Ely lost to the English, the Irish attempted to turn the screw. This came at a cost. In November 1308 Diarmait O'Dempsey's career was cut short by the soldiers of Piers

102 The Book of Howth, p. 127; Grace, p. 51; Dowling, Annals, p. 17; Chartul. St Mary's, ii, p. 333. 103 Dowling, Annals, p. 18. The description of this Murchadh Ballach as princeps Lagenie may infer that he was a brother of Muiris, king of Leinster. See also Chartul. St Mary's, ii, p. 335; Grace, p. 51, see also note f, p. 55. It seems de Cantetoun was hanged for the murder of Murchadh Ballach at Dublin in 1308; CJR, 1308–14, pp 32, 55.   104 O'Byrne, 'The Uí Bhroin of Co. Wicklow', p. 59; CJR, 1305–7, pp 354–5.   105 CJR, 1308–14, pp 200, 237. 106 Dowling, Annals, p. 18.   107 Chartul. St Mary's, ii, pp 335–6; Grace, p. 51; Ó Cléirigh, 'John

Gaveston at Tullow. The killing of O'Dempsey at Tullow and the burning of Athy by the Irish further highlights that the Barrow/Kildare region was the concentration point for Irish expansion from the midlands.[108] Without doubt Bermingham's murders of the O'Connor Falys in June 1305 had sealed the fate of the English lordships of western Kildare.

The decline of the O'Connor Falys and the O'Melaghlins resulted in the brief emergence of two new powers in the northern midlands – Muircheartach Mór MacGeoghegan of Kineleagh and Sefraidh O'Farrell of Annaly. Inevitably a power struggle developed between them. In 1310 Muircheartach Mór with probable O'Connor Faly encouragement attempted to install himself as the new regional overlord, but he was thwarted by the O'Farrells, who killed his son Ferghal, and when he attempted to pressure O'Molloy of Fearceall to accept his lordship, he also failed, as O'Molloy killed Seán MacGeoghegan in 1311.[109] Also, it seems that MacGeoghegan's expansion caused serious worries for the English, who directed a two-pronged assault against him, killing him before the end of the year.[110] (An entry for this year in the Annals of Connacht records the killing of two sons of William Liath Burke by the 'Leinster princes'; its use of the term suggests the involvement of the O'Connor Falys; given their close alliance with the MacGeoghegans, it is likely that this incident formed part of an offensive directed against Muircheartach Mór.)[111]

In the longer term, the tumultuous events of the first decade of the fourteenth century had the effect of overturning the established political patterns in both parts of Leinster, moving the focus of warfare in the midlands southwards to Laois and Munster, as evidenced by the rise of the O'Mores of Laois. The origins of the medieval power of the O'Mores can be traced back to their conquest of the Slemargy highlands, which coincided with the emergence of Laoiseach O'More as their leader in the late thirteenth century. Laoiseach managed to penetrate the Barrow frontier, destroying Leighlinbridge and Ballymore in 1297 and 1306 respectively. Other O'More raids was directed upon the Kilkenny and Carlow liberties. In 1308 Sir John de Boneville, the king's seneschal of these liberties, delivered the body of Donaghuch O'More to Kilkenny castle. It was not only English of the Barrow and of Kilkenny who were exposed to Laoiseach's expansion: the MacGillapatricks of North Ossory and the O'Ryans of Idrone also suffered. Friar Clyn later described Laoiseach as having risen from servility to the level of a prince.[112] Laoiseach was fortunate that his rise coincided with the O'Connor Faly decline, which left him the most powerful Irish noble in the midlands. As Laoiseach grew stronger, he fostered

fitzThomas', p. 179; *CJR, 1308–14*, p. 26.   **108** *Chartul. St Mary's*, ii, p. 338; Dowling, *Annals*, p. 18; *Grace*, p. 55; AClon, 1308.   **109** AClon, AConn, 1310; Dowling, *Annals*, p. 19; *Chartul. St Mary's*, ii, p. 340.   **110** AClon, AConn, 1311.   **111** MA, AConn, 1311 These princes are described as macaib/rig Laignecha. For earlier usage of this term see AU, 1249, AConn, 1249, 1289. From about 1312 the O'Connors Falys were gradually becoming more active along the marches of western Kildare, see Ó Cléirigh, 'John fitzThomas', p. 194. See also Simms, 'Gaelic warfare in the middle ages', p. 108.   **112** Clyn, *Annals*, pp 25, 29–30; *Grace*, p. 45.

good relations with the O'Connor Falys. Moreover, he seems to have become increasingly aware of the strategic value of his lordship as a link between Leinster and the Irish of north Munster. His conquests were greatly assisted through his successful exploitation of the junction-like location of Laois to create alliances and by his extensive usage of mercenary troops from Leinster and Munster.

While Laoiseach was establishing himself as the premier Irish midland lord, Murchadh O'Byrne was engaged in a struggle in East Leinster against Muiris MacMurrough (and his successor, Domhnall Riabhach). These two rising stars of Leinster politics may have met for the first time in summer 1306, when Murchadh's lordship was invaded by Justiciar Wogan in reprisal for Laoiseach's burning of Ballymore that May. As Laoiseach was establishing himself on the political landscape of the midlands, Murchadh struggled to break free of MacMurrough dominance. Both Murchadh and Laoiseach were to emerge as the real Irish winners when the English colony in Leinster dramatically con-tracted in the early fourteenth century. About summer 1315 they formed an alliance, perhaps in response to the landing at Larne of Edward Bruce on 26 May, an event that prompted an explosion of violence in Leinster as in Connacht. The Irish must have been greatly encouraged by Bruce's rout of Earl Richard Burke of Ulster at Connor during September 1315. Bruce's agreement with Ruaidhrí O'Connor (a claimant to the Connacht kingship) sparked a tremen-dous conflict in Connacht. In late 1315 Ruaidhrí claimed the Connacht kingship for himself, sacking the castles of Sligo, Ballymote, Kilcolman, Ballintober and Dunamon as well as the royal castles of Roscommon, Rinndown, and Athlone in a sustained and devastating rampage through the province. Shamed by his adherence to Burke and shocked by the dramatic rise of Ruaidhrí, the young King Féilim O'Connor took the field in early 1316. With the help of the Berminghams and Máelruanaidh MacDermot of Moylurg, Féilim on 24 February routed and killed Ruaidhrí at Templetogher, Co. Galway. Once Ruaidhrí was out of the way, Féilim turned on the English of Connacht and made wide-ranging attacks upon English settlements in the west and south of the province. This violence triggered an massive uprising of the Irish of Meath, Offaly, Thomond and Connacht after March 1316.[113] However, the return of Sir William Liath Burke to Connacht stiffened English resistance; outside Athenry on 10 August 1316, Burke annihilated Féilim's army, killing him and ending forever any O'Connor influence east of the Shannon.

After the defeat of the earl of Ulster at Connor and the advance of the Scots, many of the Leinster Irish took the field. They also had their own reasons – such as the personal ambitions of Murchadh O'Byrne and Laoiseach O'More. Moreover, the Great European Famine of 1315–17 that was raging throughout Leinster also proved to be a powerful trigger for their massive offensive upon the English of Leinster. Allying themselves with David O'Toole, they enjoyed considerable successes – burning Athy and Wicklow in autumn 1315. This forced

113 AConn, 1315; ALC, 1316.

Justiciar Edmund Butler into action. His intervention was clinical, cornering Laoiseach in late 1315 in Laois and killing 800 of his men.[114] However, Bruce's winter campaign of 1315–16 into the midlands destabilized the whole region. In December 1315 Bruce came to Laoiseach's rescue, defeating Roger Mortimer – Laoiseach's feudal overlord – at Kells. Mortimer's defeat rocked the English colony in the midlands, and encouraged the Irish to further destabilize it, though the Irish had several reverses at the hands of Butler early in the year. Bruce rocked the midland colony's remaining equilibrium on 26 January 1316 by mauling the army of Butler and John fitzThomas Fitzgerald at Ardscull near Castledermot in south Kildare.[115] After this, Bruce pushed as far as Reban in western Kildare before returning to winter in Laois, where a grateful Laoiseach welcomed him with open arms. (Bruce was not universally welcome in the midlands. The O'Dempseys treacherously led the Scots into a swamp – which indicates that they had resumed their pro-government stance.) It was probably at Laoiseach's instigation that Bruce ended any chance of an English recovery by destroying Lea, the manorial centre of the Fitzgerald lordship of Offaly, and seizing the Butler caput of Gowran in Lent that year.[116] When Bruce pulled back to Ulster, the Irish finished off what remained of the English lordships in Laois and Offaly. It may have been at this time that Laoiseach achieved his famous feat of destroying eight castles in a day, including the Mortimer fortress of Dunamase. Although the zeal of Laoiseach and his allies earned them a heavy defeat in late 1316, the English position was mortally wounded in Offaly and Laois. The seal was further set on their fate by the Bruce advance into Munster during February and March 1317, for he left in his wake a trail of destruction, stretching from Naas through Castledermot, to Gowran and on to Callan in Co. Kilkenny.[117]

The peril enveloping the English in the central midlands was further confirmed by events in north Tipperary between 1317 and 1318, where the O'Carrolls of Ely exploited the aftermath of Bruce's devastation of the English lands around Nenagh and Cashel by plundering the countryside. Although brought to heel by the English during 1317, Donnchadh Fionn O'Carroll, king of Ely, had used the interim to forge an alliance with Brian Bán O'Brien (the O'Brien dissident). They combined in the early winter of 1318 to resist a major English expedition led by Lord Edmund Butler, Sir William Liath Burke and Adam Mares. Significantly, these English magnates were aided in their efforts by King Muircheartach O'Brien of Thomond, who was keen to clip the wings of Brian Bán. The Irish trounced this impressive English expeditionary force, thereby speeding the contraction of the colony in north Tipperary.[118] The

---

114 *Grace*, pp 68–9.   **115** Curtis, *Med. Ire*, p. 186; Ó Cléirigh, 'John fitzThomas', pp 200–1.   **116** Ó Cléirigh, 'The impact of the Anglo-Normans in Laois', p. 175.   **117** *Grace*, pp 82–3.   **118** *The Book of Howth*, p. 141; *Caithreim Thoirdhealbhaigh*, ed & trans. S.H. O'Grady, Irish Texts Society, xxvii (Dublin, 1929), p. 118. There are also references to O'Brien activities in Ely, Ormond and Owney dating from about 1304, see pp 27, 36 (hereafter *CT*); AClon, AConn, 1318. The O'Carrolls were already restless in 1313. Then the sons of Philip O'Carroll attacked the Tobins of Cumsy who were well to the south of Ely.

resurgence of the O'Carrolls of Ely and the emergence of Brian Bán as a major
regional force in the midlands were reflective of what was happening among
neighbouring Irish dynasties. In Laois, this fact was finally recognized by Roger
Mortimer in 1318, when he appointed Laoiseach as custodian of the Mortimer
lands there, basing him at Dunamase, the headquarters of the Mortimer estates.
Despite his oath to uphold Mortimer interest in Laois, Laoiseach consolidated his
position and raided the Carlow liberty. Predictably, when the first opportunity arose,
Laoiseach turned on the Mortimers and the English, wiping out their interests in
Laois and carving out a greatly enlarged O'More lordship.[119] Inevitably, the
emergence of this large Irish-ruled territorial bloc in West Leinster and the
midlands, linking the Irish kings of East Leinster to the rest of Gaelic Ireland,
marked the beginning of the strangulation of Plantagenet Ireland.

---

119 Ó Cléirigh, 'The impact of the Anglo-Normans in Laois', pp 177–8; Smyth, *Celtic Leinster*,
p. 112.

CHAPTER 5

The Leinster wars, 1320–70

By 1320 Irish co-operation and collusion between both parts of Leinster in the Barrow basin was an established fact. The growth of Irish power here was greatly facilitated by Edward Bruce's expeditions, as we have seen. The weakness of the English position in the midlands was further confirmed by the victory of Donnchadh Fionn O'Carroll of Ely and Brian Bán O'Brien over the Burkes and the Butlers in winter 1318. Moreover, the MacGillapatricks of North Ossory exploited the division of the lordship of Kilkenny caused by the death of its lord, Earl Gilbert de Clare of Gloucester, at Bannockburn on 24 June 1314. These Irish reconquests were yet to peak. Indeed, all the major Irish dynasties of Leinster stood on the threshold of a dramatic advance in 1320.

It was the re-emergence of O'Brien interests in the midlands after 1320 that caused major problems for the Butlers and the Burkes. The leader of the O'Brien resurgence was not King Muircheartach of Thomond, but a rebel cousin, Brian Bán, the survivor of Muircheartach's rout of Richard de Clare on 10 May 1318, after which Brian Bán had crossed the Shannon and established himself within the Arra mountains in north Tipperary. Allying himself with the neighbouring O'Carrolls of Ely, he began to conquer territory from the Burkes and the Butlers and, in the early 1320s, he forged an alliance with Maurice fitzThomas Fitzgerald of Desmond – a union that spelt ill for the English of north Tipperary and Ormond. A great blow to the English was the death of Lord Edmund Butler in September 1321, which left his young son – a minor – as heir. The minority of James Butler (later 1st earl of Ormond) lasted from 1321 to 1326. Thomas Butler, 1st baron of Dunboyne, was given custody of the boy's lands until his coming of age, but he was confronted with a sustained Irish offensive designed to exploit the minority. By 1323 the Butlers were fighting to hold onto territory in northern Tipperary and Kilkenny; and they lost the territories of Owney, Arra and other large parts of Ormond to the Irish during the course of the fourteenth century.

Brian Bán was not the only Irish warlord on the make in the region. In nearby Ely and Ossory a simultaneous and co-ordinated offensive by the O'Carrolls and the MacGillapatricks was under way. This focused on the manor of Aghaboe on the borders of Laois and Ossory. Because of the contraction of the land of peace, Aghaboe now lay in increasingly vulnerable marchland close

87

to the MacGillapatrick heartland of Slieve Bloom.[1] The contemporary chronicle kept by the Kilkenny-based Friar John Clyn graphically illustrates the growing English consciousness of the threat of these synchronized Irish raids to the northern Kilkenny marches. Clyn tells of the Irish devastation of Ely of 1325, leaving no illusions as to the thoroughness of O'Carroll's ethnic cleansing; he says that 'in this year (O'Carroll) scarcely left a house, castle, or town in Ely O'Carroll among the English and the lovers of peace which he did not destroy by fire'. Worse followed: Brian Bán with a retinue of mixed race, some even drawn from the English families of Ely, burnt the settlements of Ossory in the same year. Action was needed, and Justiciar John Bermingham, earl of Louth, and Thomas Butler led an army against O'Carroll before the end of the year. (The death of Domhnall Dubh MacGillapatrick was probably related to this counter-offensive.)[2]

To the north of Ely and Ossory, the Irish polities of Offaly and Laois remained fractious. After the defeat of the O'Connor Falys by Andrew Bermingham on 9 May 1321 and the dynastic feuding that followed, the O'Dempseys steadily rebuilt their power.[3] In Laois, despite his reverses during the Bruce wars, Laoiseach O'More had emerged as the most powerful Irish king within the region, defeating his dynastic rivals and their settler patrons. In 1323 an inquisition as to the extent of Roger Mortimer's lands in Laois confirmed this state of affairs, revealing that Dunamase had been sacked and the remaining settlers had fled to the Newtown of Leys. After the consolidation of Laois, Laoiseach returned to his old policy of southward expansion, killing 80 men of Carlow in 1326. His activities also reveal a concerted drive into the MacGillapatrick ambit, leading to a struggle with them for regional dominance.[4] Laoiseach's advance into North Ossory may in turn have pushed the MacGillapatricks to increase their attacks upon the settlers.

Everywhere in the southern midlands, the English were in retreat; and the decline of English government was to be noticed in the growing complexity of the political relationships between individual Irish kings and English magnates. The most notorious and best example of this fraternization is that of Brian Bán and Maurice fitzThomas Fitzgerald of Desmond. In return for fitzThomas' considerable protection, Brian Bán loyally supported his endless ambition. Even more shocking was his attendance at a meeting in Kilkenny in July 1326, where it was alleged that he with the earls of Kildare and Louth as well as the future earl of Ormond and the bishop of Ossory agreed to rebel against the king, assume control of the land and elect and crown Maurice king of Ireland.

---

1 Empey, 'The Butler Lordship in Ireland 1185–1515', PhD thesis (University of Dublin, 1970), pp 160–87, 200, 207 (hereafter Empey).   **2** Clyn, *Annals*, p. 17; Curtis, *Med. Ire.*, pp 204–5. Empey dates the O'Carroll offensive and Bermingham's campaign to autumn 1323. **3** AFM, AConn, AClon, AU, 1321; *Grace*, p. 99; Clyn, *Annals*, p. 14. This Andrew Bermingham and Nicholas de la Launde were later killed by O'Nolan (Henry?) on 22 September 1322. **4** Clyn, *Annals*, p. 18, p. 27; Ó Cléirigh, 'The impact of the Anglo-Normans in Laois', p. 177.

Nothing came of this, but the pair continued their extensive extortion racket throughout much of Munster. Even more worrying for the English of Ossory was the outbreak of endemic violence among themselves in 1327, which undoubtedly facilitated the Irish advance from the north.[5]

Life was equally rough for the English of East Leinster. The gradual emergence of an Irish portal to the Shannon had increased the pressure building on the Barrow frontier. To combat this mounting pressure, Thomas of Brotherton, earl of Norfolk, in 1320 appointed the capable Henry Traherne as seneschal of his Carlow liberty. Traherne pursued a active policy against the MacMurroughs, who were keen to reconquer the arable farmland of the liberty. It is not clear who exactly was the MacMurrough king of Leinster at this point (after the death of Domhnall Riabhach in 1317, the annals do not identify his successor), but he was clearly intent on the forcible annexation of the Barrow region to his growing kingdom. Evidently, he kept Traherne busy. In 1321 Traherne delivered a Domhnall MacMurrough to imprisonment, and he enjoyed a greater success two years later, when he, with the de Valles, killed Henry O'Nolan and killed or captured the un-named MacMurrough overlord between 15 August and 8 September 1323.[6]

The new MacMurrough leader was Domhnall mac Airt, the son of the Art murdered at Arklow in July 1282. While his exact relationship with the two previous MacMurrough incumbents of the Leinster kingship is undetermined, he was a first cousin of Muiris MacMurrough (king of Leinster, *c.*1293–1314). The earliest surviving references show him in 1302 crossing the Barrow frontier to raid the liberty of Kilkenny. From the outset of his reign, he was determined to abandon the isolationist policy of his recent predecessors. One of his first actions was to repair his dynasty's damaged relationship with Murchadh O'Byrne; by 1325 he had succeeded in doing so, and both dynasties began fresh attacks on the Barrow settlers, resulting in two English expeditions into Uí Cheinnselaig that year. Nonetheless, the situation in the region remained volatile, as evidenced by government maintenance of wards at Dunlavin and Baltinglass in 1325.[7] There were times when relations between Traherne and the MacMurroughs could be cordial,[8] but these occasions were rare. Broadly speaking, it seems that the campaigns of 1324 and 1325 may have been decisive in forcing Domhnall mac Airt to shake off his isolation from the rest of the Leinster Irish. Insofar as was possible, Domhnall mac Airt continued to mend relations with Murchadh O'Byrne and David O'Toole between 1324 and 1327. Yet the exact nature of MacMurrough relations with the Irish dynasties of West Leinster remains unclear – but contact was plainly increasing.

Indeed, the election of Domhnall mac Airt MacMurrough by the Leinster Irish may represent the culmination of this rapprochement. Their election of

5 Ibid., p. 19.   **6** Ibid., pp 15–16.   **7** *Rot. pat. Hib*, no. 80, pp 31 and no. 103, 32; Otway-Ruthven, *Medieval Ireland*, p. 242; Price, *Placenames*, p. lxii; Frame, 'The Dublin government', pp 248–9.   **8** Dowling, *Annals*, p. 22. For instance, Traherne and an Art MacMurrough were captured by the Butlers in 1326.

him as king of Leinster at an assembly in early 1328 is not recorded in any Irish annal, and the absence of a set of Leinster annals forever limits our perception of what was exactly happening.[9] The contemporary relationship between the O'Brien kings of Thomond and their (MacNamara) vassals reveals a rise of vassal power. The assumption of control by a vassal at an inauguration ceremony, the development of the vassal's independent power-base and the nurturing of a network of alliances by a leading vassal allowed him to place his appointee in the kingship, and that seems to have occurred in Thomond and Connacht.[10] What happened in Leinster may actually represent the renegotiation of terms between Domhnall mac Airt and his vassals, and also the acceptance by the Leinster Irish of the redefinition of the old MacMurrough provincial kingdom. From Gerald O'Byrne's later behaviour at his and Art MacMurrough's joint submission to Richard II in January 1395, we can see that he was MacMurrough's leading vassal. This interpretation of the relationship between the O'Byrnes and the MacMurroughs is borne out by Fiach O'Byrne's much later role as kingmaker to the MacMurroughs in the last quarter of the sixteenth century.[11]

The election of Domhnall mac Airt appears to have had an enormous impact on the polity of Leinster. The fact that he embarked upon a circuit through O'Byrne and O'Toole lands before planting his banner less than two leagues from Dublin adds weight to the view that Murchadh O'Byrne's influence led to the redefinition of the MacMurrough kingship of Leinster. Traherne and Walter de Valle, realizing the danger posed by Domhnall mac Airt MacMurrough, had quickly apprehended him (David O'Toole was also captured, and ultimately executed in Dublin during 1328),[12] but they refused to release him into government custody until the reward of £100 was paid. Domhnall was then conveyed to Dublin Castle, where he remained until his escape in January 1331.[13] His long confinement cost him part of his dynastic supremacy and allowed divisions to emerge within the ruling MacMurrough family. In the meantime it left Murchadh O'Byrne as the most powerful individual Irish king in East Leinster, if not in Leinster.

If the Leinster Irish in fact did redefine the old provincial kingdom with Domhnall mac Airt MacMurrough as its titular head, it can be suggested that the government's actions against Domhnall mac Airt and David O'Toole sparked strife throughout the province during 1329. While the role of the Irish of West Leinster in the new Leinster kingdom remains not fully clear, they seem to have exploited the situation to harass the Butlers, the Mortimers and Kildare; and they may have been encouraged by events in Ormond and Ossory: from North Ossory, Brian Bán's ally, Donnchadh MacGillapatrick, burnt the Butler cantred of Odogh as far south as Moyarfe in April 1329. By early 1329, William Burke,

9 *Chartul. St Mary's*, ii, pp 365–6; *Grace*, p. 107.   10 Nic Ghiollamhaith, 'Kings and vassals in later medieval Ireland', p. 210; Lydon, *Lordship*, pp 177–8; Simms, *From kings to warlords*, p. 16; AConn, 1310.   11 Curtis, *Rich. II in Ire*, pp 167, 172; Donovan, 'Tudor rule in Gaelic Leinster', pp 138–140.   12 *Grace*, pp 106–9; Otway-Ruthven, *Medieval Ireland*, p. 246; *The Book of Howth*, pp 149–50.   13 *Chartul. St Mary's*, ii, pp 365–6, and 372.

the Brown earl of Ulster, and Muircheartach O'Brien of Thomond decided to rid themselves of Brian Bán, but, at the beginning of August 1329 Brian Bán, with Maurice fitzThomas' encouragement, hit first, burning Athassel and Tipperary before destroying his enemies at Thurles on 14 August 1329.[14]

Even without Brian Bán's activities, West Leinster was already politically unstable. In early 1329, Máelsechlainn O'Connor Faly, king of Offaly, was murdered by his nephew, Máelmorda O'Connor Faly. The O'Dempseys proceeded to exploit the internal strife among the O'Connors Falys, but their efforts in Offaly ended in a heavy defeat for them and their O'Dunne allies.[15] Even so, the O'Dempseys now emerged as the principal threat to the Fitzgeralds of Kildare, their pressure being concentrated upon Lea castle beside the Barrow, which they along with the O'Dunnes briefly captured in February 1330.[16]

There is more to this than meets the eye as the O'Dempsey action was probably linked to the outbreak of war in East Leinster in 1329. Throughout 1329, the O'Nolans stalked the Butler lands in Carlow; they captured Laurence Butler and Henry Traherne on 21 November and killed David Butler later that month. In retaliation, James Butler, 1st earl of Ormond, pillaged Richard mac Philip O'Nolan's lordship of Forth on 14 December.[17] This O'Nolan trouble was only the tip of the iceberg. Justiciar John Darcy decided to move directly against Murchadh O'Byrne. The sudden re-emergence of Murchadh's power in Leinster may have frightened many of his enemies, who included Murghut mac Nicholas O'Toole, whose family had always opposed Murchadh.[18] O'Toole and the justiciar brought O'Byrne to heel after a violent confrontation on 15 August 1329. (The fact that the justiciar was supplied by sea indicates that Murchadh had cut the overland route.) To prevent his defeated forces being hunted down, Murchadh surrendered himself and was imprisoned in Dublin Castle, but he was soon released in return for other hostages and in four months he was back terrorizing the settlers.[19] In the absence of Domhnall mac Airt MacMurrough during his own imprisonment, Murchadh rebuilt his position in Leinster, pushing the English out of east Wicklow. And instead of attacking the MacMurroughs, he opted for the subtler option of a marriage alliance. It is at this point that he

14 Clyn, *Annals*, p. 21; Otway-Ruthven, *Medieval Ireland*, pp 246–7; *Annals of Ross*, p. 44. **15** Ibid., pp 20–1. The most recent O'Dempsey leader of note was Cúilen O'Dempsey who died in 1327. See AFM, 1327. **16** Otway-Ruthven, *Medieval Ireland*, p. 247 see also p. 252 On the death of Thomas Fitzgerald, earl of Kildare, in 1328, an inquisition said that Geashill was beyond the land of peace and no rents were accruing from its lands. **17** Clyn, *Annals*, pp 20–1; *Grace*, p. 115. Henry Traherne was taken through a trick at his house of Kilbeg by Richard mac Philip O'Nolan in 1329; Otway-Ruthven, *Medieval Ireland*, p. 247. **18** Price, *Placenames*, p. lxiii; Clyn, *Annals*, p. 25; see also Frame, 'The Dublin government', p. 251; Grace, p. 129; *The Book of Howth*, p. 160. **19** Otway-Ruthven, *Medieval Ireland*, p. 247; *The Book of Howth*, p. 155; the Lawlesses were suffering the heaviest from Murchadh's aggression in east Wicklow. In 1329 John Lawless held the cantred from the earl of Kildare, see *The Red Bk Kildare*, p. 107. This John seems to have served in Darcy's armies in the campaigns against Murchadh of 1329–30. See Frame, 'The Dublin government', pp 255–7; *Grace*, p. 115; Price, *Placenames*, p. lxiii.

arranged the marriage of a daughter of his eldest son, Philip, to Art the son of Domhnall mac Airt's cousinly rival for the Leinster kingship, Muircheartach mac Muiris MacMurrough – something that represents a considerable change of policy by Murchadh. In effect, he was realigning his dynasty with the family of his bitter rival, Muiris MacMurrough (king of Leinster, *c*.1293–1314).

In West Leinster, the situation was equally turbulent. The seriousness of the warfare there in 1329–30 led to unusual roles for both Maurice fitzThomas (now 1st earl of Desmond), and Brian Bán O'Brien. In January 1330, Justiciar John Darcy asked them to restore the king's peace in the Leinster marches.[20] It was a surprising commission, but they did not disappoint. With an army said to number 1,000, they brought the war to a close, retaking Lea and forcing O'Nolan, Laoiseach O'More and O'Dempsey to submit.[21] But by May 1330 Brian Bán returned to more typical behaviour, when he killed James de Beaufo, sheriff of Limerick; and in July he fought the army of Prior Roger Outlaw of Kilmainham, deputy of Justiciar John Darcy, to a standstill. These O'Brien victories convinced the Brown earl of Ulster to raise another army against them. Others such as Ormond, equally convinced of the need for a campaign against Brian Bán, adopted a two-pronged approach. First, Brian Bán's ally, Donnchadh MacGillapatrick, was seemingly invited to come to Kilkenny, where he was murdered by the Brown earl.[22] And after a parliament held at Kilkenny in 1330, Justiciar Darcy, the Brown earl and Ormond attacked Brian Bán at Cashel; this resulted in the widespread devastation of the region. (Maurice fitzThomas lent considerable aid to Brian Bán – for which he earned attacks upon his earldom of Desmond from the Burkes.)[23]

Between 1330 and 1350, East Leinster was a sea of ever-changing alliances among the Irish, interspersed with wars against the government. Domhnall mac Airt MacMurrough's escape from Dublin Castle in January 1331 frustrated Murchadh O'Byrne's plans, but he recognized Domhnall mac Airt and helped to unleash the Leinster war of 1331–2, which began on 9 April 1331 with the English defeat of the Irish of Uí Cheinnselaig. In an co-ordinated attack, the MacMurroughs and the O'Byrnes seized Arklow on 21 April, while the O'Tooles ravaged Tallaght on the same day. The Irish, maintaining their momentum, took the castles of Newcastle Lyons, Ferns and Cowlaugh (Coillache, west Wicklow) that summer before ravaging the Wexford liberty, but, on the banks of the Slaney, English of Wexford turned them back, forcing the defeated Irish to swim for their lives.[24] This victory and the death of Richard mac Philip O'Nolan forced

---

20 For Darcy's campaigns of 1329 against the O'Connors Falys, O'Dempsey, the O'Tooles and the O'Byrnes, see *Rot. pat. Hib.*, no.17, p. 20. For Earl James of Ormond's campaigns into the lordships of the O'Mores, O'Nolans, O'Byrnes and the MacMurroughs during 1329, see ibid., no. 22, p. 20. Again for Darcy's expeditions in 1329, see the account of John de Fynchedene preserved in *DKR*, xxxxiii, pp 28–9. 21 Otway-Ruthven, *Medieval Ireland*, p. 247. *Grace*, p. 117; Orpen, *Normans*, iv, p. 231. 22 Clyn, *Annals*, p. 22; *The Annals of Ross*, p. 44; AFM, 1329; This Donnchadh mac Giollapádraig MacGillapatrick seems to have succeeded the Donnchadh MacGillapatrick, who died in 1324. See AFM, 1324. 23 *Grace*, p. 119. 24 Clyn, *Annals*,

Domhnall mac Airt to consider his options. By winter 1331, Murchadh O'Byrne and his new MacMurrough-in-laws had tired of Domhnall mac Airt. Realizing that his long confinement had reduced his influence, Domhnall mac Airt now entered English service in return for an annual exchequer fee of 40 marks. By 3 May 1332 Justiciar Anthony Lucy (appointed 27 February 1331) was ready to take the field against the O'Byrnes. On 15 June he seized Clonmore castle back from the Irish (it was located at a point where the O'Byrne and MacMurrough spheres met).[25] Between 5 and 24 August 1332, with Domhnall mac Airt's assent, he retook Arklow and proceeded to repair its damaged walls. The justiciar's activities also served as checks upon Domhnall mac Airt's rivals among the O'Byrnes, O'Tooles and those of his own dynasty. To bring Murchadh and his MacMurrough allies under control, the government acknowledged reality by recruiting Laoiseach O'More in summer 1332 to fight his old O'Byrne ally. The financial records of this campaign reveal that Laoiseach was able to put an impressive contingent into the field, including 4 men at arms, 217 light horsemen and 284 footmen between June and August, for which he gained a reward of £91. 11s. and the price of half a roll of cloth.[26] By enrolling Laoiseach against O'Byrne, the justiciar was in fact acknowledging the existence of an independent O'More territory along the western flanks of the Barrow conduit. The encircling pressure on Murchadh O'Byrne proved too much, and he was captured by his nephew, Gerald mac Dúnlaing O'Byrne, and the Lawlesses before the end of the year.[27]

Throughout the 1330s, Domhnall mac Airt tacked before ever-changing political winds. In 1334 he campaigned against the O'Byrnes and O'Tooles, receiving a reward of £40 for his capture of Murchadh O'Byrne's son Philip.[28] On 1 March 1335 Murchadh O'Byrne sent a delegation led by Robert Lawless and Gerald mac Dúnlaing O'Byrne to Justiciar John Darcy at Newcastle McKynegan. There they informed the justiciar that the now aged Murchadh had agreed to a negotiated peace whereby he and his wife would live under English protection at Wicklow or Kilmartin.[29] The apparent retirement of Murchadh and the slow emergence of his son Tadhg allowed Domhnall mac Airt MacMurrough some breathing space. That year he earned the title of 'banneret' for service in Scotland and was in receipt of a fee of 80 marks.[30] However, deep cracks opened in the alliance between Domhnall mac Airt and his cousin Muircheartach mac Muiris MacMurrough. It appears Muircheartach invited the Gabhal Siomóin sept of the O'Byrne dynasty to settle in north Carlow after a defeat by his rival kinsmen. This infusion of strength allowed Muircheartach to force a more favourable territorial division of Uí Cheinnselaig between 1335 and

pp 22–4; *Grace*, pp 121–5; *Chartul. St Mary's*, ii, pp 372, 376; *The Book of Howth*, pp 157. **25** Frame, 'Two kings', p. 163; *The Book of Howth*, p. 159; *Rot. pat. Hib*, no. 45, p. 41. **26** *DKR*, xxxxiii, pp 54–5; Ó Cléirigh, 'The impact of the Anglo-Normans in Laois', p. 177. **27** PRO E 101/239/24. Murchadh's capture is dated to 1332. **28** Philip was captured for his probable part in the burning of 80 colonists in the church of Freynestown in west Wicklow during 1332, see Lydon, 'Medieval Wicklow', p. 175; *Grace*, p. 123. **29** NLI, GO MS 191, pp 57–8. **30** Nicholson, 'An Irish expedition to Scotland in 1335', pp 197–211; Frame, 'Two kings', p. 164.

1347. In 1336 the O'Byrnes were back at war, enjoying a victory with Domhnall mac Airt over the English of Wexford.[31] (This latest outbreak of war in East Leinster was directly linked to Laoiseach O'More's conspiring with the Irish of Leinster and Munster for a war upon the English.[32] Laoiseach's rapprochement of 1332 with the Dublin government had been brief: according to Friar Clyn, he organized the treacherous killing of Sir Raymond le Ercedekne and thirteen kinsmen at a parley on 4 May 1335; by the following year, he was preaching to the Irish of Leinster and Munster about the need for a general war against the English of Ossory.) This latest O'Byrne/MacMurrough alliance continued, forcing Ormond to concentrate his forces against them in an indecisive campaign near Arklow in 1337, but it was not to last, for Murchadh O'Byrne's son, Tadhg, entered government service, and fought Domhnall mac Airt throughout 1338 and 1339.[33]

The renewal of hostility between the O'Byrnes and MacMurroughs coincides with the reactivating of O'Byrne plans to supersede the MacMurroughs as the principal Irish kings in Leinster. At some point between June 1335 and October 1337, Prior Roger Outlaw of Kilmainham, deputy to Justiciar Darcy, personally treated for the restoration of peace with the indefatigable Murchadh O'Byrne, who was acting on behalf of many of the Leinster Irish in the O'Nolan heartland of Forth.[34] By this stage, Domhnall mac Airt MacMurrough may have been dead. His son, Domhnall Óg, resumed his aggression against the English of the Barrow to rebuild his dynasty's position among the Leinstermen. The MacMurrough return to war also coincides with renewed O'Dempsey pressure along the western Barrow. There, in 1339, the O'Dempseys and seemingly some of Domhnall Óg's followers were routed by settlers after trying to force their way into Kildare.[35] Justiciar Bishop Thomas Charlton of Hereford with the local levies of the English of Kildare then added insult to injury by plundering MacMurrough Idrone in February. Another campaign was led against the MacMurroughs and the O'Nolans in Forth in April 1340, but Domhnall Óg MacMurrough in August attacked Gowran located in the strategic pass of the same name that accessed Ossory and north Tipperary.[36] Mindful of growing O'Byrne power, Domhnall Óg adopted his father's shifting policy of war and reconciliation towards the government. Between August and October 1341 he engaged the expedition of Justiciar John Morice before being rewarded with O'Tooles for service against the O'Byrnes in July 1342.[37]

31 Clyn, *Annals*, p. 27.   **32** Frame, 'The Dublin government', p. 293.   **33** *The Annals of Ross*, p. 45; Clyn, *Annals*, pp 26–8; Frame, 'The Dublin government', p. 301. Tadhg was in service with the justiciar and Bishop Thomas of Hereford against Domhnall mac Airt between 1338 and 1339. Interestingly Fynok O'Toole was also in government service against the O'Byrnes. He was part of a small expedition against the O'Byrnes in 1338, and was stationed at Newcastle MacKynegan. **34** *DKR*, xxxxv, p. 32. For Outlaw's numerous justiciarships see *NHI*, ix, p. 473.   **35** Pointedly the MacMurrough allies, the O'Nolans, killed Ormond's brother – Laurence Butler – in 1338, see Clyn, *Annals*, p. 29. For the defeat of the O'Dempseys see *Grace*, p. 133; *The Book of Howth*, p. 161.   **36** Clyn, *Annals*, p. 29; *DKR*, xxxxvii, p. 68.   **37** Frame, 'The Dublin government',

2 Another detail (see p. 79) from the Derricke woodcut (1581) showing a party of Irish
kern in an attack on an English settlement

In autumn 1342 Domhnall Óg returned to the more profitable enterprise of raiding English settlements dotted along the Barrow corridor. By autumn of 1344 the MacMurroughs, O'Nolans, O'Byrnes and the O'Tooles had mended their fences to hatch another war in Leinster.[38] Their plans ended in disaster, as Justiciar Ralph de Ufford and the royal army wreaked devastation throughout Uí Cheinnselaig and East Leinster. Typically, Domhnall Óg embarked upon repentance through service against Desmond in Munster during 1345.[39] But Domhnall Óg's defeat by de Ufford in 1344 had fatally weakened his kingship, fanning the ambitions of Muircheartach mac Muiris MacMurrough, the O'Byrne ally. Although Muircheartach and his wife were captured by the men of New Ross in 1345, he was quickly freed and probably engineered the assassination on 5 July 1347 of Domhnall Óg and his possible tanaiste, Murchadh MacMurrough.[40]

In the same period (1330–50), the Irish kingdoms of West Leinster gradually evolved into a borderland between the Irish of East Leinster and those of north Munster. As ever, Laoiseach O'More and Brian Bán fanned the flames of war. After his brief sojourn in government service in summer 1332 against the O'Byrnes, Laoiseach, as we saw, returned to his usual preoccupation of expanding O'More power. From Laois and Slemargy he orchestrated a series of anti-settler wars. He was helped in these by the collapse of Brian Bán's alliance with Earl Maurice fitzThomas Fitzgerald of Desmond in 1333. Despite his involvement in 1332 in yet another conspiracy to claim the Irish crown, Desmond had tired of his royal ambitions and now sought to become respectable; this led to a rift with Brian Bán. Such was the bitterness that Desmond led expeditions against his old friend late in 1333 and in 1335. Brian Bán, in no mood to temporize, burned Tipperary in June 1336, an attack that seems to have been directly linked to Laoiseach's contemporary war against Fulk de la Freyne, lord of Listerling and seneschal of Kilkenny, and to the attacks of Domhnall mac Airt and the O'Byrnes upon the Wexford liberty that year.[41] Laoiseach's hiring of Irish mercenaries from both Leinster and Munster to fight de la Freyne and the English of Ossory succinctly demonstrate the Irish advances. Only Henry O'Ryan and Scanlán MacGillapatrick stood with de la Freyne's forces against Laoiseach O'More and his allies;[42] still, the settlers were able to hold their own.

p. 306. Cathal O'Toole brought 7 light horsemen to this campaign, while Muircheartach MacMurrough contributed 23 light horse and 33 foot. Earlier in 1340 Fynok O'Toole received 66s. 8d. for 10 horsemen and 12 kerne for campaign against the O'Byrnes. See *Account roll of the Holy Trinity, Dublin, 1337–1346*, p. 157. **38** *Stat. Ire., John–Henry V*, p. 365; Clyn also mentions the fall of Castlekevin to the Irish in 1343, see Clyn, *Annals*, p. 30. There was fighting against the O'Byrnes, MacMurroughs, O'Nolans and the O'Tooles in 1344–5, see *The Annals of Ross*, p. 45. *Rot. pat. Hib*, no. 136, p. 47. **39** Frame, 'Two kings', p. 164. **40** Clyn, *Annals*, p. 35; *Grace*, p. 143; *The Book of Howth*, p. 165. This dates his killing to 5 June 1347. **41** Clyn, *Annals*, pp 27; *The Annals of Ross*, p. 45. **42** Ibid., p. 27. This Scanlán may have already been on thin ice with his own dynasty by 1336. In June 1333 he killed two of his first cousins and blinded and castrated a third. These were the sons of his uncle, Fionnán MacGillapatrick, see

Increasingly, English magnates were edging towards a policy whereby, in return a magnate's recognition of the territorial gains of an Irish leader, the latter would acknowledge on behalf of his dynasty the magnate's nominal overlordship. These arrangements increased after the Bruce wars of 1315–18. Roger Mortimer, lord of Laois, and Thomas Fitzgerald, 2nd earl of Kildare, respectively, acknowledged the gains made by Laoiseach O'More and Aodh Óg O'Toole as the price of their vassalage.[43] In the 1330s it was the Butlers who embraced this policy, to relieve the incessant pressure on their lands. Geographically and politically, the Butlers were fighting a two-front war against the O'Mores, Brian Bán, the MacGillapatricks, the O'Carrolls and the O'Kennedys from the north and the MacMurroughs, O'Byrnes and the O'Nolans from the east. Clearly, Ormond decided to come to terms with some of the midland Irish and with those of north Munster, so that he could concentrate against Irish pressure building along the eastern banks of the Barrow.[44] Thus, in 1336 Ormond came to terms with Ruaidhrí O'Kennedy, recognizing his gains in return for vassalage. An inquisition on the death of the Ormond in 1337 reveals dramatic losses of territory in north Tipperary to the O'Kennedys and the O'Meaghers.[45] In Ossory the situation was worse, for the Butlers had lost the western Aghadoe manors of Skirk and Rathdowney to MacGillapatrick by 1338.[46] The shift in the political landscape also forced Brian Bán to review his position. Since his break-up with Desmond he had become increasingly isolated, so he decided to bury his feud with his old rival Muircheartach O'Brien in late 1336. This proved a more wise move, for Muircheartach seemingly recognized him as his designated successor. Brian Bán's new found diplomacy did not end there. In 1337 he finally acknowledged nominal Burke overlordship in return for their recognition of his conquests, marrying a daughter of Henry Burke about this time.[47]

It must be noted that Irish expansion in Tipperary and the midlands was not uniformly successful. It made little headway within the more heavily settled central and southern Butler lands in Tipperary. Despite a major rupture with the Butlers in 1347, the O'Kennedys gained some ground at their expense, and in 1356 they made a fresh concord with the 2nd earl of Ormond, establishing a durable alliance.[48] While the earl was in England that year, Edmund O'Kennedy undertook to keep the peace and served with the earl against Art MacMurrough and the O'Mores in Laois during 1357. For his loyalty, Bernard O'Kennedy was granted two carucates of land near Nenagh in December 1358. Similarly the O'Brennans of eastern Odogh remained under the Butler thumb, binding

---

ibid., p. 24. **43** Ó Cléirigh, 'The impact of the Anglo-Normans in Laois', pp 177–8; Clyn, *Annals*, pp 29–30; *Red Bk Kildare*, no.139. **44** For the Butler lands in Tipperary and Ossory, see Beresford, 'The Butlers in England and Ireland, 1405–1515', pp 25–31. **45** Curtis, *Med. Ire.*, pp 213–4. According to Curtis, Longford, most of Westmeath, all Laois and Offaly and the northern parts of Tipperary and Kilkenny were all lost. **46** Empey, pp 208–9. **47** Nic Giollamhaith, 'Kings and vassals in later medieval Ireland', pp 201–16; AConn, 1337; *CT*, p. 171. **48** Empey, p. 200; *COD*, ii, nos. 46, 48 pp 28–30; E. Curtis, 'Some medieval seals out of the Ormond archives', pp 6–7.

themselves to the Butlers in 1359 and 1400. A similar trend reflects in the initial
O'Carroll successes and their later deals with the Butlers. In 1383, their relationship
is displayed by the marriage between Tadhg O'Carroll and Johanna, daughter of
James, 2nd earl of Ormond.[49] Other leaders such as Laoiseach O'More successfully
removed most traces of the settlers from Laois. However, Laoiseach's illustrious
career came to an ignominious end just before Christmas 1342. While intoxi-
cated, he was killed by his own servant – leaving a problematic succession.[50] The
kingship of Laois seems to have passed to Laoiseach's son, Conall O'More. But
Conall's succession was bitterly resented by his brother David (though it took
some years for this to cause problems).

Friar Clyn's commentary reveals growing co-ordination among the Leinstermen
and the Irish of north Munster in the mid-1340s.[51] In February 1345 Maurice
fitzThomas Fitzgerald, 1st earl of Desmond, summoned an assembly of magnates
to discuss his intention to take the Irish crown. Much of his anger sprang from
a serious rupture with the Butlers during 1344. After the death in 1337 of James
Butler, 1st earl of Ormond, that earldom had passed into the king's hand; on 4
February 1338 the crown delivered it into Desmond's custody for the duration
of the minority of James Butler, 2nd earl of Ormond; but in 1344, Desmond was
removed from his custodianship of the Ormond lands, and, on foot of this,
Thomas Butler in November expelled Desmond's constable from Nenagh castle.
In June 1345 Desmond attacked Edward III's supporters and the Butler lands in
Ely and Ormond, with support from Tadhg mac Ruaidhrí O'Carroll, O'Kennedy
and Diarmait MacGillapatrick,[52] but they failed to take Nenagh, and were put back
on the defensive by Justiciar Ralph de Ufford's offensive between September and
October 1345. Again the fragility of the English position was laid bare, and
matters worsened when Diarmait MacGillapatrick torched Bordwell in the
cantred of Aghaboe on 28 December 1345. (De Ufford took drastic action to
curtail the disturbances by briefly taking the liberty of Kildare into the king's
hands in December at Naas.)[53] This state of continuous war continued into
1346. Worse still for the English, Conall O'More turned his attention north-east,
focusing on the possessions of the earl of Kildare and appealing to the rest of the
Leinster Irish to aid him. By forging an alliance with O'Connor Falys and
O'Dempsey, he captured Lea and destroyed several other castles in Easter 1346.
Their actions were also linked to the burning of the manor of Aghaboe by
Diarmait MacGillapatrick and O'Carroll in summer 1346.[54] In response, the sheriff
of Kilkenny took a great prey of livestock from Cearbhall MacGillapatrick in July
1346. In Ely, the O'Carrolls under Tadhg mac Ruaidhrí exploded on the settlers.
Even though Tadhg was killed in battle against the English of Ossory, he
succeeded in expelling the Brets, Milbournes, and other English from Ely and

49 Ibid., p. 211; AClon, AFM, 1383. 50 Clyn, *Annals*, pp 29–30. 51 Ibid., pp 32, 34.
52 Otway-Ruthven, *Medieval Ireland*, p. 262. 53 Clyn, *Annals*, p. 32; Otway-Ruthven,
Medieval Ireland, pp 262–3. 54 Clyn, *Annals*, pp 32–3; *Grace*, p.141; Curtis, *Med. Ire.*,
pp 218–19; Otway-Ruthven, *Medieval Ireland*, p. 264.

occupying their lands. Fulk de la Freyne captured Ruaidhrí son of Conall O'More in battle during September 1346, but the relief was temporary.[55]

Such was the Irish power in the region at this point that Conall O'More occupied Lea castle for six months after its fall in Easter. Consequently, the Fitzgeralds of Kildare and Justiciar Walter Bermingham waged a winter war against Conall and O'Dempsey, forcing the former to submit at Athy in early 1347. The scale of his submission shows how important Conall was: he agreed to surrender 1000 cattle and to attend upon the justiciar's expeditions;[56] indeed, his submission undermined his position; he was killed by his brothers in 1348, an event that led to a struggle between his son Ruaidhrí and the killers, and which resulted in a pitched battle between Ruaidhrí (and allies drawn from the English of Ossory) with his uncle David and the English of Kildare and Carlow. Although Ruaidhrí was victorious and his rivals were either exiled or killed, his victory does not seem to have got him very far: he continued to do service with the English (which may mean that he was reliant upon their support): between 1353 and 1354 he with 68 light horsemen and 108 footmen served on government campaigns against John O'Byrne in Wicklow.[57] This weakness was the root cause of Ruaidhrí's own assassination by his brother in 1354–5. This political turmoil among the O'Mores may have led to the gradual division of their patrimony into the lordships of Laois and Slemargy.

To the south of Laois, the Butler lands in Ormond in 1347 became a palatine liberty for the 2nd earl of Ormond, with Nenagh as its capital. This seems to have prompted a massive outburst of violence from the Irish of north Tipperary led by Brian Bán and Domhnall O'Kennedy. O'Kennedy expelled the Berminghams, Cantwells and Cogans and burned Nenagh, but he failed to take its castle that December.[58] Ruaidhrí O'Carroll, Tadhg mac Ruaidhrí's probable successor, took part in these forays; according to Clyn, O'Kennedy had made pacts with Irish leaders throughout the country.[59] The English moved fast: in spring 1348 O'Kennedy was captured by the Purcells, who hanged him at Thurles. Both the O'Carrolls and Brian Bán chose to fight on after the hanging of O'Kennedy. This led to major campaigns against them until 26 July 1348.[60] In 1349 the O'Carrolls and the MacGillapatricks devastated much of northern Tipperary and Kilkenny before finally capturing the castle at Aghaboe; despite an summer expedition in 1350 by Justiciar Thomas Rokeby, that setback ensured that the cantred of the same name was effectively lost to the English of Ossory. By the 1360s, the MacGillapatricks had further cemented their gains by completely conquering Clandonagh and Clarmallagh baronies lying in the north of the cantred of Odogh.[61] As for Brian Bán, his remarkable career ended at the hands of the sons of Lorcán MacKeogh in 1350.

55 Clyn, *Annals*, p. 33; *The Annals of Ross*, p. 46; AConn, 1346; Curtis, *Med. Ire.*, p. 213. **56** *Grace*, p. 141; Frame, 'The defence of the English lordship, 1250–1450', p. 89. **57** Clyn, *Annals*, p. 37. **58** Curtis, *Med. Ire.*, pp 202, 213–14. **59** Clyn, *Annals*, p. 34. For Ruaidhrí see *COD*, ii, no. 74, p. 65. **60** Otway-Ruthven, *Medieval Ireland*, pp 266–7; Clyn, *Annals*, p. 34. A son of Brian Bán was hanged with Domhnall O'Kennedy in Thurles in June 1348. **61** Empey, pp 207, 210; Otway-

In response to the endemic violence, English policy was increasingly directed towards the establishment of friendly Irish in the lordships bordering Dublin. This policy may have been designed to prevent co-ordinated attacks of the Leinster Irish upon the English outposts. As part of this policy, Justiciar Thomas Rokeby sometime in autumn 1350 presided over the election of his protégé, John mac Taidhg O'Byrne, after a campaign into O'Byrne territory earlier in July.[62] This John stayed in English service until summer 1353, but he was determined to assert himself. John's assertion of independence frightened other Irish leaders. In particular, Muircheartach MacMurrough was so concerned that he entered English service in 1353. (Muircheartach's hold on the kingships of Uí Cheinnselaig and Leinster was far from secure, his most prominent rivals being his cousins, the sons of the slain Domhnall Óg MacMurrough, king of Leinster, c.1340–47).[63] In 1353–4 Muircheartach MacMurrough, Ruaidhrí O'More and Aodh O'Toole all supported the government, contributing large forces to a major expedition into John's country. These efforts proved successful as John came to peace on 22 March 1354, surrendering 92 cows.[64] By summer Muircheartach and John joined forces in a campaign against the English. Their actions provided ample opportunity for their respective dynastic rivals to prove their loyalty to the English. John's rivals included his cousin Murchadh mac Maghnusa O'Byrne, while Domhnall Riabhach and Diarmait Láimhdhearg MacMurrough (the sons of Domhnall Óg MacMurrough) eagerly grasped their chance to attack their father's successor.[65] The war betrayed signs of extensive co-ordination with other Leinster dynasties. Muircheartach MacMurrough was quickly captured by Patrick de la Freyne, but John mac Taidhg O'Byrne defeated Rokeby, besieging him in Wicklow castle during October 1354. He apparently requested Muircheartach's release during the negotiations, but Rokeby brought him by sea to Wicklow and executed him as a warning to John, an act that shocked not only the Leinstermen but Irish kings countrywide.[66]

Such was John's success in undermining Rokeby's alliances among the Leinster Irish that Aodh O'Toole and his brother John deserted the English and joined

Ruthven, 'Ireland in the 1350s: Sir Thomas de Rokeby and his successors', p. 49.   **62** Curtis, 'The clan system among English settlers in Ireland', pp 116–20; for the identity of this John see Pender, 'O'Clery', para. 1763, p. 131. For the campaign against O'Byrnes, see Frame, 'The Dublin government', pp 339–40.   **63** Giollapádraig O'Byrne, the probable O'Byrne tanaiste, was paid 5 marks for service in 1351, he had been in service since January that year. Also John was paid 5 marks for certain business, see Frame, 'The Dublin government', pp 342, 350. Idem, 'Military service in the lordship of Ireland', p. 121. This probability is buttressed by his service in Munster during 1352.   **64** O'More brought 68 light horsemen and 108 footmen, while O'Toole contributed 15 hobelars and 4 kerne and gained a fee of £8. 13s. 4d. And Muircheartach was drawing a fee at Michaelmas 1353. See Frame, 'The Dublin government', pp 350–2.   **65** Nicholls, 'Crioch Branach', p. 15; Frame, 'The Dublin government', p. 357. Diarmait MacMurrough was in service again in 1355, fighting Muircheartach mac Muiris' supporters and O'Byrne. See also O'Byrne, 'The Uí Bhroin of Co. Wicklow', pp 67–8. **66** AConn, AFM, AU, 1354; AClon, 1353; Frame, 'The Dublin government', pp 355–8; idem, *Ireland and Britain, 1170–1450*, p. 272.

him sometime after 9 August 1355.[67] By the close of 1355, Muircheartach's son, Art MacMurrough, had submitted, but John O'Byrne continued fighting.[68] This Art was to reconcile himself and his followers with Domhnall Óg MacMurrough's sons and the government by fighting the Leinster Irish between 1355 and 1357. John O'Byrne remained belligerent, destroying Rokeby's network of alliances and prolonging the disturbances throughout East Leinster in 1356.[69] (For his service against the Leinster Irish between February and April 1357, Art was recognized by Edward III as head of his lineage and granted a fee. Art's support for the government may have contributed to the submission of the O'Byrnes and the O'Tooles in 1357. That same year: they are soon found meekly serving on a government hosting against the troublesome O'Byrnes of Duffry in Wexford.)

Just as Leinster began to settle down, the calm was destroyed by the outbreak of a fresh MacMurrough war in May 1358, this time led by Art. Art was planning a major war (witness his realignment with John O'Byrne, his alliance with the new O'More leader, and the – undated – marriage of his daughter Gormflaith to Murchadh O'Connor Faly of Offaly).[70] The government moved quickly to neutralize this dangerous confederation by sending envoys to treat with O'More for peace, but their efforts failed. Then Art and the O'Mores of Laois and Slemargy openly defied the English by raiding throughout the Barrow valley, resulting in a major O'More victory in July 1358.[71] In September, English attempts to placate these allies failed at a parley near Athy. Through shrewd diplomacy, Art brought the Leinster Irish under his leadership, and from the safety of the Leinster mountains raided English outposts. There were, however, setbacks. Although in August 1358 John O'Byrne, captured by Ormond, promised fealty and repentance, we soon find him cutting northward into the Dublin marches and aiding Art and the O'Mores to sever the royal highway through the Barrow artery.[72] More ominous for the English lordship was Art's campaign in aid of O'More in Laois. The alliance of the MacMurroughs and the O'Mores threatened Ormond's lands around Leighlinbridge, particularly the Gowran pass, which accessed Ossory and north Munster. There, an Irish hegemony opened up possibilities of expansion up the Barrow and into Kildare. In 1359, amid a fierce offensive upon Ormond's earldom, the earl, now justiciar,[73] defeated Art and the O'Mores in a pitched battle in Laois. A general

---

67 *Rot. pat. Hib*, no. 11, p. 59 and no. 129, p. 63. See also Frame, 'The Dublin government', p. 358. **68** For the genealogy of this Art see Pender, 'O'Clery', p. 128. *NHI*, ix, p. 149. He may be the man captured with Henry Trahene by the Butlers in 1326. See Dowling, *Annals*, p. 22. **69** O'Byrne, 'The Uí Bhroin of Co. Wicklow', p. 68. See also the attack of Adam Dodyng of Ballymore's attack on the Gabhail Raghnaill O'Byrnes in 1356, see *Rot. pat. Hib*, no. 33, p. 59. **70** *Rot. pat. Hib*, no. 5, p. 66, nos 29, p. 77; for the marriage of Gormflaith to Murchadh O'Connor Faly, a later king of Offaly, see *Cal. papal letters*, iv, p. 341. This records the papal legitimation of their marriage in 1390. For the alliances with the O'Byrnes and the O'Mores see Frame, 'Two kings', p. 165. Lydon, 'Medieval Wicklow', p. 176. **71** AConn, AClon, AU, 1358. **72** Frame, 'The Dublin government', pp 373–4. **73** Frame, 'Two kings', p. 166; idem, Frame, 'The Dublin government', p. 372. There was a campaign against the O'Mores of

peace was made on 12 August 1359 and John voluntarily submitted at Carlow, where in fact he was knighted.[74]

The Butler lands were exposed to the migration of Irish settlers across the Barrow. Art's reverse did not lessen the crisis faced by English within the Barrow valley. By 1360, traffic on the royal highway through the Barrow needed armed escorts because of the omnipresent dangers posed by the MacMurroughs. This crisis is best illustrated when Ormond granted Rower to the Roches on condition that they would forcibly eject any encroaching Irish settlers.[75] The pressure on the settlers of the Barrow brought Lionel of Clarence to Ireland on 15 September 1361. Despite an initial reverse inflicted by the (recently knighted) Sir John O'Byrne in Wicklow, Clarence shored up the English position along the Barrow by refortifying Carlow and defeating of Art. Later, at a parley, he treacherously captured Art and his tanaiste, Domhnall Riabhach MacMurrough, confining them in Trim, where they were either murdered or died naturally in July 1362.[76] Clarence sealed the English commitment to Carlow by relocating the exchequer and the common bench there before campaigning separately against the O'Mores and the O'Byrnes. The MacMurrough threat was continued by Art's successor, Diarmait Láimhdhearg. His persistence was exploited by Sir John O'Byrne to curry further favour with the English. For Sir John's services against Diarmait Láimhdhearg in 1365–6, he received a fee, while his son Tadhg and a John O'Toole were knighted. By 1367 relations had improved, as evidenced by Edward III's recognition of Diarmait Láimhdhearg in July as leader of the Leinster Irish.[77] Peace was short-lived, for the threat to the Barrow corridor re-emerged. Separate campaigns were launched against the O'Tooles and the MacGillapatricks throughout 1367–8.[78] The potency of the MacMurrough threat to the Barrow region required drastic action. After his arrival in Ireland on 20 June 1369, Justiciar William of Windsor captured Diarmait Láimhdhearg and executed him later that year.[79]

Slemargy in 1359, see *Rot. pat. Hib.*, no. 57, p. 69.   **74** Otway-Ruthven, *Medieval Ireland*, p. 283; idem, 'Two kings', p. 166; Otway-Ruthven, 'Ireland in the 1350s', p. 56; For the probable dating of John O'Byrne's knighting, see Nicholls, 'Crioch Branach', p. 16. See also *Rot. pat. Hib*, no. 7, p. 66. There were also 10 O'Byrne hostages housed in Dublin Castle between February and July 1360. Adam de Gratham, constable of Dublin Castle, was paid 57*s*. 9*d*. for the hostages of MacMurrough, O'More of Laois and Maurice Boy on 28 May 1360, see *Rot. pat. Hib*, no. 53, p. 78.   **75** *COD*, ii, no.64, p. 58.   **76** Gilbert, *Viceroys*, p. 218; O'Byrne, 'The Uí Bhroin of Co. Wicklow', p. 69; AConn, AClon, AU, 1361.   **77** Rymer, *Foedera* (1816–20 ed.) III, 2, p. 830; Simms, *Kings to warlords*, p. 38.   **78** In 1367 Máelsechlainn mac Sefraidh MacGillapatrick was killed by the English. See AClon, AConn, 1367. David O'Toole was killed by the English of Dublin in 1367. See AFM, 1368.   **79** AFM, 1368, 1369; AU, AConn, 1369.

CHAPTER 6

Leinster and the kingship of Art MacMurrough, 1370–1420

Despite the surgical actions of Lionel of Clarence and William of Windsor, by 1370 the English lordship in Ireland was in danger of being cut in two by Irish pressure originating in north Munster, West Leinster and East Leinster. To the west of the Barrow, the power of the O'Briens, O'Kennedys and O'Carrolls of north Munster had re-emerged. This was compounded by the dramatic rise of the O'Mores of Laois and MacGillapatricks of North Ossory. In East Leinster, the MacMurroughs, O'Nolans, O'Tooles and O'Byrnes threatened to clog the Barrow artery. The government's actions to counter the coalescing of Irish powers along the Barrow were sporadic and limited by lack of finance. One of its tactics was to exploit the fissures within Irish polity by enlisting the service of rival dynasts against their own lords. Very often the settlers, however, were left to combat the Irish on their own, as shown by the efforts of Henry Traherne and Fulk de la Freyne. This often meant making deals with their enemies to preserve their positions, which in turn led to incidents such as Brian Bán O'Brien and the English of Ely attacking the English of Ossory in 1325, and the intervention of the English of Ossory, Kildare and Carlow in O'More politics in 1348. These policies often worked to great effect, preventing wider co-operation among the Irish. Despite these clever strategies, the Leinster wars of 1329, 1336, 1344, and 1354–9 augured ill, as we shall see, for the settlers and the government.

During the last three decades of the fourteenth century, the Leinstermen finally gained the upper hand over the government and conquered the strategic Barrow valley before launching offensives upon the vulnerable earldom of Kildare. Much of this success was due to their alliances with the Irish of Munster – particularly those in the north of that province. The MacMurroughs, the O'Byrnes, the O'Briens of Arra and the O'Carrolls of Ely combined for major offensives aimed at the English of Kildare, Carlow and the Dublin borders. A proof of this greater flexibility in Irish politics is the fact that in 1371 and 1384 King Brian Sreamach O'Brien of Thomond conspired with the Irish of Connacht and Leinster against the government. Collusion of the Irish of Munster and Leinster is also to be seen in the service of MacGillapatrick and O'Meagher mercenaries with the MacMurroughs and O'Byrnes of East Leinster. Furthermore, there was an increase in marriage alliances between the

Leinster nobility and those of north Munster.[1] Symptomatic of this process was the career of Art MacMurrough. During his kingship of Leinster, the Irish effectively corralled the government's authority into a slender enclave surrounding Dublin. The resultant crisis in Leinster distracted Richard II's attention from England at a crucial time, contributing to the fall of the house of Plantagenet and the accession of Henry Bolingbroke as Henry IV in September 1399.

Art's parents were Art MacMurrough, king of Leinster (*d*.1362), and a daughter of Philip O'Byrne. According to Thomas D'Arcy Magee, a nineteenth-century antiquarian, Art was born about 1357.[2] Seemingly he had an elder brother and a sister, Gormflaith, who was married to Murchadh O'Connor Faly of Offaly. Jean Creton, who witnessed Art's parley with Thomas le Despenser, earl of Gloucester, in summer 1399, described him as a tall handsome man with a stern countenance but wondrously active.[3] This perception of Art is caught in a stereotypical snapshot (in Creton's manuscript) of the meeting of Latin Europe and the face of the barbarian, in which Art is transformed into a symbol of die-hard Irish resistance, brandishing a spear at the ordered rows of English knights. But the figure of Art is more complex than this. We sometimes find him described as the self-styled king of Leinster and a piratical outsider. The Leinster Irish saw it otherwise. It is clear, though, that Art, like Janus, had two faces. Curtis has pointed out that he was not an implacable foe of the English: at various times throughout his career he willingly accepted English kings as his overlords. Elizabeth de Veel, probably Art's second wife, was of English stock, and his heir Donnchadh married Aveline Butler, daughter of the 3rd earl of Ormond.[4]

Art was not predestined for the Leinster kingship. From early in his career, he was close to the O'Byrnes, his mother's people, and his O'Byrne cousins unflinchingly supported him. The extensive intermarrying of Art's children with the O'Byrnes also demonstrates the O'Byrnes' importance to him. Gerald, Art's third son, married Sadhbh, daughter of Donnchadh mac Braen O'Byrne of Newrath.[5] Uná, probably a daughter of Art, married Donnchadh mac Braen's heir, Murchadh; and Gormflaith MacMurrough married Edmund O'Byrne, Donnchadh mac Braen's brother.[6] After Art's father's mysterious death in Trim castle in July 1362, the Leinster kingship passed to his sometime rivals, the sons of Domhnall Óg MacMurrough (king of Leinster, *c*.1340–7). The rapprochement hammered out about 1357 between the two MacMurrough branches held; in 1364 Diarmait Láimhdhearg, the eldest of Domhnall Óg's sons, and Art the elder's brother, Donnchadh, both received fees from Lionel of Clarence. However,

---

1 For example, Donnchadh O'Byrne's second wife was of the O'Meagher dynasty of the north Tipperary territory of Ikerrin; see *Cal. papal letters, 1417–31*, vii, p. 343; *Holinshed's Chronicle*, p. 235; AConn, 1401.   2 D'Arcy McGee, *A memoir of the life and conquests of Art MacMurrough*, p. 18.   3 Webb, 'The deposition of King Richard II', p. 40.   4 Frame, 'Two kings', p. 173; Curtis, *Med. Ire.*, pp 246–7, 262–5; idem, 'The barons of Norragh, Co. Kildare, 1171–1660', pp 88–91; *COD*, iii, no. 85, p. 70.   5 *Cal. papal Reg., 1427–47*, viii, p. 78.   6 *Cal. papal Reg, 1417–31*, vii, p. 519. She was his second wife. His first being Joan O'Connor Faly. See ibid., p. 221; RIA MS 1233 (23/Q/10): An Leabhar Donn, f. 11.

it seems that Diarmait Láimhdhearg's provincial kingship was not well received by the O'Byrnes and the O'Tooles; this led him to seek government approval, which came in 1367. He was now recognized by Edward III as leader of the Leinster Irish. But peace was short-lived, as for the MacMurrough threat to the Barrow region re-emerged. After his arrival in Ireland on 20 June 1369, Justiciar William of Windsor captured Diarmait Láimhdhearg and Gerald MacMurrough, brother of Art the elder, executing them later in the year.[7]

This latest MacMurrough disaster resulted in the Leinster kingship passing to another brother of Art the elder, Donnchadh. The emergence of Donnchadh and his nephew Art as the principal MacMurrough leaders was generally welcomed by the Leinster Irish. Unlike Diarmait Láimhdhearg, Donnchadh and Art were more inclined to look for support among the O'Byrnes and O'Tooles. The Leinster kingship began to be confined within Donnchadh's family, to the exclusion of their cousins. This was a considerable political evolution, steering the dynasty away from the creation of a multiplicity of power bases which would inevitably lead to weakness. This concentration of power in a single kingly line strengthened the MacMurroughs immeasurably, laying the groundwork for their advances of the early fifteenth century. Donnchadh demonstrated his new regional status in 1371, when he joined Brian Sreamach O'Brien of Thomond and the Munster Irish in a furtive plot to conquer Ireland.[8]

Unlike the MacMurroughs, the O'Byrnes became victims of their success, for their dynastic unity began to disintegrate in the 1330s. After the death of their greatest king, Murchadh O'Byrne, about 1337, infighting increased. Instead of succession through a single line, it alternated between descendants of Murchadh's sons – Philip and Tadhg. The effect of this rotating succession subdivided power within the lordship. Still, the O'Byrne decline was delayed by the emergence of a series of talented leaders such as Sir John O'Byrne and his successors. Paradoxically, the eventful emergence of Art MacMurrough as king of Leinster papered over the O'Byrne cracks, for his close relations with the O'Byrne leaders may have cowed many of their dissidents. The death of Sir John O'Byrne in the late 1360s did lead to a dynastic civil war, but this discord did not prevent the O'Byrnes from exploiting William of Windsor's preoccupation with the Munster wars of Brian Sreamach O'Brien of Thomond: they took Wicklow and Newcastle McKynegan castles in summer 1370 and, although these fortresses were quickly retaken, it was not before the O'Byrnes razed Wicklow.[9] Sometime after this, the O'Byrnes and the government agreed a truce. The signatory to this peace was their next recorded overlord was Braen mac Philip O'Byrne, Art's uncle. The agreement was confirmed on 27 March 1371. In coming to this

7 Simms, *Kings to warlords*, p. 38; AFM, 1369.   8 Curtis, *Med. Ire.*, p. 242. Then the council of Ireland reported to the king in 1371 that O'Brien, MacNamara and nearly all the Irish of Munster and Leinster were confederated to make a universal conquest of all Ireland. The earl of Kildare, the justiciar, offered Donnchadh MacMurrough 20 marks and an English cloak worth 71s. for the safe keeping of the roads between Carlow and Kilkenny.   9 *Chartul. St Mary's*, ii, p. 397; Price, *Placenames*, p. lxvii.

peace, it was clear that Braen mac Philip was motivated by a need to deal with his rebellious cousins. By the terms of the peace, he also agreed to never obey any MacMurrough, to rebuild the church of Wicklow, and to acknowledge the rights of the archbishop of Dublin.[10] Unsurprisingly, once Braen mac Philip had silenced his rivals and renewed his alliance with Aodh O'Toole, he soon turned his back on this agreement and embarked on the a conquest of north Wicklow.[11] In 1374 he captured and demolished the castles of Wicklow and Newcastle McKynegan. A prompt English campaign retook both castles by September, but Braen mac Philip maintained his pressure, seizing them again during 1376, and he grabbed Kindlestown castle in 1377. The only notable reverse suffered by the Wicklow Irish in these years was the killing of Aodh O'Toole by the English in 1376. Despite this reverse, the seemingly smooth transition of the O'Toole leadership to Sir John O'Toole, Aodh's brother, further underlines the strength of the Irish ruling families of East Leinster. By the time of Braen mac Philip's death in 1378, his power extended from Bray to Tullow.[12]

After the killing of Donnchadh MacMurrough on 6 October 1375 by Sheriff Geoffrey de Valle of Carlow, Art MacMurrough emerged as the leading figure of his dynasty.[13] However, another Art, Diarmait Láimhdhearg's son, succeeded Donnchadh as overlord. In early 1377, this Art mac Diarmait received government recognition as MacMurrough leader and was granted a fee of 40 marks.[14] It is clear, though, that his leadership was disputed by Art, and, with the help of the O'Byrnes and O'Tooles, he undermined his rival. The foundation of Art's success was shaped by the previous sixty years of Irish expansion. As in East Leinster, his later power in West Leinster and north Munster was to be founded on diplomacy, marriage and military success. By exploitating previous MacMurrough advances into the Barrow and the midlands, Art consolidated a diplomatic and military web that stretched from the mountains of East Leinster to the mountains of Arra in north Tipperary. Like no other Leinster ruler since Diarmait MacMurrough (king of Leinster *c.*1129–71), Art was able to recruit mercenaries on large scale from West Leinster and the midlands.

---

10 TCD, MS E.3.25 (588), ff 202v–204. From the names of the O'Byrne branches supporting Braen mac Philip, it is clear that he drew his support from the southern lands of the O'Byrnes. He seems to have been predominately opposed by those branches living in the north of the lordship.   **11** Gilbert, *Viceroys*, p. 233. The Carrickmines ward suffered a prolonged attack from the O'Byrnes between 1371 and 1373. John de Colton marched to Newcastle McKynegan's relief in 1373. For de Colton's role, see *Rot. Pat. Hib*, no. 60, p. 87.   **12** *Chartul. St Mary's*, ii, pp 283–4; Gilbert, *Viceroys*, p. 293; Otway-Ruthven, *Medieval Ireland*, p. 302; Price, *Placenames*, p.lxviii; Frame, *English lordship*, p. 314. In February 1376 Wicklow Castle could only be supplied by sea going barge, see *Rot. pat. Hib*, nos 33–4, p.100b. For the killing of Aodh O'Toole, see AFM, AConn, 1376; this Sir John was assassinated in his own house by a person of his household in 1388, see AConn, 1388. O'Byrne, 'The Uí Bhroin of Co. Wicklow', pp 69–71. For Curtis' definition of the territorial extent of the O'Byrne kingdom, read Curtis, *Med. Ire.*, p. 241.   **13** Frame, 'Two kings', pp 169–71; Richardson and Sayles, *Parl. and councils Med Ire*, i, pp 99, 124–5; AConn, 1375.   **14** *Rot. Pat. Hib*, no. 2, p. 99b, nos 27, 30, p.100b, no. 35, p. 104. Curtis, *Med. Ire.*, p. 246.

Art was able to exploit the increasing contacts between the Irish of East Leinster and those of West Leinster and north Munster – capitalizing on the weakness of the government during the late 1370s. In late 1377 he ravaged much of Kildare, Wexford and Carlow, forcing the government to offer him a fee of 80 marks. After his submission in January 1378, Art accepted this sum.[15] In February 1378 he burnt Carlow before linking up with Murchadh na Raithnighe O'Brien of Arra in March to ravage the region yet again, driving the government into crisis. Such was the devastation that James Butler, justiciar of Ireland and 2nd earl of Ormond, directed the parliament convened at nearby Castledermot to buy off Murchadh na Raithnighe with 100 marks.[16] Murchadh na Raithnighe readily agreed and swore a oath before the council to go back to whence he came. Naturally, this abject government defeat only fuelled Irish rapacity and increased Art's ambitions. By June, Murchadh was back prowling on the borders of Leinster. This time he had Tadhg Ailbhle O'Carroll (he seems to have succeeded William Alainn O'Carroll) with him. They ravaged and plundered much of Kildare, Carlow and Kilkenny, enforcing the Leinster king's hegemony over the Barrow valley, so much so that in late 1378 the English appointed the Leinster king keeper of the roads between Carlow and Kilkenny with a fee of 80 marks. This marked the beginning of his emergence both as the undisputed king of Leinster and as a fixed point on the political landscape. By 1381 he was acknowledged as head of his dynasty, outmanoeuvring his rivals through a policy of execution and coercion.[17]

It was Art's diplomacy that underpinned his success. One of his favourite diplomatic methods was the traditional ploy of marriage – giving the hands of several of his kinswomen to Irish kings. Through these marriages as well as military aid against the English, Art created a network of friendly Irish lordships, stretching from the Leinster coast to the Shannon. In north Munster, he promoted close relations with the MacGillapatricks of North Ossory, the O'Briens of Arra and the O'Carrolls of Ely; this undoubtedly helped him to take up where Donnchadh MacMurrough had left off, and in 1384 he formed alliance with Brian Sreamach O'Brien of Thomond.[18] However, it was the marriage of Art's daughter, Sadhbh, to Fionnán MacGillapatrick of North Ossory that really solidified the link between north Munster and Leinster. Art used his considerable military muscle to shield the MacGillapatricks, as evidenced by his victory in 1386 over the English of Ossory.[19] Furthermore, he

---

15 Ibid., nos 31–2, p. 100b, nos 38–9, p. 104. Art also accepted £40 for the killing of his uncle, Donnchadh, in 1375. Richardson and Sayles, *Parl. and councils Med Ire*, i, p. 99. In 1384 he extracted £10 for attacks on his tenants during a parley. *Rot. Pat. Hib.*, no. 22, p. 122b. And in 1389 he charged the colonists of Carlow 10 marks for attacks, see ibid., no. 177, p. 146. See also Frame, 'Two kings', p. 169. **16** Curtis, *Med. Ire.*, p. 243; AFM, 1383. **17** AFM, AU, 1380. **18** Otway-Ruthven, *Medieval Ireland*, p. 317. **19** The precise date of Sadhbh MacMurrough's marriage to Fionnán MacGillapatrick of North Ossory is unknown. See AConn, 1410. However, Art's defeat of the English of Ossory in 1386–7, suggests there was an effective alliance by this date. For Art's victory over the English of Ossory, see AU, 1386.

also used the MacGillapatrick lordship as a recruiting ground for mercenaries.[20] To the north of Ossory, he also actively promoted an alliance with the O'Mores of Laois, who had been in decline since the death of Laoiseach O'More in 1342. By 1360, Laoiseach's kingdom had been subdivided into two lordships centred on Slemargy and Laois. Their decline in power is shown also by their defeat in 1381 by Lord Lieutenant Edmund Mortimer, lord of Laois and earl of March, and James Butler, 2nd earl of Ormond.[21] This possibly prompted them sometime in the 1380s to renew their old alliance with the MacMurroughs. (Among the O'Mores there was a lot of support for Art, as shown by their attendance on his campaigns and his good relations with the O'More lords of Laois and Slemargy.)

Parallels can also be detected in Art MacMurrough's relationship with the O'Connor Falys. Unlike the O'Mores, they were steadily re-emerging as the major power-brokers in West Leinster from mid-century, pushing into western Kildare and Meath.[22] Significantly, Murchadh O'Connor Faly, king of Offaly after 1384, was married to Art's sister, Gormflaith.[23] This O'Connor Faly/MacMurrough alliance must have been designed mainly to facilitate the inroads of both dynasties into Kildare, but it also bound the O'Carrolls of Ely and the O'Mores closer to Art. As with the MacGillapatrick alliance, Art used this O'Connor Faly alliance to fish for mercenaries (among their O'Dunne vassals).[24] Both the O'Dunne overlord and Art O'Dempsey accepted Art's agreement with Richard II on 7 January 1395 and on 21 April 1395.[25] This suggests that the MacMurroughs had thrown a protective umbrella over West Leinster and the midlands. If so, it greatly increased the stability among the Irish kingdoms there. This conclusion is supported by the noticeable interchange of nomenclature among these dynasties, the increasing frequency of wars among the Irish, and their allocation of scarce resources for the erection of churches and for the protection of shrines. Such stability was ominous for the earldoms of Ormond and Kildare.

MacMurrough marriages reveal a pecking order among Art's allies. For instance, there were none with the O'Tooles and O'Mores – indicating that Art placed them in the same bracket as the O'Ryans, the O'Nolans, the Kinsellas and the O'Murphys. However, the submissions of 1395 of the Leinster nobility to Richard II demonstrate clearly that Art spoke for them all; the hostage taken

---

20 AConn, 1398.   **21** Curtis, *Med. Ire.,* pp 253–4. Mortimer forced an unnamed O'More lord to recognize that he was his hereditary vassal; see also *Liber Primus Kilkenniensis*, p. 127. When they were defeated by Ormond – the O'Mores were in alliance with the O'Nolans and lost some 440 men.   **22** AFM, 1385. See Ó Cléirigh, 'The O'Connor Faly lordship of Offaly, 1395–1513', pp 87–102.   **23** Muircheartach O'Connor Faly died in 1384, see AU, 1384. However, there was another quite powerful O'Connor Faly lord called Muiris Maol about. But he was killed by the O'Kellys of Laois in 1389, see AU, 1389.   **24** AConn, 1398. Then Cearbhall and Eóghan, the sons of Donnchadh O'Dunne, were killed in MacMurrough's defeat.   **25** Curtis, *Richard II in Ire.*, pp 31, 43. An earlier O'Dunne overlord was killed by the O'Molloy of Fearceall in 1381. See AFM, 1381 Diarmait O'Dempsey, lord of the O'Dempseys (*d*.1383) was married to Be Binn, daughter of Domhnall O'Dunne. See AConn, 1376.

by Richard for Art's loyalty included Gerald mac Taidhg O'Byrne, John O'Nolan and Máelsechlainn O'More. Murchadh O'Connor Faly and Fionnán MacGillapatrick, Art's allies in West Leinster and the midlands, remained at large – which suggests that his influence there was considerably less than along the Barrow and East Leinster. The O'Byrne relationship with Art was different from that of the other hostages. During the ratification ceremony of the agreement with Richard on 7 January 1395, both Art and Gerald mac Taidhg O'Byrne on behalf of the Leinster Irish affixed their seals to the parchment, suggesting that they considered each other as equals.[26] There were other faces to Art's kingship. A key to his success was his insurance of the acquiescence of stronger allies through pragmatic good relations; if, however, he had sufficient power to enforce his lordship over a weaker lord, he did so, as Féilim O'Toole found out in 1395, when he complained to Richard of attacks upon his lands from Hy Kinsella, a lordship within Art's kingdom; earlier, he had accepted Art's agreement with Richard, but he now stated that he was subject to none but Richard.[27]

Art's military power, too, was impressive. It enabled him to exercise his authority over the English of central Wexford, by extracting black rents from New Ross. This MacMurrough pressure on Wexford was evident by the fact that another Art, described as 'roydamna of Leinster', was killed there by the English in 1383. His power over Carlow is demonstrated in 1389, when he received 10 marks from the English there as compensation for the killing of some followers.[28] However, it was Art's control of the Barrow region that ultimately made him the target for royal intervention. Through the Barrow valley (as we have seen) ran the royal highway that kept Dublin in contact with southern Ireland. Art was in control of this strategic artery by 1378, and this encouraged him to expand into Kildare. Indeed, the classic ingredient of his later expansion was the weakness of the Fitzgerald earldom of Kildare. Art's thrust into southern and central Kildare coincided with those of the O'Connor Falys and O'Dempseys from the west and the O'Byrnes and O'Tooles from the east.[29] The MacMurrough threat to Kildare was not just military: about 1390, Art married Elizabeth de Veel, heiress to the Kildare barony of Norragh, which Art now claimed through his wife (it was held in chief from the earl of Kildare). According to the Statutes of Kilkenny of 1366, however, Elizabeth's lands were forfeit because of her marriage to Art (provisions in the Statutes prohibited mixed-race marriages); Art was unsuccessful in his 1391 petition to have this decision reversed. In retaliation, Carlow

26 AFM, 1394; Price, *Placenames*, p. ix; Curtis, *Richard II in Ire.*, pp 31, 166–7. 27 Curtis, *Richard II in Ire.*, pp 125–6; Frame, 'Two kings', pp 169, 171–2; Johnston, 'Richard II and the submissions of Gaelic Ireland', p. 7. This shows that Art had lordship over Englishmen such as Henry Tallon. 28 AFM, 1383; *Rot. Pat. Hib*, no. 177, p. 146. 29 AFM, 1383. Diarmait, lord of the O'Dempseys, was killed by the English of Leinster in 1383. Later in 1394 Aodh and Thomas O'Dempsey were killed while pursuing English raiders, see AFM, 1394. Earlier in 1392, Donnchadh O'Dempsey died. See ALC, 1392; The stability of the O'Connor Falys is evident as they erected a church at Killeigh for the Franciscans in 1393. See AFM, 1393. An Calbhach O'Connor Faly captured the earl of Kildare in 1398, and held him hostage for a

was destroyed by Art, O'Ryan, O'Nolan and Tadhg Ailbhle O'Carroll in 1391–2, and in 1392 Art with Gerald mac Taidhg O'Byrne, Féilim O'Toole, and O'More again devastated the counties of Kildare and Carlow.[30] On this occasion their burning extended deep into Kildare as far as Naas in the north of the country, while the fearful townsfolk of Castledermot paid him 84 marks to go away. It is highly probable that Art's offensive was directly linked to the war in Munster between Toirdhealbhach Maol O'Brien of Arra and Ormond. Having learned its lesson, the government shortly afterwards returned the revenues of Norragh to Elizabeth. Art and his allies also moved again against James Butler, 3rd earl of Ormond. Over the previous century, Butler supremacy had been forced out of a variety of territories stretching from the Wicklow coast, the Leinster mountains, the Barrow conduit, North Ossory, Laois, Offaly and, finally, from north Tipperary. To consolidate their borderlands, successive earls of Ormond and the Burkes from the 1330s entered into agreements with individual Irish kings, particularly those of north Tipperary. But the emergence of Art's father, Art the elder, in the 1350s led to further conflict. What antagonized the Butlers were Art MacMurrough's interests in the Barrow region, West Leinster and north Tipperary, threatening the stability of Ormond's already contracting northern frontiers. Despite their best efforts, the Butlers were unable to roll back the MacMurrough tide flowing into the midlands through the strategic pass of Gowran. The fact that Gowran town was the residence of the earls of Ormond up to 1391 added further insult to the injured Butler pride.

From the middle of the 1380s, the MacMurrough/Butler struggle was approaching its climax. It was helped on its way by two important events: first, Ormond was appointed keeper or governor of the counties of Tipperary and Kilkenny in autumn 1389; then, in 1391, a Sir Hugh le Despenser sold to Ormond, Kilkenny castle and manor along with Callan and other lands scattered in the liberty. In the same year Richard II, at the request of Thomas, 3rd earl of Stafford, granted the earl's share of the liberty to Ormond – thus firmly establishing Ormond as the English counterpoise to the MacMurroughs. The intentions of the Butlers became clear when Ormond's brother in the parliament of January 1393 successfully petitioned for a grant to reconquer the river valleys of the Nore, the Suir and the Barrow.[31] The Butlers were determined to reassert their lordship over the Irish of North Ossory and the O'Carrolls, thereby undermining the relative automony of the MacMurroughs. The MacMurroughs and the Butlers were on a collision course.

On 2 October 1394, Art's kingship of Leinster received its first serious test. The occasion was the landing of Richard II at Waterford. Art greeted the king's arrival by burning New Ross, but the combined strength of the king's army and

---

period, see AFM, 1398.   **30** *A roll of the proceedings of the king's council in Ireland*, p. 41. Robert Wadley, archbishop of Dublin and Chancellor of Ireland, attempted to defend Co. Carlow, bringing 200 men at arms and archers. This encouraged the Irish to pull back. He was also compelled to resist a six-day Irish siege of Naas in Kildare.   **31** Curtis, *Med. Ire.*, p. 256; *A roll*

Ormond proved too strong, and Art was forced to submit by 30 October. When he did so, Ormond insisted on his incarceration, but Art was soon released in return for Gerald mac Taidhg O'Byrne, John O'Nolan and Máelsechlainn O'More. On 7 January 1395, Art and Gerald near Tullow promised to evacuate Leinster and conquer fresh lands as royal mercenaries. At a later meeting on 16 February at Balgory near Carlow, both men pledged to forfeit 20,000 marks each if the deal was broken. In return, Richard returned Norragh to Elizabeth de Veel, Art's wife. Through Art's encouragement, many of Leinster nobility accepted the agreement. But even before that, peace was jeopardized by Ormond, who sought to reclaim lands within Irish kingdoms (Ormond aggression in Wicklow caused Gerald mac Taidhg O'Byrne on 18 January 1395 to write to the king).[32] Clearly, Ormond was maximizing this opportunity to force many of his former clients among the Irish lords of north Tipperary, now Art's allies, to acknowledge his temporary supremacy. Tadhg Ailbhle O'Carroll of Ely, trying to turn this situation to his advantage, wrote to the king, to request that he be recognized as the king's immediate subject, and asking for aid against his dynastic rivals; he also sought protection from the Butlers (Ormond's plans were clear from his role in the negotiation of the submissions of the Irish lords of Tipperary to Richard). On 25 April 1395, Tadhg Ailbhle O'Carroll along with Toirdhealbhach Maol O'Brien of Arra, the two O'Dwyers and three O'Kennedy leaders submitted as Butler clients to Richard at Kilkenny. Ormond, however, had in mind to enforce his own suzerainty more forcefully over Tadhg Ailbhle O'Carroll and these Irish lords once Richard departed. Even though Art and other Irish kings were knighted by Richard at Christchurch in March, the Irish interpretation of the concord substantially differed from that of the English.

When Richard left for England in May 1395, his agreement with the Irish came under pressure. In summer 1395, the English instigated clashes with the O'Connor Falys and the O'Carrolls. Tension was further increased by an unsuccessful kidnap attempt upon Art MacMurrough in Dublin.[33] In spite of this provocation, peace held until 1396. The commitment of Art, the O'Byrnes and the O'Carrolls to the agreement was clear. In February 1396 Donnchadh mac Braen O'Byrne of Newrath travelled to the English court, where Richard warmly welcomed him, granting him a fee of 80 marks.[34] Tadhg Ailbhle O'Carroll also took full opportunity of the relative peace in Ireland by embarking on pilgrimage to Rome in early 1396. On his way home, he met Donnchadh mac Braen at Richard's court in London. Together they joined the king's campaign in August 1396 to Calais and performed good service in France.[35] It seems they eventually came home either in late 1396 or early 1397 to a country in crisis.

of the proceedings of the king's council in Ireland, pp 220–2; Lydon, *Lordship*, pp 173, 205–6. **32** Curtis, *Richard II in Ire*, p. 31; Johnston, 'Richard II and the submissions of Gaelic Ireland', p. 6. **33** AFM, 1395. **34** *CPR, Rich II*, v, p. 670. Donnchadh mac Braen was granted the fee on 17 February 1396, and he returned to Ireland in the company of James de Cottenham keeper of the Kindlestown ward. This James was keeper of the castles of Wicklow, Newcastle and Kindlestown between 1397 and 1399, see *CPR, Rich II*, vi, pp 187, 480. **35** Johnson, 'The

Richard's dispatch to Ireland of his heir, Roger Mortimer, earl of March, as lord lieutenant was a catalyst in the crisis. Once in Ireland, Mortimer behaved more like a great magnate than Richard's representative, campaigning against the Irish in a series of expeditions that alienated them. But in the headstrong Mortimer, the formerly besieged earls of Kildare and Ormond found the perfect ally who was determined to enforce their claims to lands lying among the Leinster Irish. Incursions by Ormond and Mortimer into the Leinster mountains brought the crisis to the boil. Féilim O'Toole turned on the English in summer 1396, as did the O'Byrnes in early 1397.[36] For the early part of 1398, Art MacMurrough outwardly remained loyal, but he approved of the O'Byrne and the O'Toole attacks. The strife came to a dramatic climax in Kellistown in Carlow on 20 July 1398, when the O'Byrnes and the O'Tooles along with Art's troops cornered Mortimer, killing him. In West Leinster, the crisis was further exacerbated by the capture in 1398 of Gerald Fitzgerald, 5th earl of Kildare, by An Calbhach O'Connor Faly, Art's nephew. The government struck back, burning Glendalough that summer and killing Art's ally, Domhnall O'Nolan, king of Forth. In response, Art led his allies and mercenaries against the English of Leinster and Meath.[37]

On hearing of Mortimer's death, Richard decided upon another campaign to Ireland and revoked the 1395 agreement. Meanwhile Art MacMurrough's position in Leinster was weakening: annalistic evidence shows that in 1398 many of his allies either naturally expired or were killed. The O'Nolans were deprived of their leader, Gerald mac Taidhg O'Byrne, who died sometime in 1398, leaving a problematic succession between Donnchadh mac Braen O'Byrne and the relatively unknown Domhnall O'Byrne.[38] And west of the Barrow, the O'Mores lost both their leaders that year, when both Máelsechlainn O'More of Laois and the son of Muircheartach Buidhe O'More of Slemargy seemingly died of natural causes. Ironically, however, their deaths strengthened the dynasty by causing the reunification of the O'More lordships under Giollapádraig mac Fachtna O'More. And in north Munster Art MacMurrough's influence was reduced by the deaths of MacGillapatrick of North Ossory in 1398 and Toirdhealbhach Maol O'Brien of Arra the following year.[39] So, on the face of it, Art stood little chance of providing an effective resistance to Richard. However, what really unified these Irish dynasties behind Art was the danger from Ormond.

The campaign against Richard's army was aided by Art's choice of battle-ground. He used the protection of the Leinster mountains and the Wicklow region as the staging-point for those forces who came to his banner – thereby making up for deficiencies in men and material. Richard landed at Waterford on 2 June 1399, and had the better of the early exchanges, but he took the disastrous

Interim: Richard II and Ireland 1395–1399', p. 178.   **36** Ibid., p. 181; eadem, 'Richard II and the submissions of Gaelic Ireland', pp 9–11; AFM, 1396; *Ancient Irish histories*, ii (*Marleburrough's Chronicle*), p. 15.   **37** AFM, ALC, AConn, 1398.   **38** AClon, AConn, 1398.   **39** ALC, AFM, 1398, 1399.

3 Greater seal of Art MacMurrough's grandson, Domhnall Riabhach MacMurrough-
Kavanagh (*JRSAI*, 6, 1883–4).

decision to pursue Art into the Leinster mountains. Once in this intimidating
landscape, the hunter became the hunted. From this naturally protecting
environment Art inflicted considerable losses upon Richard's army, whose ill-
considered trek ended near Arklow with starving troops wading out to waiting
supply ships in search of bread. And at a famous parley, Art and the O'Byrne
leader denounced Richard and rejected any offer of peace, much to the king's
fury. However, things came to a halt when Henry Bolingbroke landed at
Ravenspur to challenge for the English crown, forcing Richard to quit and
embark for England on 27 July 1399.

Richard, as it turned out, was deposed and Bolingbroke took the crown as
Henry IV. Despite Richard's departure, Art remained at war, promising his wife
never to rest until her barony was restored. He now resolved to attack Ormond,

travelling to Munster in August 1399 to aid Maurice Fitzgerald, 5th earl of Desmond, against him. Apparently, Art was also able to unleash Tadhg Ailbhle O'Carroll upon the Butler lands. Ormond quickly neutralized O'Carroll, capturing and imprisoning him (he eventually escaped from Gowran in 1400).[40] Ormond also allied with the Burkes of Clanwilliam to secure his earldom's north-western flank, by marrying his daughter Elizabeth to Theobald Burke in 1401.[41] But an infusion of mercenary forces from Munster strengthened the resolve of Art MacMurrough and Domhnall O'Byrne. The O'Byrnes set to the conquest of north Wicklow and took Newcastle McKynegan that year[42] (they consolidated their gains by settling the mercenaries just south of Bray). This O'Byrne advance into the southern Pale was paralleled by Art's assault upon Wexford in 1401; however, the O'Byrne threat to the Pale evaporated when the mercenaries, led by Tadhg O'Meagher, were annihilated by the Dublin citizens in July/August 1401 at Bloody Bank near Bray. Stung by this reverse, Domhnall O'Byrne submitted to Lord Lieutenant Prince Thomas of Lancaster on 8 November 1401.[43]

In the following years, the Leinster wars reverted to the trends which were emerging during the last thirty years of the fourteenth century. Now that the Irish lordships throughout the province were fairly stable, much of their pressure focused on eroding the Kildare earldom. Art MacMurrough resumed his routine of extracting blackrents from the English towns of East Leinster.[44] At this stage his power and fame was such that there exists a strong possibility that the letter captured from the Welsh leader, Owain Glyndwr, at Waterford in November 1401, urging Irish kings to join him in a struggle against the English, was meant for Art.[45] The Leinster dynasties did not get involved in this grandiose scheme, but they maintained an intense pressure upon Kildare. From the west Murchadh O'Connor Faly and the O'Dempseys continued to push into the earldom. However, English resistance was stubborn. In 1403 they attacked the O'Connor Falys of Offaly and killed three O'Dempsey leaders, while the 5th earl of Kildare cut down Eóghan O'Connor Faly sometime the following year. To the south, Murchadh O'Connor Faly's son-in-law, Giollapádraig O'More of Laois, also made inroads into English territory; he defeated the English in 1404 at Blackford and killed Richard Hardfoot Butler in 1405.[46]

The year 1405 saw a most determined and co-ordinated Irish assault upon the English of Leinster. Again Art MacMurrough was to the fore, ravaging Castledermot, Wexford and Carlow until his fee of 80 marks was paid.[47] In addition, that year it seems his O'Connor Faly cousins burnt the Kildare territory of Oghgard, while the new O'Byrne leader, Donnchadh mac Braen of Newrath, captured

40 ALC, 1400.   **41** Cosgrove, 'Ireland beyond the Pale', p. 581.   **42** *The Book of Howth*, pp 480–1; AConn, 1401.   **43** AConn, 1401. Donnchadh mac Braen's second wife was Siobhan O'Meagher of Ikerrin. See *Cal. papal letters, 1417–31*, vii, p. 343; *Holinshed's Chronicle*, p. 235.   **44** AConn, 1401. See also Frame, 'Two kings', p. 169.   **45** Lydon, *Lordship*, p. 245; Curtis, *Med. Ire.*, fn. 3 p. 286. This suggests Glyndwr had been in Ireland with Richard.   **46** Ó Cléirigh, 'The O'Connor Faly lordship of Offaly, 1395–1513', p. 90; AConn, 1403, 1404; AFM, 1404, 1405.   **47** AFM, 1405.

Newcastle McKynegan.[48] Ó Cléirigh says that 1405 was a watershed year for the embattled English of the midlands. In response to the O'Connor Faly attacks on Kildare and Meath, Ormond, the serving justiciar, in late summer led an another expedition into Offaly, but he, soon afterwards fell ill and died – which probably contributed to the growing O'Connor Faly hegemony over Offaly, western Kildare and Meath.[49]

In 1406, the Irish pressure intensified upon the English settlements in East Leinster (the deaths that year from plague of four nobles of the O'Nolan, O'Toole, MacMurrough and O'Byrne dynasties indicate the close contract of the Irish with the colonists);[50] the ongoing danger of Irish attacks forced the government to launch a series of campaigns to alleviate the pressure on the Pale. That year the Dublin citizens routed a large Irish force, while the prior of Connell defeated 200 Irish on the Kildare plains.[51] These successes laid the groundwork for an offensive against Art. Then Lord Lieutenant Thomas of Lancaster, James Butler (4th earl of Ormond), Thomas fitzJohn Fitzgerald, 6th earl of Desmond, and Prior Thomas Butler of Kilmainham campaigned into the Barrow region to loosen Art's grip there – with some success, for they captured O'Nolan and his son.[52] They failed in their main objective, but this did not prevent them from trying again. During an invasion in late August and early September 1407 of the MacMurrough heartland, Deputy Lieutenant Stephen Scrope (Lancaster's deputy), Ormond and Desmond fought an inconclusive battle with Art. They had one notable victory: in August 1407, after defeating a branch of the O'Kennedys traditionally allied with the Butlers, Tadhg Ailbhle O'Carroll seems to have marched to the aid of Art and on 9 September English forces at Callan destroyed the army of Tadhg Ailbhle and William Burke of Clanwilliam as they tried to enter Leinster.[53] Given the time and place of these events, it would seem that the O'Carrolls and the Clanwilliam Burkes were either coming to Art's aid or were trying to divert government forces away from its campaign against the MacMurroughs.

The perilous condition of the English lordship in Ireland was graphically shown in 1408, when Thomas of Lancaster barely escaped death during a surprise Irish attack upon Kilmainham.[54] All and all, though, Art MacMurrough seems to have weathered this storm and emerged stronger: he was bold enough to level charges of bad faith against the English of Wexford for non-payment of his fee in 1409.[55] Even more worrying for the government was the dramatic collapse of a campaign in 1410 against the O'Byrnes. Instead of bringing them to their knees, half of the troops of Prior Thomas Butler of Kilmainham, Lancaster's deputy, deserted to the Irish, causing him to beat a hasty retreat to the Pale.[56] The power of the Leinster Irish was further demonstrated in 1413, when

48 *Holinshed's Chronicle*, p. 236; AConn, 1405. **49** Ó Cléirigh, 'The O'Connor Faly lordship of Offaly, 1395–1513', p. 90. **50** AClon, AConn, 1406. **51** *Holinshed's Chronicle*, p. 236. **52** *Ancient Irish histories*, ii (*Marleburrough's Chronicle*), p. 21; Dowling, *Annals*, p. 26. **53** *Holinshed's Chronicle*, p. 237; AFM, 1407. **54** AFM, AConn, 1408. **55** Frame, 'Two kings', p. 174; the seneschal of Wexford was appointed to investigate this matter. **56** Dowling,

Art destroyed Wexford and Donnchadh mac Braen O'Byrne defeated an English hosting.[57] As has been outlined, Art's kingship saw the Irish of Leinster reach their territorial and military apex. (In East Leinster, these successes were heavily reliant upon the continuation of good relations between Art and the O'Byrnes.) Towards the end of Art's life there were signs of decline, indicating that his career possibly had over-extended MacMurrough resources. This process was further accelerated through a series of dynastic deaths, misfortunes and the fact that his sons lacked his abilities.[58] Their attempts to maintain Art's kingdom were further doomed to failure by their later bitter divisions. This emerging MacMurrough weakness became clear in 1414, when the English of Wexford burnt much of Idrone and captured Art's son, Gerald MacMurrough. Although Art's eldest son Donnchadh MacMurrough, defeated the raiders to secure his brother's release, it was a sign of decline.[59]

Another factor is important to consider – the fact that during this period, Art and the Butlers became allies. This Butler policy has its origins in the 1330s in north Munster. A linguistic shift is also apparent within the Butlers; for example we find the 3rd earl of Ormond acting as an interpreter in 1395 for the Irish during their submissions to Richard II; also the Butler cadet branch of Dunboyne married increasingly into the ruling family of the O'Dwyers; and there was the marriage of Tadhg Ailbhle O'Carroll and Johanna Butler, daughter of the 2nd earl.[60] As with the Irish of north Munster, the Butlers changed their attitude to the MacMurroughs, grudgingly making the pragmatic decision to accept the loss of territory in Leinster. Instead of waging a continual war with the Leinster nobility, the Butlers now sought allies among their ranks. But this Butler rapprochement with the MacMurroughs was decidedly forced. Its architect may have been Prior Thomas Butler of Kilmainham, half-brother to the 4th earl of Ormond. Lord Lieutenant John Talbot's arrival in Ireland during 1414 could have had something to do with this policy. Talbot, faced by a financially strapped administration, attempted to alleviate this pressure by seeking payment of Ormond of long-standing debts. In February 1415 Ormond was summoned before the exchequer to explain his arrears, and in 1417 Talbot seemingly authorized the seizure of the Butler earldom for non-payment of the arrears.[61] This probably speeded Ormond's quest for Irish allies. The improvement in MacMurrough/Butler relations probably happened before Art's death in 1416/7, being the first real substantive piece of evidence for this rapprochement was the union of Art's son, Donnchadh, and Aveline Butler, Ormond's half-sister;[62] this marriage, which probably took place in 1416/7; heralded an alliance between the MacMurroughs and the Butlers that would last into the sixteenth century.

Annals, p. 27. This records that 800 out of 1500 hired Irish kerne deserted to the O'Byrnes. *Holinshed's Chronicle*, p. 240.   **57** AFM, AConn, 1413.   **58** Art son of Art died in 1414, see AFM, 1414. In 1417 Diarmait Láimhdhearg son of Art died, see AFM, 1417.   **59** AConn, AU, 1414.   **60** Blake-Butler, 'The barony of Dunboyne', 2, no. 3 (October, 1945) pp 80–1; AClon, AFM, 1383 Empey, p. 210.   **61** Griffith, 'The Talbot-Ormond struggle for control of the Anglo-Irish government', pp 376–97.   **62** *COD*, iii, no. 85, p. 70. See H. Nicholas (ed.),

The effects of this alliance were felt throughout Leinster. Talbot's Leinster campaigns of 1415–19 reveal a pattern of aggression against the allies of Art and the Butlers. In 1414 government forces defeated the O'Mores near Kilkea in Kildare,[63] and Talbot's attacks of 1415 upon Giollapádraig O'More, the McKeoghs and the Walshes of the Welsh mountains in Kilkenny may have forced Art to dispatch his son, Gerald, to declare fealty to Henry V.[64] Talbot's expeditions into West Leinster also caused major diplomatic readjustments, as evidenced by Giollapádraig O'More's service later in 1415 on the lord lieutenant's campaign against the MacMahons of Oriel. In this context Art's 1416 devastation of the Wexford liberty belonging to Gilbert Talbot, the lord lieutenant's elder brother, makes some sense.[65] To the north, Donnchadh mac Braen O'Byrne matched the MacMurrough offensive by capturing Wicklow with the aid of Ormond's governor of Arklow and killing Talbot's constable. This indicates that the O'Byrnes were tracking the shift in the king of Leinster's diplomatic policy. Signs of closer relations between the O'Byrnes and the Butlers become clearer when Edward Perrers, a Butler client, was reappointed constable of Wicklow on 27 August 1416.[66] And Talbot's reaction to the fall of Wicklow confirmed the rise in Butler diplomatic influence in East Leinster: Talbot forced Donnchadh mac Braen O'Byrne and Diarmait mac Aodha O'Toole to submit at Castledermot.[67] Shortly, after these events Art died in mysterious circumstances. The annals are divided on the date and manner of his death; one account tells that he died naturally during December 1416, while another records that in January 1417 he and his chief brehon was poisoned by a woman at New Ross. Talbot's involvement is not recorded,[68] but Art's death was an unexpected blessing for the Dublin government.

The improvement in MacMurrough/Butler relations is also evident in West Leinster and north Munster. Allegations of Butler collusion with the O'Connor Falys made by Talbot cast some light upon the nature of midland politics. The Talbot party also claimed that Margaret O'Carroll, An Calbhach O'Connor Faly's wife, had lordship over Ormond's manor of Ougterany. (This is understandable as Margaret was probably a child of the union of Johanna Butler and Tadhg Ailbhle O'Carroll and therefore a cousin of Ormond.[69] Also there was another marital link between the O'Connor Falys and the Butlers: John

Proceedings and ordinances of the privy council, ii (London, 1834), p. 301.   **63** *Holinshed's Chronicle*, p. 241.   **64** AFM, 1415, see also note o. AConn, 1415. This speaks of Furnival's destruction of Laois and Cullentragh Castle. See also *The charters of the abbey of Duiske*, p. 139.   **65** AConn, AFM, AU, 1416. See also Matthew, pp 123–4.   **66** *CPR Hen V, 1416–22*, ii, p. 42. This notes that Wicklow was situated among the O'Brynnes and far distant from any aid of the English. John Liverpool was reappointed as constable of Wicklow on 30 September 1414. There is no mention of him after 1415. Griffith, 'The council in Ireland 1399–1452', p. 152. For the Perrer's appointment, see *CCR. Hen V, 1413–19*, i, p. 317. In 1428 John Perrers was constable of Wicklow castle and was an Ormond supporter. *CPR Hen VI, 1422–29*, i, p. 478.   **67** TCD, MS E.3.18 (581), fol. 54; Nicholls, 'Crioch Branach', p. 21.   **68** AConn, 1416; AU, AFM, 1417. After Art's death a great war broke out between the Irish and English of Leinster, see AFM, 1417.   **69** Gilbert, *Viceroys*, p. 315; AClon, 1383; Empey, p. 210.

Butler of Dunboyne, seneschal of the liberty of Tipperary between 1429 and 1433, was married to Ellen, An Calbhach's sister.) Significantly, MacGillapatrick of North Ossory, the traditional enemy of the Butlers, offered Talbot his services in January 1418 to fight the O'Connor Falys.[70] Moreover, Prior Thomas Butler was accused of parleying with Murchadh O'Connor Faly in May 1418. As the 1422 complaints of James Butler, 4th earl of Ormond, demonstrate, Prior Thomas' parley was at a time when the Butlers were virtually at war with Talbot's government. Indeed, Ormond alleged that, prior to 1419, Talbot instructed Prior Thomas to disband the Butler forces before allowing Tadhg O'Brien of Thomond and Walter Burke attack the defenceless earldom.[71] The prior was canvassing support among the O'Connor Falys, who were openly at war with the king's government. Furthermore, in winter 1416 Talbot antagonized the O'Connor Falys by destroying their castles of Edenderry and Croaghan.[72] However, the first definite proof of an O'Connor Faly/Butler alliance was in May 1418 when Prior Thomas was sheltered from Talbot by Murchadh O'Connor Faly before joining Murchadh's ally, William Ruadh O'Kelly, tanaiste of Uí Maine in Connacht, to besiege the royal castle of Roscommon.

This Butler/O'Connor Faly alliance was further confirmed by events in 1419, when An Calbhach O'Connor Faly gave military assistance to the Butlers: and Talbot later accused Ormond of handing Thomas Talbot, the lieutenant's cousin, to the O'Connor Falys. Clearly, Talbot identified both Donnchadh MacMurrough, the provincial king of Leinster, and An Calbhach as the leading Irish allies of the Butlers. Therefore it is not surprising to find that Talbot was intimately involved in the captures of both men: in May 1419 Donnchadh was captured and dispatched to the Tower of London. Talbot also seems to have organized the kidnapping of An Calbhach (however, An Calbhach escaped).[73] Also in 1419 Talbot led a large army against the O'Tooles after their raid on Ballymore, destroying Castlekevin.[74] He was intent on neutralizing Butler power and the legacy of Art MacMurrough.

70 Otway-Ruthven, *Medieval Ireland*, p. 353; AConn, 1417.   **71** Griffith, 'The Talbot-Ormond Struggle', pp 393–4.   **72** AConn, 1416.   **73** AFM, AConn, 1419. An Calbhach was captured by a son of Libind Freyne who sold him to Talbot, see AU, 1419. Diarmait Láimhdhearg a another son of Art MacMurrough died earlier in 1417, see AConn, AU, 1417.   **74** *Ancient Irish histories*, ii (*Marleburrough's Chronicle*), pp 27–8; *Holinshed's Chronicle*, pp 242–3.

CHAPTER 7

The Butlers and the Leinstermen, 1420–70

After the death of Art MacMurrough, the greatest medieval king of Leinster, the decline of MacMurroughs was rapid. The reasons for this are complex, one being Donnchadh, who clearly did not enjoy his father's influence with the Leinster nobility. Symptomatic of this decline was the MacMurrough/Butler alliance of about 1416/17, a union that utterly transformed the political complexion of Leinster, marking the start of greater integration of Irish and English interests in Leinster. The MacMurrough decline was accelerated when Talbot captured Donnchadh (1419), and sent him to the Tower of London – a confinement that lasted until 1427.[1] Donnchadh's capture had three major long-lasting effects: it split the MacMurroughs until 1447 into two rival camps; it damaged their relationships with the O'Connor Falys and the O'Byrnes; and it allowed Ormond to deconstruct Art's diplomatic nexus by winning over former MacMurrough allies.

By 1420 when Ormond returned from France as justiciar, MacMurrough weakness became even clearer.[2] Ormond realized that Art's network of alliances was rapidly breaking down, and he saw that this spelt danger for his government of Ireland and for his earldom. Another consequence of MacMurrough decline was the emergence of Art's stronger allies – particularly An Calbhach O'Connor Faly in West Leinster and the O'Byrnes, who nursed aspirations to the provincial kingship. Ormond therefore sought to maintain good relations with both these dynasties. Ormond now launched a new initiative in Leinster. By confronting the MacMurroughs, he demonstrated his ability to govern but also a desire to utilize them under his suzerainty. He concentrated his efforts in the strategic Barrow conduit where the Irish polities of East and West Leinster met: Art MacMurrough had built his success upon the control of this region, Ormond attempted to do likewise. Indeed, Holinshed's *Irish Chronicle* records that Ormond defeated MacMurrough in 1420: this cannot refer to Donnchadh, Ormond's imprisoned brother-in-law; it must mean Gerald MacMurrough, Donnchadh's brother and deputy. Ormond's later campaigns in this region confirm his intent to reopen the Barrow highway; he seized from the O'Dempseys the strategically important Lea castle and returned it to Kildare.[3]

---

1 AFM, AConn, 1419; *Proceedings and ordinances of the privy council*, ii, p. 301. This source preserves a letter from Donnchadh to Henry V, petitioning for his release from the Tower during 1421. **2** *Holinshed's Irish Chronicle*, p. 243. **3** Ibid. In this text MacMurrough is called

Ormond's successful campaign of 7–11 June 1421 against the O'Mores bears similar hallmarks.[4] His victory was a result of good timing, for he campaigned at a time when the O'More leadership was uncertain. Giollapádraig mac Fachtna seemingly died in the late 1410s, but the identity of his successor is unsure.[5] To the north of Laois, the O'Connor Faly dynasty, allies of the Butlers, was also in crisis. In summer 1421 Murchadh O'Connor Faly died after defending the weak O'More lordship against a de la Freyne/MacGillapatrick expedition. Before his death Murchadh alienated his son, An Calbhach, by appointing his own brother, Diarmait, king of Offaly. But the declaration of the Annals of Connacht in 1422 of An Calbhach's kingship of Offaly indicates tension between him and Diarmait – the reigning king.[6] This strife was short-lived, for both parties seemingly came to an understanding, leaving Diarmait as nominal king and An Calbhach as the most powerful of his name – a situation that was clarified when An Calbhach defied the invasion of the midlands by James Fitzgerald, 7th earl of Desmond, challenging him to attack Offaly.[7] Ormond's success in the Barrow region was due to his ability to capitalize upon the dynastic troubles besetting these three dynasties. A testimony to the revival of government power there was Ormond's inspection in June 1421 of the Barrow's defences.[8]

Ormond's alliance-building among the Leinster Irish was a continuation of the strategy of his half-brother, Prior Thomas Butler of Kilmainham. His pursuit of this strategy transformed his dynasty's role in both parts of Leinster, securing his position greatly against his enemy, the lord lieutenant John Talbot. Ormond's alliances with the Irish of West Leinster also had the effect of releasing pressure upon the northern and western borders of his earldom, solidifying his midland frontiers. His fear of Talbot was well justified. On 10 April 1422 Ormond's lieutenancy expired and he was replaced in November as justiciar by Talbot's brother, Archbishop Richard of Dublin. Ordered to England to answer Talbot's charges of misgovernance, Ormond arrived there in early summer 1423.[9] Significantly, his departure from office was greeted by an unprecedented avalanche of Irish violence directed at the interim justiciar, William fitzThomas Butler, and the Talbots. Prominent in these events was Gerald MacMurrough, who plundered Talbot's liberty of Wexford and destroyed Wexford town (the Wicklow Irish also seem to have been involved). Additionally, the O'Tooles raided the Dublin and Kildare marches throughout summer. In June Gerald MacMurrough, Donnchadh mac Braen O'Byrne and the O'Connor Falys evinced a desire to submit, but only Gerald MacMurrough did so in fact.[10]

Art; Dowling, *Annals*, p. 28.   **4** Ibid., p. 246; Dowling, *Annals*, p. 29; *Original letters illustrative of English history*, i, pp 31–2; Matthew, pp 136–8.   **5** There are two possible candidates for the O'More leader – a Fachtna (*viv.*1449) and a Cétach (*d.*1464). On the whole, Fachtna may be the more likely candidate. See Curtis, 'Richard, duke of York', p. 167.   **6** AFM, 1421; AConn, 1421, 1422; Ó Cléirigh, 'The O'Connor Faly lordship of Offaly, 1395–1513', p. 90; Matthew, p. 162.   **7** Cosgrove, 'Ireland beyond the Pale, 1399–1460', p. 571.   **8** Matthew, p. 138. **9** Ibid., p. 140; Otway-Ruthven, *Medieval Ireland*, p. 362.   **10** Ibid., p. 154; *Rot. pat. Hib*, no. 22, p. 225; Cosgrove, 'The emergence of the Pale, 1399–1447', pp 543–5; Otway-Ruthven,

The violence after Ormond's departure for England was not confined to East Leinster. In West Leinster, the O'Mores and An Calbhach made parallel raids in 1422–3. An Calbhach's power during Ormond's absence mushroomed; we find him raiding Meath with the O'Reillys and Berminghams in 1423.[11] An Calbhach's position was strengthened by his connections with both Irish and English lords in Connacht and Ulster. Examples of his alliance-building are the prestigious marriage (before 1424) of his daughter Fionnuála to Niall Garbh O'Donnell of Donegal, while another daughter, Mór, married MacWilliam Burke of Clanrickard.[12] Recognizing the power of the O'Connor Falys, Talbot concluded on 27 March 1425 an indenture with An Calbhach, by terms of which An Calbhach promised to restore lands to the English, to cease levying blackrent upon Meath and to pay a 1,000 mark fine.[13] This arrangement was soon disregarded. In 1426 An Calbhach again raided Meath, and he went on to burn Mullingar with Hubert Tyrrell in September 1427.[14] His connections with Niall Garbh O'Donnell also drew him into an alliance with the Clandeboy O'Neills. Inevitably, these northern alliances placed him at odds with the Great O'Neill dynasty of Tyrone. After 1427, Niall Garbh O'Donnell allied with the Clandeboy O'Neills against the O'Neills of Tyrone. The ramifications of An Calbhach's Ulster alliances only became clear in 1430 when he submitted with other midland lords to Eóghan O'Neill of Tyrone during the latter's circuit of the region.[15]

In East Leinster after 1424 Ormond's position was threatened by dynastic rivalries within that polity. Donnchadh mac Braen O'Byrne, seeing MacMurrough weakness as his opportunity, clashed during the late 1410s and early 1420s with the O'Connor Falys in Kildare, but the combatants seem to have concluded a shaky peace through the marriage before 1421 of Donnchadh mac Braen's son, Murchadh, to Joan O'Connor Faly.[16] Donnchadh's ambition soured relations between himself and his son-in-law, Gerald MacMurrough.[17] Furthermore, on 10 April 1425 Donnchadh confirmed his indenture of 1424 with Earl Edmund Mortimer of March, lord lieutenant of Ireland, by entering into an agreement with Talbot, now lord lieutenant, recognizing the jurisdiction of Archbishop Talbot within his domains and, importantly, agreeing to protect the tenants of the Talbot liberty of Wexford – a clear challenge to the MacMurroughs.[18] When Ormond replaced Talbot as lord lieutenant three weeks later, on 28 April 1425, the earl endeavoured to reverse Talbot's inroads. Because of governmental commitments elsewhere, Ormond was not to turn to the affairs of the Leinster

Medieval Ireland, pp 362–3. **11** Cosgrove, 'Ireland beyond the Pale, 1399–1460', p. 571. **12** Empey, pp 589–90; AFM, 1452. **13** *Rot. pat. Hib*, no. 112, p. 238b; Cosgrove, 'Ireland beyond the Pale, 1399–1460', p. 571; Otway-Ruthven, *Medieval Ireland*, p. 364. **14** AConn, 1426; Cosgrove, 'Ireland beyond the Pale, 1399–1460', pp 571–2; *Rot. pat. Hib*, no. 32, p. 246. **15** AFM, 1430, 1447. For Fionnuala's dispensation to marry Aodh Buidhe O'Neill. See *Cal. papal letters*, ix, p. 97; Empey, pp 592, 760; Cosgrove, 'Ireland beyond the Pale, 1399–1460', p. 573. **16** *Cal papal letters*, vii, p. 221. **17** O'Byrne, 'The rise of the Gabhal Raghnaill' p. 56; *Cal papal letters*, viii, p. 78; see Nicholls, 'The Kavanaghs' (1977), p. 436. **18** *Rot. Pat. Hib*, no. 113, p. 238; O'Byrne, 'The Uí Bhroin of Co. Wicklow', pp 84–5; Lydon, *Lordship*, p. 241;

Irish until the last third of the year, when he took the submissions of Diarmait O'Toole and Donnchadh mac Braen O'Byrne on 8 August and 6 December respectively. No military pressure seems to have been brought to bear upon the O'Byrnes: not only did Donnchadh declare himself a liege subject of Henry V, but he acknowledged that he was Ormond's man and promised to protect merchants entering his lordship;[19] in return, Ormond promised that as long as the O'Byrnes observed the peace, they were entitled to his protection.

Ormond's favouring of the O'Byrnes possibly contributed to MacMurrough insecurity. As part of his dual policy of good government and self-interest, Ormond took the field in autumn 1426 against Gerald MacMurrough,[20] but in fact he achieved reconciliation by means of negotiation. Ormond's policy had visible results in East Leinster, resulting in the lodgment in August of O'Toole hostages in Dublin Castle without a campaign.[21] So, it would seen that the O'Byrne/Butler alliance and Ormond's probable arrangement with Gerald not only strengthened the earl's position in East Leinster but improved the relations among the Irish nobility, thawing out the frosty relations between Donnchadh mac Braen and his MacMurrough son-in-law. This renewal of the old MacMurrough/ O'Byrne alliance may have been sealed with the marriage of Murchadh, Donnchadh mac Braen's son, to an Uná Kavanagh, possibly Gerald's sister.[22]

Gerald and Donnchadh mac Braen confirmed their membership of Ormond's party after the arrival on 31 July 1427 of John, Lord Grey, which resulted in the termination of Ormond's lord-lieutenantship and his embarkation for England. Ormond did not take his loss of power easily. Gerald MacMurrough, Donnchadh mac Braen and Diarmait O'Toole now began raiding again. Late in 1427 the archbishop of Armagh wrote to the English government, informing them that this triumvirate with 3,000 troops had invaded Talbot's liberty of Wexford, Carlow, Kildare, and Meath, taking the towns of Connell and Castledermot. When Grey made peace with them after the fall of Castledermot, his entourage included Donnchadh MacMurrough, Ormond's brother-in-law. Although the Annals of Ulster mention that Donnchadh was ransomed by his province in 1427, many of the Leinster nobility, however, were not glad to see him.[23] Donnchadh's return changed Ormond's policy in Leinster; he now became anxious for Donnchadh to regain his position, and ignored Gerald. Cosgrove argues that to aid Donnchadh's bid to recover his kingdom, the English granted him a fee in July 1427 of 80 marks in the hope that he would be strong enough to curb his brother and Donnchadh mac Braen O'Byrne.[24] The change in Ormond's policy becomes evident after his return to Ireland during summer

Otway-Ruthven, *Medieval Ireland*, p. 364.   **19** Matthew, pp 191–2. See also ibid., appendix III, no. i, pp 574–6.   **20** Ibid., p. 201; Otway-Ruthven, *Medieval Ireland*, p. 365.   **21** Otway-Ruthven, *Medieval Ireland*, p. 365; *Rot. pat. Hib*, no. 119, p. 239.   **22** *Cal papal letters*, vii, p. 519. **23** *Reg Swayne*, pp 109–10. See also *Rot. pat. Hib*, no. 34, p. 246; Cosgrove, 'The emergence of the Pale, 1399–1447', p. 544; AU, 1427; AFM, 1428.   **24** *Rot. pat. Hib*, no. 31, p. 246; Cosgrove, 'The emergence of the Pale, 1399–1447', p. 544.

1428. By that autumn Donnchadh MacMurrough and the lord lieutenant, John Sutton, an ally of Ormond, were campaigning against the O'Byrnes. Any remaining doubts of Donnchadh MacMurrough's attachment to Ormond were dispelled by his attack upon the earldom of Kildare, burning Naas on 26 September 1429.[25] MacMurrough's assault had much to do with the continuing struggle between the Talbot and Ormond parties. At this time Ormond and his ally, Sutton, were under sustained attack from the Talbot faction within the government who sent charges to England concerning the earl's behaviour.[26] Moreover, the 5th earl of Kildare was allied to the Talbot faction through the marriage of his daughter, Elizabeth Fitzgerald, to Grey – a Talbot supporter. Soon afterwards, in the winter of 1429–30, Ormond left for England again.

In Ormond's absence, there was an upsurge in Irish violence – probably in sympathy with him. As for Donnchadh MacMurrough, he established himself to some degree within the MacMurrough heartland but needed Butler support. Because of his sack of Naas and the absence from Ireland of both Sutton and Ormond, the royal service proclaimed in 1430 at Mullaghmast was probably directed against him.[27] Donnchadh MacMurrough was only to regain his kingdom when Gerald died in 1431.[28] After this, deep rifts opened between the O'Byrnes and Donnchadh MacMurrough. Predictably, Donnchadh's reign was characterized by wars with the O'Byrnes and an unhealthy dependence on Ormond. Furthermore Donnchadh mac Braen O'Byrne's alienation from Ormond and Donnchadh MacMurrough was clear from his non-attendance on the latter's raid with Diarmait O'Toole into the Dublin marches in 1431 and his absence from the MacMurrough victory of 1432.[29]

In 1432 Ormond returned from England and set about immediately re-establishing his influence. During his absence, his power within the midlands and West Leinster had weakened because of continual Irish attack. The Four Masters record that he defeated Máelruanaidh mac Taidhg O'Carroll of Ely in 1432, breaking down his two castles. Seemingly Donnchadh MacMurrough supported this reassertion of power by Ormond, his brother-in-law. (In that year Donnchadh was mentioned as capturing Walter Tobin, a leading English figure in the southern Tipperary cantred of Comsey).[30] After forcing the O'Carrolls to submit and the re-establishing of his writ in Tipperary, Ormond took a longer view in the midlands. While the Ormond earldom was strong enough to weather Irish assaults, the neighbouring earldom of Kildare was verging on disintegration. Ormond realized that the prospect of the Kildare earldom fracturing under Irish pressure would threaten the stability of his own earldom. While the government in 1430 had allocated funds for the refortification of the Kildare marches, the Irish pressure upon Kildare was becoming irresistible.[31] Evidence of this is

25 *Stat. Ire., Hen VI*, pp 36–9; Price, *Placenames*, p. lxxviii. **26** Matthew, pp 241–6. **27** Otway-Ruthven, *Medieval Ireland*, p. 369; Frame, 'The defence of the English lordship, 1250–1450', map 4.3, p. 81. **28** Cosgrove, 'The emergence of the Pale 1339–1447', p. 544; AFM, 1431; Nicholls, 'Late medieval Irish annals' (1430), p. 99. **29** AFM, 1431, 1432; O'Byrne, 'The rise of the Gabhal Raghnaill', p. 57. **30** *MacFirbis' Annals*, 1444, 1448; Cosgrove, 'Ireland beyond the Pale, 1399–1460', p. 582. **31** *Stat. Ire., Hen VI*, pp 32–5.

Margaret O'Carroll's feasts at Killeigh and Rathangan during 1433: the fact that these actually occurred succinctly demonstrates the Kildare decline, as Rathangan belonged to the earl of Kildare; moreover, the fact that Margaret could be so bountiful during a year of famine indicates that the O'Connor Falys had access to considerable resources and that the wider Irish midland world enjoyed a considerable degree of stability. In 1433 we find Cathaoir O'Connor Faly attempting to extract blackrents from Kildare town.[32] Also, Tullow and Lea castles fell after 1435 to the O'Byrnes and O'Dempseys respectively, while Castledermot was destroyed about 1443.[33] Although Ormond was on friendly enough terms with An Calbhach, the latter's success at the expense of Kildare was unpalatable.

In autumn 1432, Ormond married Elizabeth Fitzgerald, daughter and heiress of Gerald Fitzgerald, 5th earl of Kildare[34] (and ironically the widow of Lord Grey, Ormond's former enemy). Through his wife, Ormond became the protector of the Kildare earldom upon the death of the earl on 13 October 1432, acquiring two-thirds of it while one-third went to the widowed countess.[35] This was seemingly achieved with the blessing of Kildare, who realized his earldom's perilous condition: his brother and successor, John, would die soon after him,[36] and the next in line, Thomas fitzMaurice Fitzgerald, Kildare's grandnephew, was still a minor. As part of the deal, Ormond seems to have undertaken to foster and educate Thomas fitzMaurice in his household and marry him to his second daughter, Elizabeth. But in the process of acquiring control of these Kildare lands, Ormond ignored the 5th earl's entail of 1397 (this entail was an attempt by Kildare to distribute various lands among his brothers and nephews). Understandably, Ormond's actions outraged these Fitzgeralds.[37]

While Ormond profited personally from his marriage, it did improve the defence of the English lordship. Significantly, Ormond's deputy, the prior of Kilmainham, assisted by the English of Meath, inflicted a defeat upon An Calbhach in 1436 (this prompted a struggle in 1437 between An Calbhach and his brother Cathaoir, who had English support).[38] Also, Ormond's resurgence in the midlands, his Kildare marriage and the MacMurrough alliance checked his opponents in East Leinster. Donnchadh mac Braen O'Byrne was now surrounded by either Butler allies or Butler-held territory. In response, he prudently avoided trouble, nursing his lordship to his death in 1434. Edmund O'Byrne, his brother and successor, was also alienated from Ormond and Donnchadh MacMurrough, even though he bore a traditional Butler forename and was

---

32 AFM, AConn, 1433; *Rot. pat. Hib*, no. 94, p. 258b.   33 Ellis, *Tudor frontiers*, p. 111. This was confirmed in 1531 by the letter of Piers Butler, earl of Ossory, stating that Tullow had been in the hands of the Irish for the previous 200 years, see *S.P. Hen VIII, 1515–38*, pp 153–4; *Cal. papal letters*, ix, pp 241, 330; *Cal. papal letters*, xii, p. 137; Ó Cléirigh, 'The O'Connor Faly lordship of Offaly, 1395–1513', pp 92–3.   34 AFM, 1452. Elizabeth's death is dated to 6 August 1452.   35 *COD*, iii, no. 99, p. 82. On 18 July 1432 Henry VI licensed Elizabeth to marry Ormond.   36 Ibid., p. 86.   37 *Red Bk Kildare*, no. 158, pp146–7; Frame, *Eng Lordship*, p. 24; *COD*, iii, no. 101, pp 83–5.   38 AConn, 1436; AFM, 1437; Ó Cléirigh, 'The O'Connor Faly lordship of Offaly, 1395–1513', p. 93.

probably a brother-in-law of the MacMurrough.[39] That said, Edmund was never in the Talbot camp, either, but, from the 1430s he actively supported the enemies of the Butlers such as Thomas fitzMaurice Fitzgerald, the Kildare heir.[40] Initially however, Ormond and Thomas fitzMaurice were friendly, as the young Fitzgerald heir spent some time living in the earl's household. Over time, relations declined, culminating in Ormond's banishment of Thomas fitzMaurice from Kildare, probably before Ormond's departure in winter 1434–5 for England.[41]

Ormond's trouble with Thomas FitzMaurice Fitzgerald was a separate thing from his feud with Talbot. The source of Thomas' rancour towards Ormond was the latter's appropriation of the Kildare lands. Their dispute crucially influenced provincial politics during this period. After his expulsion from Kildare about 1434/5, Thomas found refuge among those Leinster nobles disaffected with Ormond; these included the O'Byrnes, O'Mores, O'Tooles and Cathaoir O'Connor Faly, the disgruntled brother of An Calbhach. In aligning himself with these lords, Thomas ound a ready-made support base to challenge Ormond. He appears to have bound himself to the O'Mores, marrying first Dorothea, daughter of Uaithne mac Giollapádraig O'More.[42] In a sense, he modelled his later network of alliances upon Ormond's earlier system. Herein, maybe, lies the genesis of the later Kildare party in Leinster. The first public sign of Fitzgerald dissatisfaction came in 1439, when at Kilcock in Kildare the brothers of Prior Thomas Fitzgerald of Kilmainham and Cathaoir O'Connor Faly captured William Welles, deputy of the lord lieutenant, Lionel Welles – Ormond's ally.[43] Furthermore Thomas fitzMaurice's O'More marriage connected him to another anti-Ormondist force – the O'Byrnes. The most active young warlord of this dynasty at this time was Donnchadh mac Braen's son, Braen of Newrath. Not insignificantly this Braen was married to Elizabeth O'More;[44] while Elizabeth's parentage remains obscure, she and Dorothea were at least cousins, if not sisters. Therefore Thomas fitzMaurice Fitzgerald and Braen were possibly brothers-in-law. One thing is certain: though before September 1440 they were both terrorizing the Pale, burning the Kilgobbin lands of the Walshes. Accordingly, they were both outlawed on 6 September. One of the reasons for Thomas fitzMaurice's

39 O'Byrne, 'The rise of the Gabhal Raghnaill', pp 56–60; RIA MSS 1233 (23/Q/10) An Leabhar Donn, f. 11. **40** *COD*, iii, no. 135, p. 119; *CPR, 1441–46*, iv, p. 97; *A roll of the proceedings of the king's council in Ireland, 1392–93*, pp 303–4. **41** Pender, 'O'Clery', para. 2221, p. 183. John Cam, Thomas fitzMaurice's father, may have died already. Thomas fitzMaurice was not recognized as earl until 1455. **42** Matthew, p. 471; Fitzgerald, 'Historical notes on the O'Mores and their territory of Leix', appendix x. Although in later years he was to repudiate her. Interestingly the compilers of the Four Masters referred to the 8th earl of Kildare as Gearoid mac Tomais Uí Morda, see AFM, 1493. **43** Matthew, p. 284, see also pp 274–5, 347; AFM, 1439; *Rot. pat. Hib*, no. 11, p. 262. **44** Genealogia Joannis Byrne Armigeri apud Burdigalam in Galliarum Regna, Microfilm of Ms 162, reel; no. 971, Pos 8301. Conn O'Connor Faly, lord of Offaly (1458–1471), was also married to a daughter of O'More – probably Cétach. See *MacFirbis' Annals*, AConn, 1462.

alliance with the O'Byrnes and also the O'Tooles was their impressive military strength – evidenced by their destruction in 1442 of a large English hosting.[45]

Although Thomas fitzMaurice was pardoned in March 1442 by Henry VI for his offences,[46] his activities and those of his allies forced Ormond to shore up his position yet again in West Leinster and the midlands. His new midland policy was directed at the O'Carrolls of Ely and was similar to those adopted with the O'Connor Falys and the MacMurroughs. As usual, marriage lay at the heart of this latest realignment. Ormond ensured future O'Carroll attachment to the Butlers by arranging a double marriage alliance with the family of Máelruanaidh mac Taidhg O'Carroll. Playing an important role in Ormond's latest scheme was the Butler family of Polestown, whose manor lay astride the strategic junction from Gowran and Kilkenny to Carlow; they were very much a frontier family, living upon the pressurized northern frontiers of the Ormond earldom, facing the O'Carroll, MacGillapatrick, and the O'More lordships. In 1440 the head of the Polestown family was Edmund MacRichard Butler, Ormond's lieutenant entrusted with the earldom's defences during the earl's absences from Ireland. For Ormond, it was therefore imperative that Edmund MacRichard's family conclude marriage alliances to stabilize the northern borders. About 1440 Edmund MacRichard and his sister Mary respectively married Gylys (Catherine) and Seán, children of Máelruanaidh O'Carroll.[47] The drawing of Seán O'Carroll into the Butler nexus reveals long-range planning, as Seán succeeded his father as O'Carroll overlord in 1443 upon the latter's death. Also marriage into the Irish nobility was a natural progression for Edmund MacRichard, as his own mother was an O'Reilly. There was another level to this Butler alliance-building: it not only bound the O'Carrolls to the Butlers but it also drew the O'Connor Falys, O'Kennedys and the MacGeoghegans closer.[48]

This Butler policy cannot but have immeasurably strengthened their position in West Leinster, allowing them to adopt a much harder line against their enemies within the region – particularly the MacGillapatricks, O'Mores and Fitzgeralds of Kildare. This Butler tacking resulted from the re-emergence in north Munster and the midlands of the influence of James Fitzgerald, 7th earl of Desmond. The first mention of Desmond's resurgence comes in 1440, coinciding roughly with the formation of the Butler/O'Carroll alliance. Then Desmond, with MacGillapatrick of North Ossory, successfully defended the O'Mores from an O'Connor Faly onslaught.[49] Desmond's alliance with MacGillapatricks and the O'Mores (two dynasties with long histories of hostility to the Butlers) indicates that he was building a client base to oppose Ormond's growing influence in the midlands. MacGillapatrick's dealings with Desmond were to cost him dear, as the alarmed citizens of Kilkenny invaded his country and pulled down

---

45 *COD*, iii, no. 135, p. 119; AFM, 1442.   46 *CPR, 1441–46*, iv, p. 97.   47 *COD*, iii, no. 191, p. 175, no. 234, p. 212; Pender, 'O'Clery', para 2045, p. 158; Empey, p. 387.   48 *MacFirbis' Annals*, 1443, 1445, 1454. Lodge, *Peerage*, ii, pp 13–14.   49 AFM, 1440; Cosgrove, 'Ireland beyond the Pale, 1399–1460', p. 582.

his castle of Cullahill before July 1441. Whether Desmond's actions were connected to the struggle between Ormond and the Fitzgeralds of Kildare is uncertain;
more likely, they can be traced to the gradual breakdown of Ormond's alliance
with Desmond. Earlier, in an indenture dated 10 May 1429, both earls proposed
a marriage alliance between Ormond's daughter Anne and Thomas, Desmond's
son; Empey suggests that this was fuelled by their mutual fear of Talbot. The
proposed marriage alliance was to never come to fruition. The first cracks may
have appeared after Anne's death in 1434, but Ormond substituted another
daughter, Elizabeth.[50] While outright hostility between Ormond and Desmond
did not break out until 1444, the pressure for conflict was building.

Edmund MacRichard Butler, as Ormond's deputy, was a ruthless enforcer,
who played a crucial part in the political maelstrom gathering in West Leinster
and the midlands. It was his actions in 1443 that drew the various anti-Butler
parties together. The security afforded him by the O'Carroll alliance made him
bold enough to attack the MacGillapatricks. Thus, in 1443 he summoned
Fionnán and Diarmait MacGillapatrick to Kilkenny and had them beaten to
death before going on to sack North Ossory. Shortly afterwards he defeated a
confederation of MacGillapatricks, O'Mores, some O'Carrolls, Fitzgeralds of
Kildare as well as Cathaoir and Conn O'Connor Faly at Slieveardagh in east
Tipperary.[51] (The surprising involvement of Conn O'Connor Faly, An Calbhach's
son, may be explained by his father's inability to control him. The O'Connor
Faly/Butler friendship in fact still held firm, as evidenced by Ormond's
patronage that year of the Berminghams, An Calbhach's allies in his attack on
Meath that year.) However, Edmund MacRichard's victory was pyrrhic, for the
O'Mores routed the Butlers in Kilkenny later that year.

The destabilization of the midlands also affected the Irish polity of East
Leinster, where the provincial kingship of Ormond's brother-in-law, Donnchadh
MacMurrough, was weakening, as was, indeed, his leadership of his own
dynasty.[52] Worse still, Edmund O'Byrne also seemingly fanned the ambitions of
the sons of Gerald MacMurrough. Confirmation that the Wicklow Irish were at
the centre of opposition to Ormond in Leinster came in 1443, when we find
Prior Thomas Fitzgerald of Kilmainham seeking O'Toole and O'Byrne aid to
kidnap his Ormond-sponsored rivals. Probably as result of Prior Thomas'
activities and also because of Fitzgerald involvement in the 1443 assault upon the
Ormond earldom, in 1443–4 Ormond imprisoned Prior Thomas at Dublin.
Dramatically, Thomas fitzMaurice Fitzgerald and his allies humiliated Ormond's
administration by attacking Dublin Castle and helping Prior Thomas to escape
to England to present charges against Ormond's governance of Ireland.[53]
Ormond's position in East Leinster now worsened. In 1444, the apple of discord

---

50 *COD*, iii, no. 88, pp 72–3; Cosgrove, 'Ireland beyond the Pale, 1399–1460', p. 582; Empey,
p. 273.   **51** *MacFirbis' Annals*, 1443, 1462; AConn, 1462.   **52** AFM, 1442. See also Nicholls,
'The Kavanaghs' (1981), p. 189.   **53** *A roll of the proceeding of the king's council in Ireland,
1392–1393*, pp 303–4; *COD*, iii, pp 142–3.

ripened among the MacMurroughs. Against a background of considerable violence in the midlands, Gerald's sons revolted against Donnchadh; this upsurge in violence may have been connected to the recall of Ormond in 1444 by Henry VI to face the charges laid by Prior Thomas and Treasurer Thorndon. Again Donnchadh was forced to rely on mercenaries to maintain himself.[54] In 1444, the political volatility in West Leinster ignited East Leinster. At its heart was a war in Slieveardagh between Desmond and Ormond. In preparation for this struggle Desmond cultivated support among the Leinster nobility.[55] Ormond's position was further weakened by the rebellion of Walter Tobin of Comsey and the Butlers of Cahir,[56] the main result of which was Ormond's decision to make a truce with Desmond – lasting one year. Ormond was careful to ensure that this truce was in place before his departure for England after September. It was a truce that Desmond turned to his advantage by using it to ally with MacGillapatrick, O'More and Domhnall Riabhach, a son of Gerald MacMurrough. (The emergence of Domhnall Riabhach MacMurrough-Kavanagh was a most significant event in the politics of this period. His ability to form an alliance with Desmond suggests considerable government weakness.)

Donnchadh MacMurrough's kingship of the Irish of Leinster was further hobbled when Ormond's deputy, Richard Nugent, Baron Delvin, was replaced in January 1445 by Archbishop Richard Talbot. (This was not part of the Ormond/Talbot feud as that had been ended by both parties the previous year, resulting in the marriage of Ormond's daughter Elizabeth to John Talbot's son.) John Talbot, now earl of Shrewsbury, was appointed lord lieutenant in 1446 – a development that probably encouraged the enemies of Ormond and Donnchadh to attack them before Talbot arrived. Talbot was determined to stamp out the last embers of his feud with Ormond, but Ormond's enemies were equally determined to damage the Butler party. Predictably, war broke out during 1446 in East Leinster between the O'Byrnes and Donnchadh. The O'Byrnes had the best of it, killing a prominent MacMurrough noble and raiding Uí Cheinnselaig by sea.[57] The problems for Donnchadh continued as the sons of Gerald (in alliance with Desmond) expanded their power with relative impunity in Leinster. The first signs of a concord between Domhnall Riabhach MacMurrough and Desmond appeared in 1445, when his forces attacked English lords in Leinster and Munster, probably Butler clients.[58] In 1446 Domhnall Riabhach joined with Desmond to exploit Ormond's absence from Ireland by launching devastating attacks upon Butler lands in Tipperary and Kilkenny. Such was the power of this combination that Edmund MacRichard Butler could not stop them. The plight of Ormond's deputy was not helped by the fact that the junior Butlers and the Tobins aided Desmond.[59]

---

54 Matthew, pp 356–7; *MacFirbis' Annals*, 1444; see also Nicholls, 'Late medieval Irish annals' (1443, 1445), p. 99.   55 Empey, p. 273; Nicholls, 'Late medieval Irish annals' (1444), p. 87. 56 *MacFirbis' Annals*, 1444, 1448; Beresford, 'The Butlers in England and Ireland, 1405–1515', p. 125.   57 AFM, 1446; RIA MSS 1233 (23/Q/10): An Leabhar Donn, f. 11.   58 PRO E101/248/15; Griffiths, *The reign of Henry VI*, p. 418; *MacFirbis' Annals*, 1445.   59 PRO

Talbot arrived in Ireland during summer 1446, and campaigned widely in Ulster and Leinster the following winter. (It appears from the petitions of the communities of Kilkenny and Tipperary in January 1447 that one of the attacks upon the Butler earldom occurred before Talbot's arrival.)[60] The submissions secured by Talbot in winter 1446–7 illustrate that he behaved even-handedly towards both the allies and enemies of Ormond. In Leinster, Donnchadh MacMurrough, An Calbhach O'Connor Faly, Fachtna O'More, O'Dempsey and O'Nolan submitted, while, oddly, no submission was asked of Edmund O'Byrne or Theobald O'Toole.[61] Another sign of Talbot's desire to publicly proclaim the end of the feud with Ormond was the ordinances of his parliament of January 1447, when he outlawed Thomas fitzMaurice Fitzgerald,[62] an action that must have strengthened Ormond's claim to the lands of Kildare earldom. But the experiences of 1446 convinced the Butlers to change their policy in Leinster. Sometime early in 1447 Donnchadh MacMurrough (perhaps encouraged by Edmund MacRichard Butler) came to terms with his nephews, seemingly recognizing Domhnall Riabhach as his successor. This detached him from the anti-Butler host and ended the budding ascendancy of Edmund O'Byrne in East Leinster. Because of the reconciliation of Donnchadh and Domhnall Riabhach, Edmund's successor Dúnlaing mac Gerald was unable to exploit his advantage. By 1447 this change of direction was evident when Domhnall Riabhach's brother Art and Edmund MacRichard were captured by Walter Tobin of Comsey and Butlers of Cahir.[63]

After his release, Edmund MacRichard changed his attitude to the MacGilla-patricks. This shift was probably speeded up by Ormond's return from England in early 1449. This latest U-turn saw Fionnán MacGillapatrick marry a daughter of Edmund MacRichard Butler about 1448/9.[64] (Edmund MacRichard's diplo-matic acrobatics probably would not have been possible without MacMurrough assistance.) This Fionnán was probably the offspring of Fionnán MacGillapatrick and Sadhbh MacMurrough, Art MacMurrough's daughter. This would have made him a nephew of Donnchadh and first cousin to Domhnall Riabhach. The resurgence of the Butler party is confirmed by the response of Pope Nicholas V in 1450 to an earlier petition of the abbot of Graiguenamanagh. In it, the abbot had complained of the plundering by Ormond, Donnchadh, Domhnall Riabhach, Domhnall O'Ryan and a Tadhg MacGillapatrick.[65] Nicholas V ordered the bishops of Ossory and Leighlin and the abbot of Laois (Abbeyleix) to summon the earl and his accomplices before them to determine the truth of

E101/248/15; Empey, pp 258, 275, 321.   **60** Empey, pp 273–4. Also the people of Carrick on Suir in 1450 stated that their town had been attacked by English rebels twice in the previous fifteen years. See *Stat. Ire., Hen VI*, pp 243–5; Empey, p. 278.   **61** *MacFirbis' Annals*, 1446; Matthew, p. 393.   **62** *Stat. Ire., Hen VI*, pp 94–5; see note. 2, p. 94.   **63** *MacFirbis' Annals*, 1447.   **64** Lawlor, 'Calendar of the Liber Ruber of the diocese of Ossory', p. 170; Edwards, 'The MacGiollapádraigs (Fitzpatricks) of Upper Ossory', p. 329; for Fionnán see Pender 'O'Clery', para 1785, p. 134. He is described as 'Finghin na cul choilledh'.   **65** *Cal. papal letters*, x, pp 497–8; see Lawlor, 'Calendar of the Liber Ruber of the diocese of Ossory', p. 170.

the accusations. This shift in the regional balance had the effect of isolating the Tobins of Comsey and the Butlers of Cahir, contributing to the relative ease of Edmund MacRichard's victory in 1448 over them. The equality of the MacMurrough/Butler partnership was affirmed about 1449, when Donnchadh's daughter Gormflaith, Ormond's niece, married Henry O'Neill of Tyrone. Her marriage to such an important prince illustrated the central role of her dynasty in the crafting of Butler policy countrywide.[66]

On 9 December 1447 Duke Richard of York replaced Talbot as lord lieutenant of Ireland, though he did not take up his post until July 1449. In August of that year York devastated Wicklow, forcing the submission of Dúnlaing mac Gerald's successor, Braen O'Byrne of Newrath. In an elaborate indenture Braen agreed that his family would adopt English custom and tongue, and promised to disgorge loot garnered from shipwrecked cargoes washed up on the coastline between Delgany and Arklow. In a flourish Braen gallantly presented two choice ponies to York's wife. As time proved, his gallantry was pragmatic and deceptive. Significantly, though, at the time of Braen's submission several Leinster nobles, anxious to avoid similar attacks, travelled to Kiltimon to submit before York; these included Theobald O'Toole, Fachtna O'More, Cathaoir O'Dempsey, Féilim O'Nolan, O'Murphy, and Domhnall Riabhach, who came as Donnchadh MacMurrough's representative.[67]

Because of his concord with Donnchadh, Domhnall Riabhach now regarded his O'Byrne cousins as enemies. The struggle between the MacMurroughs and the O'Byrnes continued into the 1450s. Ormond's death in August 1452 removed a restraint from the O'Byrnes. O'Byrne aggressiveness is detected in the papal appointment in 1451 of Tadhg O'Byrne, the Benedictine prior of Glascarraig, as bishop of Ferns; this was objected to by the diocese's 'grave and noble men' – most probably the MacMurroughs.[68] York also realized that the O'Byrnes would pursue their own independent ambitions in East Leinster, so he determined to brake their drive, outlining his intentions during his parliament of April 1450. To his loyal retainer Sir Edmund Mulso, seneschal of his liberty of Meath, York granted permission to found a town in the O'Toole mountainous heartland of Fercullen, and Mulso leased a castle near Bray close to the uplands, as a base for his conquest of that territory. However, Mulso was more often than not absent – fighting Henry VI's wars. In spite of this, attempts – albeit unsuccessful ones – were made throughout the 1450s to conquer Fercullen.[69]

Government activities in West Leinster and the midlands reveal a similar desire to contain the Irish threat to English centres. Even before Ormond's death, the Irish polities of West Leinster were displaying signs of decline. (An

66 _MacFirbis' Annals_, 1448; Empey, p. 760. A peace had been concluded between the O'Neills and Ormond in 1444. Matthew dates the marriage to 1449. See Matthew, p. 413; AFM, 1452. 67 Curtis, 'Richard, duke of York', pp 166–8; Gilbert, _Viceroys_, p. 353. 68 _NHI_, ix, p. 312; It transpired that Bishop Robert of Ferns was still alive and Tadhg had obtained his appointment through fraud, resulting in its reversal in 1453. _Cal. papal letters_, x, pp 244–5. 69 _Stat. Ire., Hen VI_, pp 214–21; _Stat. Ire., 1–12 Edw IV_, pp 228–31; _Ancient Records of Dublin_, i, pp 252–3.

Calbhach was certainly not the force he had been ten years earlier. After the death of his wife Margaret O'Carroll in 1451, he married Catherine O'Kelly of Uí Maine – a sign of a growing reliance upon allies west of the Shannon.)[70] A new ring of castles was under construction to pen in the Irish. When he left Ireland in late 1450, York installed Ormond as his deputy. In 1452 Ormond embarked upon the pacification of the midlands, erecting two castles close to Thurles, while Edmund MacRichard Butler built one at Buolick in Slieveardagh.[71] The second phase of Ormond's strategy came during that summer, when on a circuit of the midlands he took Lea castle from O'Dempsey, burnt Irry in Offaly, and parleyed with An Calbhach before taking the submissions of the O'Farrells and O'Reillys.[72] Finally, he travelled into Tyrone to chastise Henry O'Neill for having abandoned his wife, Gormflaith MacMurrough, the earl's niece. In an effective demonstration of his power, Ormond forced O'Neill to take her back. However, Ormond's death on 23 August 1452 dramatically changed the political climate.[73]

It is not without significance that Thomas fitzMaurice Fitzgerald gained his pardon sometime in 1452, thereby bolstering his claims to his inheritance.[74] This pardon and Ormond's death transformed Thomas fitzMaurice from an outlaw living in the twilight worlds of both Irish and English society into a major player within the English lordship; but in spite of his pardon, he was denied his inheritance. The reason for this was the continuing Butler dominance of the English government. Although York was reappointed as lord lieutenant on 11 February 1451, his tenure of that office was challenged in 1453. On 12 May 1453 Ormond's son, James Butler, earl of Wiltshire and Ormond, a Lancastrian, was appointed lieutenant of Ireland for ten years, while York remained protector of the lordship. Crucial to Wiltshire's appointment was Henry VI's favour.[75] Wiltshire had no intention of relinquishing his grip upon the Kildare lands, much to Thomas fitzMaurice's frustation. Unsurprisingly, Thomas fitzMaurice in 1453–4 fought him for them, centring the dispute on the manors of Maynooth and Rathmore.[76] The Butlers and Fitzgeralds were aided by their respective Irish allies in this struggle for the Kildare earldom.[77] In the ensuing melee Thomas fitzMaurice, with the aid of a mixture of English and probably O'Byrne allies, successfully wrested back the Kildare manors from Edmund MacRichard, William fitzJames Butler, 7th baron of Dunboyne, and their Irish allies (probably the MacMurroughs).[78] Fitzgerald fortunes further improved when York was restored as lieutenant of Ireland in 1454, forcing Wiltshire on 15 April to surrender all claims to the lieutenancy. Thomas

---

70 AFM, *MacFirbis' Annals*, AConn, 1451.   71 *Stat. Ire, Hen VI*, pp 284–7. For instance, the parliament of 1450 granted subsidies to aid the erection of Usk castle in Kildare; Dillon, 'Laud Mss 610', no. lxx, p. 147.   72 AFM, *MacFirbis' Annals*, 1452.   73 AFM, *MacFirbis' Annals*, 1452; Griffiths, *The reign of Henry VI*, p. 422; Dillon, 'Laud Mss 610', no. lxx, p. 147.   74 *Stat. Ire., Hen VI*, p. 94. See note 2.   75 *CPR*, 1452–61, p. 102.   76 Ellis, *Tudor frontiers*, p. 111.   77 *Stat. Ire., Hen VI*, p. 293; H. Ellis (ed.), *Original letters illustrative of English history*, 2nd series (London, 1969), i, pp 117–21; Beresford, 'The Butlers in England and Ireland, 1405–1515', p. 135; Empey, p. 301.   78 Empey, p. 303 In 1475 Sir John Butler renounced Butler claims to the manors of

fitzMaurice responded to York's rise by supporting his cause.[79] The Fitzgerald victory over the Butlers is confirmed by the fact that Thomas fitzMaurice was both 7th earl of Kildare and York's deputy by October 1454.[80]

However, the struggle between the Fitzgerald and Butler parties was far from over. Indeed, in that year the seneschal of the Wexford liberty appealed for protection to Kildare as York's deputy. He reported that he had repelled (with O'Byrne aid) Domhnall Riabhach, Thomas Fitzgerald, later 8th earl of Desmond, O'Meagher and MacGillapatrick. Undeterred, Domhnall Riabhach with Donnchadh MacMurrough and the Butlers of Polestown, Cahir and Dunboyne returned to raze Wexford before 18 October 1454.[81] This sequence of events shows Domhnall Riabhach to be politically skilled, utilizing his full complement of allies – some of whom were deadly enemies of each other. Before Christmas, Edmund MacRichard seemingly campaigned with the MacMurroughs against some unnamed Leinstermen, probably O'Byrne raiders, in Uí Feilme (the northern Wexford barony of Ballaghkeen). All this violence almost certainly arose from the Butler failure to defeat the earl of Kildare in 1453–4. Kildare eventually presided over the attainder of the Butlers on 20 April 1455.[82] This period of intense turbulence also brought about changes in the internal polities of the MacMurroughs and the O'Byrnes. The pressure showed among Kildare's O'Byrne allies when Braen was assassinated at Wicklow by his nephew during 1454.[83] Furthermore, shortly after 1455 Donnchadh MacMurrough abdicated (perhaps due to the onset of his blindness) in Domhnall Riabhach's favour; he died in 1478. Domhnall Riabhach continued the alliance with the Butlers, marrying two of his children to those of Edmund MacRichard.[84]

Now York's deputy, Kildare's attitude to the Irish changed; he distanced himself from his past and embraced a future of service to the English crown. His policy of good government, self-interest, and affinity-building was similar to the old Butler policies. He knew that the vulnerability of the Pale and the government were linked to that of his own earldom. The strategic value of the Kildare estates being their proximity to the royal highway through Carlow and Kildare, Kildare decided that a revived Kildare earldom would act as the Pale's shield.[85] The first step came in 1454–5 when the Dublin assembly legislated for the introduction of a series of anti-Irish laws. Another important event was the suspension, at Easter 1455, of the timber trade between the Wicklow Irish and Dublin as well as the cessation in September of the supplying of Wicklow castle. (These actions were presumably due to O'Byrne hostilities. This must be taken as the end of the

Rathmore and Maynooth.   **79** *Proceedings and ordinances of the privy council*, vi, pp 172–3; Otway-Ruthven, *Medieval Ireland*, p. 386; Empey, p. 303.   **80** *Stat. Ire., Hen VI*, p. 301; AFM, *MacFirbis' Annals*, 1454; Curtis, *Med. Ire.*, p. 321; Ellis, *Tudor frontiers*, p. 112.   **81** *COD*, iii, no. 190, pp 173–5; *Stat. Ire., Hen VI*, pp 361–5; Curtis, 'Richard, duke of York', pp 178–9.   **82** *Stat. Ire., Hen VI*, pp 522–31, 735–41. Kildare also presided over the repeal of the Butler attainder on 26 January 1458.   **83** *MacFirbis' Annals*, 1454.   **84** Nicholls, 'Late medieval Irish annals' (1478, 1487, 1489, 1508), p. 99; *Cal. papal letters*, xii, p. 699; Nicholls, 'The Kavanaghs', (1977), p. 437–8; Nicholls, 'The Kavanaghs', (1981), p. 190. Curtis, *Med. Ire.*, p. 319.   **85** Ellis, *Tudor*

O'Byrne alliance with Kildare.) Also, in December 1457 the Dublin assembly prohibited Irish horsemen from staying within the walls of the city after nightfall.[86] Further signs of Kildare's hardline attitude to his former allies was his energetic programme of encastellation in the Dublin and Kildare marches.

Another factor that reinforced Kildare's presence within his own earldom and the wider sphere of West Leinster was O'Connor Faly decline. In 1452 Sir Edward Fitzeustace captured and released An Calbhach, while an internal power struggle produced an O'Connor Faly civil war three years later. The question of An Calbhach's successor was solved in 1458 when he passed the baton to his son, Conn O'Connor Faly. Like his father, Conn was confronted by the gradual fencing-in of Offaly by fortifications. Reversal of fortune was shown in Kildare's defeat and capture of Conn in 1459, which signalled the commencement of the earl's recovery of his north-western frontier.[87] Although Conn later recouped his losses, this defeat put a brake on the O'Connor Faly renaissance. Kildare also improved his earldom's eastern fortifications such as Kilcullen and Ballymore, and Naas was later enclosed.[88] In the longer term, the resurgence of Kildare effectively isolated the Irish of East Leinster from those of West Leinster, thereby increasing the Pale's security.

The English lordship in Ireland was gradually being drawn into the English civil war between the houses of Lancaster and York. While York had been victorious at St Albans in 1455, his fortunes were reversed by his defeat at Ludford Bridge on 12 October 1459. After York's attainder by the English parliament, Wiltshire was reappointed as lord lieutenant of Ireland, but his appointment proved ineffective as because on 8 February 1460, York, attended by Kildare, held a parliament at Drogheda which confirmed his appointment as lord lieutenant dating from 1457. On hearing of the Yorkist victory at Northampton on 10 July 1460, York created Kildare his deputy and sailed for England. By October he had forced Henry VI to recognize him and his heirs as next in line to the throne. Henry VI's supporters would have none of it; they killed York on 30 December at Wakefield. In March 1461 London acclaimed Earl Edward of March, York's son, as Edward IV. On 29 March 1461 Edward IV defeated the Lancastrians at Towton. Yorkist forces found Wiltshire among the prisoners, and executed him on 1 May 1461.

The war between York and Lancaster was reflected in the struggle between Kildare and the Butlers. Edmund MacRichard Butler's position as Wiltshire's deputy posed a considerable obstacle to the governance of the earl of Kildare, who was a confirmed Yorkist. Kildare profited from Wiltshire's destruction when Edward IV divided the Ormond lands: by 1468 Kildare acquired the Butler lands of Oughterard, Oughterany, Castlewarden and Clintonscourt.[89] The Butlers now

frontiers, p. 113; *Stat. Ire., Hen VI*, pp 298–9.   **86** *Ancient Records of Dublin*, i, pp 284–9, 298. **87** *MacFirbis' Annals*, 1452, 1458; AFM, AConn, 1458; AFM, 1459.   **88** *Stat. Ire., 1–12 Edw IV*, pp 606–7. (Dated to 1469–70), see ibid., pp 582–5, 609; Ellis, *Tudor frontiers*, p. 114.   **89** *Stat. Ire., Edw 1–12*, pp 586–7. Wiltshire and his brothers were attainted on 4 November 1461 by

allied themselves with another Kildare enemy – Conn O'Connor Faly. The most significant indication of the Butler/O'Connor Faly determination to check Kildare's government was their joint devastation of Meath during summer 1461. Kildare managed to check their threat by having the English gentry of Meath purchase the O'Connor Faly hostages in Bermingham hands – an act that swiftly brought Conn to peace and saw him serve against Edmund MacRichard that year.[90] The Lancastrian challenge did not end: in winter 1461–2, Wiltshire's brother, John Butler, 6th earl of Ormond, arrived in Ireland to gauge the support of a pro-Lancastrian revolt in Ireland. As for Kildare, he was replaced as justiciar in March 1462 by his brother-in-law, Thomas fitzJames Fitzgerald, earl of Desmond, deputy of Duke George of Clarence. In spite of considerable initial success, Ormond failed to re-establish his grip upon his earldom, and his enterprise was ended by the earl of Desmond's defeat of the Lancastrians under Edmund MacRichard Butler at Pilltown in Kilkenny during summer 1462. This led to a Butler attainder by the Dublin parliament and confiscation of Ormond's earldom on 15 October 1462. Although Ormond did not leave Ireland until after 17 August 1464, the Butler cause was lost;[91] this was confirmed by the subjugation of the Butlers of Polestown in 1463, the death of Edmund MacRichard in 1464, and the acceptance, by 1465, of Edmund fitzJames Butler, 8th baron of Dunboyne of Kildare patronage.[92]

In Desmond's parliament late in 1463, Kildare, now chancellor, was rewarded for service against Ormond with grants of the lordships of Carlow and Ross. He used the Carlow grant to further fortify the southern frontiers of his earldom.[93] However, the tables were turned in 1466: Kildare and Desmond led an army into Offaly in pursuit of Conn O'Connor Faly, only to be completely destroyed. However, Conn's victory was soured when Tadhg (Kildare's brother-in-law), allowed the earl to be rescued by the Dublin citizens.[94] The fact that Tadhg was Kildare's brother-in-law highlights how Kildare had modelled his party in the midlands upon the 4th earl of Ormond's prototype. As mentioned already, Kildare had earlier created links with O'Mores by marrying Dorothea O'More. By the late 1450s it appears that Kildare had taken a new wife, Joan, sister of the earl of Desmond, and he seems to have used a daughter from his O'More marriage to cement an alliance with Tadhg O'Dunne – presumably to check Conn.[95] Kildare's regional position in

---

parliament, stripping all their lands and titles. See *CPR, 1461–7*, p. 178.   **90** AFM, 1461; Ó Cléirigh, 'The O'Connor Faly lordship of Offaly, 1395–1513', pp 96–7. This good service earned him respite but he was soon back raiding the English of Meath, killing the baron of Galtrim in 1460, see AFM, 1460. Cúilen O'Dempsey was killed by the English in 1464, see AConn, 1464.   **91** *Stat. Ire., 1–12 Edw IV*, pp 25–7; Empey, p. 304; Butler, 'The battle of Pilltown', pp 206–8.   **92** Empey, p. 304; Beresford, 'The Butlers in England and Ireland, 1405–1515', p. 225; Blake-Butler, 'The barony of Dunboyne', 2, no. 4 (October, 1946), p. 115. **93** Curtis, *Med. Ire.*, pp 327–8; also 10 marks were granted in 1465 to Baron Edmund Wellesley of Norragh to build a castle there against the Irish. *Stat. Ire., 1–12 Edw IV*, pp 368–9. **94** AFM, AConn, *MacFirbis' Annals*, 1466.   **95** AFM, 1464; Nicholls, *O'Doyne MS*, p. 126.

the midlands improved yet again when his former father-in-law, Uaithne O'More, became a leading figure in the lordship of Laois after 1468.[96]

Meanwhile in East Leinster, O'Byrne expansion after 1454 continued, often in co-ordination with the Harolds. Kildare took firm action in his 1456 parliament against Dublin's rebellious marchers, outlawing Henry Walsh of Carrickmines and Geoffrey Harold. As in West Leinster, the Dublin government took action to curb Irish inroads into the Pale, ordering the building of Bray castle in 1459. At the request of the commons in 1460, Archbishop Tregury of Dublin along with Henry Walsh erected fortifications to protect Rathdown and Newcastle Lyons. Orders were also issued for the erection of towers on Kilmainham and Lucan bridges, while a tower was constructed alongside the walls of St Mary's abbey to protect Fingal from raiders.[97] In spite of these considerable efforts, the crisis on the Dublin marches peaked in the 1460s. Since his arrival in Ireland in 1450, Archbishop Michael Tregury of Dublin had been intent upon the revival of his diocesan rights within the lands of the Wicklow Irish and the marchers, complaining to the pope in 1451 of the desolation of his archbishopric. In 1460 he obtained a grant for recovery of archiepiscopal lands and apparently began to revive his rights in Harolds' Country and O'Byrnes' Country.[98] His plans badly backfired, ending in kidnap, an alleged beating and a dismal imprisonment at the hands of Patrick O'Byrne and Geoffrey Harold, who were later excommunicated for their actions.[99] The events of Tregury's kidnap may have been the reason for the Dublin assembly's prohibition in 1461 of communication between citizens and the Harolds. A proof of the ability of the Wicklow Irish to penetrate the Pale was their attack in 1462 upon Holy Trinity (Christchurch cathedral).[100] However, the northward march of the O'Byrnes received a setback in 1463: despite having routed the Walshes and other English, the unnamed O'Byrne overlord was killed at the moment of victory.[101] Bray was taken by the Irish and then retaken by Desmond before August 1464. It is clear also that Kildare was pushing Walshes against the O'Byrnes and Harolds, for a list of the Walshes of Kilgobbin in 1467–8 refers to a Maurice Walsh as the servant of Kildare.[102]

Kildare's ability to alleviate O'Byrne pressure upon the Pale may have lessened when the O'Byrnes and the MacMurroughs made up their differences

96 In 1464 Cétach O'More died after contracting plague, see AConn, 1464. Similarly, Domhnall O'More died of plague in 1468, see AFM, AConn, 1468. **97** *Stat. Ire., Hen VI*, pp 402–5, 440–7, 632–3. **98** *Cal. papal letters 1447–55*, x, p. 99; *Stat. Ire., Hen VI*, pp 768–773; H.F. Berry (ed.), *Registers of wills and inventories of the diocese of Dublin in the time of Archbishops Tregurry and Walton, 1457–1483* (Dublin, 1898), pp xx–xxi. **99** O'Byrne, 'The rise of the Gabhal Raghnaill', p. 63; *Alen's Reg.*, p. 242. **100** *Ancient records of Dublin*, i, p. 309; 'The Christchurch Deeds', in *DKR*, xx (Dublin, 1888). no. 297, p. 90. **101** AConn, *MacFirbis' Annals*, 1463. It seems the unknown O'Byrne overlord was succeeded by Tadhg Mór – son of Braen O'Byrne of Newrath. *McFirbis' Genealogies*, Microfilm no.473 (UCD), p. 475. However, William Harold and Robert Harold's burnings throughout 1463 ensured that the Dublin marches remained disturbed see *Stat. Ire., 1–12 Edw IV*, pp 67–9 and pp 215–17. **102** *Ancient*

in the late 1450s or early 1460s. It seems that the successor of the fallen O'Byrne overlord of 1463 was Tadhg mac Braen of Newrath, and that Domhnall Riabhach MacMurrough, an adroit diplomat, contracted an alliance with Tadhg by giving him his daughter in marriage. Domhnall Riabhach remained at peace throughout much of the 1460s and was conspicuously absent from the Butler defeat in summer 1462 at Pilltown. Indeed, he breathed new life into the MacMurroughs and the provincial kingship, by establishing himself in Enniscorthy castle.[103] Domhnall Riabhach also maintained good relations with the Butlers, the Fitzgeralds of Desmond and the O'Byrnes. In contrast to Domhnall Riabhach's quiet diplomacy, the O'Byrnes remained turbulent, conducting a lucrative business of extortion and ransom along the marches. The recurring theme of the parliament of 1465 was the need to defend the Pale from them (the case of the unfortunate Piers Cruys of Crumlin was typical: he was kidnapped by the O'Byrnes and forced to pay a large ransom, which bankrupted him). Because of the persistence of the danger from the Irish, fresh fortifications against them were commissioned at Ballinateer. More interesting was parliament's listing of requests of the people of Co. Dublin, in which they asked that the government prevent foreign fishing fleets from exploiting waters under Irish control, without a licence: clearly the Irish had developed naval abilities, and were able to enforce a tax on these continental fishermen exploiting their coastal waters. The O'Byrnes put this newly found revenue to great use by buying large quantities of new and improved armour and weaponry. No doubt the O'Byrnes were also benefiting from the blackrents levied upon Wicklow town, and their trade in timber and cereals was equally lucrative.[104] These advantages helped the Irish of Wicklow to see off Desmond's twin campaigns of 1466 following his disaster in Offaly that year and to repulse Lord Lieutenant John Tiptoft's offensive of September 1467 and briefly capture Bray two years later.[105]

The O'Connor Faly victory of 1466 over Thomas fitzMaurice Fitzgerald, 7th earl of Kildare, elevated Conn to the status of Irish enemy number one in Leinster. Tiptoft strove to capture him, but dramatic splits within the government delayed him: during the parliamentary sessions on 4 February 1468, Tiptoft arrested and attainted Desmond, Kildare and Sir Edward Plunkett, accusing them of being in league with the Irish, and on 15 February Tiptoft had Desmond beheaded.[106] By the end of February he had further success, for Edmund

records of Dublin, i, pp 141–3; _Stat Ire._, _1–12 Edw IV_, pp 444–5.   **103** Genealogia Joannis Byrne; Curtis, _Med. Ire._, p. 311.   **104** _Stat. Ire._, _1–12 Edw IV_, pp 320–3 & 352–5; _Cal. Carew MSS_, _1515–74_, pp 193–4; Ronan, 'The ancient churches of the deanery of Wicklow', p. 142. For the timber trade see _Account roll of the priory of the Holy Trinity, Dublin, 1337–1346_, pp 36, 167. In 1461 the Dublin Assembly banned the sale of corn to the Irish. See _Ancient Records of Dublin_, i, p. 309. Butter was also traded by Wicklow's Irish with the people of Dublin, see ibid., p. 193. An interesting incident in 1390s records that Gerald mac Taidhg O'Byrne paid a merchant of Dublin, Esmond Berle with a sea going barge. Was this used for trade? See _A roll of the proceeding of the king's council in Ireland, 1392–1393_, p. 181.   **105** _MacFirbis' Annals_, 1466; _Ancient records of Dublin_, i, pp 327–8; O'Byrne, 'The rise of the Gabhal Raghnaill', p. 64.   **106** AFM,

fitzJames Butler, 8th baron of Dunboyne, captured Conn O'Connor Faly, thereby opening the door for Kildare's brother-in-law, Tadhg O'Connor Faly, to establish himself. However, this did not prevent Tiptoft from again campaigning during May in Offaly against Tadhg.[107] In June, Gerald Fitzgerald attempted to avenge his brother Desmond's death by burning Meath, an action that panicked the government. Treasurer Roland Fitzeustace released Kildare, and with him fled to Gerald. By the time Worcester mustered his forces to challenge Gerald, he faced a formidable confederation. Significantly, the Desmond and Kildare forces were reinforced by Domhnall Riabhach and Tadhg O'Connor Faly.[108] Once Gerald had returned to Munster, Tiptoft accepted the submissions of Kildare and Fitzeustace; his acceptance of Kildare's submission for the sake of peace clearly illustrates Kildare's alliance-building among the Irish. Tiptoft wrote to Edward IV expressing the hope 'that your subiectes shoulde continue in the more tranquillitie and peas from the daiely sautes of your Irishe enemyes and English rebelx such as was bounden in affinitie to the saide Erle of Kildare'.[109] Kildare then left for England and obtained the reversal of his attainder at the end of July.[110] The terms of Kildare's pardon demonstrate that he inherited the mantle formerly worn by the earls of Ormond when dealing with the Leinstermen. In return for his pardon, Kildare undertook to render loyal service and 'to make the Irishmen of Leinster to be at peace, according to his power'.[111]

1467; Cosgrove, 'The execution of the earl of Desmond, 1468', pp 22–3. **107** AFM, AConn, 1468; *Ancient records of Dublin*, i, p. 328. **108** Ó Cuiv, 'A fragment of the Irish annals', p. 97. **109** Otway-Ruthven, *Medieval Ireland*, p. 393. There was a general movement among the Pale nobility for Kildare's pardon, see I. Thornley (ed.), *England under the Yorkists* (London, 1920), p. 257, citing Lords of Ireland to Edward IV, 28 June 1468 (PRO, 'Ancient correspondence', LVIII, no. 50). **110** Curtis, *Med. Ire.*, p. 332. **111** *Stat. Ire., 1–12 Edw IV*, pp 586–7.

CHAPTER 8

The Kildares and the Leinstermen, 1470–1520

In the midst of a renewed English civil war, Tiptoft was recalled to England – with Sir Edward Dudley staying on in Ireland as his deputy. By the end of that summer Dudley too had embarked for England, leaving the way clear for Kildare's elevation to the justiciarship. There were few suitable candidates: Ormond was in disgraced exile, while the Desmonds increasingly pursued an isolationist policy following the execution in February 1468 of Thomas Fitzgerald, 8th earl of Desmond. Even though Kildare now was the only remaining great English magnate involved in the affairs of state, his election was nonetheless an affirmation of the belief that he could protect the Pale and extend English jurisdiction. The fact that Edward IV left him as justiciar between 1470 and 1475, and reappointed him in 1477, indicates the earl had his king's confidence. Kildare's election in 1470 therefore marked a decisive point in his career, enabling him and his successors to create a stable English heartland from which to strike at the Irish of East Leinster. Kildare's fortification of the Pale was copied throughout his own earldom, thereby threatening the spheres of the Irish dynasties of West Leinster and the midlands. Under Kildare and his better known son and grandson, Fitzgerald power would become persuasive through-out Leinster, forcing a great territorial wedge between the overlapping polities of the east and west parts of the province, and allowing the earls to exert their overlordship through a combination of violence and marriage. Although Kildare power was meant to advance hand in hand with royal power, outside the Dublin council the earls of Kildare were the real power in the English lordship in Ireland – playing successive kings with a potent mix of charm, connections and controlled violence.

As in 1456, the major problem now facing Kildare's government was the continued advance of the Irish of East Leinster into the Pale. At times during the 1470s, the Wicklow Irish and their allies threatened to eradicate any government control over the Dublin marches, but, with the support of Edward IV, Kildare and the Dublin council continued the construction of a defensive system around the Pale. By 1470 the government was so weak that Edmund mac Theobald O'Toole compelled Saggart to pay him protection money. Furthermore, collectors of parliamentary subsidies in Harolds' Country (the area between

Saggart and Kilmashogue) feared that the Harolds would deliver them to the Irish. No doubt this situation contributed to the decree of Kildare's parliament of November/December 1470, commanding Saggart's townsfolk to abandon their agreement with the O'Tooles.[1] Saggart paid the ultimate price for its compliance, when the O'Byrnes and O'Tooles sacked it in 1471/2 – forcing many to abandon it. The rape of Saggart spurred frantic English activity to enclose the town with defensive ditches, while a fortified dyke was dug from Tallaght to Saggart.[2] Indicative of the confidence of the Irish of East Leinster and their alienation from the English archbishopric of Dublin and the government was their attempt to resurrect the dormant bishopric of Glendalough, which was granted papal approval in 1481. The main movers behind this were Domhnall Riabhach MacMurrough and the O'Byrnes – indicating improving relations between the O'Byrne and MacMurrough dynasties.[3] Yet in the face of such provocation Kildare stuck to his task, one of his most innovative actions being to create an embryonic standing force to punish their incursions: his parliament of 1471–2 granted him 80 archers for his retinue, 40 of whom Kildare undertook to maintain. Three years later Kildare's parliament went on to authorize the establishment of a permanent fighting force, the 'Fraternity of St George', comprising 160 archers and 63 spearmen, whose captains included Kildare's son, the young Gerald Fitzgerald. Kildare's fortification of the Pale limited the freedom of the Irish to make raids upon it; however, when they did penetrate the Pale defences, they were devastating. It was Kildare's clients such as Maurice Walsh of Kilgobbin who bore the brunt of their wrath: in 1476, the O'Byrnes and O'Toole destroyed Jamestown castle, leaving Walsh destitute.[4]

In West Leinster, Kildare's task was no less daunting. After his defeat of Conn O'Connor Faly in 1458, he slowly re-established Fitzgerald power over the west of his earldom – a dangerous process, as the earl's capture during Conn's 1466 victory showed. On that occasion, Kildare's allies (led by Conn's brother, Tadhg, Kildare's brother-in-law) freed him. Ironically, at the time of Kildare and Desmond's arrest by Tiptoft in February 1468, Kildare's midland position improved, for the Dunboyne Butlers delivered Conn to gaol, allowing Tadhg to establish himself. Also during Gerald Fitzgerald of Desmond's devastation of Leinster (1468) in revenge for the execution of his brother, Tadhg's actions showed him to have been a dedicated Kildare supporter. He joined the offensive upon Tiptoft's government that produced Kildare's release and eventual pardon. But in 1471 Kildare somewhat surprisingly released Conn, who determined to reclaim his lordship. His release led to civil war in Offaly, with Tadhg invoking the support of Kildare; however, Tadhg's death from plague late that year probably resulted in a truce between Kildare and Conn.[5]

1 *Stat. Ire., 1–12 Edw IV*, pp 664–9.   2 Ibid., p. 809. This coincides with Dublin Assembly's suspension in 1471 of the cereal trade with the Irish of Glendalough, see *Ancient records of Dublin*, i, p. 347.   3 *Alen's Reg*, pp 38, 245; *Cal. papal letters 1471–84*, xiii, part 2, p. 744.   4 *Stat. Ire., 12–22 Edw IV*, pp xlv, 130–5, 516–19, 715–7, see also pp 444–5. Maurice was described as Kildare's servant in 1467–8; Curtis, *Med. Ire.*, p. 334.   5 AFM, AConn, 1471.

In autumn 1474 Conn died, clearing the path for the succession of his son, Cathaoir O'Connor Faly. Cathaoir inherited a lordship in decline within a region still affected by the Butler collapse of the early 1460s. Although in 1475 Cathaoir joined his cousin Aodh O'Donnell of Donegal to burn throughout west Meath and Longford, his dynasty was fragmenting.[6] Cathaoir's brother Art cut out a fiefdom for himself and Cathaoir imprisoned Art briefly in 1476 because of the latter's alliance with the Butlers of Dunboyne.[7] But the absence of the stabilizing influence of Ormond over the midlands, combined with the dawn of Kildare hegemony, had profound effects there. Furthermore, the three junior Butler branches (Dunboyne, Cahir and Polestown) were exposed to Kildare aggression under the guise of Yorkist government. The absence of Ormond also promoted infighting among his kinsmen that only further destabilized the region. The differing attitudes of these Butler houses towards Kildare were illustrative of the inner confusion within their ranks: the Butlers of Dunboyne and Cahir alternated between being anti-Kildare to being neutral, while those of Polestown allied with the Kildares.[8] Although John, 6th earl of Ormond, renounced all claims to the Kildare estates in 1475, and on 21 June that year was restored to his own,[9] the Kildares remained hostile towards his brother and successor, Earl Thomas Butler, 7th earl of Ormond.

After the death of Kildare on 25 March 1478, his son Gerald was elected to take his place as justiciar. This seamless passage of government office from father to son raised the eyebrows of Edward IV, who reversed the election – dispatching Lord Henry Grey to Ireland in July 1478 as deputy lieutenant.[10] Kildare, in no mood to relinquish his office, held a parliament between May and September that extended government control over the Ormond earldom through an act of resumption, and he passed a similar bill in his 1479/80 parliament.[11] Although Grey's appointment was vigorously opposed by Kildare, Grey managed to hold a parliament in November 1478 at Trim; exasperated by Kildare's resistance, Grey embarked for England early in the new year – prevailing on Robert Preston, 1st Viscount Gormanston, to take over his office. Subsequently Kildare travelled to London to see the king, to return in triumph as lord deputy later that year. About this time, James fitzEdmund Butler of Polestown, Ormond's lieutenant, decided to make a personal alliance with Kildare by fostering his son Piers, then aged about eleven, in the earl's household. Kildare's eagerness to foster the boy indicated that he believed Piers would succeed to the Irish lands of Ormond.[12] However, Edward VI dismissed the acts of the rival parliaments of 1478, but allowed those of the 1479/80 parliament, thereby enabling Ormond to petition for the restoration of his Irish lands. While it is unlikely that the return of the

---

6 AFM, 1474, 1475; Ó Cléirigh, 'The O'Connor Faly lordship of Offaly', pp 97–8.   7 Ó Cléirigh, 'The O'Connor Faly lordship of Offaly', p. 98; AConn, 1476.   8 AU, 1489; Beresford, 'The Butlers in England and Ireland, 1405–1515', pp 229–2; Empey, p. 334.   9 *COD*, iii, no. 213, pp 190–2, no. 242, pp 216–17; *Stat. Ire., 12–22 Edw IV*, pp 270–5.   10 Ellis, *Tudor Ireland*, p. 62.   11 *Stat. Ire., 12–22 Edw IV*, pp 672–7, 685–95.   12 *COD*, iv, appendix,

Ormond lands was Kildare's true ambition in guiding the acts of resumption through parliament, he recognized the lands' potential value and was slow to restore them to Ormond. Indeed, it took a letter from Edward IV, dated 6 April 1481, ordering him to do so forthwith before he complied.[13]

The most pressing problem for Kildare, as for his father before him, was the ability of the Irish of East Leinster to obstruct his governance of the English lordship. The Kildare/Polestown alliance gave him the key to solve these difficulties; it was as politically important as the formation of the earlier Butler/MacMurrough alliance. By hitching his family's fortunes to the Kildare star, James fitzEdmund Butler of Polestown effectively sidelined his family's alliances with the O'Carrolls, O'Mores, O'Connor Falys and MacMurroughs, thereby exposing them to growing Kildare aggression. In doing so, he may have exacted a measure of revenge for the studied neutrality in 1461–2 of his father-in-law, Domhnall Riabhach MacMurrough-Kavanagh. Significantly, though, James fitzEdmund Butler's alliance with the Kildares occurred after Domhnall Riabhach's death in 1476.[14] Domhnall Riabhach's successor was James's brother-in-law, Murchadh Ballach MacMurrough-Kavanagh, and it occurred at the time of the realignment of the Polestown Butlers with Kildare. While Murchadh Ballach's marriage to Joan Butler of Polestown probably cushioned him from the worst of the impending Fitzgerald offensive, he was determined to oppose Kildare in East Leinster, and to this end he may well have constructed a defensive league to combat Kildare, by allying with Uaithne O'More and Cathaoir O'Connor Faly; also he married his daughter Honora to the increasingly powerful lord of the Gabhal Raghnaill O'Byrnes, Réamain Garbh O'Byrne of Glenmalure.[15]

Uaithne O'More[16] and Cathaoir O'Connor Faly had good reason to ally with Murchadh Ballach. The late 1470s saw a dramatic increase in Kildare's presence along their respective borders. In Kildare, during 1477, a tower was erected at Galmorestown,[17] while Kildare's parliament of 1478 granted his father-in-law, Sir Roland Fitzeustace, a subsidy for the walling of Kilcullen and Calverstown. Two years later Kildare's parliament gave £10 to Prior Nicholas of Connell to build a castle against the Irish at Bolablught. And later the parliament of 1480–1 authorized the sheriff of Kildare to empower the serjeants of each Kildare barony except Kilcullen, Naas, and half Norragh, to take men for two days to block the O'Connor Faly routeway into the lands of the earldom. No doubt the O'More and O'Connor Faly lords were also deeply concerned by the Polestown/Kildare alliance. War between these competing interests was inevitable. In 1479 Murchadh Ballach and these allies warred in southwestern Kildare against Sir Roland Fitzeustace[18] – a conflict that was a prelude to

---

no. 53, pp 344–5. **13** Ibid., iii, no. 249, pp 234–5; ibid., no. 252, pp 243–4. **14** AFM, 1476; Nicholls, 'Late medieval Irish annals' (1476) p. 99; Dowling, *Annals*, p. 31. **15** AU, 1489; Nicholls, 'Late medieval Irish annals' (1489) p. 99; *Stat. Ire., 12–22 Edw IV*, pp 708–9; Price, 'Armed forces of the Irish chiefs in the early sixteenth century', pp 201–2. **16** In 1473 O'More (probably Uaithne) was captured by MacGillapatrick, see AConn, 1473. See also AFM, AConn, 1477. **17** Ellis, *Tudor frontiers*, p. 114. **18** *Stat. Ire., 12–22 Edw IV*, pp 708–9,

Kildare's offensive of 1480, when a royal service was proclaimed in Kildare against the Irish. That September that year the justiciar rode into the Leinster mountains, burning the O'Byrne lordship as well as seizing Leighlinbridge from Murchadh Ballach.[19] The parliament of 1481 casts some light upon the extent of Kildare's success: it empowered the earl to take possession of vacant lands in Kildare and Carlow 'namely from Calverston to Carlow Castle and thence to Leighlin bridge which the Earl had recovered from the Irish'. It seems also that in the 1480s Kildare was also pushing down the east bank of the Slaney, establishing control sometime before 1483 over Rathvilly and Clonmore castles.[20]

There were further indications of a substantial change in the military balance in Leinster. The Leinster Irish was reliant, as we know, upon large infusions of mercenaries drawn from Munster or Connacht. There was a massive influx of galloglass into Leinster during the 1480s – giving one 'battle' of galloglass each to the MacMurroughs, O'Byrnes, O'Connor Falys, MacGillapatricks and O'Mores. The increasing prevalence of these galloglass in the service of the Leinster lords was linked to the gradual break-up of the MacDonnell lordship in the Western Isles. We know that it was the Kildares who first employed these MacDonnell galloglass in Leinster (they were importing these forces into Leinster from 1466 at least).[21] The employment of these MacDonnells possibly tilted the balance decisively in Kildare's favour, leading the Leinster Irish to find mercenaries for themselves. This state of affairs may also suggest that Kildare's power in West Leinster was denying the Leinster lords access to sources of mercenaries in Munster and Connacht. Still, Kildare's campaigns in the early 1480s were not conclusive. Indeed, the continuing existence of the bishopric of Glendalough suggests that the Wicklow Irish had drawn the fire out of Kildare's offensive. Moreover, Kildare was prudent enough to take time to consolidate his gains by underpinning them with castles. In Kildare during 1484 he built Lackagh tower and strengthened Kildare castle.[22] Possibly as a reaction to Murchadh Ballach's recruiting of galloglass, Kildare constructed a castle at Castledermot, thereby reinforcing the budding Kildare suzerainty over north Carlow.[23] While in West Leinster the earl had achieved supremacy over the O'Connor Falys; and Cathaoir, for his service, accepted a blackrent of 40d. a ploughland for Meath from Kildare's parliament of March 1485.[24]

711, 764–7; Ellis, *Tudor frontiers*, p. 114.   **19** Otway-Ruthven, *Medieval Ireland*, p. 400; *Ancient records of Dublin*, i, p. 357; O'Byrne, 'The rise of the Gabhal Raghnaill', pp 68–71; *The Annals of Ross*, p. 46; in 1481 Cathaoir MacMurrough killed by the English of the liberty of Wexford, see AFM, AU, 1481.   **20** Curtis, *Med. Ire.*, p. 342; Price, 'Armed forces of the Irish chiefs in the early sixteenth century', p. 203; *Alen's Reg*, p. 276; Bryan, *Great earl of Kildare*, pp 60–1.   **21** Price, 'Armed forces of the Irish chiefs in the early sixteenth century', p. 202; Lynch, *Scotland, a new history*, p. 168; Nicholson, *Scotland the later middle ages*, p. 542. During Kildare's defeat in 1466 at the hands of Conn O'Connor Faly, 'John son to Mac-donell' was killed, see *MacFirbis' Annals*, 1466; Curtis, *Med. Ire.*, p. 341.   **22** Ellis, *Tudor frontiers*, pp 114, 119.   **23** NAI, PRO 7/1 c.15. See also NLI, MS 8008 (ii); Ellis, *Tudor frontiers*, p. 119.   **24** NAI, PRO 7/1 c.18. See Ellis, 'Parliament and great councils, 1483–99: addenda et corrigenda', p. 102;

Kildare's activities to strengthen his earldom were not all military in nature; he also sought to establish clear legal title to lands lying on the fringes of his earldom as well as to gain title to lands in Irish possession. For instance, Kildare's first marriage to Alison Fitzeustace, daughter of Sir Roland, achieved a jointure of estates in east Kildare, bordering the O'Toole upland territory of Imaal. This marriage also afforded Kildare the opportunity to extend his authority into O'Toole lands.[25] The parliament of 1483 formally legalized Kildare's claims to the lands belonging to absentee landowners located in the Irish lordships around Kildare, Carlow and west Wicklow. Although he encouraged absentees to return, few came. While the 1483 legislation may have been also originally designed to protect churchlands in the region, Kildare benefited from it. As a pretext to his advance into Wicklow, Kildare bought from the Butlers of Dunboyne the mesne tenures of lands deep in O'Toole territory at Castlekevin, Coillache and Ballymore. These purchases within this region legally underpinned his impending conquest there. And after the death of Archbishop Walton of Dublin in June 1484, Kildare flexed his muscle by seizing 24 townlands belonging to the lordships of Ballymore and Castlekevin.

The turmoil that was to envelop the monarchy after the death of Edward IV in 1483 strengthened Kildare's authority. Richard, duke of Gloucester, Edward IV's brother, deposed the new king Edward V, imprisoned him with his brother, Duke Richard of York, and took the crown as Richard III. He was eager to conclude an agreement with Kildare, who dispatched John Estrete to him with proposals, including a request for the constableship of Wicklow castle.[26] Richard III agreed to this, but stipulated that Kildare appear before him in August 1484 – which he did; but the details of their agreement does not survive. Kildare used the king's approval to consolidate his power, and although he incurred Edward IV's censure for meddling within the Butler earldom in 1481, this did not prevent him in 1484 from attempting to obtain two-thirds of the profits accruing to Ormond from his earldom.[27] Moreover, in 1485 Kildare confirmed his alliance with the Polestown Butlers through the marriage of his daughter, Margaret, to Piers, the son of James fitzEdmund. This marriage also suggests that Kildare was supporting and developing the Polestown Butlers as an alternative within the Ormond earldom to the absentee earl.[28] This sealing of the Polestown/Kildare alliance was vitally important for the extension of the earl's power into West Leinster and the midlands. The success of Kildares in establishing their hegemony in this region was conditional upon the continued maintenance of their alliance with Butlers of Polestown.

Ó Cléirigh, 'The O'Connor Faly lordship of Offaly', p. 98. In 1485 Art O'Connor Faly killed by Cathaoir, see AFM, AConn, 1485.   **25** Lennon, *Sixteenth century Ire.*, p. 71.   **26** Clarke, 'The Black Castle, Wicklow', p. 7. See Quinn, 'Aristocratic autonomy, 1460–94', p. 609; Otway-Ruthven *Medieval Ireland*, p. 401.   **27** *COD*, iii, no. 261, pp 253–5.   **28** Empey, p. 334; Curtis, *Med. Ire.*, p. 344; *COD*, iii, no. 191, pp 175–6; James fitzEdmund's brother, Walter, the sometime sheriff of Kilkenny, was married to Grainne – daughter of Uaithne O'More. See Beresford, 'The Butlers in England and Ireland, 1405–1515', pp 239, 241, 272.

However, Kildare's plans received a jolt when Richard III was swept from the throne in August 1485 by Henry Tudor. In November that year, Tudor, now Henry VII, passed an act of parliament restoring Ormond's estates. An open dispute between Ormond and his deputies, the Butlers of Polestown, came in 1486–7 when Lambert Simnel, a Yorkist pretender to the English throne, landed in Ireland and declared himself to be Edward VI's nephew, Earl Edward of Warwick (the real Warwick was a prisoner in the Tower of London and Henry VII publicly exhibited him in London to disprove Simnel's claims). In an act of open defiance, Kildare and his fellow Yorkists accepted Simnel as Edward VI at Christchurch on 24 May 1487. On 4 June, a force comprised of Yorkists and Irish troops sailed for England from Dublin; it included Sir Thomas Fitzgerald, Kildare's brother, who was killed fighting at Stoke on 16 June. Throughout the Simnel crisis, the Polestown Butlers were unshakeable in their loyalty to Kildare – which must have proved embarrassing for Ormond. However, Mayor John Butler of Waterford, and many of the other Butlers and the O'Byrnes declared for Henry VII. Although James fitzEdmund died in April 1487, he left his commission as Ormond's deputy to his son Piers,[29] whom Edward VI (Simnel) appointed sheriff of Kilkenny on 13 August 1487, two months after Stoke. Despite Henry VII's victory at Stoke, and Kildare's stubborn resistance until the end of the year, the king did not intervene in Ireland.[30] Kildare eventually recognized the king's authority, confirming Piers' office as sheriff of Kilkenny on 20 March 1489 in Henry VII's name.[31] The king left Kildare as justiciar for the time being, but Ormond was anxious to remove Piers from office.

When requesting the constableship of Wicklow castle in 1484, Kildare stated his intention to conquer the O'Byrnes. Henry VII's acceptance of Kildare's submission, and hence the status quo, encouraged the earl to make war in East Leinster. The O'Byrnes under Tadhg and later Gerald mac Dúnlaing proved difficult to dislodge, so Kildare seemingly pushed the O'Tooles against the O'Byrnes. The O'Tooles were in an unenviable position, lying directly in Kildare's path. Their lord, Edmund, may well have agreed to co-operate with Kildare; if so, his alliance with the O'Byrnes ended – resulting in his death in 1488 at their hands. The O'Toole/Kildare alliance endured.[32]

By the late 1480s, opposition was mounting among many Irish dynasties to Kildare's government and his alliance with the Polestown Butlers. After the death of his father in April 1487, Piers hoped to assume control of the Butler inheritance in Ireland, but Ormond and his clients had other ideas. Clearly, Ormond was in contact with the Irish allies of his house (Empey marks this confederation of Kildare's enemies as the origins of the 'Anti-Geraldine League' of 1504). During the Simnel crisis of 1487, Seán O'Carroll of Ely, the old ally of

29 Otway-Ruthven, *Medieval Ireland*, p. 403. See also *CSPI, 1601–1603*, p. 669; *Cal. Carew MSS Miscellaneous*, p. 473; see also Empey, p. 335; Curtis, *Med. Ire.*, p. 339; AFM, 1486.   **30** *COD*, iii, no. 272, pp 261–2; Beresford, 'The Butlers in England and Ireland, 1405–1515', p. 235; Otway-Ruthven, *Medieval Ireland*, p. 403.   **31** Ibid., no. 274, pp 265–6.   **32** AU, 1488.

the Butlers, wrote to Ormond, stating that he was opposed to Kildare and had recruited 200 galloglass. In addition he allied with the O'Briens, the MacWilliam Burkes, the MacDermots, the O'Kennedys, O'Dwyers, MacBrien of Coonagh, and Cormac MacCarthy Mór to resist Kildare. O'Carroll told Ormond that he would also encourage O'More to war against 'your grette empney therle of kyldare and his maynteners'.[33] The emergence of this Irish confederation seems to have been a reaction to Kildare's encroachments into the midlands. In 1488 Kildare stamped his authority on the northern midlands, using artillery to force Muircheartach MacGeoghegan to surrender his castle,[34] and in the following year the Fitzgeralds of Desmond attacked the O'Carrolls, killing Seán and routing his MacSweeney galloglass. Empey argues that the Desmond offensive was probably an attempt to destroy this 'Anti-Geraldine League'.[35] Furthermore, the death in 1489 of Joan Butler, the wife of Murchadh Ballach MacMurrough-Kavanagh, effectively suspended ties between the provincial king and his nephew, Piers. In spite of the breach with Piers, Murchadh Ballach did not end the Ormond/MacMurrough alliance. This growing opposition to Kildare was reflected among Murchadh Ballach's neighbours, the O'Byrnes. In 1490 Gerald mac Dúnlaing O'Byrne died, and was succeeded by his brother, Cathaoir, who proved bitterly opposed to Kildare.[36]

Although Henry VII judged it useful to retain Kildare in office, he viewed him with intense suspicion, and he was goaded by fears of Kildare's involvement in the landing of another Yorkist pretender, Perkin Warbeck, on the Cork coast in November 1491. (Warbeck claimed to be Richard, duke of York, Richard III's prisoner.) On 6 December 1491, Henry appointed Sir James Butler of Ormond and Captain Thomas Garth as commanders of an English army to crush the rebels in the counties of Kilkenny and Tipperary, allowing them to act without reference to Kildare[37] – in effect, removing the Ormond earldom from his governor's jurisdiction. Henry VII's action encouraged the English-based Thomas Butler, 7th earl of Ormond, to begin the reform of his Irish earldom. He now reinforced the position of Sir James Butler of Ormond, by appointing him on 7 December by the king's licence as his deputy and attorney in Kilkenny and Tipperary.[38] This enraged Piers, because it threatened the position his family had built up. Sir James Butler of Ormond was the natural son of John, 6th earl of Ormond and Ragnailt O'Brien and therefore a nephew of the 7th earl; he had been fostered in the house of Morgan (Máelruanaidh?) O'Carroll. Upon his arrival in Ireland from England, he found a ready support base among the O'Briens, MacWilliam Burkes, and O'Carrolls.[39] With them he campaigned

---

33 Empey, pp 336–7; the O'More lord still seems to be Uaithne. In 1489 Uaithne's son, Ross, was killed by Cathaoir mac Laoiseach O'Dempsey see AFM, 1489; Ruaidhrí son of David O'More, described as Tanaiste of Laois, died naturally in 1489, see AU, 1489. In 1489 Geoffrey mac Fionnán MacGillapatrick, king of North Ossory, also died. See AU, 1489; *COD*, iv, appendix no. 9, pp 315–6. **34** AFM, 1488. **35** Empey, p. 337; AFM, 1489 Murchadh and Maelmuire MacSweeney, clearly galloglass, were killed by Desmond in Ely that year. **36** AFM, 1490. **37** *CPR, 1485–94*, p. 367. **38** *CCR, 1485–1500*, no. 580, p. 168. **39** *COD*,

throughout the Ormond earldom and Leinster, subduing the Butler branches and taking hostages from the Leinster Irish. His actions further infuriated Piers, who regarded himself as Earl Thomas' rightful deputy.[40] These campaigns isolated the Poletown Butlers, for those of Dunboyne and Cahir recognized Sir James Butler of Ormond as the earl's deputy. It was probably at this time that Sir James captured and imprisoned Piers; in June 1492 Kildare and Sir Roland Fitzeustace were removed by Captain Garth from their positions as lord deputy and treasurer,[41] Archbishop Fitzsimons becoming deputy lieutenant, and Sir James treasurer and governor. The Four Masters illustrate a familiar reaction, stating that 'as soon as the Earl abandoned them [the English], they were universally plundered and burned from every quarter'.[42]

Relations between Kildare and Sir James Butler of Ormond worsened because of the former's support for Piers. The arrival of Sir James of Ormond threatened the Kildare hegemony in Leinster. Significantly, it was in the vital midland theatre that Sir James of Ormond and Garth's campaigns attempted to undermine Kildare's party. In winter 1492 Sir James of Ormond and Garth successfully attacked Cathaoir O'Connor Faly and killed his son, An Calbhach.[43] Kildare responded quickly and brutally. (Kildare's subsequent capture of Garth and his hanging of Garth's son was completely in line with the earl's obligations as overlord to O'Connor Faly.)[44] Kildare's edginess was revealed in 1492, when his followers killed the unfortunate Conn O'Connor Faly after he had thrown a pole in jest at the earl.[45] Sir James of Ormond's struggle with Kildare spread into neighbouring Ely. In 1492/3 Morgan (Máelruanaidh?) O'Carroll wrote to Henry VII, complaining that Kildare and perhaps the O'Byrnes or the O'Brennans had devastated Ely O'Carroll because he supported Sir James as the king directed.[46] In 1493 Kildare's ruthless extension of his power throughout Leinster continued, when he directly interfered among the O'Mores of Laois (who, given their past, were probably allied to 7th earl of Ormond's deputy). Then Kildare's troops killed their lord, Conall mac David O'More, at Kilberry castle in Kildare, before installing Niall mac Domhnaill O'More in his place. Also that year Kildare attacked the MacMurroughs, but Murchadh Ballach beat him off. As a consequence of the earl's behaviour, Sir James of Ormond launched a devastating attack upon the Kildare earldom, burning Kildare town itself.[47]

Plainly, the king could not allow this anarchy to continue. When Archbishop Fitzsimons' deputy lieutenancy was transferred to Robert Preston, 1st Viscount Gormanston, in September 1493, Henry VII appointed his son, Henry, duke of York, as lord lieutenant. And on 13 October 1495, Sir Edward Poynings, Duke

---

iv, appendix no. 15, pp 319–20.   **40** AFM, 1492; Empey, p. 341.   **41** *COD*, iv, appendix, no. 31, p. 332; Quinn, 'Aristocratic autonomy, 1460–94', p. 616; AFM, 1492.   **42** AFM, 1492. **43** AFM, 1492.   **44** Ó Cléirigh, 'The O'Connor Faly lordship of Offaly', p. 99; Ellis, *Tudor Ireland*, p. 73.   **45** AFM, 1492.   **46** *COD*, iv, appendix no. 15, pp 319–20. In this text Kildare's allies are known as the 'Brenenses' Máelruanaidh O'Carroll later married Kildare's sister – Joan. See Curtis, *Med. Ire.*, p. 338; for Máelruanaidh's pedigree see Pender, 'O'Clery', para 2045, p. 158; Vennings, 'The O'Carrolls of Offaly', p. 182.   **47** AFM, AU, 1493.

Henry's deputy, landed in Ireland with a expeditionary force and marched quickly against the O'Hanlons of southern Ulster. Strong suspicions lingered of Kildare's incitement of his clients and of covert collusion with O'Hanlon. In late February 1495 Poynings arrested Kildare, sending him to England in March. Sir James Fitzgerald, Kildare's brother, then seized Carlow castle, displaying Kildare's banner. In response, Poynings parliament (1 December 1494–February 1495) attainted both Fitzgerald brothers. In November, Kildare was charged with encouraging O'Hanlon's resistance as well as with prompting his brother's rebellion.[48]

Earlier in June, Perkin Warbeck besieged Waterford, but Poynings broke the siege in August, forcing the pretender to flee into Desmond. (He was captured in 1498 and executed the next year.) Against this disturbed background the government sought friends among the Leinster nobility. A Franciscan friar was dispatched to spy on the O'Byrnes and to ascertain the views of Cathaoir mac Dúnlaing O'Byrne. The friar's report was favourable, as the Dublin council sent messengers to ask Cathaoir mac Dúnlaing to campaign against the Fitzgeralds. Instead of joining Kildare's supporters, Cathaoir O'Connor Faly, like Murchadh Ballach, aligned himself with Sir James of Ormond, earning jointly £43 6s. 8d. in the latter half of 1495 and a further £4 13s. 3d. by March 1496.[49] Also at some point during 1495, with the help of Cathaoir and Edmund fitzJames Butler, 8th baron of Dunboyne, Sir James of Ormond retook Carlow after a siege, but Kildare's brother escaped.[50] Moreover, in the Dublin marches Theobald Walsh of Carrickmines and the Harolds organized forces to resist the rebels, while the baron of Dunboyne led a campaign into Wicklow late in 1495, capturing Art mac Edmund O'Toole, a Kildare client.[51] Even Murchadh Ballach's brother, Gerald MacMurrough, who was married to Kildare's natural sister, sided with Sir James of Ormond and was given custody of Carlow castle.[52]

After the death of Gerald MacMurrough in early 1496, Poynings entrusted Carlow castle to Murchadh Ballach and Cathaoir O'Connor Faly. But the loyal service of the MacMurroughs, O'Connor Falys and O'Byrnes fell victim to high politics. By summer 1496, Kildare was back in favour because nothing had been proved against him. Moreover, Henry VII came round to the realization that

---

48 Quinn, 'The hegemony of the earls of Kildare, 1494–1520', p. 641; Gilbert, *Viceroys*, p. 454; AFM, 1494. Sir James Fitzgerald is mentioned burning Meath in 1494. This reference must pertain to 1495. For the attainder of the Fitzgeralds, see Quinn, 'The bills and statutes of the Irish parliaments of Henry VII and Henry VIII', p. 94.   **49** Conway, *Henry VII, Scot & Ire.*, pp 84, 173. citing accounts of William Hattecliffe, under treasurer of Ireland, 1495–6 (BL, Royal MS C XIV, ff 133–44). Cathaoir mac Dúnlaing may have been in government service in 1494. To influence his decision, a length of velvet was presented to his wife. A common problem is the mistaken labelling of O'Byrnes as O'Briens; Gilbert, *Viceroys*, pp 457–8.   **50** Carlow Castle was entrusted to Gerald Cavanach by the government, see Gilbert, *Viceroys*, p. 458; Conway, *Henry VII, Scot & Ire.*, p. 156.   **51** Ellis, *Tudor frontiers*, p. 73. See also Gilbert, *Viceroys*, pp 610–1. This is an account of Garth's Leinster command in 1496, see Conway, *Henry VII, Scot & Ire.*, pp 196–7; Poyning's parliament declared that Wicklow castle should have an English-born constable, see Quinn, 'The Kildare hegemony, 1494–1520', pp 640–1.

Kildare was the only English magnate capable of governing Ireland in his name, and was a considerably cheaper option than direct intervention, so he made a new concord with Kildare, whereby he was restored to the deputyship and granted any crown lands he could reconquer from the Irish. A fresh mark of the king's favour was Kildare's new wife, Elizabeth St John, the king's cousin. These new conditions ended the war of Kildare's brother, Sir James Fitzgerald, who submitted in July 1496. Kildare landed in Ireland in mid-September 1496. Characteristically, he was soon in the saddle, taking pledges from both English and northern Irish lords at Drogheda and Dundalk. In Leinster, where there was resistance, he retook Carlow from Murchadh Ballach MacMurrough-Kavanagh and Cathaoir O'Connor Faly after two attempts, before embarking on a circuit throughout Leinster. Bereft of protection and without an option, Murchadh Ballach, Cathaoir mac Dúnlaing, Cathaoir O'Connor Faly, O'More and O'Dempsey dispatched the envoys to make submissions on their behalf at Dublin during October 1496.[53]

This signalled the beginning of the restoration of the Kildare hegemony in West Leinster and the midlands. Two incidents set the seal on it – the murder of Sir James of Ormond by Piers on 17 July 1497,[54] and Kildare's successful petitioning of Thomas Butler, 7th earl of Ormond (28 January 1498), for the reappointment of Piers as his deputy. The Polestown/Kildare pact was back in place[55] and Kildare was free to pursue the establishment of an effective overlordship in Leinster; he now attacked the O'Mores, who were now probably led by Máelsechlainn mac Uaithne (before the end of the century, Kildare enforced his suzerainty over them, recovering the castles of Lea, Morett and Dunamase).[56] The only major problem now on the midland horizon was the emergence of the powerful Toirdhealbhach Donn O'Brien of Thomond, Sir James of Ormond's cousin, who, in 1499, revenged him by defeating Piers.[57] In East Leinster, Kildare, supported by Henry VII's approval and his resources, systematically conquered the O'Tooles and O'Byrnes, expelling them from the territories of Fercullen and Ferter that adjoined the southern Pale. Kildare's first major incursion into Wicklow was probably in 1497. That year, the Four Masters record that the O'Byrnes killed O'Hanlon's son, Kildare's ally – which suggests that Kildare had used his Irish clients to attack the Wicklow Irish.[58] It also seems hardly a coincidence that the bishopric of Glendalough ceased to exist that year: Bishop Denis White of Glendalough resigned his office before Kildare's chancellor, Archbishop Fitzsimons, while Geoffrey Fyche, a high-ranking official of the

---

52 Nicholls, 'The Kavanaghs' (1981), fn. 9, p. 190; Cathaoir MacInnycross is described as Cahir McGerald upon his accession to the Leinster kingship in 1531, see Dowling, *Annals*, p. 35. **53** O'Byrne, 'The rise of Gabhal Raghnaill', pp 72–3; Conway, *Henry VII, Scot & Ire.*, pp 232–5; Ellis, *Tudor Ireland*, p. 85.   **54** Ellis, *Tudor Ireland*, p. 86; Curtis, *Med. Ire.*, p. 356. **55** *COD*, iv, appendix, no. 35, p. 335; Conway, *Henry VII, Scot & Ire.*, p. 240. **56** Máelsechlainn's date of death is given as 1502, see Fitzgerald, 'Historical notes on the O'Mores of Leix', appendice x; Carey, 'The end of the Gaelic order', p. 213.   **57** AU, 1499. **58** AFM, 1497.

archbishopric, was appointed archdeacon of Glendalough.[59] White's resignation indicates that Kildare's offensive had greatly weakened the bishop's patrons, the O'Byrnes and the MacMurroughs.[60]

By 1500 Kildare's conquest of the Wicklow Irish was well under way. Indeed, Toirdhealbhach mac Airt O'Toole, in a petition of 1540 to Henry VIII, confirmed that Kildare conquered Wicklow forty years earlier.[61] To establish a stable buffer zone between the Irish heartlands and the southern Pale, Kildare recovered and garrisoned Fassaroe and Castlekevin castles. Testifying to his determination to enforce his conquest, he built Powerscourt castle by 1500 at the expense of 4,000 or 5,000 marks.[62] In addition, before 1513 he enforced his hegemony over the O'Tooles, by settling his MacDonnell galloglass and their commander, James Boyce, near Baltyboys in west Wicklow. Furthermore, he regularly levied impositions and military service upon the Irish. He may also have forced the O'Tooles to retreat to their old Imaal heartland (something that probably contributed to a later internal O'Toole struggle for increasingly scarce resources).[63] During Kildare's conquest, the cohesiveness of the O'Byrne dynasty began to shatter. In 1500 Cathaoir mac Dúnlaing O'Byrne was assassinated by some of his kinsmen, who may have been anxious to come to terms with Kildare.[64] This marked the effective extension of Kildare's overlordship over the entire Wicklow region and the fatal weakening of the military machine of the senior O'Byrne dynasty. The next clearly identifiable overlord of the O'Byrnes, we know of, was Tadhg mac Gerald O'Byrne of Kiltimon, who made an indenture in January 1536 with Lord Deputy Leonard Grey.[65] The extent of the O'Byrne decline can be seen from the ease with which Kildare punished the O'Byrnes for their looting of Robert Suttrell's shipwrecked cargo off Wicklow between 1510 and 1513 (the O'Byrnes had the active assistance of John Dryman, Kildare's constable of Wicklow, in relieving Suttrell of his goods; after hearing Suttrell's complaints, Kildare marched into O'Byrne territory and arrested the unknown O'Byrne overlord's son for his part in the larceny.[66] This overlord died shortly afterwards and was succeeded by an unidentified kinsman, indicating the extent of Kildare's dominance).

On the other hand, Murchadh Ballach MacMurrough-Kavanagh managed, with difficulty, to maintain himself; he was strong enough to secure the abbacy of Duiske for his son, Cathaoir. In 1503, after his return from England, Kildare was powerful enough to compel the Leinster Irish to join him on campaign in Antrim.[67] It is not

59 *Alen's Reg*, pp 253–4; *The Fasti of St Patrick's*, p. 88.   **60** The pope continued to appoint Italians as bishops of Glendalough, see *Cal papal letters*, xvii, part 1, no. 579, pp 372–3. It is unlikely they ever arrived in Ireland, see *NHI*, ix, p. 313.   **61** Landsdowne MSS 159, f.13; J. Morrin (ed.), *Cal. Pat. Rolls Ire.*, i (Dublin, 1861), no. 109, pp 80–1 (hereafter *Cal.Pat.Rolls Ire.*). **62** Lyons, *Gearóid Óg Fitzgerald*, p. 13; *S. P. Hen VIII, 1515–38*, no. xcviii, p. 264; Price, 'Powerscourt and the territory of Fercullen', pp 117–20.   **63** Price, 'Placename study as applied to history', pp 26–9; *Crown surveys, 1540–1*, pp 266, 326, 335; AFM, 1517.   **64** AU, 1500.   **65** *Cal. Carew MSS, 1515–74*, no. 72, pp 88–9.   **66** *L. & P. Hen.VIII*, i, no. 297, pp 84–5. **67** Nicholls, 'Late medieval Irish annals' (1501) p. 100; AFM, 1503. On this expedition they

known whether Murchadh Ballach was part of this campaign, but it angered him that Kildare's power was undermining his provincial kingship. In fact, Murchadh Ballach in August 1504 travelled to Galway to join a confederation of Kildare's enemies, a league that was decidedly midland in character and which included Máelruanaidh O'Carroll, the O'Brien and O'Kennedy lords of Arra and Ormond. However, these forces, along with Murchadh Ballach, Toirdhealbhach Donn O'Brien and Ulick Burke, were defeated by Kildare at Knockdoe on 19 August. (Kildare brought large contingents of Leinster Irish with him, most notably Cathaoir O'Connor Faly.)[68] After this reverse, Murchadh Ballach seemingly accepted Kildare's suzerainty to his death in 1511/2, as did his successor, Art Buidhe, Domhnall Riabhach's son.[69] The Kildares took full advantage of Murchadh Ballach's weakness after the defeat of Knockdoe by buying lands between 1508 and 1526 in Wexford and in Carlow: in Wexford, the earls bought lands particularly in Roche's Country and in the manors of Fasaghbentry, Deeps and Old Ross and established a garrison in New Ross; they also purchased Clonogan castle (Wogan's castle) on the east bank of the Slaney, and Cloghgrenan castle in Carlow. Other purchases included Drumroe castle at Mount Loftus, Co. Kilkenny, from Theobald fitzRobert Butler in April 1509, and Kildare later even settled a sympathetic MacMurrough branch there.[70] Moreover, Kildare's dominance over the Irish of East Leinster effectively ended the great rivalry between the O'Byrnes and the MacMurroughs.

It was always the inherent instability of the critical midland theatre that threatened to unravel Kildare's overlordship. Throughout much of the first decade of the century, the earl's position was unassailable; we find him, for example, encouraging the O'Connor Falys to batter the MacGeoghegans into submission.[71] Kildare was at the height of his powers in 1510, when he brought the Leinster Irish on campaign in Munster. In spite of successes against the MacCarthys in that campaign, the O'Briens inflicted a significant reverse on Kildare's forces in Limerick;[72] there can be no doubt this was a decisive moment in the earl's career, sending shockwaves through his Irish clients. Unsurprisingly it was in West Leinster and the midlands that cracks first began to appear in Kildare's pedestal. In 1511 he supported the assassination of Cathaoir O'Connor Faly by his cousins, An Calbhach and Brian O'Connor Faly. Two years later he faced more trouble from a combination of the O'Mores and O'Carrolls. In August 1513 his artillery failed to reduce Máelruanaidh O'Carroll's castle of Leap; he had to return to Kildare for reinforcements; but on his way back to Leap, he was shot by the O'Mores.[73] His wound proved fatal, causing his death on 3 September 1513. Kildare's now shaky dominance over the Leinster Irish

demolished the castle of Belfast.   **68** Dowling, *Annals*, p. 33; Empey, p. 337; ALC, AFM, AConn, 1504; Ó Cléirigh, 'The O'Connor Faly lordship of Offaly', p. 100.   **69** Ibid., p. 33; AFM, 1511; Nicholls, 'Late medieval Irish annals' (1512), p. 100. For the obit of Art Buidhe, see AFM, 1518.   **70** Quinn, 'Irish Ireland and English Ireland', p. 635; Dowling, *Annals*, p. 35; Nicholls, 'The Kavanaghs' (1981), p. 193, see also fn. 35.   **71** Ó Cléirigh, 'The O'Connor Faly lordship of Offaly', p. 100.   **72** AFM, ALC, AConn, 1510.   **73** AU, 1511; Nicholls, 'Late

was passed to his son Gerald, 9th earl of Kildare. On 4 September, Gerald was elected justiciar by the Dublin council, an appointment confirmed by Henry VIII on 26 November.

The new Kildare earl's first priority was to re-establish himself in West Leinster and the midlands. During 1513, in the traditional Irish manner, he distributed gifts of tuarastal in the form of armour and horses among the midland lords such as the MacGillapatricks, O'Dempseys, O'Connor Falys and Giollapádraig O'More.[74] Sometime that year Piers Butler, joined by the MacMurroughs and O'Carrolls, burnt Desmond's lands in the Limerick territory of Connelloe: this suggests that Piers attempted to take advantage of the death of the elder Kildare in order to strengthen his position with the traditional Irish allies of his house. In 1514 the new earl of Kildare made his first substantive effort to shore up his midland affinity, attacking the O'Mores and capturing Cullentragh castle and Abbeyleix; while he suffered some losses, he subdued the O'Mores, for we know that Giollapádraig O'More accepted the earl's gifts that September. Kildare also lent his support to Piers to drive off Desmond and the O'Carrolls. In spite of Kildare and Piers' success, the O'Carrolls still extracted a blackrent from the English of Tipperary and Kilkenny in 1515.[75]

Trouble loomed on the horizon for Kildare. From 1515, his stewardship of Tudor Ireland increasingly fell under closer official scrutiny. That year a serious body of criticism emerged from within the Dublin government, the most prominent of the dissidents being Sir Thomas Darcy of Platten. Darcy had been a loyal supporter of Kildare's father and served as deputy treasurer between 1504 and 1513, but he did not enjoy the same intimacy with the new earl (shortly after his election to the justiciarship in September 1513, Kildare had removed him from office and from the council). Another of Kildare's sharpest critics was Robert Cowley, a Kilkenny lawyer. In May, Kildare arrived at the court of Henry VIII, where his enemies, led by Darcy, blamed him for the decline of the English lordship and the king's natural preoccupation with English affairs. More seriously, before the English council on 24 June, Darcy accused Kildare of making war and peace against the Irish without the Dublin council's consent, and of extracting coign and livery (that is, imposing billeting) upon the Pale.[76] Kildare's enemies created the impression that he was subverting royal government to further his own ends, and they also alleged that he had tried to usurp the crown's judicial, military and fiscal powers within his own earldom. The king heard them out and dismissed their charges and confirmed Kildare as deputy.[77]

The death in August 1515 of Thomas Butler, 7th earl of Ormond, presented Kildare with a poisoned chalice. In December the king gave the Ormond lands

medieval Irish annals' (1510), p. 100; Fitzsimons, 'The lordship of O'Connor Faly, 1520–1570', p. 208; Ó Cléirigh, 'The O'Connor Faly lordship of Offaly', p. 100; Lyons, *Gearóid Óg Fitzgerald*, p. 9. **74** *Crown surveys, 1540–1*, pp 319, 327, 332. **75** AU, 1513, 1514; ALC, AConn, 1514. See also Dowling, *Annals*, p. 33; *Crown surveys, 1540–1*, p. 331; Nicholls, *Gae Ire.*, p. 167. **76** *Carew MSS 1515–74*, no. 2, pp 6–8. **77** Ellis, *Tudor Ireland*, pp 102–3; Lyons, *Gearóid Óg Fitzgerald*, p. 30; Quinn, 'Henry VIII and Ireland', p. 321.

in Ireland, Wales and England to Ormond's daughters, Anne St Leger and Margaret Boleyn, but on 6 April 1516 Kildare and the Dublin council gave Ormond's Irish estates to Piers. In July, however, Henry VIII instructed Kildare to support the daughters' claims against Piers.[78] Although there was considerable advantages for Kildare in Piers' succession, he was compelled to support Margaret Boleyn's son, Thomas; otherwise he risked losing the support of Henry who later became successively involved with Thomas Boleyn's daughters, Mary and Anne Boleyn. The case was again heard by the Dublin council during the Michaelmas term of 1516, but was suspended until the king issued further instructions; this left Piers in possession of the Irish lands. At first, the controversy did not harm the Kildare/Polestown axis, for their interests were rooted in each other's success. Kildare needed Piers' goodwill if he was to reassert his father's midland overlordship; and Piers required his brother-in-law's aid, if he was to enforce his claims to the Ormond earldom. During 1516 Kildare defeated their mutual enemy, Máelruanaidh O'Carroll, taking Leap castle. Piers' predicament was highlighted when Edmund Butler of Cahir successfully defied him that year.[79] In 1517, the Kildare/Polestown alliance proved too strong for their opponents: Kildare quashed Máelruanaidh O'Carroll after he attacked the earl's O'Melaghlin clients, while Piers forced the submission of the Cahir Butlers in August.[80] The seal on Kildare's dominance in the midlands was set when he seems have been influential in the election of An Calbhach O'Connor Faly as lord of Offaly.[81]

During this period, East Leinster was peaceful – indicating the effectiveness of Kildare's overlordship. The reform treatise penned in 1515 by Patrick Finglas proposed that the king reconquer the province, stating that the Irish were 'but feeble in regard of the strength they have been of in former time'.[82] In Wicklow, Kildare settled his brothers to ensure Irish obedience. To James, he granted the western manors of Hollywood and Three Castles, and to Oliver lands nearby; Richard received the manors of Fassaroe, Powerscourt and Crevaghe as well as lands in Fercullen. Also, an internal family agreement stipulated that if Richard died without heir, his lands would pass to Walter. Furthermore, Thomas held lands at Dunboyke and Tulfarris in the manor of Ballymore. Throughout this region, Fitzgerald stewards were also collecting rents from the O'Byrnes and O'Tooles. However, in 1516 they may have caused tension in the O'Toole lands of Imaal and Glencapp.[83] The earl's distraction with his midland campaigns possibly provided some of the impetus for O'Toole restlessness; but it was the killing of Seán O'Toole of Imaal by Kildare's troops that primed the region. The

78 RIA MS 24. H.17; Ellis, *Tudor Ireland*, p. 103.   **79** AFM, ALC, AConn, 1516; Vennings, 'The O'Carrolls of Offaly', p. 183; *Ancient Irish histories*, i (Campion's *Historie of Ireland*), p. 159. **80** AFM, 1517; *COD*, iv, no. 40, pp 43–51, no. 119, pp 106–7; Empey, p. 293.   **81** Fitzsimons, 'The lordship of O'Connor Faly, 1520–1570', p. 208; AFM, 1517.   **82** *Carew MSS 1515–74*, no. 1, p. 5.   **83** *Crown surveys, 1540–1*, p. 235.

following year Seán Óg O'Toole revenged this attack, killing some of Kildare's men after they had attacked Imaal.[84] Worse was to follow when Kildare's client, Art O'Toole, was killed probably by his Imaal kinsmen, while in 1517/18, Art's son, Toirdhealbhach, defeated an expedition led by Mayor Christopher Ussher of Dublin, a Kildare client.[85] Political uncertainty within the MacMurroughs also possibly contributed to the instability in Wicklow: on 25 November 1517 Art Buidhe MacMurrough, king of Leinster, died leaving a disputed succession between two candidates, Art Buidhe's brother, Gerald, and Murchadh Ballach's son, Muircheartach. Gerald won.[86]

This violence in East Leinster occured against in the context of steadily deteriorating relations between Kildare and Piers. Although Piers was in possession of the Ormond lands and was styled earl, Henry VIII refused to recognize his title. Apparently, Piers nursed grievances arising from Kildare's diplomacy in 1515–16 during the aborted resolution of Ormond's estates. Piers clearly felt hard done by, having expected his brother-in-law's total support. Ultimately the falling out of Piers and Kildare began a deadly power struggle. In effect, the collapse of their partnership marked time upon the Kildare's monopoly of the highest government office and consequently the earl's hegemony in Leinster. Piers raised the stakes, refusing to compensate Kildare's government for two-thirds of the income from the Ormond estates which the Polestown Butlers had received while Earl John and Earl Thomas were absentees. The ill-feeling increased when Piers took Robert Cowley into his service and used his legal skills to undermine Kildare's government, probably in the hope that the king might formally recognize Piers' disputed title of earl of Ormond as a reward for his loyalty. By late 1518, Cardinal Wolsey convinced Henry VIII of the necessity of reform in Ireland. Accordingly, Kildare was ordered to appoint a deputy and come to England to answer charges of misgovernance. Before he left for England, Kildare appointed Maurice Fitzgerald as his deputy; he arrived at court in late 1519 or early 1520.[87]

84 O'Toole, *A history of the Clan O'Toole*, p. 223; *Holinshed's Irish Chronicle*, p. 253. See also *Ancient Irish histories*, i (Campion's *Historie of Ireland*), p. 159.   85 AFM, 1517; O'Toole, *A history of the Clan O'Toole*, p. 223.   86 BL Egerton MS 1782, p. 3; AFM, 1518. Muircheartach died in 1521, see Nicholls, 'Late medieval Irish annals' (1521), p. 101. In 1519 Donnchadh Kavanagh, Muircheartach's brother, died, see AFM, 1519; *S.P. Hen. VIII, 1515–38*, iii, p. 36; Nicholls, 'The Kavanaghs' (1981) p. 190.   87 *Red Bk Kildare*, no. 201, pp 188–9; Lennon, *Sixteenth century Ire.*, pp 85–7; Quinn, 'The Kildare hegemony, 1494–1520', p. 660; *COD*, iv, no. 61, p. 60; McCorristine, *The revolt of Silken Thomas*, p. 39.

CHAPTER 9

The advance of Tudor rule into Leinster, 1520–70

In 1520 the Kildares stood at the height of their power, both in Leinster and throughout the country. But within fifteen years their achievements had been irreversibly undone by Henry VIII. Before the council of the Star Chamber in early 1520, Kildare was accused of creating a personal power-base despite his oath to the king, and was removed from office. On 10 March 1520 Thomas Howard, earl of Surrey, was appointed lord lieutenant as part of a plan to reform the Dublin government. After his arrival in Dublin on 23 May, Surrey embarked upon a series of campaigns against Irish lords throughout the country. In East Leinster some lords such as the O'Byrnes and Toirdhealbhach mac Airt O'Toole welcomed Surrey when he advanced into their territory that autumn, hoping to curry favour with him in Kildare's absence in England;[1] but Surrey was faced by an entirely different set of circumstances in West Leinster and the midlands, where he met a systematic and organized campaign of opposition.

Financial problems hindered Surrey in his attempts to combat this opposition. During the course of his campaign, it transpired that Kildare had orchestrated these outbursts of endemic violence. Among Kildare clients opposing Surrey's army were Máelruanaidh O'Carroll of Ely, Conall O'More, a noble of Laois, and Brian O'Connor Faly of Offaly.[2] Surrey's suspicions of Kildare's involvement were confirmed to him by Máelruanaidh O'Carroll at a July parley before handing over his brother, Donnchadh O'Carroll, and his own son as hostages. Moreover, Donnchadh (in a later statement that September) told government officials that the abbot of Monasterevin had brought letters to Máelruanaidh from Kildare in England during Easter 1520, encouraging him to war upon the earl's English enemies.[3] Surrey managed to detach O'Connor Faly from Kildare's party, and it was probably during this period that Surrey invested him as lord of Offaly.[4] These amicable relations were brief. With Kildare still out of favour and

---

1 *Cal. Carew MSS, 1515–74*, no. 9, p. 16. See also *L. & P. Hen VIII*, xvi, no. 272, p. 116. Toirdhealbhach mac Airt later described himself as Norfolk's old servant. 2 Vennings, 'The O'Carrolls of Offaly', pp 181–3; Conall was married to Gormflaith O'Carroll. See poem 'Tnuth Laighean re laimh gConaill' RIA 2 (23/F/16), p. 113. 3 *Cal. Carew MSS, 1515–74*, no.5, p. 9. 4 Fitzsimons, 'The lordship of O'Connor Faly, 1520–1570', p. 209. This Brian

in England, Piers Butler under the cover of extending royal authority sought to spread his influence in the midlands. In 1521 he attacked Ely, capturing Máelruanaidh's son, Fearganainm; and in July that year Máelruanaidh with the O'Mores and O'Connor Falys raided Co. Kildare, forcing Surrey to lead an inconclusive campaign against them, his only notable success being the wounding of Conall of Laois in July by Sir Edward Plunkett, Baron Dunsany. By mid October, however, the three again submitted, and O'Connor Faly pledged his loyalty to Surrey before the end of the year. Still, the growth of Piers Butler's power among the midland lords convinced many to place themselves in the Butler camp; and after Surrey's departure from Ireland in winter 1521–2, O'Connor Faly and Máelruanaidh cultivated relations with Piers,[5] who on 26 March 1522 was appointed lord deputy.

Like Surrey before him, during 1522 Piers concluded that he could not govern effectively because of the activities of the earl's clients, so he requested that Kildare be allowed to return to Ireland. Granted permission to do so, Kildare arrived on 1 January 1523, and he wasted no time in reasserting his suzerainty over his Leinster clients. This was quickly achieved in East Leinster as evidenced by the acceptance that month of gifts of horses made by the earl to leading O'Byrnes and O'Tooles.[6] However, a residual threat remained from Piers, and the Kildares themselves exacerbated the situation when James Fitzgerald, the earl's brother, murdered Piers' partisan, Robert Talbot, on his way to spend Christmas 1523 in Kilkenny. This murder brought the deputy's army into the Wicklow highlands in pursuit of James. He succeeded in expelling James from the region, destabilizing Kildare's eastern frontier and loosening his grip upon the O'Tooles and the O'Byrnes.[7] The struggle spread, dragging various O'Byrne factions into the vortex, with different leaders aligning themselves on either side. However, Kildare's restoration was completed by his reappointment as lord deputy in May 1524.[8]

Kildare also faced growing problems from the MacMurrough kings of Leinster; these coincided with the growing rapprochement between Piers and his MacMurrough uncles, the sons of Domhnall Riabhach MacMurrough-Kavanagh. In January 1523, Piers' uncle, Gerald MacMurrough, king of Leinster and husband to Katharine Butler, died at Leighlinbridge and was succeeded by his brother Muiris.[9] An indication of Kildare's desire to stamp his overlordship

---

O'Connor Faly was the son of Cathaoir, lord of Offaly (*d.*1511), and Siobhan O'Connor Faly see poem 'Failghigh chosnas clu Laighean' NLI G 992, sff. 256–266; RIA I (23D/14), p. 62. **5** *S.P. Hen VIII, 1515–38*, no. xii, pp 78–82; ibid., no. xxv, pp 85–8; Fitzsimons, 'The lordship of O'Connor Faly, 1520–1570', p. 210. **6** *Crown surveys, 1540–1*, pp 335. **7** Quinn, 'The re-emergence of English policy as the major factor in Irish affairs, 1520–34', p. 671; *L. & P. Hen VIII*, iv, part 3, no. 5795, p. 2590; O'Byrne, 'The rise of the Gabhal Raghnaill', p. 79. **8** O'Byrne, 'The rise of the Gabhal Raghnaill', p. 76; *Crown surveys, 1540–1*, p. 326. Yet he maintained considerable control over the O'Byrnes as confirmed by the death of An Calbhach O'Byrne of Cronroe on the earl's expedition of that year against the O'Donnells of Donegal. See AFM, 1524. **9** Dowling, *Annals*, p. 34; Nicholls, 'Late medieval Irish annals' (1523), p. 101;

on the MacMurroughs was the murder of Bishop Maurice Doran of Leighlin in
1525: Abbot Cathaoir MacMurrough of Duiske, Murchadh Ballach MacMurrough-
Kavanagh's son, allegedly encouraged his own son, Murchadh, to murder the
bishop in order to procure the see for himself.[10] Kildare's reaction was ferocious;
he invaded Carlow and forced Abbot Cathaoir to flee to his cousin – Piers.
Kildare then subjected Murchadh to a horrific death, disembowelling him and
flaying him alive.[11] This rocked the wider MacMurrough dynasty and must have
proved humiliating for Muiris, its overlord, so it is hardly coincidental that
Muiris completely aligned himself with Piers, symbolically returning Arklow to
the latter in August 1525. Kildare also cultivated MacMurroughs who were
sympathic to him, most particularly his cousin Cathaoir MacInnycross.[12] By 1526
Kildare was clearly hostile to Muiris, and was cultivating another MacMurrough
leader – Cathaoir mac Airt MacMurrough of Sliocht Diarmada Láimhdeirg, to
whom he gave the hand of his daughter, Lady Alice Fitzgerald.[13]

But Kildare's position in West Leinster and the midlands had been damaged.
One of the disaffected Irish lords was Conall O'More of Laois, who seemingly
succeeded to the lordship of Laois upon the death of his cousin Cétach mac
Laoiseach in 1523.[14] Like O'Connor Faly, he had allied with Piers after 1521,
and he had devastated southern Kildare in March 1522 after hearing rumours of
Kildare's return.[15] After his return to Ireland on 1 January 1523, Kildare realized
that he had to again establish his presence in the midlands or face the continued
erosion of his hegemony, so he led his army into the midlands against Conall of
Laois and O'Connor Faly. After a short struggle and the brinkmanship of Conn
Bacach O'Neill of Tyrone, both nobles accepted Kildare's overlordship, but
although Conall of Laois resented Fitzgerald dominance he still recognized
Kildare's overlordship by accepting his horses on 21 and 26 January 1524.[16]
Kildare was determined to draw O'Connor Faly more firmly into his camp;
sometime 1523 and 1526 he gave his daughter, Lady Mary Fitzgerald, to O'Connor
Faly as his wife. This O'Connor Faly/Kildare midland alliance did much to
repair the damaged Kildare hegemony in Leinster, but these moves of Kildare
could not prevent West Leinster and the midlands becoming the vital arena for
his struggle with Piers in 1525.

In that year Piers dispatched gunners to Máelruanaidh O'Carroll of Ely to
defend Leap castle, but Kildare and O'Connor Faly had the best of the conflict

---

COD, iv, p. 158.   **10** ALC, AFM, AConn, 1525; Dowling, *Annals*, p. 34.   **11** AFM, ALC, 1525;
Dowling, *Annals*, p. 34; Nicholls, 'Late medieval Irish annals' (1523), p. 101; Nicholls, 'The
Kavanaghs', (1981), p. 190.   **12** COD, iv, no. 118, pp 102–3; *S.P. Hen VIII, 1515–38*, lix, p. 157;
Nicholls, 'The Kavanaghs', (1981), p. 192.   **13** Lansdowne Ms 159, f. 13; Hughes, 'The fall of
the Clan Kavanagh', p. 295. That year Cathaoir mac Airt first appears in the written record,
burning Drumore castle in Kilkenny and killing its occupants. See Nicholls, 'Late medieval
annals' (1526), p. 101; Dowling, *Annals*, p. 35. Although this was Kildare property, it housed
Abbot Cathaoir's nephew – Cathaoir. Perhaps Cathaoir mac Airt was delegated by Kildare to
eject the tenant who may have switched into the Butler camp.   **14** AU, 1523.   **15** L. & P.
Hen VIII, iii, part 2, no. 2197, p. 934.   **16** *Crown surveys, 1540–1*, pp 338 & 340.

in the midlands, forcing Máelruanaidh O'Carroll to renew his alliance with the earl, thereby reaffirming the Kildare midland suzerainty. The struggle, however, between Kildare and Piers was far from over. Unlike O'Connor Faly, Conall O'More of Laois played an unknown part in the earl's reconquest of 1525. Certainly, the friendship between Conall and O'Connor Faly had cooled and a considerable mistrust evolved between them. During this period Conall realigned again with Piers. His discontent with Kildare manifested itself in sporadic raiding into Kildare between 1525 and 1526.[17] The actions of Máelruanaidh O'Carroll of Ely succinctly display the unenviable position of the midland lords, caught, as they were, along the faultline of the conflicting ambits of the Fitzgerald and Butler houses. However, he successfully walked the diplomatic tight-rope, and managed two politically advantageous marriages: Feargananim, Máelruanaidh's heir, was married off to another daughter of Kildare, while the hand of Grainne, Máelruanaidh's daughter, was given to Ulick Burke (later 1st earl of Clanricarde), Piers' nephew. And when Burke tried to back out of the marriage, Máelruanaidh coerced him into keeping his word. For much of the late 1520s, Máelruanaidh, like his neighbours, was forced to flit between the rival camps.

By 1526 Kildare had the upper hand. Realizing this, Piers submitted complaints to court about Kildare's behaviour – forcing Kildare to present counter-allegations in summer 1526. But by August Henry VIII, having enough of the anarchic state of Ireland, summoned both Kildare and Piers to account for their actions. Kildare left for England in November; Piers had been there since September. Henry planned to reduce Kildare's power, and he also sought to resolve the Kildare/Butler rivalry, as it was affecting the peace of the English lordship in Ireland. Moreover, the disputed succession to the Ormond earldom between Piers and Sir Thomas Boleyn demanded resolution. Henry VIII also wished to discuss with them how to put an end to the plotting of James Fitzgerald, 11th earl of Desmond, with the French. While Kildare was in England during autumn 1527, Sir Thomas Fitzgerald, his brother and deputy, was replaced by Richard Nugent, 12th Baron Delvin, a prominent Kildare opponent. In response, Kildare encouraged his supporters and Irish clients to wreak havoc throughout Leinster to force Henry VIII to send him home.[18]

This struggle culminated in O'Connor Faly's capture in May 1528 of the acting lord deputy, Delvin. But this only steeled Henry to reduce Kildare's power. To this end, Surrey, now duke of Norfolk and Henry's principal adviser on Irish affairs, weakened Kildare's position in Leinster by leasing lands in Carlow and Wexford to Piers, the newly created earl of Ossory.[19] This represented an attempt by the government to create an effective opposition to Kildare

---

17 Ibid., p. 345. On 22 February 1526, Conall accepted horses from Kildare. For Conall's attacks on the liberty of Kildare, see Lyons, *Gearoid Óg Fitzgerald*, p. 40.   **18** His later attainder of 1536 is dated to 1528. Clearly he was judged to have committed treasonable acts in 1528. See *Cal. Inquisitions*, Hen VIII 107/8, p. 58. *S.P. Hen VIII, 1515–38*, no.lvi, pp 145–7.   **19** COD, iv, no. 140, pp 128–9; Quinn, 'The re-emergence of English policy as a major factor in Irish affairs, 1520–34', p. 675.

in the strategic midland region. Exasperated by the widespread disobedience of Kildare's clients, the king, against the counsel of Norfolk and Wolsey, reappointed Ossory lord deputy in August 1528. Ossory now made overtures to the disgruntled clients of Kildare, drawing Conall O'More of Laois and O'Connor Faly's brother, Cathaoir, to his side; and his new-found influence in the midlands was evidenced by the attendance of Cathaoir, Máelruanaidh O'Carroll of Ely, and Conall of Laois at his investiture as deputy in October. In East Leinster Ossory also drove wedges between Kildare and his brothers who governed Wicklow's western highlands on the eastern flank of the Fitzgerald earldom. The crisis facing Kildare here was heightened by the defection of his brother Sir Thomas Fitzgerald to Ossory in January 1529.[20] Sir Thomas' acceptance of a government pardon underlined the difficulties faced by the Kildare clients. Shortly after this O'Connor Faly released Delvin, and the government agreed to resume payment of blackrent to him.[21] And the weakening of Kildare's grip roused the O'Tooles to raid Kildare's earldom for the first time in decades.

By June, Henry VIII, adopting a different tack, appointed a mere youth, his natural son, Henry Fitzroy, duke of Richmond, as lord lieutenant. Ossory was discharged in August and replaced by a secret council consisting of Lord Chancellor Archbishop Alen of Dublin, Chief Justice Patrick Bermingham and Treasurer John Rawson; but in November his position as a Tudor agent in the midlands was significantly bolstered by his appointment as a justice of the peace in Tipperary and Kilkenny. In late summer Henry dispatched Sir William Skeffington to assess the Irish situation militarily. After a campaign against the O'Mores in March/April 1530, Skeffington returned to England to report to his royal master, following which he was appointed lord deputy on 22 June 1530. A deal was also struck with Kildare whereby the earl was pardoned for his nefarious activities of 1527–8 and was licensed to return home.[22] In return, Kildare promised his utmost co-operation with Skeffington; he arrived back in Ireland with him on 24 August. Kildare's first action signalled his intentions in East Leinster: he launched a successful attack upon the O'Tooles.[23]

Quickly assessing the danger posed by Ossory's party in West Leinster and the midlands, Kildare determined to recover his position through a course of diplomacy and military aggression. He also rewarded O'Connor Faly and the other loyal midland lords.[24] With Skeffington's approval, he launched several campaigns against his former clients under the pretext of protecting the Pale, forcing Conall of Laois to accept his (Kildare's) overlordship in November. This time, perhaps mindful of the danger of Ossory, Kildare was more far-sighted in his approach to the midlands. By 1532 he had soothed the grievances of Conall

20 Ibid., no. 144, pp 131–2.   21 Fitzsimons, 'The lordship of O'Connor Faly, 1520–1570', p. 212.   22 *L. & P. Hen VIII*, v, no. 398, p. 198; ibid., iv, part 3, no. 6490 (22), p. 2919; ibid., iv, part 3, no. 6363, p. 2856; *S.P. Hen. VIII, 1515–38*, no. lvii, p. 150; Quinn, 'The re-emergence of English policy as a major factor in Irish affairs, 1520–34', p. 679.   23 J. Hooker, 'The description of the conquest and inhabitation of Ireland', in Holinshed's *Chronicles* (1587), ii, p. 87; Lennon, *Sixteenth century Ire.*, p. 102.   24 *Crown surveys, 1540–1*, pp 346–50.

of Laois; Máelruanaidh O'Carroll of Ely also returned to Kildare's camp, and this led Ossory to promote the claims of O'Carroll's rivals. Between 1530 and 1532 Kildare buttressed his position in East Leinster against Ossory, by securing his candidate's succession to the Leinster kingship after the 1531 death of Muiris MacMurrough. This was Cathaoir MacInnycross, Kildare's cousin, who was described by Ossory as 'thErl of Kildares servaunt and norishe'.[25]

In spite of Kildare's military resurgence, he faced a new threat when Archbishop Alen of Dublin legally challenged his rights to former archiepiscopal and secular lands lying within the Wicklow mountains. This challenge was the culmination of earlier campaigns waged by his predecessors, Archbishops Rokeby and Inge in 1514 and 1521 respectively. During the parliamentary sessions of September and October 1531, Alen successfully sought the repeal of the 1483 statute legalizing Kildare's claims to lands of absentees throughout Kildare, west Wicklow and Carlow. Alen encouraged absentee owners to re-occupy these lands but also attempted to establish his own rights where title had fallen vacant. This was a tremendous blow to Kildare, who was convinced of Skeffington's collusion, and the blow was compounded when Thomas Howard, duke of Norfolk, then leased all his lands within the region to Ossory, thereby allowing the latter to interfere within the Fitzgerald liberty of Kildare.[26]

Kildare struck back by mobilizing his clients, an act which reduced Skeffington to impotence, and (perhaps through Kildare's connivance) Alen was burdened with a huge praemunire fine in spring 1531.[27] Only the rise of Henry VIII's new favourite, Thomas Cromwell, prevented the archbishop's ruin. Ironically, the hobbling of Alen further weakened Kildare's hold on north Wicklow: to pay his debts, Alen sought to claw back rents due to the archiepiscopal coffers from the marcher families there, many of whom were Kildare's clients (Kildare authorized them to hit back, unleashing them with the O'Byrnes and O'Tooles to raid Alen's estates).[28] Then Kildare turned on Piers Butler (Ossory), encouraging the Butlers of Cahir to oppose him in Tipperary, and he sought to weaken Ossory's position among the Irish of East Leinster by seeking a lease of Tullow from Ossory's overlord, Thomas Boleyn, earl of Ormond and Wiltshire.[29] Kildare's actions were in response to Ossory's growing influence among the O'Byrne leadership who wanted to be rid of Kildare. Probably because of Kildare's active interference among the O'Byrnes living close to Tullow, Seán mac Lorcán O'Byrne of Clonmore burnt much of southern Kildare in early 1532.[30] Kildare's response, effective and brutal, was to hang two of Seán mac Lorcán's sons, but

---

25 Nicholls, 'Late medieval Irish annals' (1531, 1532), p. 101; Dowling, *Annals*, p. 35; *S.P. Hen. VIII, 1515–38*, no. lix, p. 157; Nicholls, 'The Kavanaghs' (1981), fn.9, p. 190; *Crown surveys, 1540–1*, p. 335.   **26** Quinn, 'The re-emergence of English policy as a major factor in Irish affairs, 1520–34', p. 680.   **27** Murray, 'Archbishop Alen, Tudor reform and the Kildare rebellion', pp 14–5.   **28** *Alen's Reg*, pp 172 & 242; O'Byrne, 'The rise of Gabhal Raghnaill', p. 83.   **29** Lyons, *Gearóid Óg Fitzgerald*, p. 49; *S.P. Hen. VIII, 1515–38*, no. lix, pp 153–5.   **30** *L. & P. Hen VIII*, v, no. 1061, p. 480. Seán mac Lorcán earlier accepted a horse from Kildare on 4 September 1515, see *Crown surveys, 1540–1*, p. 325.

this only served to increase the enmity of the O'Tooles and O'Byrnes towards the earl: throughout May 1532, Edmund O'Byrne of the Downes subjected Kildare's clients in the Dublin marches to a regime of nightly terror, while in west Wicklow Art Óg O'Toole publicly mocked Kildare's faltering overlordship by burning the town of Donard that year.[31]

On 5 July 1532 Henry VIII reappointed Kildare (yet again) as lord deputy to succeed the now discredited Skeffington. Incapable of sharing power, Kildare set out, under the pretext of good government, to re-establish his suzerainty over the midlands. It was here that the rivalry between Ossory and Kildare reached a deadly climax. Their struggle focused upon the race to succeed the deceased Máelruanaidh O'Carroll of Ely during 1532. Before he died, Máelruanaidh nominated his son Fearganainm as his successor. This was vehemently resisted by Máelruanaidh's brothers, Donnchadh and Uaithne, who were actively encouraged by Ossory; this compelled Fearganainm to request Kildare's support in 1532–3. Two factors were to propel Kildare and Ossory into outright war – the killing of Ossory's son, Thomas Butler, by Diarmait MacGillapatrick, Kildare's ally, in late 1532; and the wounding of Kildare (during his siege of Birr castle) by Ossory's O'Carroll supporters in winter 1532–3.[32] However, Kildare succeeded in re-establishing Fearganainm in his lordship by bringing Donnchadh O'Carroll to heel in 1534 (he took Shinrone castle). But news of Kildare's wound worked against him among the Leinster nobility: the lord of North Ossory, Brian MacGillapatrick, promptly switched sides, handing over Diarmait, his brother, to the Butlers, and himself marrying Margaret Butler, Ossory's daughter.[33] The effect of Brian MacGillapatrick's realignment turned the midland war in favour of the Butlers. The fall-out of Kildare's wound was soon felt in East Leinster. There the O'Tooles routed Kildare's brothers, while Edmund O'Byrne exposed Kildare's inability to defend the Pale by audaciously attacking Dublin Castle, releasing prisoners and generally terrifying the citizens during a rampage through the city.[34] Infuriated by the chaos and suspicious of Kildare, Henry VIII demanded the presence of Kildare and Ossory at court in September 1533. Kildare delayed his departure for England until spring of the next year; he appointed his son, Thomas Fitzgerald, Lord Offaly, as vice-deputy in his absence. Once in England both Kildare and Ossory accepted reforms that would have the effect of considerably limiting their personal power. In May 1534 Henry VIII finally dismissed Kildare as lord deputy, and Skeffington was provisionally reappointed. Kildare also had to surrender his recent palatine liberty of Kildare

31 Ibid; N. White (ed.), *Extents of Irish monastic possessions 1540–1* (Dublin, 1943), p. 63. 32 ALC, 1532; Fitzsimons, 'The lordship of O'Connor Faly, 1520–1570', p. 213; Vennings, 'The O'Carrolls of Offaly', pp 185–6; *Ancient Irish histories* i (*Campion's historie of Ireland*), p. 173; Edwards, 'The MacGiollapádraigs (Fitzpatricks) of Upper Ossory', pp 327–9. See also *S.P. Hen VIII, 1538–46*, no. ccxxxii, pp 24–5, see also fn.1, p. 25. Conall O'More's third son Giollapádraig was party to the murder of Thomas Butler by Kildare clients in 1532. 33 AFM, ALC, 1532; Edwards, 'The MacGiollapádraigs (Fitzpatricks) of Upper Ossory', p. 328. 34 *S.P. Hen. VIII, 1515–38*, no. lxiv, p. 169; *L. & P. Hen VIII*, v, no. 1061, p. 480.

and accept Skeffington's appointment without reservation.[35] Even so, he was not allowed to return home, and his son Offaly was summoned to court. In spite of close surveillance, Kildare advised Offaly to create a stand-off between Fitzgerald and English forces in Ireland. On 11 June 1534, Offaly denounced Henry VIII before the Dublin council, and rebellion broke out.

At first Offaly enjoyed considerable support among the Leinster Irish (the O'Mores, for example, prominently figured in Offaly's victories over Ossory at Thomastown and Tullow during the summer, forcing the Butlers to flee to Waterford).[36] During September, Offaly ordered his Irish clients, including Conall of Laois, Cathaoir MacInnycross, the O'Byrnes and the O'Connor Falys, to protect Co. Kildare, while he laid siege to Dublin. In December, Offaly and the O'Mores burnt Trim and Dunboyne;[37] but their failure to take Dublin, and the arrival of Skeffington, caused many Leinster nobles to realign themselves with the government. On account of these reverses, Offaly became dependent on the reconciled O'Connor Faly brothers, but fractures were evident in Offaly's camp when early in 1535 Conall O'More of Laois and Cathaoir O'Connor Faly formed an alliance. The Kildares' position became increasingly untenable when Skeffington captured Maynooth in late March 1535; this opened up the midlands to the lord deputy's armies, allowing Ossory (Piers Butler) to strike at the wavering allies of Offaly, and to turn two brothers of Conall of Laois on him. Conall of Laois was forced to withdraw his support from Offaly in April, and to give hostages to Ossory.[38] Also, Skeffington praised the O'Tooles and O'Byrnes for their hounding in March 1535 of the weakening Kildare forces. Even though the Kildares were on the run, Conall of Laois retained considerable sympathy for Offaly, his foster-son; and early in August O'More forces captured, but then released, Sir John Burnell and Féilim Buidhe O'Connor Faly, Offaly's principal supporters. It was also reported that in the same battle O'More troops allowed Offaly, now 10th earl of Kildare, to escape capture (this prompted Lord Leonard Grey to complain to Thomas Cromwell, the chief minister of Henry VIII, on 15 August).[39] But the end was near: within days, Cathaoir O'Connor Faly surrendered to Ossory, while on 24 August Kildare and O'Connor Faly finally surrendered to Grey.

The fall of the Kildares created a countrywide political vacuum; and the execution of Kildare with five uncles at Tyburn during February 1537 completed the implosion. With the destruction of the Kildare Geraldines, the political balance of the previous six decades in East Leinster and West Leinster and the midlands ceased to exist. The Dublin government's first priority following the

---

35 Brady, *The chief governors*, p. 4.　**36** At Thomastown Cétach Ruadh, Conall O'More's son, wounded Lord James Butler – the son of Ossory. *S.P. Hen. VIII, 1515–38*, no. xcii, pp 251–3. **37** *S.P. Hen. VIII, 1515–38*, no. xciii, pp 251–3; *L. & P. Hen VIII*, vii, no. 1573, p. 586.　**38** Ibid., pp 251–4.　**39** *The Book of Howth*, pp 193–4; *L. & P. Hen VIII*, viii, no. 382, p. 152; *S.P. Hen. VIII, 1515–38*, no. lxxxvi, p. 234. This relationship is mentioned in *S.P. Hen. VIII, 1538–46*, no. cccxxvi, p. 258. *S.P. Hen. VIII, 1515–38*, no. xcvi, p. 261, no. xcviii, p. 265; *Cal. Carew MSS, 1515–74*, no. 57, p. 71; *L. & P. Hen VIII*, ix, no. 98, p. 28.

Kildare defeat was to shore up the frontiers of the Pale. Consequently, in the two decades after 1536, the policies pursued by successive lord deputies were dictated by the need to secure stability. The Tudors, in effect, had to slip into the shoes of the Kildares to fill the political void: at one time the Kildares would have checked and punished unwarranted Irish incursions into the Pale; now the task fell to a financially-strapped government.

The turmoil was most acutely felt in West Leinster and the midlands, a region that had been destabilized by the chronic political upheaval of recent years. Instead of a Kildare hegemony in the region, three powers now vied with each other – the leaderless Kildare party, Ossory's (Piers Butler's) faction and the government party. But under the steerage of Grey, Skeffington's successor as lord deputy, reform was attempted. As has been argued, if the reform of the Irish lordship was to be ultimately successful, the Irish polities of West Leinster and the midlands had to be stabilized. Therefore, a government hegemony in the midlands was deemed of the utmost importance; if the midland lords failed to be amenable to the cause of reform, then they would have to be convinced by coercion. The study of Grey's governorship and his relations with the Irish of West Leinster is crucial to a clear understanding of the progress of Henrician reform. Deserving especial consideration are the government's dealings with the O'Connor Falys and the O'Mores, the effects of which were to reverberate throughout Leinster; it would became clear that the government was determined to reduce the power of local elites, and bring the days of the warlords to an end.

Grey knew that over-reliance on Ossory could not advance the reform of the English lordship. To Ossory's disgust, the lord deputy developed the now leaderless Kildare party as a counterweight to Butler power – a policy that the Butlers read as tantamount to a rejection of their efforts.[40] Although they actively sought to impede him as well as seek his downfall, Grey showed himself to be an able and active governor, achieving the acceptance of English authority by a series of countrywide military campaigns. The midlands proved particularly difficult: after his release probably in late 1535, Brian O'Connor Faly exploited the political instability for his own ends, banishing his brother Cathaoir from Offaly between 1536 and 1537; in May 1537, Grey's armies overturned O'Connor Faly's restoration, exiling him in neighbouring Ely between June and November, during which time Grey gave the lordship to a grateful Cathaoir as part of his policy to stabilize the wider region. Grey's victory reduced O'Connor Faly to desperate straits, but he found safety with other former Kildare adherents such as Fearganainm O'Carroll, lord of Ely, and O'Meagher.

Grey now attempted to flush O'Connor Faly out from Ely through cultivating Fearganainm O'Caroll. Throughout the Kildare rebellion, Fearganainm had loyally supported his brother-in-law, the 10th earl. In contrast, his uncle Donnchadh O'Carroll joined the Butler and the English forces in the pursuit of

40 Brady, *The chief governors*, pp 18–22.

the Kildares – a persistence that paid off, for Donnchadh, with Butler support, eliminated the challenge of Uaithne O'Carroll and deposed Fearganainm in 1536. Fearganainm was not to regain his position until Donnchadh's death after May 1538. Grey then continued to extend his government's influence in the midlands by lending Fearganainm military assistance against Ossory's clients in summer 1538. Grey took Birr and Modreeny castles – and promptly handed them over to Fearganainm.[41] As a preamble to his restoration, Fearganainm agreed with Grey at Dublin on 12 June 1538 to hold Ely as a tenant of the king. In 1539 Fearganainm moved closer to Grey by making a treaty whose terms determined his relationship with the English crown: he was to pay a fixed rent for his lordship, and he agreed to provide a fixed number of soldiers each year for military service; in return, Grey quelled the turmoil between the O'Carroll factions, taking Moldreeny castle in November from the sons of Donnchadh.

With regard to the O'Connor Faly lordship, in autumn 1537 the Dublin council forwarded plans to London for its settlement, proposing that Cathaoir O'Connor Faly be created a baron and given the lordship of Offaly or that he be settled outside Offaly and that it be planted. These proposals came to nought when Brian O'Connor Faly regained his lordship by force in November.[42] This, and the threat of an O'Connor Faly/Ossory alliance, forced Grey to treat with O'Connor Faly before allowing him to submit in March 1538. As part of this policy Grey concluded an indenture with Brian MacGillapatrick of North Ossory in November 1537, detaching him from the Butler party by granting him government protection; to bolster the government's position in the midlands, Grey formally recognized Brian MacGillapatrick's lordship and, importantly, declared it not to be part of the Butler-dominated Co. Kilkenny.[43]

Unlike Brian O'Connor Faly, Conall O'More of Laois, his enemy, adopted a different approach, flitting between Ossory and the government. Both Ossory and Grey realized that the O'More lordship west of the Barrow conduit was one of the keys to the wider region. (The Kildare collapse increased the strategic importance of Laois.) Tellingly, both sought to court the O'More overlord, and as a result Conall of Laois was elevated beyond his normal status in midland politics. On 21 March 1536 it was reported that Conall and many of the Leinster nobility were deeply disturbed by the arrest of Sir James Fitzgerald, Kildare's uncle. However, the presence of government troops in the midlands and Grey's parley at Kilkea with Conall of Laois and Cathaoir MacInnycross MacMurrough, king of Leinster, prevented trouble.[44] This did not prevent Conall from taking the field against Brian MacGillapatrick of North Ossory in June and July (Grey had to

---

41 Vennings, 'The O'Carrolls of Offaly', pp 187–8; AFM, 1536; Fitzsimons, 'The lordship of O'Connor Faly, 1520–1570', pp 214–6.   **42** Fitzsimons, 'The lordship of O'Connor Faly, 1520–1570', pp 214–5; AU, 1537.   **43** *S.P. Hen VIII, 1515–38*, pp 514–15; Edwards, 'The MacGiollapádraigs (Fitzpatricks) of Upper Ossory', p. 335.   **44** *Cal. Carew MSS, 1515–74*, no. 74, p. 90; *S.P. Hen. VIII, 1515–38*, no. cxx, p. 307. This Cathaoir MacInnycross who was also known as Cathaoir Glais received horses from Kildare on 4 September 1513 and on 16 January 1523, see *Crown surveys, 1540–1*, pp 320, 335.

intervene to stop the conflict and negotiate a peace between the pair). At this stage, Ossory (Piers Butler) remained the only noble in Ireland able to control the Irish of the midlands. Testifying to this state of play was Conall of Laois and Ossory's presence as sureties to the submission on 14 July of Cathaoir MacInnycross, and the earl's role in the negotiations with Brian MacGillapatrick to end his feud with Conall.[45] The latter placated Grey by campaigning against Conchobhar O'Brien of Thomond and the Munster Geraldines in July/August 1536 before fighting O'Connor Faly in June 1537.[46] Yet it would be wrong to say that Conall's service realigned his lordship with the government: Conall died shortly after June 1537 and was succeeded by his brother Piers O'More, a client of Ossory (Piers ensured his succession to the O'More lordship through a combination of Ossory's support and by bribing Grey).[47] Once he became lord of Laois, he tacked before prevailing political winds. To appease and gain the support of Grey, Piers O'More agreed to maintain government galloglass in Laois, a decision probably taken to check the activities of Conall O'More's sons. In spite of the killing before the close of 1537 of Laoiseach, Conall of Laois' eldest son and also lord of Slemargy, the O'More civil war was to rage unabated.[48]

The shifting policies of the O'Mores are a fairly accurate reflection of the turbulence affecting the midlands. The discord in Laois also created opportunities for the government to gain a foothold there. On 14 January 1538 Grey negotiated a peace between Piers O'More and his nephews, Ruaidhrí Caoch and Cétach Ruadh O'More. In these brothers, Grey found willing accomplices to combat the Butlers in the midlands. Unsurprisingly, peace among the O'Mores proved short-lived. That same year Grey sent a series of complaints to court, accusing Ossory of attacking the sons of Conall of Laois. In reality, Grey had encouraged these new friends and other former Fitzgerald clients to attack Piers O'More and the Butler lands in Carlow.[49] In June, Piers complained of the activities of his nephews to the local army commander at Athy, Co. Kildare. Ruaidhrí Caoch O'More suddenly arrived and attempted to kill his uncle, forcing the army to arrest Piers for his own safety. Grey then arranged a conference for the warring parties in Dublin. Piers, accompanied by Ossory, arrived in Dublin to attend the conference in early June. Once there Grey

---

45 *Cal. Carew MSS, 1515–74*, no. 83, p. 97; *S.P. Hen VIII, 1515–38*, no. ccxxxii, pp 334–5. In 1546 Walter Cowley, a Butler ally, stressed the adherence of the O'Mores to Ormond, see *L. & P. Hen VIII*, xxi, part 1, no. 920, p. 450.   **46** *S.P. Hen VIII, 1515–38*, no. cxlii, p. 354; *Cal. Carew MSS, 1515–74*, no.86, p. 106.   **47** *L. & P. Hen VIII*, xiii, part 2, no. 1271, p. 522.   **48** In October 1537 Ruaidhrí Caoch O'More was served with a subpoena to give evidence in a murder case in the king's court at Kilkenny. To the horror of the official who served the subpoena, Ruaidhrí irreverently threw the writ in the mud and stood upon it. See *L. & P. Hen VIII*, xii, part II, no. 859 (2), p. 303.   **49** *CSPI, 1509–73*, no. 3, p. 36; *Cal. Fiants Hen VIII*, no. 171. This pardon dated 24 March 1540/1 records Edmund Ashbolde of Maynooth's encouragment of Cétach Ruadh to attack the Butlers. In 1538 Ossory described this Edmund Asbolde as a servant of Grey. See *S.P. Hen VIII, 1538–46*, fn. 1, p. 26. Also he alleged that Edmund had joined the O'More attack on Tullow. On 13 May 1538 Peter Fitzgerald of Great Grange was charged with instigating Cétach Ruadh to attack Ossory, see *CSPI, 1509–73*, no.55, p. 40.

arrested Piers, placing him in handcuffs and confining him in Maynooth.[50] This allowed Cétach Ruadh and Ruaidhrí Caoch a free hand to attack the Butlers and their uncle's tenants upon their return to Laois. On 22 August Piers was released; he renewed his submission two days later;[51] the king's commissioners confirmed his lordship of Laois, but his nephews expelled him from Laois and shortly afterwards Cétach Ruadh was inaugurated as lord of Laois in his place. However, substantial divisions quickly emerged among the brothers: Ruaidhrí Caoch remained closely allied to Cétach Ruadh, while a third brother Giollapádraig entered into an alliance with O'Connor Faly, marrying his daughter.[52]

In East Leinster, Grey pursued the cause of reform with similar zeal. As in West Leinster, this meant the introduction of English common law into the Irish lordships. To aid the furtherance of reform, Grey adopted a policy of divide and rule, patronizing relatively minor dynastic figures in an attempt to undermine their overlords. A prime example of this policy was the government's attitude to Cathaoir mac Airt MacMurrough. By 1534 Cathaoir mac Airt was already a major power among the MacMurroughs, and he was the son-in-law of the 9th earl of Kildare.[53] His Kildare client status was confirmed by his active role in the Kildare rebellion of 1534–5 which led to his pursuit by Ossory (Ossory complained that Cathaoir mac Airt had committed destruction totalling some 3,000 marks to the king's subjects during the rebellion). This led to his imprisonment in Dublin Castle (significantly, he allegedly escaped later with the aid of Grey). After the failure of the Kildare rebellion, the English regularly pressed Cathaoir mac Airt to reform his country and abolish Irish legal custom and dress. With government encouragement, Cathaoir mac Airt exploited internal MacMurrough dissension to increase his own power. On 12 May 1536 the ailing king of Leinster, Cathaoir MacInnycross MacMurrough, entered into an agreement with Grey that substantially curbed his power, thereby allowing Domhnall mac Cathaoir Kavanagh of Garryhill and Cathaoir mac Airt to become the dominant figures among the MacMurrough-Kavanaghs.[54]

To the north of MacMurrough country, the O'Byrnes also faced the advance of English power into their lands. In January 1536, Tadhg mac Gerald O'Byrne of Kiltimon, the O'Byrne overlord and a Butler client, drew up a series of indentures with Grey and proved his loyalty by campaigning in Munster during

---

50 *S.P. Hen. VIII, 1538–46*, no. ccxxxii, pp 24–5; ibid., no. ccxxix, p. 18.   **51** *CSPI, 1509–73*, no. 8, p. 41. In particular Cétach Ruadh attacked Ossory's lands of Oteryn and Tullowphelim, see *Cal. Carew MSS, 1515–74*, no. 121, p. 140. On 20 June 1538 Ossory's son, Lord James Butler, mentioned that Grey's troops actually joined with Cétach Ruadh to attack Oughter Inn. See also ibid., no. ccxl, pp 48–9. See also *CSPI, 1509–73*, no. 38, p. 45; *S.P. Hen VIII, 1538–46*, no. ccli, pp 88–9.   **52** *S.P. Hen VIII, 1538–46*, no. cccxxiii, p. 242.   **53** Cathaoir, a son of Art MacMurrough, a principal captain of the Sliocht Diarmada Láimhdeirg, was the most politically astute Irish lord of East Leinster from the late 1530s to his death. In 1526 Cathaoir first appears in the written record, burning the castle of Drumore in Kilkenny. Dowling, *Annals*, p. 35; Lansdowne Ms 159, f. 13; Hughes, 'The fall of the Clan Kavanagh', p. 295.   **54** Hughes, 'The fall of the Clan Kavanagh', p. 295; *Cal. Carew MSS, 1515–74*, no. 77, p. 93.

August. Ossory, however, was not content to let friendly relations blossom between Grey and his O'Byrne supporters. He now encouraged Tadhg to attack his O'Byrne cousins of Newrath who were firmly allied to Grey: this led to serious fighting in east Wicklow. In June 1538, Ossory complained to the king of Grey's attacks upon the lands of Tadhg. Two years later, James Butler, 9th earl of Ormond, Ossory's son and successor (James succeeded him upon the latter's death in August 1539), bitterly attacked Grey because of his patronage of the O'Byrnes of Newrath.[55] Clearly, much of the O'Byrne lordship was in chaos resulting from this deadly feud – a further indication of the increasing fragmentation of the ruling elite.

One completely unexpected result of the collapse of the Kildares in Leinster was the rise of the mercurial Toirdhealbhach mac Airt O'Toole and his allies, the Gabhal Raghnaill O'Byrne lords of Glenmalure. Their sudden appearance further complicated this chaotic situation in a region still reeling from the collapse of the Kildares. Eager to establish his dominance over all the O'Tooles, Toirdhealbhach sought to create alliances with the neighbouring O'Byrne lords of Glenmalure, the Kavanaghs of Garryhill and the Art Boy Kavanaghs. The whole period after 1535 was characterized by the dramatic rise of traditionally weaker Irish families in East Leinster. For instance, Toirdhealbhach himself was married to a daughter of Muircheartach mac Airt Buidhe MacMurrough, leader of the Art Boy Kavanaghs and the dynastic overlord between 1544 and 1547.[56] The rise of the Art Boy Kavanaghs happened because government attention was focused upon reducing of the power of Cathaoir MacInnycross MacMurrough, king of Leinster. However, part of the explanation for it may lie in the nexus of interfamilial alliances forged by Toirdhealbhach and later by the O'Byrnes of Glenmalure with other Leinster dynasties. During this period Toirdhealbhach and his allies flirted with both the Butler and Fitzgerald camps. But for the most part this alliance of junior Irish lords operated independently in East Leinster in these years. The creation, and success, of allegiances of this sort and their ability to be a nuisance to the government, however, were conditional on the presence of a protagonist leader with the necessary charisma and initiative. In this sense, therefore, Toirdhealbhach can be seen as a precursor to the later more powerful Gabhal Raghnaill O'Byrne warlords.

Toirdhealbhach and his confederates were determined to eradicate any form of restraint already existent within the Leinster mountains, their first objective being to undo the Kildare conquest of O'Tooles' Country. From the middle of the 1530s to Toirdhealbhach's submission in November 1540, this nexus was in intermittent conflict with the Dublin government.[57] In the aftermath of the Kildare rebellion during 1535, when the now unrestrained O'Tooles waxed

55 *Cal. Carew MSS, 1515–74*, no. 72, p. 89; *S.P. Hen VIII, 1538–46*, iii, pp 74–5; *L. & P. Hen VIII*, xvi, no. 304 (22), p. 131.   56 Nicholls, 'The Kavanaghs' (1979), p. 732. In 1538–9 a son of Muircheartach had sought help from Toirdhealbhach mac Airt to burn the Pale see *S.P. Hen VIII, 1538–46*, no. cccxxvi, p. 256.   57 *S.P. Hen VIII, 1538–46*, no. cccxxix, p. 266.

strong, Toirdhealbhach exploited the power vacuum by treacherously capturing and destroying the former Kildare castle of Powerscourt.[58] Even though a member of the Geraldine League (a party of Kildare supporters seeking the restoration of Gerald Fitzgerald as 11th earl), Toirdhealbhach steadfastly sought permanent confirmation of his gains through protracted negotiations with Fitzgerald rebels and the government. An example of these changed circumstances can be seen in May 1538, when Toirdhealbhach defeated John Kelway, constable of Rathmore, and a large force of Co. Kildare gentlemen at Three Castles near Blessington. During his lord deputyship (1536–40), Grey led several expeditions against Toirdhealbhach. In December 1537 Toirdhealbhach had agreed to peace for three years and promised to contribute to government hostings, being allowed in return to enjoy the lands his father held before the Kildare conquest and promising he was not to aid any Fitzgerald rebels.[59] Again Ossory's (Piers Butler's) influence can be detected, as he and his son, Lord James Butler, acted as sureties to the agreement. Peace did not last, with the result that the O'Tooles were pushed back into the Fitzgerald camp. During 1538 the English learned that the Kildare heir, Gerald Fitzgerald, accepted from Art Óg O'Toole gifts of a saffron shirt, an English cloak edged with silk, and also money, at Maghnus O'Donnell's castle in Donegal. Also, a confession by Conchobhar Mór O'Connor, Grey's servant, reveals that the O'Toole brothers obtained a promise of Powerscourt and Fassaroe from Gerald. Moreover, Thomas Lynch, a Galway merchant, later confirmed that he had seen the messenger of the O'Tooles in O'Donnell's castle. Consequently, Grey led a campaign into the mountains against them and the Gabhal Raghnaill O'Byrnes of Glenmalure during May 1539.[60]

Toirdhealbhach also made common cause with some Irish leaders of the midlands and West Leinster. For the first time in decades, these dynasties extended helping hands to each other across the Barrow frontier. In Kildare days, the power of the earls was sufficient to prevent such co-ordination, so this combination of the Irish of both parts of Leinster is reminiscent of the days of Art MacMurrough in the late fourteenth and early fifteenth centuries; and despite Grey's attempts to strangle this alliance at birth, it now posed a substantial obstacle to the military subjugation of Leinster. Then in late 1539 Grey's enemies, led by Ormond, accused him of favouring former Fitzgerald clients such as Fearganainm O'Carroll of Ely and of being under O'Connor Faly's influence, and the following April Grey was recalled to England after the fall of Thomas Cromwell, his patron.[61] O'Connor Faly along with Giollapádraig

58 In 1536 Toirdhealbhach's brother Art Óg along with Edmund Óg O'Byrne was still in the service of the government, see *L. & P. Hen VIII*, xi, no. 934, p. 373; *S.P. Hen VIII, 1515–38*, no. xcviii, p. 264.   59 *L. & P. Hen VIII*, xiii, part 1, no. 1136, p. 425. Piers Ruadh sent messengers to Glendalough in June to negotiate for release of prisoners; ibid., no. 1138, p. 426. Toirdhealbhach killed Kelway for his treachery and his earlier hanging of two O'Tooles; ibid., no. 1160, p. 433. Over sixty Kildare gentlemen were slain. See also AU, 1538.   60 *S.P. Hen VIII, 1538–46*, no. cclxxi, p. 135, fn.1, p. 139; *L. & P. Hen VIII*, xiv, part 1, no. 1245, p. 553.
61 O'Byrne, 'The rise of the Gabhal Raghnaill', pp 89–92; *S.P. Hen VIII, 1538–46*, no. cccxxvi,

O'More and Toirdhealbhach then proceeded to burn part of the Pale, causing much government concern.[62] The government's reaction was sharp and effective: Lord Justice Sir William Brereton brought an expedition into Offaly, forcing O'Connor Faly to submit. On 1 May, Ormond, also, complained that the lands of his earldom and the Pale had suffered attacks from a co-ordinated Irish offensive; he mentioned the O'Tooles and O'Connor Falys in particular. O'Connor Faly continued burning in Kildare throughout early May, while Tadhg mac Gerald O'Byrne of Kiltimon (a government supporter) foiled a huge O'Toole raid on the Pale by warning the Palesmen.[63] Eventually, a government army was dispatched during the middle of June to O'Toole's Country, where it was confronted by the combined forces of Toirdhealbhach, Domhnall mac Cathaoir Kavanagh of Garryhill and probably Seán mac Rhéamain O'Byrne of Glenmalure. Due to the strength of the Irish and a lack of supplies, the government made a peace of six weeks.[64] A more illustrative example of the extent of Irish co-ordination came in July, when Ormond's invasion of Idrone forced Toirdhealbhach to hasten to the aid of Domhnall mac Cathaoir Kavanagh of Garryhill; however, the size of Ormond's army convinced Toirdhealbhach that a truce was a better option.[65]

Sir Anthony St Leger, appointed as Grey's successor in August, adopted a different countrywide policy towards the Irish lords. He recognized that their major concern was secure tenure of their respective lordships, and that military force alone could not produce long-term stability. St Leger determined to steer a new course through an adept combination of diplomacy and force. This policy, known as Surrender and Regrant, involved the lord's submission, his rejection of the pope, and his acknowledgement of Henry VIII as head of the church. In return, the Irish lord was granted back his lands, often with a title. In pursuit of this political stability and to foster personal relations with the Irish lords, St Leger supported primogeniture among the ruling families.

After subduing the MacMurrough-Kavanaghs in early September, St Leger and Ormond crossed the Barrow into the midlands, where they concentrated their attention on Laois and Offaly, campaigning against both the Butler party and the former Kildare clients. By 22 September, St Leger had secured the submissions of all the principal midland lords, including Cétach Ruadh O'More of Laois and all his brothers. This reassertion of government power over the O'Mores had rapid results – evidenced by their service on campaigns in Ulster and Munster.[66] In June 1541 Cétach Ruadh attended parliament and, with his family, was pardoned and given a grant of English liberty.[67] In Offaly, Brian

pp 248–63.   **62** *S.P. Hen VIII, 1538–46*, no. ccc, p. 202.   **63** Ibid., no. ccxcviii, p. 199, no.cci, p. 203; *CSPI, 1509–73*, no. 21, p. 53.   **64** Domhnall mac Cathaoir fired Athy, burning the Dominican house there in June 1540, see *Extents of Irish monastic possessions 1540–41*, p. 172; *L. & P. Hen VIII*, xv, no. 815, p. 386.   **65** *S.P. Hen VIII, 1538–46*, no. cccxv, p. 226.   **66** *L. & P. Hen VIII*, xvi, no. 70, p. 20; see ibid., xx, part 2, p. 382. *CSPI, 1509–73*, no. 52, p. 55.   **67** *Cal. Fiants Hen VIII*, nos 205–6. Also a Dorothy O'More was granted English liberty during 1542 in

O'Connor Faly and his clients of O'Dunne and O'Connor Irry were also forced to make peace that September.[68] Henry VIII then ordered St Leger to banish Brian and restore Cathaoir; St Leger balked at this, arguing that O'Connor Faly's exile would greatly undermine the new treaties and thus destabilize the midlands region. In November O'Connor Faly proffered his own solution to the impasse by offering to hold Offaly of the king with the title of baron of Offaly.[69] Furthermore, he submitted his feud with Cathaoir to St Leger's judgment. The lord deputy then recommended that Offaly be divided between them. Accordingly on St Leger's recommendation, Henry VIII pardoned O'Connor Faly in 1541, but he did not issue him a grant of Offaly.

An example of the strengths and frailties of St Leger's policy is the case of Toirdhealbhach O'Toole. After securing the adherence of the Irish of the midlands, St Leger brought his army into the Leinster mountains to confront Toirdhealbhach (that September the O'Toole truce with the government expired). St Leger's army was able to secure the submissions of most of the O'Byrnes and MacMurrough-Kavanaghs, but the O'Tooles remained elusive, making St Leger more determined to subdue them. To that end, he sought money from England to rebuild two castles facing the mountains of the O'Tooles.[70] After a four-week campaign in November 1540, St Leger and Ormond cornered Toirdhealbhach and his O'Byrne allies in the Wicklow highlands. There Ormond convinced the tired O'Toole leader to come to terms. As the price of his obedience Toirdhealbhach requested the formal recognition of his claims, demanding that the ancestral lands of the O'Tooles be granted to him and his brother, Art Óg. At the same time the O'Byrnes renewed their submission. After Toirdhealbhach's submission, St Leger dispatched him to court, where he made his submission to Henry VIII before April 1541.[71] In return Henry VIII confirmed Toirdhealbhach's tenurial rights and those of his brother; thus, O'Toole claims to the castles of Castlekevin and Powerscourt and to ancestral lands lying in north and central Wicklow were legitimized.[72] Henry VIII's confirmation of the articles of the St Leger/O'Toole agreement greatly ameliorated the grievances of the Irish of the central Wicklow highlands. Now St Leger turned to the O'Byrnes. On 4 July 1542, Tadhg O'Byrne and his leading nobles agreed to the gradual introduction of English rule into their lordship as part of Surrender and Regrant, which meant that the O'Byrnes had a great deal of autonomy over their own affairs. But as time proved, the reality was to be otherwise and, as has been noted, the

---

order that she may marry the son of Thomas Eustace. See *Cal. Fiants Hen VIII*, no. 305. **68** *L. & P. Hen VIII*, xvi, no. 70, p. 20.   **69** *S.P. Hen VIII, 1538–46*, no. cccxxvii, pp 264–5, no. cccxliii, p. 316.   **70** St Leger estimated Toirdhealbhach the elder levied black rents of 400 or 500 marks yearly, see *L. & P. Hen VIII*, xvi, no. 272, p. 116. For the castles see also ibid., xvi, no. 70, p. 20. Archbishop Brown of Dublin lamented that Toirdhealbhach the elder with 200 men continually devastated his Tallaght lands and killed his tenants, see *S.P. Hen VIII, 1538–46*, no. cclxiv, p. 123.   **71** *S.P. Hen VIII, 1538–46*, no. cccxxix, pp 266–71; H. Nicholas (ed.), *Proceedings and ordinances of the privy council of England*, vii (London, 1837), pp 92–3.   **72** *Proceedings and ordinances of the privy council of England*, vii, pp 92–3.

change in English policies, combined with the political fragmentation of the O'Byrne lordship, paved the way for its being replaced by an English seneschalcy.[73]

Peace was short-lived, as strife among the O'Tooles again destabilized the Irish of East Leinster. In early 1542 Toirdhealbhach forcibly attempted to exert his rights within the territory of his cousin, Toirdhealbhach mac Seaáin O'Toole of Imaal,[74] but he was killed by his rival in a surprise morning attack upon his encampment. His death destroyed the equilibrium he had been building for the best part of a decade among the Irish of the mountains. Toirdhealbhach's death and the later killing of his heir, Toirdhealbhach Óg, by Toirdhealbhach mac Seaáin before May 1543,[75] opened up considerable opportunities for Seán mac Rhéamain O'Byrne of Glenmalure, 6th lord of Críoch Raghnuill (the land of Raghnall), and his son, Aodh. Theirs was a discontinuous territory, anchored by the chief residence of its lords at Ballinacor lying at the mouth of Glenmalure, ranging from Glendalough southwards to Shillelagh and westwards into Carlow. After 1542, they positioned themselves to fill Toirdhealbhach's leadership role among the Irish of the Leinster mountains; this led them into direct conflict with the Butlers of Ormond and later the government.[76]

After the collapse of Kildare power in 1535, the Butlers planned to extend their authority into the Wicklow district known as Cosha lying to the northeast of Shillelagh, a territory where all the senior O'Byrne branches held lands.[77] By doing so, the Butlers were resurrecting claims dating from the thirteenth century. However, the O'Byrnes of Glenmalure had also moved into Cosha, and seized a large slice of this territory centred in the parishes of Kilcommon and Preban adjacent to Aughrim and Tinahely. They were now the major obstacle to the Butler advance. The expansion of the O'Byrnes of Glenmalure also irritated the senior O'Byrne families who were allied to the Butlers. Thus, in 1543 the Butlers decided to challenge those territorial gains, focusing particularly upon Preban and Kilcommon. In October 1543, Sir John Travers, a Palesman, was appointed as constable of Arklow with instructions to enforce old Butler claims to these lands.[78] Although Travers failed in this objective, his attacks upon the O'Byrnes of Glenmalure, combined with separate forays against some of the O'Tooles and the MacMurrough-Kavanaghs, seriously disturbed the Irish leaders within the region.

Having said that, the O'Byrnes of Glenmalure had some links to the Butlers. Seán O'Byrne's grandmother was Joan, daughter of Edmund MacRichard Butler of Polestown, which made him cousin to the earls of Ormond. They also had

---

73 *Cal. Carew MSS, 1515–74*, no. 170, pp 193–4; Nicholls, 'Crioch Branach', pp 8 & 16. **74** *S.P. Hen VIII, 1538–46*, no. ccclxxxiii, pp 438–9.   **75** *L. & P. Hen VIII*, xviii, part 1, no. 553, pp 321–2.   **76** O'Brien, 'Feagh McHugh', p. 13; idem, 'The Byrnes of Ballymanus', pp 305–7; see also Father Richard Galvin's 1872 transcription of the 1631 will of Féilim mac Fiach O'Byrne in Archivium Parochiale de Rathdrum, Liber II. This records the gifts made by Féilim to his sons.   **77** O'Rourke, p. 9. See also Nicholls, 'Crioch Branach', p. 11.   **78** *COD*, iv, no. 311, i, and ii, pp 256–7.

links to the Butlers through Aodh O'Byrne's first marriage during the early
1540s to Sadhbh, daughter of Féilim Buidhe O'Byrne of Clonmore; this Sadhbh
was the niece of the prominent enemy of the 9th earl of Kildare, Seán mac
Lorcán O'Byrne of Clonmore, who had pillaged southern Kildare during 1532;[79]
and both Seán mac Lorcán and his brother Féilim Buidhe were clients of the
Butlers, an alliance continued by Sadhbh's brother Aodh Geangach O'Byrne.
Sometime in the early 1540s, Aodh and Sadhbh became the parents of Fiach
mac Aodha O'Byrne (Fiach's exact date of birth is unknown, but it is thought
that he was born in 1544).[80] By August 1550, however, Aodh had married
another Sadhbh, daughter of Art Óg O'Toole of Castlekevin, while his ex-wife
Sadhbh was later to marry Diarmait Dubh Kinsella. Many of the factors that
forced the separation of Aodh and his first wife may be connected to his
increasingly fraught relations with the Butlers.[81]

In this ever-shifting political world of East Leinster, the ambitions of the
O'Byrnes of Glenmalure grew. Having withstood the Butler assault of 1543, they
now saw themselves as the emerging regional power, and, instead of remaining
content with their relatively minor position, they sought to expand their influence
southwards by interfering among the MacMurrough-Kavanaghs. During the
1540s, Cathaoir mac Airt MacMurrough, with the encouragement of the Dublin
government, steadily undermined the position of his weakening overlord,
Cathaoir MacInnycross.[82] His favour in the eyes of the government was evident
by the fact that he sat in the parliament of 1541; moreover, his name also
appeared along with those of other Irish lords whom it was proposed to elevate
to the peerage. In 1543 he received a grant of the lordship of St Mullins, on the
condition that he build a house at Polmonty, maintain the usual fairs there, and
ensure travellers free and safe passage through the nearby pass. Cathaoir
MacInnycross' treaty with St Leger of 3 September 1543 also facilated Cathaoir
mac Airt's rise, for in it Cathaoir MacInnycross relinquished much of his personal
power. Cathaoir mac Airt's rising confidence was confirmed in 1544, where he
dispatched Edmund Kavanagh and nineteen kerne to serve at the English siege
of Boulogne in France. After the death of Cathaoir MacInnycross that year,
Cathaoir mac Airt MacMurrough began to assert his supremacy. In 1545 he
defeated Gerald mac Cathaoir Kavanagh of Garryhill and his allies, the O'Byrnes
of Glenmalure, in a pitched battle near Hacketstown.[83] But the MacMurrough
title still eluded Cathaoir mac Airt as he had to recognize the dynastic primacy
of Muircheartach mac Airt Buidhe MacMurrough. Meanwhile the safety of the
forested and hilly fastness of their homeland allowed the O'Byrnes of
Glenmalure to recover and to rethink their strategy. Despite their reverse near
Hacketstown, they soon re-emerged from Glenmalure to begin a lucrative

79 *L. & P. Hen VIII*, v, no. 1061, p. 480; Nicholls, 'The genealogy of the Byrnes of Ranelagh',
p. 110.   **80** *DNB*, xvi, p. 786.   **81** *Cal. Fiants Edw VI*, no. 537; Price, 'Notes', p. 141.
82 Moore, 'The MacMurrough-Kavanaghs', pp 7–8.   **83** Dowling, *Annals*, pp 37–8; O'Byrne,
'The rise of the Gabhal Raghnaill', p. 99.

business in levying protection money from the English settlements located amid the foothills of the western and northern Leinster mountains. In late 1545 a dramatic increase in Irish attacks upon the Pale compelled Archbishop Browne of Dublin to dispatch complaints to Henry VIII in February 1546.[84] This upsurge in violence was paralleled by the attacks made by Brian O'Connor Faly and Giollapádraig O'More in late 1546 on the settlers in the midlands. These attacks coincided with the recall of St Leger to England in spring 1546 to answer charges. Before his departure, he appointed Lord Justice Sir William Brabazon to govern Ireland in his absence. Despite St Leger's declaration that the O'Byrnes and the O'Tooles were spent forces, clearly there had been a dramatic increase in the military strength of the O'Byrnes of Glenmalure.[85]

This influx of military strength into Críoch Raghnuill had its origins in the political turmoil sweeping West Leinster and the midlands. By 1542 this region was the great battlefield for the phoney war between Ormond and the reformers within the government, one of the underlying reasons for which was the recent strengthening of the Ormond party in late spring or early summer 1541, when Tadhg O'Carroll, along with the O'Molloys, slipped through a secret tunnel into Clonlisk castle and assassinated Fearganainm O'Carroll of Ely (a son-in-law of the 9th earl of Kildare and a government supporter).[86] In North Ossory the situation was somewhat different. There St Leger endeavoured to keep Brian MacGilla-patrick in the government camp. Thus, in June 1541, MacGillapatrick, through St Leger's patronage, was granted the title of baron of Upper Ossory. This allowed him to take his place among his fellow barons in the Irish house of lords at the opening sessions of the 1541 parliament.[87] However, the struggle between Ormond and St Leger became concentrated in the lordships of Laois and Offaly. In Laois, the O'More overlords were targeted by St Leger because of their usual loyalty to Ormond. In 1542, Ruaidhrí Caoch O'More succeeded Cétach Ruadh as lord of Laois, when the latter was killed in Carlow by the followers of Domhnall mac Cathaoir Kavanagh of Garryhill.[88] After his inauguration, Ruaidhrí Caoch submitted before the council at Dublin on 13 May 1542, promised military service to the government, and concluded an agreement about the lordship of Slemargy with Robert St Leger, sub-constable of Carlow castle. On 10 November Ruaidhrí Caoch again submitted before the Dublin council and confirmed his concord with Robert St Leger.

Ruaidhrí Caoch inherited his father's mistrust of Brian O'Connor Faly and became convinced that St Leger encouraged O'Connor Faly's raids into Laois.[89] Ostensibly O'Connor Faly's attacks were in support of his son-in-law,

84 *S.P. Hen. VIII, 1538–46*, no. cccxxxv, p. 557; O'Byrne, 'The rise of the Gabhal Raghnaill', p. 96. **85** *S.P. Hen VIII, 1538–46*, no. cccxlv, p. 569. **86** AFM, 1541. **87** Bradshaw, *The Irish constitutional revolution of the sixteenth century*, p. 238. **88** *CSPI, 1586–8* no. 34, p. 117. The three O'More brothers, Cétach Ruadh, Giollapádraig and Ruaidhrí, were recorded as being at peace in November 1541, see *S.P. Hen VIII, 1538–46*, no. cccliv, p. 348. For Cétach Ruadh's killing see *L & P. Hen VIII*, xx, part 2, no. 797, p. 382. **89** *Cal. Carew MSS, 1515–74*, no. 163, pp 185–6; *L. & P. Hen VIII*, xx, part 2, no. 797, pp 382–3.

Giollapádraig O'More; but they also masked a government offensive against Ormond's clients, of whom Ruaidhrí Caoch was one. In June 1544 Ruaidhrí Caoch outlined his grievances in a letter to Henry VIII, accusing St Leger of complicity in O'Connor Faly's actions. To protect himself, Ruaidhrí Caoch moved closer to Ormond, marrying Margaret Butler in 1543/4.[90] This alliance so alarmed O'More's neighbour, Brian MacGillapatrick, 1st baron of Upper Ossory, that he now allied himself with O'Connor Faly to prevent encirclement by Ormond and his clients. St Leger and O'Connor Faly then encouraged him to exploit Ruaidhrí Caoch's struggle with his brother, Giollapádraig O'More, attacking Laois. This resulted in Brian's brief imprisonment in Dublin on the orders of Ormond's friends in the government. Brian now realized that he needed to be more ambivalent in his dealings with St Leger, and to play both sides.[91]

However, St Leger's success in achieving some stability in the midlands was conditional upon the continuance of good relations with Brian O'Connor Faly, who had been pardoned and received a regrant of the Offaly lordship in 1544. In 1545 St Leger encouraged the English government to create O'Connor Faly a peer for life. By June 1545 the London government had prepared letters patent for the grant of a viscountcy to O'Connor Faly. But St Leger's recall in 1546 radically changed the situation. In March, as we saw, St Leger returned to England to answer charges of misgovernment. He asked O'Connor Faly to accompany him as a symbol of what could be achieved through tough but humane government. After considering Grey's fate, O'Connor Faly seemingly assumed that St Leger was destined for the block and did not travel to London. Fearing the fall of his patron, he, along with Giollapádraig O'More, attacked Co. Kildare for the first time in six years in late 1546. However, Lord Justice Brabazon with Ruaidhrí Caoch successfully crushed their rebellion. During the fighting, Ruaidhrí Caoch killed O'Connor Faly's eldest son and forced Giollapádraig to flee into Offaly, and O'Connor Faly to flee to Connacht. St Leger returned to Ireland in December 1546 and made Ruaidhrí Caoch, Giollapádraig and O'Connor Faly submit, bringing the two O'More brothers to Dublin to settle their dispute.

During Ruaidhrí Caoch's detention in Dublin, O'Connor Faly again devastated Laois and constructed forts there. Ruaidhrí Caoch O'More wanted to return home, but St Leger forcibly detained him in Dublin. In a letter to Henry VIII, Ruaidhrí Caoch accused St Leger of encouraging O'Connor Faly and Robert St Leger to attack his lands. During 1547 Ruaidhrí Caoch faced another revolt led by Giollápadraig. Initially, Ruaidhrí Caoch was successful, forcing Giollapádraig to flee. Before summer 1547 Giollapádraig returned with his O'Connor Faly allies, killed Ruaidhrí Caoch, and seized the lordship.[92] However, St Leger still viewed O'Connor Faly as crucial to the peaceful rule of the midlands. In summer 1547 O'Connor Faly was received into the king's

90 *CSPI, 1509–73*, no.49, p. 70; *L. & P. Hen VIII*, xix, part 2, no. 531, ii, p. 323.   **91** Edwards, 'The MacGiollapádraigs (Fitzpatricks) of Upper Ossory', p. 338; *CSPI, 1509–73*, no. 1, iii, p. 71. **92** *Cal. Pat. Rolls. Ire*, i, p. 505.

peace by the deputy and was granted lands in Dublin for his private use.[93]
However, the government's policy in West Leinster and the midlands was
becoming more hard-line; when O'Connor Faly rebelled again in October, the
London government instructed St Leger not to accept his surrender. On a wider
scale, St Leger's position, however, was weakened by the death of Henry VIII in
January 1547, and during that year Edward Seymour, Protector Somerset, the
guardian of the minor Edward VI, defeated the court faction that patronized St
Leger. O'Connor Faly had made a serious error of judgment. In May 1548
St Leger was replaced as lord deputy by Sir Edward Bellingham – an appoint-
ment that ushered in a new era of English government. Throughout 1548, the
O'Mores and O'Connor Falys waged a bloody but ultimately unsuccessful war
with Bellingham's army; it led to the surrenders of O'Connor Faly and
Giollapádraig O'More in November 1548, and they were transported to
Marshelsea prison near London, where Giollapádraig died in 1549.[94] Cathaoir
O'Connor Faly remained in rebellion but was captured and later executed at
Dublin during 1549. Bellingham issued pardons to all the remaining O'Connor
Faly and O'More leaders and embarked upon the plantation of Laois and Offaly
in November 1550.

Bellingham and many of the New English captains were firm believers in
plantation, determining that the intrusion of prototype plantations in the
lordships of O'Mores and O'Connor Falys would in the long term stabilize the
grip of the English monarchy upon the island. The proposed plantation of Laois
and Offaly had effects throughout the midlands. It was also intended that the
plantations would curb the resurgent power of the O'Carrolls of Ely. Leading the
O'Carroll revival was the capable Tadhg Caoch – husband of Egidia Butler. After
the assassination of his father Fearganainm O'Carroll at Clonlisk castle during
1541, Tadhg Caoch's succession had been bitterly disputed, and, in response, the
Irish privy council summoned the rival claimants to a meeting on 2 July 1541 at
Dublin, where it was decreed that Seán and Tadhg O'Carroll should lay aside
their claims and they be given varying degrees of yearly compensation. In the
end the lordship was divided between Tadhg Caoch and An Calbhach
O'Carroll. Within a short period Tadhg Caoch outpaced his rival and was
generally regarded as the lord of Ely. In June 1542 he visited London, seeking the
status of tenant-in-chief from Henry VIII. He was cordially received by the king
and was presented with a gift of £20.

Although upon his return home Tadhg Caoch maintained his loyalty to the
English government, he took advantage of feuds between the O'Melaghlins and
the O'Maddens to extend O'Carroll power, rebuilding Banagher castle despite
their opposition in 1544. In 1546 Tadhg Caoch showed his regard for St Leger
by attending his farewell reception in Dublin. In spite of such loyalty, the greatest
threat to Tadhg Caoch and his lordship came from government officials such as
Edmund Fahy, captain of the king's kerne. The danger to the O'Carrolls was also

93 *Cal. Fiants Edw VI*, nos 68, 78.   **94** PRO, SP 61/1/129; Lennon, *Sixteenth century Ire.*, pp
164–6; AFM, 1548.

increased by the government's campaigns in the midlands against the O'Connor Falys and the O'Mores during 1547–8, and by its government's erection of Fort Governor in Offaly and Fort Protector in Laois as well by the appointment of Bellingham as lord deputy. As a prelude to the impending trouble, An Calbhach O'Carroll, Tadhg Caoch's representative, was arrested while visiting Dublin in 1548. Shortly afterwards, Fahy and Sir Francis Bryan invaded Ely, forcing Tadhg Caoch to demolish Banagher castle and abandon nearby fortresses. However, this invasion of Ely ran out of steam, enabling Tadhg Caoch to retake these castles and roll back the English gains. This gave Tadhg Caoch a chance to exploit his victories by burning Nenagh and plundering the lands of his rivals. In turn, the government released An Calbhach, to have him check Tadhg Caoch. But once he was free, An Calbhach refused to obey the government, which meant that the English had to treat Tadhg Caoch favourably. With the support of some of the O'Kellys, O'Melaghlins and the MacMurrough-Kavanaghs, Tadhg Caoch negotiated a peace with the government at Limerick during 1549. However, when chance arose later in 1549, he took full advantage of it to expel Fahy from Ely in 1549.[95]

Either in 1551 or 1552, Tadhg Caoch's attempts to avoid the fate of the O'Connor Falys were rewarded by the grant of a tenancy-in-chief and a knighthood on his submission before Sir William Brabazon at Limerick. In addition he was also granted the title of lord baron of Ely, and several manors. This grant of a peerage was seen as a threat by Tadhg Caoch's rivals with the result that he was killed by An Calbhach O'Carroll in mid 1553. Within a year An Calbhach was deposed by William Odhar O'Carroll, Tadhg Caoch's brother. William Odhar was gravely concerned about government attempts to subdue the Irish of Laois and Offaly, to whom he sent troops to in 1556.

In the face of such tremendous military opposition from the midland lords, the plantations were legally established in Laois and Offaly in late 1556.[96] During summer 1557, Thomas Radcliffe, earl of Sussex and lord deputy of Ireland, devastated Offaly and expelled the O'Connor Faly leaders, forcing them to seek refuge at William Odhar's castle of Leap. But the English advance into Ely caused William Odhar to review his options, and he decided to ride to safety rather than risk capture. Indeed, Sussex's presence in Ely saw William Odhar adopt a more conciliatory tone: he joined the English campaign in July. Sussex then installed his brother, Sir Henry Radcliffe, as lieutenant of Laois and Offaly with extensive powers of martial law over the newly created shires and the neighbouring Irish lordships. Sir Henry's appointment evidenced a more forceful

---

95 Vennings, 'The O'Carrolls of Offaly', pp 189–91; AFM, 1544, 1547, 1548, 1549.
96 Fitzsimons, 'The lordship of O'Connor Faly, 1520–1570', pp 220–34. For the reaction of the O'Mores to the Laois plantation, read Carey, 'The end of the Gaelic political order', pp 213–57; Brady, 'Court, castle and country: the framework of government in Tudor Ireland', p. 45. For a series of pardons of the early 1550s relating to the O'Mores, see *Cal. Fiants Edw VI*, nos 598, 678, 717, 1041, 1163, 1188.

government approach spearheaded by New English captains to the midland Irish. (In doing so, the claims of the newly restored Gerald Fitzgerald, 11th earl of Kildare, were ignored).[97] But once Sussex returned to Dublin, William Odhar isolated the English garrisons in Ely, cutting their communications before retaking these fortresses. Relief was all too brief. By late summer 1558, Sussex was back, replacing William Odhar with Tadhg O'Carroll. Again William Odhar managed to unravel Sussex's plans, by expelling Tadhg from Ely in January 1559. The English, concerned for their plantations in Laois and Offaly, then made peace with William Odhar, granting him the captaincy of Ely.

If the violent imposition of the plantations profoundly disturbed the Irish of West Leinster and the midlands, they also affected East Leinster and the rest of Ireland. The fighting in West Leinster and the midlands was to irrevocably redefine Irish politics. Through the harsh application of martial law throughout Leinster, combined with the dispossession and execution of various Irish lords, a seething hatred arose among the Leinstermen towards the government. The effect of the plantations on the Leinster chessboard caused a decisive eastward shift in the provincial centre of gravity to its edge, the Wicklow mountains.[98] From there Aodh O'Byrne offered refuge to the dispossessed in his virtually impenetrable territory of Glenmalure, hoping to harness their military manpower for his own purposes. His aim was to become the leader of Leinster, and he advanced his own family's status through his patronage of poets and his military support of the O'More and O'Connor Faly opponents of the plantations. On a more local level, he also shrewdly used them to expand his growing income, by enlisting them to extract protection money from Irish and English alike.[99]

It was not merely events within the midlands and West Leinster that propelled Aodh to the forefront of Leinster politics.[100] Even before the wars in West Leinster between 1546 and 1550, the power of the O'Byrnes of Glenmalure was increasing there – as evidenced by their contact with the O'Mores and O'Connor Faly from the early 1540s. This seems borne out by the report that Ruaidhrí Caoch fostered his son Ruaidhrí Óg in the Ballinacor household of Seán O'Byrne, Aodh's father. The O'Byrne rise was helped also by the death of Art Óg O'Toole of Castlekevin before November 1546, which left them able to pose as the leaders of the mountain lords.[101] Their incomes from extortion and timber enabled them to buy firearms. An indication of the growth of his house's importance is the fact that Aodh, independently of his father, patronized poetic families, particularly the McKeoghs, to have them compose a corpus of bardic poetry celebrating his military prowess and that of his family from the middle of

97 Carey, *Surviving the Tudors*, p. 101. **98** O'Byrne, 'The trend in warfare in Gaelic Leinster' p. 137. **99** His use of these fugitive warbands even earned Spenser's grudging admiration. See A. Hadfield & W. Maley (ed.), *A view of the state of Ireland*, p. 113. **100** *Cal. Fiants Edw VI*, no. 301, and nos 537–8. These record pardons for Aodh and his followers between 1549 and 1550. **101** Carey, 'The end of the gaelic political order', p. 237; *L. & P. Hen*, xxi, part 2, no. 476, p. 234. In November 1546 Brian mac Toirdhealbhach O'Toole was granted his father's lands, and Fiach O'Toole of Castlekevin was to gain those belonging to his father.

the 1540s.[102] Between 1 April and December 1546 Lord Justice Brabazon led an expedition against them, which they seem to have successfully defied.[103]

Another factor that propelled these O'Byrnes of Glenmalure to provincial prominence was the resurrection of Butler claims to lands lying within the Irish lordships in East Leinster. These claims were one of the main obstacles to the success of Surrender and Regrant during the late 1540s. The government moved to curb Ormond's power. In September 1546 it was proposed that his patent to lands reconquered from the Irish be withdrawn. In 1547 the crisis in East Leinster came to a head, sparked by the mysterious death of Ormond at a banquet in London during October 1546.[104] That event and the minority of Ormond's his son, Thomas Butler, later 10th earl of Ormond, allowed the government a free hand to implement its polices in the midlands. Violence was also fuelled and ignited by the resurgence of the activities of Fitzgerald dissidents among the O'Mores, O'Connor Falys, O'Tooles and O'Byrnes in 1546–7. Sometime during 1546 some Fitzgeralds, with the probable help of the O'Tooles of Imaal, burnt Rathvilly in Carlow as well as Rathangan and Ballymore in Kildare,[105] but it is not clear whether these activities can be linked to the warring of O'Connor Faly and Giollapádraig or to Brabazon's 1546 campaign against the Gabhal Raghnaill O'Byrnes. In Wicklow there seems to have been at least two major outbursts of violence: early in 1547 St Leger destroyed an O'Byrne force and killed their leader, while Toirdhealbhach mac Seaáin O'Toole of Imaal was killed by the Talbots before May 1547. More seriously, a force led by Henry and Maurice Fitzgerald was defeated at Three Castles near Blessington by Brian mac Toirdhealbhach O'Toole of Powerscourt.[106]

Bellingham realized the strategic significance of the midlands and West Leinster, and his tenure of the office was characterized by the violent extension of martial law into Leinster. The southern and western borders of the Pale were fortified, and seneschals were introduced into the Irish lordships of East Leinster; these latter were in fact policemen, but many possessed their own agendas. Seán and Aodh O'Byrne embarked upon a two-pronged strategy. To the south they consolidated their hold upon their threatened lands of Kilpipe and Preban and

102 *Leabhar Branach*, no. 4, ll.477–80 p. 19, she is called d'inghin Fhéilim. See also no 11, ll. 1109–116, p. 43. She is referred to as hinghin Fhéilim Buidhe. This dating can be confirmed as two poems dedicated to Aodh contain envois to his first wife Sadhbh from whom he had separated by 1550.   103 HMC, Halliday MSS: *Irish Privy Council, 1556–71* (London, 1897), p. 278 (hereafter HMC *Ir. Privy Council Bk*).   104 Price, 'The Byrnes' Country and Arklow', p. 57; Edwards, 'The death of the ninth earl of Ormond', pp 30–9; *COD*, iv, no. 352, p. 292. 105 Brady, *The chief governors* p. 57; AFM, 1546. O'Toole links Toirdhealbhach mac Seaain to the burning of Ballymore but he incorrectly assigns this act to 1548, see O'Toole, *A history of the Clan O'Toole*, pp 274–5.   106 Price, 'The Byrnes Country', p. 227; O'Toole, *A history of the Clan O'Toole*, pp 274–5; *Cal. Inquisitions, Edw VI*, 43/10, p. 135; AFM, 1547; *Cal. Fiants Edw VI*, no. 72. Brian mac Toirdhealbhach was pardoned on 2 April 1549. He was also known as *Brian An Coggey*, dying on 23 Mar 1549. He was succeeded by his younger brother Féilim mac Toirdhealbhach, who was killed on 14 May 1603. See *Cal. Fiants Edw VI*, no. 264; *Cal. Inquisitions* J 1 11/18, p. 326; *S.P. Hen VIII, 1538–46*, no. ccccxlv, p. 570.

exploited the collapse of the O'Tooles of Imaal to move into the political vacuum in west Wicklow and east Kildare caused by the fall of the Fitzgeralds. Their activities did not go unnoticed by the Butlers, who in 1548 moved to halt the development of an O'Byrne hegemony over the Leinster mountains. This proved a major factor in the growing destabilization of the Irish of East Leinster, the Butlers justifying their assault by pointing to their claims to long-lost lands lying within Críoch Raghnuill. While the details of this latest Butler offensive remain obscure, it is clear that the lords of Glenmalure vehemently resisted this intrusion.[107] In the early stages of this struggle, Aodh enjoyed the support of his wife's family (the O'Byrnes of Clonmore) against the Butler threat, but this soon changed.[108] In July 1548 the Butlers unleashed Tibbot Walsh, constable of Arklow, and the O'Byrnes of Newrath; their invasion of Crioch Raghnuill proved successful as their troops were quartered throughout the territory, forcing Seán and Aodh to retreat, along with their cattle, higher into the Wicklow uplands. Facing defeat, Seán dispatched a letter begging protection from Bellingham.[109] In response, Bellingham intervened with the Butlers and their allies, depriving them of victory. By September 1548, Seán recovered, benefiting from this breathing space, and authorized Aodh to begin a fresh assault upon the Pale. Seán and Aodh changed their tactics, beginning a double game with the English. While the son remained aloof from their overtures, the father, diplomatically, concluded a peace at Dublin during October 1548.[110]

Similar unrest was caused by Butler enroachments into MacMurrough-Kavanagh lands. Spearheading this attempted reconquest was Richard Butler, later Viscount Mountgarret. In 1538, he obtained a grant of the lands of the duke of Norfolk within the MacMurrough-Kavanagh homeland. Standing directly in his way was Cathaoir mac Airt MacMurrough, who, on Muircheartach mac Airt Buidhe MacMurrough's death in 1547, was finally elected dynastic overlord.[111] A three-cornered struggle for regional suzerainty now emerged, involving Cathaoir mac Airt, the Butlers and local English officials. In 1548 Sir Anthony Colclough complained to Bellingham that Cathaoir mac Airt refused to hang a man for theft, preferring to use the Brehon law of restitution. Cathaoir mac Airt's explanation was deemed sufficient, as he was thanked for his good service. More serious, though, was his feud with Richard Butler, who accused him of launching raids upon his lands in Kilkenny. Bellingham moved quickly to defuse this explosive situation by writing soothingly to Cathaoir mac Airt, affirming the government's faith in him. Unsurprisingly Aodh O'Byrne now patched up his

107 *Cal. Fiants Edw VI*, no. 301. Aodh and his brother Patrick were pardoned for unspecified activities on 12 May 1548.   108 *Cal. Fiants Edw VI*, no. 301. Aodh and his brother Patrick were pardoned for unspecified activities on 12 May 1548; *Cal.Pat.Rolls.Ire*, i, no. 101, p. 185. This mentions the pardons of Aodh's brother in laws, Terence McFeolim, Charles McFeolim Bowy McLorcane and Hugh Geangaghe McPhilip Bwy, between 10–11 May 1548. 109 PRO, SP 61/73/43; *CSPI, 1509–73*, no. 43, p. 81. For Walsh's pardon of 1550, see *Cal.Fiants Edw VI*, no. 560; O'Byrne, 'The rise of the Gabhal Raghnaill', p. 100.   110 *CSPI, 1509–73*, no. 101, p. 89.   111 AFM, 1547.

differences with his old enemy Cathaoir mac Airt; together they attacked a series of English settlements, and went on to spend their plunder on silks and saffron in the markets of Kilkenny.[112]

In 1550 the government continued to make steady inroads into Leinster. In March, Cathaoir mac Airt MacMurrough's feud with Richard Butler exploded when he seized Ferns castle, the most important fortress in East Leinster. This led to widespread disturbance, culminating in Sir James Croft's invasion and ravaging of his country. On 4 November before a great council at Dublin, Cathaoir mac Airt acknowledged his offence and publicly renounced his title of MacMurrough. His possessions were considerably reduced, but on his own request he obtained permission to make his explanations in person to Edward VI. On 8 February 1554 he was created baron of Ballyanne, which allowed him to sit in the Irish house of lords. A second title, that of captain of his country, was also granted to him, but he never enjoyed this privilege as his patent was only issued shortly before his death sometime after February 1554.[113] He was succeeded by Murchadh mac Muiris MacMurrough, baron of Coolnaleen. The coercion of Cathaoir mac Airt was mild in comparison to the steady hardening of the government's position towards the Leinster nobility after 1556. In 1557, to their horror, Murchadh mac Muiris endured the indignity of public execution at Leighlinbridge. Also, in Wicklow, the senior O'Byrnes and the O'Tooles, undermined by the imposition of the English seneschalcy, were compelled to regularly maintain government troops and forced to render a military tax known as the cess.[114] In 1557 Aodh's allies, Fiach mac Airt Óig O'Toole of Castlekevin and his cousin Féilim mac Toirdhealbhach O'Toole of Powerscourt were ordered by the English to desist from levying traditional dues from the freeholders of the Glencapp uplands of north Wicklow. Even more shocking was the crucifixion of Conall Óg O'More, lord of Laois, as well as the hanging of Domhnall mac Laoiseach O'More, lord of Slemargy, at Leighlinbridge in March of the same year.[115] The grisly fates of these Irish leaders polarized the situation in Leinster, facilitating Aodh's rise and steeling his resolve to preserve his power at all costs.

On the other hand, there were often good relations between the Leinster Irish and the government. In 1544–5 Dúnlaing O'Byrne of Newrath and An Calbhach O'Byrne, probably with Ormond's encouragement, served Henry VIII

112 *CSPI, 1509–73*, no. 111, p. 90, see also no. 17, p. 101; Moore, 'The MacMurrough-Kavanaghs', pp 8–9. **113** Hughes, 'The fall of the Clan Kavanagh', p. 284. Cathaoir mac Airt died in 1554, see AFM, 1554. **114** Moore, 'The MacMurrough-Kavanaghs', p. 9; AFM, 1557; *Cal. Carew MSS, 1515–74*, no. 170, pp 193–4; HMC, Halliday MSS: *Ir. Privy Council Bk 1556–71*, pp 67, 74, 109, 124, 126, and 143–4. **115** HMC, Halliday MSS: *Ir. Privy Council Bk 1556–7*, p. 39; PRO, SP 61/1/28, 29; Dowling, *Annals*, p. 40; AFM, 1547; Carey, 'The end of the Gaelic political order', p. 222; See also Fitzsimons, 'The lordship of O'Connor Faly, 1520–1570', pp 226–7. For the plantations read Dunlop, 'The plantations of Leix and Offaly', pp 61–96. This Conall Óg O'More with William Odhar O'Carroll killed An Calbhach O'Carroll, lord of Ely, see AFM, 1554. In 1556 he with Donnchadh O'Connor Faly were separately taken prisoner in 1556, but were released for guarantees of good behaviour, see AFM, 1556.

against the Scots.[116] And as has been already mentioned, Brian mac Toirdhealbhach O'Toole of Powerscourt acted as sheriff of Co. Dublin in 1545, earning deserved praise from St Leger. Moreover, Braen mac Taidhg Óig of Newrath was appointed as sheriff of O'Byrnes' Country in 1558.[117] There were also good relations between the Irish and individual English families. Testifying to this sometime in the 1550s, Fiach mac Airt Óig O'Toole of Castlekevin married Rose Basnett, daughter of Dean Edward Basnett of St Patrick's cathedral, while Tadhg Óg O'Byrne, the dynastic overlord between 1566 and 1577, fathered a son, John Falconer, by an woman of Lancashire during a stay there.[118] Even though Aodh was at odds with the English for most of his career, he did enjoy good relations with individual English. Often English observers described him as having a likeable enough character: he was friendly with Sir Francis Agarde, seneschal of the O'Byrnes and O'Tooles since May 1566, while the poets of the *Leabhar Branach* boasts of the infatuation of a young Englishwoman with Aodh.[119]

These occasional good relations with the English did not distract Aodh from copper-fastening his dynasty's position among the Irish of Leinster. From the late 1550s, he groomed his eldest son Fiach to inherit his position as the most powerful Irish lord in Leinster. To the same end he built a network of marriages between his children and the important Irish dynasties in Leinster. Links with the MacMurrough-Kavanaghs were obviously high on his agendum. Thus, in the early 1560s Fiach was married to his cousin Sadhbh, daughter of Domhnall mac Cathaoir Kavanagh of Garryhill in Carlow. Their union proved fruitful, yielding at least four sons and two daughters by 1569. Sometime in the 1560s Fiach's sister Elizabeth was married to Cathaoir mac Airt's second son, Brian mac Cathaoir Kavanagh of St Mullins in Co. Carlow, the MacMurrough-Kavanagh overlord from 1557.[120] After Brian Kavanagh's death in 1578, Elizabeth married Féilim mac Toirdhealbhach O'Toole of Powerscourt; and Eleanor, a daughter of Elizabeth and Brian Kavanagh, was later to marry Fiach's ally, Domhnall Spainneach Kavanagh.[121] Aodh's nexus also stretched into the midlands. In November 1573 Fiach's favourite sister Margaret was escorted by her family for her marriage to Ruaidhrí Óg O'More of Laois, the great friend of Aodh and his son. Another unnamed sister of Fiach became the wife of Cathaoir Dubh Kavanagh, a leader of the Art Boy Kavanaghs based at Clonmullen;[122] after the death of her husband about 1581, she married Tadhg mac Giollapádraig

---

116 Blake–Butler, 'Henry VIII's Irish army list', pp 3–5. **117** *S.P. Hen VIII, 1538–46*, no. ccccxlv, p. 570; AFM, 1547; *Cal.Fiants Philip & Mary*, no. 203. **118** *Calendar of the patent and close rolls of chancery*, ii, ed. J. Morrin (Dublin, 1862), no. 63, p. 595. Rose Basnett was still alive in July 1601. Then she was included along with her son Féilim O'Toole of Fartry and his wife, Margery Byrne, in the pardon of that date (hereafter *Cal.Pat.Rolls.Ire.*, ii); Nicholls, 'Crioch Branach', p. 24. **119** Lennon, *Sixeenth century Ire.*, p. 200; *Leabhar Branach*, ll. 1373–76, p. 53, ll. 1337–40. This refers to Aodh's forcible abduction of English wives including '… a woman with a gold-embroidered headdress' after burning their homes, see ibid., p. 353. **120** *Leabhar Branach*, pp x, 373. See Brian's obit AFM, 1578. **121** *Cal. Fiants Eliz*, no. 3713; O'Brien, 'Feagh McHugh', p. 14. **122** *DNB*, xvi, p. 786; Nicholls, 'The Kavanaghs', (1979), p.731.

Donolle obreane the messenger

4 Lord Deputy Sidney receiving a messenger from an Irish lord (Derricke, 1581)

O'Connor Faly of Offaly. The hand of a fourth sister, Honora, was given to Robert Walsh of Leopardstown, a leading figure of the prominent marcher lineage of south Dublin.[123] This marital nexus, reinforced by diplomacy, persuasion, and military might, spun a web of discontent, involving many of those in Leinster bitterly opposed to English rule. Thus, Ballinacor became the virtual epicentre of intrigue in Leinster against English government.

To proclaim his new status, Aodh increased the production of poems in his honour, recruiting such well-established poets as Tadhg Dall O'Higgins to record his heroism, reflecting the rising military and social capital of the O'Byrnes of

123 Nicholls, 'The genealogy of the Byrnes of Ranelagh', p. 111; Lane Poole Papers, NLI MS 5378. This describes the Byrnes and the Walshes as closely related.

Glenmalure. This corpus of poetry projected Aodh and the Gabhal Raghnaill as protectors of the Leinstermen and of the Irish from English incursions and aggression – beginning his transformation to an important regional leader.[124] This was the atmosphere in which Fiach grew up. Dispossessed warlords who sought his father's protection amid Crioch Raghnuill's great belts of mountainous forest must have made Fiach very conscious of the dramatic changes facing his world. Fiach benefited immensely from the tutelage and experience of his father, but there were differences between father and son. It is not possible to gauge the extent of Aodh's religious convictions, but Fiach seems to have been an extremely devout Catholic. The evolution of his Catholic political and religious ideology may have been shaped by an education by, or a exposure to, Counter-Reformation priests. His first-hand experience of the rough justice meted out by the seneschals, and his family's links with Irish and Catholic militants in Munster and Ulster, proved important to the formation of his political outlook.[125] The growth of their influence in Leinster was leading the O'Byrnes onto the stage of countrywide politics, and they were to gradually immerse themselves in the struggle to preserve the Catholic identity of the Irish and Old English nobility from the twin advances of Protestantism and Anglicization. According to the seventeenth-century historian, Philip O'Sullivan Beare, the O'Byrne lords of Glenmalure were incredibly devout and fervent Catholics, and 'this Fiach, like his father, was the bitterest enemy of the Protestants'.[126] It would seem that the O'Byrnes of Glenmalure and many of the Leinster nobility began to link the struggle to maintain the power of the Irish aristocracy with that to preserve the Catholic faith. The identification of these twin struggles as one led Fiach to increasingly view himself as a leader with potential countrywide status, rather than just as a regional figure.[127] In a sense the posture that Fiach began to take may be viewed as a continuance of that adopted by Seán (Shane) O'Neill in 1561, when O'Neill took issue with Lord Lieutenant Sussex about the executions of several Irish leaders.[128] The New English officials noted that the young Fiach inherited his father's charm; they even described him as loquacious; but they prophetically noted that his facade masked a considerable hostility to them; this proved true as the 1560s wore on. Unsurprisingly, Aodh's attacks also became more predatory – indicating Fiach's growing influence on his father.

The young Fiach first caught the government's attention in January 1563, when he and Aodh received pardons for their involvement in Richard Keating's disturbances in Wexford the previous summer.[130] In either December 1562 or

---

124 *Leabhar Branach*, pp 54–6, see ibid., pp 1–73, see also no. 32, p. 130–5; Bradshaw, 'Native reaction to the westward enterprise', n. 8, p. 72.   **125** T. O'Laidhin (ed.), *The Sidney state papers, 1565–70* (Dublin, 1962), p. 56; *CSPI, 1509–73*, no. 57, p. 329; Donovan, 'Tudor rule in Gaelic Leinster', pp 118–50.   **126** P. O'Sullivan Beare, *Ireland under Elizabeth*, ed. M. Byrne (Dublin, 1903), p. 63 (hereafter O'Sullivan Beare).   **127** Ibid., pp 18–19, 66.   **128** *CSPI, 1509–73*, no. 22, p. 176; see also Brady, *Shane O'Neill*, pp 35–59.   **130** Price, 'Notes', p. 134.

January 1563 Aodh and his son had captured two junior garrison captains, George Harvey and Henry Davells (who they later released unharmed); but then the O'Byrnes and the O'Tooles killed several Talbots on 22 September 1563,[131] and in August 1564, along with some Kavanaghs, they drove their old enemy Tibbot Walsh from his lands near Aughrim, an action that led to government concern.[132] In late 1565 Aodh's followers killed some men of Sir Francis Harbert. (When called to account in February 1566, Aodh promised to surrender Fiach, but he defaulted on this pledge.)[133] Clearly the O'Byrnes were removing threats lying close to their heartland, but these attacks were part of a strategy devised by Aodh and his brother-in-law Fiach mac Airt Óig O'Toole of Castlekevin to gain control of extensive forestlands within the Wicklow mountains. Ostensibly these actions of theirs were designed to facilitate the growth of their lucrative timber trade with Dublin and the towns of Wexford, but, with Aodh's encouragement, Fiach was using that income to recruit, train and arm a private army. The government appeased them, granting them pardons in May 1567 and April 1569: Sir Francis Agarde, the seneschal, realized the danger that Fiach posed, but his friendship with Aodh inhibited him from taking any punitive action.[134]

Two factors are crucial to understanding the rise of Aodh and Fiach to the helm of Leinster. First, in the midlands Ruaidhrí Óg O'More had begun to emerge as one of the principal leaders of the O'Mores, particularly of those disaffected with the plantations. Unlike his half-brothers, An Calbhach and Cétach, who had comfortable existences in Dublin, Ruaidhrí Óg returned to Laois from Glenmalure either in the late 1550s or the early 1560s. The young man quickly found a friend and a patron in the planter holding the Stradbally lands of his father, Ruaidhrí Caoch[135] – Sir Francis Cosby, sheriff of Laois since 1564 and seneschal from 1566. The two of them combined to extort black rents from both planters and Irish. During the early 1560s, Ruaidhrí Óg's first cousins, Niall mac Laoiseach and Cétach mac Conaill Óig O'More, encouraged by Seán O'Neill, led a campaign of resistance to the planters, whereas other cousins like

---

131 *Cal. Fiants Eliz*, no. 579; *CSPI, 1509–73*, no. 15 p. 195; PRO, SP 63/9/17; *CSPI, 1509–73*, no. 17, p. 222; *Leabhar Branach*, p. 65.   **132** PRO SP 63/11/73; *CSPI, 1509–73*, no. 73, p. 244. **133** HMC, Halliday MSS: *Ir. Privy Council Bk 1556–71*, pp 150–4. Sir Nicholas Bagnel wrote to the earl of Leicester, complaining that the country of the Byrnes, Tooles and the Walshes was waste and full of robbers in February 1566. This trouble seems to have demanded the appointment of Sir Francis Agarde as seneschal of the Toole and Byrne countries in March 1566, see *CSPI, 1509–73*, no. 33, p. 289.   **134** Price, 'Notes', pp 136–7; *CSPI, 1509–73*, no. 86, p. 529; Donovan, 'Tudor rule in Gaelic Leinster', p. 131.   **135** *CSPI, 1509–73*, nos 17–8, p. 414; This An Calbhach is described as being of Grey's Inn. In July 1569 he petitioned for the continuance of his pension of 40 livres. He also asked to be restored to the Laois lands of his father, Ruaidhrí Caoch O'More. Another brother Cétach is also mentioned. Later in April 1571 Ormond addressed An Calbhach as his cousin, confirming that these boys were half–Butlers. See idem, no. 4, p. 443; For the executions of several O'Byrnes and O'Mores including Laoiseach mac Cétach and Cathaoir mac Cétach in May 1570, see idem, no. 52, p. 430; Carey, 'The end of the Gaelic political order', p. 238.

Muircheartach mac Laoiseach, now lord of Slemargy, actually benefitted from the plantation and lent it military support.[136] What effect the plantation had on Ruaidhrí Óg cannot be discerned, for his Cosby alliance protected him from the worst of planter revenge. Indeed, Ruaidhrí Óg, like other O'More dissenters of the ruling dynasty, determined to secure a place for himself. Central to his grievances was the exclusion of his particular O'More family, the mac Ruaidhrí branch, from the new order brought by the plantations to West Leinster and the midlands. Previous opposition by Ruaidhrí Óg's uncles and cousins to the advance of authority into Laois had led to their being either exiled or denied a shareholding with full tenurial rights under common law within the plantation of Laois: effectively, in 1563–4 their lordship had been dismantled and parcelled out to a combination of their former vassals and English settlers, turning the traditional order on its head.

The government's refusal to accomodate these O'Mores within the Laois plantation, as also the exclusion of the mac Briain and mac Giollapádraig branches of the O'Connor Falys of Offaly, created an explosive scenario within the region. In 1566 the turbulence caused by the wars waged by the excluded Laoiseach mac Cétach Ruadh and his brother Cathaoir led Lord Deputy Sir Henry Sidney to offer new terms: in July 1566 he granted them some lands in the Gallen uplands of southwest Laois. This left only Ruaidhrí Óg excluded from the plantation, and Ruaidhrí Óg's growing disillusion with the situation is manifested by the fact that he and his followers were granted a pardon on 17 February 1566 to him and his followers, which coincided with the grant of a commission to the earl of Kildare, to make war upon O'More dissidents in March 1566.[137] Ruaidhrí Óg was encouraged by the incorporation of his two cousins into the new order, so he opened direct negotiations with the authorities to seek a similar accommodation, but by late 1566 it was clear to the government that there were no lands left within the plantation to grant to him and his kinsmen. During this period Ruaidhrí Óg still maintained close links with the O'Byrnes of Glenmalure. Perhaps symptomatic of his growing discontent at his exclusion was the increasing prominence of Aodh and Fiach within midland politics.[138]

Unlike Ruaidhrí Óg and the mac Briain and mac Giollapádraig branches of the O'Connor Falys of Offaly, William Odhar O'Carroll, lord of Ely, continued to thrive by playing both sides. In 1564 he cemented his hold on his lordship by procuring the death of Máelruanaidh O'Carroll in 1564. Ormond was the biggest threat to William Odhar (perhaps this may have prompted his marriage to Sadhbh MacGillapatrick of Upper Ossory). At the same time, William Odhar's stock was rising, as he was knighted on 30 March 1567 and, that May, Sidney

136 *CSPI, 1509–73*, no. 17, p. 230, no. 31, p. 232, no. 4, p. 238, no. 52, p. 242; Carey, 'The end of the Gaelic political order', p. 227.   **137** HMC, Halliday MSS: *Ir. Privy Council Bk*, pp 156–7; Carey, 'The end of the Gaelic political order', pp 237–9; See also Fitzsimons, 'The lordship of O'Connor Faly, 1520–1570', pp 232–3. See also Carey, *Surviving the Tudors*, pp 126–7. **138** *Leabhar Branach*, ll. 1730, ll. 1733, p. 66.

recommended that he be granted an baronetcy, and the queen (Elizabeth) was favourable to the idea. But little progress having been made by October, Sir William Odhar went with Sidney and other Irish lords to visit the English court. His efforts reaped rewards, as in December 1567 he was granted some special rights of jurisdiction – privileges reserved for prominent Irish loyalists. Even so, these honours did not prevent the renewal of hostilities between the O'Carrolls and the Butlers in summer 1568. The rapacity of the Butlers was blunted by their involvement in the first Desmond rebellion in 1569; this allowed Sir William Odhar O'Carroll to strengthen himself through a combination of legal and violent measures: it seems that he sheltered several dissidents drawn from the other main midland Irish families, skillfully unleashing them from time to time on the Butler earldom. However, Sir William Odhar's success at playing the hand dealt to him was the exception rather than the norm.

The norm in the midlands was represented by the increasingly discontented Ruaidhrí Óg O'More. The O'Byrnes of Glenmalure were determined to exploit the anger of Ruaidhrí Óg at his exclusion from the plantation of Laois. He did stay at peace for the remainder of the 1560s, but he was gradually realigning himself with the O'Byrnes. What clinched this alliance was the decision of Sidney (Ormond's rival) to award to Sir Peter Carew the elder the Idrone lands of the MacMurrough-Kavanaghs along with those of Sir Edmund Butler of Cloghgrenan in December 1568, a decision that had serious ramifications for the Irish of both parts of Leinster. The bad blood between the Butlers and Sidney stemmed from April 1566, when Sidney had Sir Edmund and his followers charged in the Kilkenny courts with robbery and exhortion. The bringing of a Butler to book in a Kilkenny court was a direct attack upon their hegemony. On 10 July Sidney rubbed salt into the injured Butler pride, by bringing Sir Edmund again before the courts to bind him to the peace. Later in the year Sidney struck at the pillar of Butler power, by ordering that the practice of coign and livery be abandoned throughout the Ormond earldom.

In response, Sir Edmund with Piers Grace in November raised the stakes by parading 1,400 troops through Wexford. On 17 December the Irish judiciary by an act of state awarded Idrone to Carew; five days later at Newcastle McKynegan in east Wicklow, Sidney signed the act into law. From there he marched to Kilkenny and declared Sir Edmund and his confederates outlaws. Indignant with rage and while his brother Ormond was in England, Sir Edmund rebelled in June 1569. With Irish help, he engaged in a series of devastating raids, plundering and killing many of the English planters of Laois before ravaging much of Wexford, Carlow, Kildare and the southern Dublin Pale; but it was a campaign that ran out of steam after the fall of his castle of Cloghgrenan and his failed siege of Kilkenny in July. After suffering defeat at Kilmocar and burning Arklow, Sir Edmund submitted on 1 September 1569 to the newly returned Ormond, and was imprisoned in Dublin Castle, but the war dragged into 1570.[139] It was

---

139 Edwards, 'The Butler revolt of 1569', pp 253–4; *CSPI, 1509–73*, no. 12, p. 426. See also

one in which the O'Byrnes of Glenmalure and many of the O'Mores, particularly Laoiseach mac Cétach Ruaidh, supported the Cloghgrenan Butlers. In truth though the O'Mores and other Irish dissidents in the midlands were now increasingly reliant upon the relieving effects of military expeditions of the O'Byrne lords of Glenmalure into the region.[140]

Brady, *A viceroy's vindication?*, pp 62–3.   **140** PRO, SP 63/30/52. O'Byrne interference within this region is confirmed by the charge levelled at Aodh in February 1569, accusing him of supporting and supplying Muircheartach O'More's forces against the settlers, see *CSPI, 1509–73*, no. 37, p. 403. *An Leabhar Branach* also throws further light upon Aodh's activities, mentioning raids in Laois and Ossory, his kidnap of the daughter of O'Connor Faly and his killing of An Calbhach O'Molloy of Fearceall as well as contemptuous references to the latter's dynasty and his neighbours, the O'Melaghlins of west Meath. *Leabhar Branach*, no. 18, ll. 1730, ll. 1733, p. 66. See also ll. 1749, p. 67, this mentions his plundering of the coarb of Ballyduff in the Laois parish of Kyle in the barony of Clandonagh. For the references to the O'Melaghlins and the O'Molloys, see no. 5, ll. 541–4 p. 22.

CHAPTER 10

War and peace, 1570–90

Lord Deputy Sir Henry Sidney, determined to exact vengeance upon the O'Mores who took part in the Butler revolt of 1569, launched a manhunt throughout Laois for those still left in the field.[1] But it was not to be through military means but through cunning that Sidney achieved his goal. On 2 February 1570 Ruaidhrí Óg O'More along with his cousin Laoiseach mac Cétach Ruaidh O'More appeared before Sidney at Strabally, Co. Laois, to put in their pledges. In doing so, Ruaidhrí Óg was clearly pressing his claims to be incorporated into the plantation.[2] Even though Sidney pronounced the government's willingness to forgive Laoiseach mac Cétach Ruaidh's acts, he was biding his time to take his revenge. In his memoirs written in 1583, Sidney recalled how he 'got to come to me (without protection or other assurance) two brothers, dangerous men, called Kaer mac Kedo O'Moore, and Lysagh mac Kedo O'Moore, sons of Kedo, sometime captain of Leysh, and died in rebellion'. Once in Sidney's presence, the trap were sprung on the hapless brothers. After a trial, Sidney oversaw the hanging of Laoiseach mac Cétach Ruaidh at Carlow in May 1570; as for Cathaoir, he brought him to Dublin to face a trial for treason, where he was duly found guilty and hanged, drawn and quartered. 'In this journey', Sidney recalled, 'I did as good service as ever I did in any peaceable progress.'[3] But there was one O'More leader left alive – one that was eminently capable of hitting back.

Ruaidhrí Óg had survived Sidney's purge because of his continued service with Cosby. The executions of his cousins, and his own survival, guaranteed his emergence, under O'Byrne patronage, as a force to reckoned within the region. Effectively, the executions sealed Aodh O'Byrne's influence in the midlands, as Ruaidhrí Óg was only the principal O'More leader left alive, with the exception of Muircheartach of Slemargy.[4] Ruaidhrí Óg was greatly embittered by the actions of Sidney, a kinsman of Cosby, and therefore he soon became embroiled in a vicious feud with Cosby, seneschal of Laois and representative of the Sidney faction. By late 1570 Ruaidhrí Óg was fast establishing himself as the principal threat to the New English in West Leinster and the midlands, recruiting large

---

1 PRO, SP 63/30/52.   2 HMC, Halliday MSS: *Ir. Privy Council Bk*, p. 241.   3 Brady, *A viceroy's vindication?*, p. 76.   4 Dowling, *Annals,* p. 41; for the relationship between the Cosbys and the Sidneys, see Cosby, 'The English settlers in Queen's County', p. 323. Dorcas Sidney was married to Alexander Cosby.

bands of swordsmen as well as refusing to parley with Cosby. In April 1571 he was elected as lord of Laois (in the presence of Fiach O'Byrne), perhaps as a response to the declaration of martial law there in March.[5] The emergence of Ruaidhrí Óg created opportunities for the O'Byrnes. The O'Byrnes had been active; they had taken part in the rebellion of Sir Edmund Butler of 1569. Fiach had exploited the situation by supporting Butler's attacks near Ferns and Arklow as well as threatening Newcastle McKynegan between July and August 1569.[6] After Butler's submission on 1 September 1569, Aodh O'Byrne's sons helped him escape to Glenmalure from Dublin Castle in November 1569; this proved to be a mixed blessing for the O'Byrnes, particularly Fiach, for, while in Glenmalure, Fiach's wife Sadhbh became enamoured with Sir Edmund during the winter of 1569–70; this led to her divorce from Fiach (and her subsequent relationship with Butler) and caused considerable enmity between the two men.[7]

In 1571 Ruaidhrí Óg joined Fiach in attacks upon the Pale, and later Fiach was indicted along with his brother-in-law Brian Kavanagh, and several Old English landowners of southern Wexford in connection with the killing of Robert Browne of Mulrankan, Co. Wexford, a prominent government supporter, on 21 April 1572.[8] Fiach's alleged accomplices were Matthew and John Furlong of Horetown and Matthew Fitzharris of Macmine. These raids by Fiach were parallelled by Ruaidhrí Óg's burnings in Laois, and his incitement of the O'Mores and the O'Connor Falys in May. On hearing of Robert Browne's death, Sir Nicholas White, his father-in-law and seneschal of Wexford, went to London; in early August 1572, armed with Elizabeth's support, he returned to Ireland, thirsting for revenge.[9] The previous month, Sir Francis Agarde (seneschal of O'Byrnes' Country) had successfully attacked the followers of Fiach, killing his brother. Within days of his return from England, White attacked Críoch Raghnuill, but failed to bring Fiach to book. His assault undermined attempts being made by Kildare and Agarde to make a deal with Fiach O'Byrne and Brian Kavanagh (who, it would seem, had agreed to betray the Furlongs of Horetown, Co. Wexford, in return for immunity from prosecution), and it sparked the outbreak of a wider war.[10] Meanwhile in Laois, the government, advised by Ormond and Kildare, adopted different tactics with the O'Mores. In August 1572 the two earls held a conference with Ruaidhrí Óg in Kilkea castle, during which Ruaidhrí Óg denounced the brutality of the settlers and the government. But in spite of his anger, Ruaidhrí Óg's demands were remarkably moderate and consistent: crucially, he accepted the permanence of the Laois plantation and expressed his willingness to be accommodated within it. In particular, he wished for a grant of the Gallen lands of his executed cousins. In

---

5 PRO, SP 63/31/33; PRO, SP 63/32/2, 9; *CSPI, 1509–73*, no. 9, p. 444. **6** Ibid., no. 40, p. 416; *Calendar of the manuscripts of the marquis of Salisbury*, i (London, 1883), no. 1320, p. 417. **7** *Cal Carew MSS, 1575–88*, no. 501, p. 350; *CSPI, 1509–73*, no. 81, p. 423; O'Byrne, 'The rise of Gabhal Raghnaill', p. 104; see also Brady, *A viceroy's vindication?*, p. 77; *Acts Privy Council*, xix, p. 410. **8** PRO, SP 63/36/16; Fiach was mentioned as the killer of Browne, see PRO, SP 63/37/13. **9** PRO, SP 63/37/59. **10** *CSPI, 1509–73*, no. 13, p. 477; PRO, SP 63/37/44.

return for settlement of his grievances, Ruaidhrí Óg submitted and accepted a pardon.[11] Meanwhile Fiach and Brian Kavanagh responded to White's assault by ravaging Wexford, defeating the Wexford freeholders in August and September 1572; however, they along with Aodh O'Byrne came to peace in December 1572 (deserting Matthew and Robert Furlong of Horetown who were later executed) and were pardoned.[12]

By early January 1573, Ruaidhrí Óg, realizing that his claims were to be ignored yet again, returned to war, and launched an offensive to overthrow the Laois plantation. His purpose was to force the authorities to incorporate him within the new order, but these latest attacks only convinced them to adopt a much harsher policy towards him. They now proposed to plant the loyalist Eóghan O'Dempsey in Ruaidhrí Óg's Gallen heartland. This further fuelled the already enflamed region, ensuring the bitterest fighting yet between Ruaidhrí Óg and the planters. Throughout 1573, Aodh and Fiach renewed their diplomatic contacts with Gerald Fitzgerald, 15th earl of Desmond. Desmond hoped that Ruaidhrí Óg (who had helped him to escape from Dublin earlier in 1573) and the O'Byrnes would return to war in 1574.[13] In preparation for the forthcoming war, Aodh recruited mercenaries and made two strategic marriage alliances that strengthened his position in East Leinster: sometime in 1573, Fiach married Rose, daughter of Fiach mac Airt Óig O'Toole of Castlekevin and Rose Basnett.[14] And in November 1573 the lords of Glenmalure gave the clearest sign yet of their approval of Ruaidhrí Óg's struggle against the planters, when Fiach escorted Margaret, his favourite sister, to Laois to marry Ruaidhrí Óg; for Ruaidhrí Óg, marriage to Fiach's sister was further confirmation of his high status among the Leinster Irish.

To the government the O'More/O'Byrne union was profoundly disturbing. In December, Sir Piers Fitzgerald, sheriff of Kildare, ambushed Fiach upon his return from Laois, but Fiach's bodyguard routed the sheriff's horsemen and kerne and carried Fitzgerald off to Glenmalure.[15] Once back in Glenmalure, Fiach and Aodh were defiant, refusing Agarde's demands for a parley to negotiate the sheriff's release and demanding a massive ransom of £800. They were determined to keep their captive in order to strengthen their hand for when they moved to war – as they did, early the next year, in the face of several English rescue attempts. On Desmond's prompting, Fiach burnt to the gates of Dublin throughout January to March 1574, while Ruaidhrí Óg, the O'Connor Falys and the O'Tooles terrorized the Pale's southern borders. By May, it was estimated that Fiach and his allies could put up to 600 men into the field. The growing confidence of the Irish leaders was clear when Fiach penetrated the Pale defences, and set the town of Kilmainham aflame before retreating back into the mountains.[16] The frustration of the New

11 PRO, SP 63/37/37; *CSPI, 1509–73*, no. 41, p. 481. 12 Donovan, 'Tudor rule in Gaelic Leinster', pp 125–6; *CSPI, 1509–73*, no. 51, p. 490; Price, 'Notes', p. 138. 13 *CSPI, 1574–85*, no. 42, p. 7, no. 4, p. 11; *CSPI, 1509–73*, no. 88, p. 529; PRO, SP 63/42/88. 14 Lane Poole Papers, NLI MS 5378; *CSPI, 1509–73*, no. 6, p. 530. 15 PRO, SP 63/43/13. 16 PRO, SP 63/45/41;

English at their inability to contain the attacks of the mountain Irish was palpable. That June a party led by John Crawhall violently protested before Lord Deputy Fitzwilliam about the ease of Fiach's success, accusing the old marcher families of the Dublin Pale of connivance in these attacks.[17] However, in early October Aodh, having decided to come to terms with the English, opened negotiations with Ormond. His tactics were double-dealing, reflecting his own father's actions of October 1548, when Seán O'Byrne travelled to Dublin to negotiate his submission, while leaving Aodh to guard their lordship. This time Aodh played the role of the father; leaving Fiach in charge, he gave himself into Ormond's custody, arriving in Dublin on 24 October.[18]

The widespread disorder in Leinster between 1571 and 1575 and the ease of the Irish attacks raised serious reservations about the loyalty of the earl of Kildare, the governor of the Pale's southwestern borders. During these years, a strong party of opposition to Kildare had grown around Lord Deputy Sir William Fitzwilliam; this included figures among the gentry of Co. Kildare, New English officials and several prominent midland planters, many of whom believed that Kildare was conspiring to restore the old Fitzgerald overlordship over the Leinster Irish and that he coveted the office of lord deputy. Most of them also believed that the earl was in league with Ruaidhrí Óg, Fiach and the O'Connor Falys. Indeed, Fitzwilliam (an avowed enemy of the earl) later lambasted him as the 'the procurer and maintainer of the storm, disorder and rebellion of the Pale since [the beginning] of my government'.[19] Between November 1574 and February 1575, the enemies of Kildare assiduously gathered information purporting to show that he had orchestrated the midland war to undermine the plantations and to destroy the adminstration of Fitzwilliam.

In West Leinster and the midlands, Kildare was accused of having open communication with the O'Mores and the O'Connor Falys, and of having encouraged them to attack the New English planters and those Kildare gentry opposed to the extension of the earl's power. The earl was also known to be eager to affirm his power in Offaly; in January 1574 he asked for its seneschalship – a move vehemently resisted by the Offaly planters.[20] From the middle of the 1560s Kildare had, in fact, gradually evolved into a powerful government representative on the Wicklow marches. On 16 July 1565 he was appointed captain of Imaal, and he was granted the constableship of Shillelagh on 12 December 1570, which meant that he now came into closer contact with the O'Byrnes of Glenmalure. Kildare's links with the lords of Glenmalure and their O'More protégé resulted in his holding of several all-night conferences with them in Kilkea castle between 1572 and 1575.[21] What resulted was a mutually beneficial and pragmatic relationship facilitated by Kildare's position as the natural leader of the Old English Catholic community of the Pale and East Leinster. From time

PRO, SP 63/43/14; PRO, SP 63/45/46; PRO, SP 63/46/64. **17** PRO, SP 63/46/51. **18** PRO, SP 63/48/53; PRO, SP 63/48/70 (i); PRO, SP 63/48/7. **19** Bodl., Carte MS 55, f.30. **20** Carey, *Surviving the Tudors*, pp 163–4. **21** PRO, SP 63/51/26 (i).

5 The dispossessed Ruaidhrí Óg O'More as seen by the illustrator of Derricke's *Image of Ireland* (1581)

to time it seems that Kildare employed the services of Fiach to terrorize his enemies. Fiach relished the chance given to him by Kildare's dirty war to wreak havoc; in particular, he played a prominent role in the roughing up of some of the gentry of Co. Kildare in December 1572, burning parts of Castledermot and attacking the Wellesleys of Bishopscourt. Later, Eóghan O'Dempsey, Kildare's enemy, alleged that in 1573 the earl even tried unsuccessfully to have the O'Byrnes murder the captive sheriff of Kildare.[22] In these charges there was little substantive evidence of Kildare's alleged orchestration of violence between 1572 and 1575 or of his conspiracy to wrest back the lord deputyship for his house. In fact, the evidence was coloured by the agendas of Kildare's accusers, but it all tends to illustrate the realities and practical problems faced by English officials attempting to rule these rowdy borderlands. Fitzwilliam, though, pressed ahead, and at a privy council meeting on 8 May 1575, he arrested Kildare and committed him to Dublin Castle before transferring him to the Tower in London. Under examination in England, Kildare successfully defended himself from these charges of treason by explaining his actions in the context of government service. As nothing was proved, Kildare returned to Ireland in 1577.

During Kildare's absence, his erstwhile friends, Ruaidhrí Óg and Fiach, burned throughout Kildare. Later, during Lord Deputy Sidney's circuit through East Leinster in November and December 1575, Ruaidhrí Óg submitted before him at Kilkenny, and Aodh also met him without protection; but Fiach remained aloof.[23] This stratagem of the father going to plead the son's cause reflects their earlier tactics of 1548 and 1574. It is difficult at times to distinguish between Fiach's actions and those of his father in this period, but Aodh seems to have gradually taken a less active part, adopting the role of an elder statesman. To the English administrators there was little doubt that Aodh was a figurehead and Fiach the real power in Críoch Raghnuill.[24] From 1575 Fiach was on a collision course with the government. Unfolding events in the midlands further alienated him. In December 1575 Sidney concluded that the Laois plantation would never stabilize unless Ruaidhrí Óg was given a stake. He was now prepared to give Gallen (located on the Laois/Kilkenny borders) to Ruaidhrí Óg, but was not prepared to countenance his traditional rights as ruler of Laois. In June 1576 he pardoned Ruaidhrí Óg; but he still delayed the settling of his estates. Then, in the hope of addressing Fiach's discontent, Sidney dispatched Agarde in July 1576 to bring him by any means to Dublin. Soon, Fiach was lodged in Dublin Castle.[25] By January 1577, the political situation in the midlands had considerably worsened because of Sidney's delay of Ruaidhrí Óg's case. Moreover, renewed intimidation shown to Ruaidhrí Óg by Cosby signalled the rejection of his claims – forcing him again into revolt in February 1577. On 3 March 1577, Ruaidhrí Óg sealed his fate by burning Naas in the Pale.[26]

22 PRO, SP 63/49/62; PRO, SP 63/43/20; PRO, SP 63/52/24; PRO, SP 63/49/60.
23 *CSPI, 1574–85* no. 4, p. 11, no. 36, p. 14; see ibid., no. 38, p. 25, nos 59–63, p. 53; ibid., no. 24, p. 70; Price, 'Notes', p. 139; *Cal Carew MSS, 1575–88*, no. 33, p. 32.   **24** O'Byrne, 'Glenmalure', p. 154.   **25** PRO, SP 63/56/6.   **26** PRO, SP 63/57/39; O'Sullivan Beare, pp 7–8.

A savage war ensued. In autumn 1577 Ruaidhrí Óg burnt Leighlinbridge and Carlow before capturing Alexander Cosby and Sir Henry Harrington (the lieutenant of the Offaly plantation) at a parley. Harrington had been a thorn in Ruaidhrí Óg's side, and had enjoyed some considerable successes against him. He was also Agarde's son-in-law and a nephew to Sidney – something not lost upon Ruaidhrí Óg. While Ruaidhrí Óg had the perfect opportunity to revenge himself upon Sidney, he was not slow to grasp the strategic importance of his captives; accordingly, he used them as levers to negotiate redress for his losses and set a high price for their freedom. In September, he outlined his grievances in a document which he dispatched to Sidney. Principally, he directed his anger at the New English captains bordering his lands. Until Sidney met Ruaidhrí Óg's demands for a pardon and a grant of Gallen, the O'More leader refused to consider freeing his prisoners. To ensure Sidney's compliance, Ruaidhrí Óg also demanded that he be given Richard Harrington and the sons of Robert Harpoole and Walter Butler as hostages. His demands also reflected the concerns of his O'Byrne allies; for he targeted government supporters throughout Leinster. Then he audaciously demanded that Viscount Roland Fitzeustace of Baltinglass, Barnaby MacGillapatrick, 2nd baron of Upper Ossory, Sir Francis Agarde, Lord Montgomery, Robert Pipho and John Fitzeustace of Castlemartin be fined £500 apiece for attacks into Irish lands. Continuing with this pan-Leinster agenda, he requested that Conchobhar O'Connor Faly be pardoned and restored to his lands in Offaly, and he then went on to ask for the restitution of personal effects taken by the New English settlers.[27]

Sidney would not agree to this. A resentful Ruaidhrí Óg then insulted Sidney by parading Harrington and Alexander Cosby like slaves through his territory – which only made Sidney more determined to catch him. The feud between the two men climaxed when, with the help of a disaffected O'More, Sidney finally cornered Ruaidhrí Óg during mid December 1577. And in a night-time attempt by Sidney to rescue Harrington and Cosby, Ruaidhrí Óg's wife Margaret was beheaded and two of their sons killed. After seeing their slaughter, Ruaidhrí Óg, although seriously wounded, fought his way through the English and escaped but not before mutilating Harrington. The killing of Fiach's brother John by English soldiers within three days of Margaret's death suggests that the O'Byrnes intervened to support Ruaidhrí Óg.[28] Shortly afterwards, either in late 1577 or early 1578, Muircheartach O'More of Slemargy (Ruaidhrí Óg's alleged ally) and his unarmed followers were massacred by Sir Francis Cosby and Robert Harpoole, sheriff of Carlow. This outrage sparked fighting that spread into

---

27 HMC, *De L'Isle and Dudley MSS*, ii (1934), pp 70-1; O'Sullivan Beare, p. 7. **28** *Carew MSS, 1575–1588*, no. 501, p. 356. For the Harringtons in general, see I. Grimble, *The Harrington family* (London, 1957); ALC, 1578; O'Byrne, 'Glenmalure', p. 155; Brady, *A viceroy's vindication?*, p. 98. For the reaction of the O'Byrnes to the deaths of Margaret and John, see *Leabhar Branach*, no. 68, pp 259–63. Interestingly the Wicklow based poet, Donnchadh McKeogh, criticizes the lords of Glenmalure for making such a faraway match for Margaret. It also predicts that they will be avenged.

Kildare and Carlow. After his recovery from his wounds, Ruaidhrí Óg led revenge attacks from Críoch Raghnuill upon Carlow and Kildare until his death in a skirmish with the soldiers of Barnaby MacGillapatrick, 2nd baron of Upper Ossory, on 30 June 1578. While the O'Mores quickly elected as the new lord of Laois Ross O'More, the leader of the mac Lochlainn O'Mores, they had suffered a massive setback.[29]

The deaths of Ruaidhrí Óg and his wife disrupted the plans of the O'Byrnes and deeply affected Fiach, who swore revenge and undertook to bring up the pair's remaining children in Glenmalure. Another man whose life was profoundly affected by the death of Ruaidhrí Óg was his victim Sir Henry Harrington. On 28 April 1578 he became seneschal of the O'Tooles and the O'Byrnes, succeeding Agarde, who died on 26 November 1577.[30] After a long convalescence, Harrington travelled south to Newcastle McKynegan to take up his duties. Armed with a rigorous commission of martial law, Harrington, in contrast to Agarde, adopted a more hard-line policy towards the O'Byrnes, attempting to establish himself as the sole fulcrum of power in Wicklow by eradicating the traditional privileges of the Irish nobility.[31] One of his first actions set the tone. In April 1578, Fiach mac Airt Óig O'Toole of Castlekevin died. Harrington then approached the government, who, with considerable insensitivity to the O'Tooles, granted him the guardianship of Barnaby O'Toole, Fiach's son and heir.[32] In July 1578, Harrington was also granted the constableship of Shillelagh (this infuriated Kildare, who had held this office from December 1570 until his arrest in 1575; in November 1579 Kildare successfully appealed to the English privy council for the restoration of this office; this only served to intensify his feud with Harrington).[33] Harrington's behaviour in east Wicklow created a poisonous situation with the senior O'Byrnes and their leader, Dúnlaing mac Edmund O'Byrne of Cronroe. On his accession to the seneschalship, he appropriated the traditional rents due to Dúnlaing, thereby rendering him politically impotent. This act exacerbated Dúnlaing's grievances and, combined with Harrington's excessive brutality, created a volatile political atmosphere within the formerly loyal senior O'Byrne leadership.[34]

---

29 *Cal. Carew MSS, 1575–88*, no. 101, p. 137; O'Byrne, 'Glenmalure', p. 155; AFM, 1578; *CSPI, 1574–85* no. 41, p. 138; O'Sullivan Beare, p. 8; *Calendar of the manuscripts of the marquis of Salisbury*, ii (London, 1888), pp 186–7.   30 In November 1577 he was later viciously attacked by Ruaidhrí Óg during the rout of the O'Mores. Harrington's injuries consisted of several deep head wounds, a broken arm and the loss of a finger to Ruaidhrí Óg's sword. So severe were Harrington's wounds that Sidney feared that his nephew would not survive the journey back to Dublin. However, he was permanently scarred. See *Cal. Carew MSS, 1575–88*, no. 501, p. 356; *Cal. Fiants Eliz*, nos 3266, 3612. For Agarde's date of death, see *Cal. Inquisitions*, Eliz 100/75, p. 235.   31 HMC, *De L'Isle and Dudley MSS*, ii (1934), p. 82; Nicholls, *Gaelic. Ire.*, p. 173.   32 Donovan, 'Tudor rule in Gaelic Leinster', p. 134; Brady, *The chief governors*, p. 276. 33 J. Hogan & N. McNeill (eds), *The Walsingham letter book, May 1578–December 1579*, p. 237; *Cal. Fiants, Eliz*, nos 3372, 3707; O'Byrne, 'The rise of the Gabhal Raghnaill', pp 157–8; Carey, *Surviving the Tudors*, p. 199.   34 AFM, 1578; O'Byrne, 'The rise of the Gabhal Raghnaill', p. 158.

Ruaidhrí Óg's death, which coincided with the natural death of Brian Kavanagh[35] and the execution of Fiach mac Airt Óig O'Toole during 1578, left Fiach as the only lord powerful enough to lead the Leinstermen. To counter the encroachments of the government, he now sought to create a unified provincial opposition. Even though he was the most powerful Leinster lord, he could not claim its kingship without losing support among the MacMurrough-Kavanaghs; so he chose to play kingmaker among them, advancing his clients in several dynastic struggles as well as compelling them to swear loyalty to him. During summer 1578 Sir Thomas Masterson, seneschal of Wexford since 1573, along with Sir Peter Carew the younger, led raids upon Críoch Raghnuill. This struggle spiralled out of control, and much of Wexford was destroyed by Fiach's revenge attacks. On 21 September 1578 Fiach submitted in Christchurch. The text of his submission reveals his bitterness towards Masterson.[36] Subsequently, Fiach was committed to the custody of Harrington. Within days he was freed, submitting alongside his father at Castledermot on 30 September 1578. A further sign of their elevated position among the Leinster nobility was that this latest submission signalled the ensuing submissions of Brian Kavanagh, Conchobhar O'Connor Faly, Tadhg mac Giollapádraig O'Connor Faly and Ruaidhrí Óg's marshal.[37] Masterson, however, plotted for Fiach to be assassinated at a proposed parley, but through his spies Fiach learned of Masterson's intent and laid a snare of his own, ambushing Masterson's troops on their way to the meeting.[38] As for Aodh, he outwardly co-operated with the government throughout 1578–9, lavishly entertaining Lord Justice Sir William Drury at Ballinacor in February 1579. In addition, he agreed to the inclusion of his lordship within the government's plans to shire the territories of Wicklow and Ferns. However, any moderating influence exercised by Aodh over Fiach was extinguished by the old lord's death in summer 1579.[39]

If Aodh or Ruaidhrí Óg had not played the Catholic card, Fiach was to. As the 1560s and 70s wore on, it would seem that Fiach linked the struggle to preserve his rights and privileges and those of the Leinster nobility with the growing resentment of Catholics at the discrimination practised towards them by the government. Although several poems dedicated to Aodh contain many traditional motifs common in bardic poetry, they reveal a hardening in the attitude of the lords of Glenmalure towards the new religion and the New English. The poems are marked by an increase in the use of religious imagery and evidence particular devotion towards the Virgin Mary. Tellingly, they contain are numerous references to the burning of English villages and to suppression of the English language among the Irish. The main corpus of bardic material relating to Fiach may postdate 1587, continuing until summer 1597.[40] In spite of

---

35 AFM, 1578. Brian died sometime after October 1578. **36** PRO, SP 63/63/1. **37** *Cal. Carew MSS, 1575–88*, no. 109, pp 140–1. Ruaidhrí Óg's marshal was Seán mac Ruaidhrí. **38** O'Byrne, 'Glenmalure', p. 155; AFM, 1578. **39** AFM, 1579; *Calendar of the manuscripts of the marquis of Salisbury*, ii, no. 701, p. 235. **40** *Leabhar Branach*, no. 10, ll. 1013–6, p. 39; see all of no. 33; ibid., no. 4, pp 15–9; no. 7, pp 25–32; no. 8, ll. 797–800, p. 31; no. 14, pp 45–50; no.

these difficulties in dating, there is little reason to doubt Bradshaw's essential point that, through their patronage of poets and by their actions, the O'Byrnes were promoting a new nationalistic ideology fiercely opposed to the extension of New English rule. The declaration of Fiach as leader of the Leinster nobility to fight for the Catholic cause in 1580 was a new and most significant development in Irish history, signalling the gradual fusion of an embryonic Irish nationalism and Catholicism against a government mainly dominated by New English Protestants.[41] In July 1580 Fiach and his 28-year-old Old English ally, James Fitzeustace, 3rd Viscount Baltinglass, went to war with the government in defence of Catholicism as well as to avenge the wrongs done to the Leinstermen since the 1550s. This alliance and crusade shocked the government. One observer prophetically noted that the alliance of Fiach and Baltinglass and their public beating of the Catholic drum heralded a new era in the Irish wars, for it was fuelled by political, cultural and, now, religious grievances. Indeed, Fiach declared to officials in 1581, that he would not come to peace unless 'religion might be at liberty'.[42]

In Fiach's decision to embark upon a major war with the government in summer 1580, the bloody events of 1577–8 played no little part in. Likewise, Baltinglass had become steadily disaffected with the administration's harsh policies towards his class, the Catholic Old English nobility. Throughout the 1570s, Baltinglass' father, Roland Fitzeustace, 2nd Viscount Baltinglass, had been a prominent opponent of the levying of the cess upon Catholic lands and towns by the army. More worrying for the Old English Catholics was their growing exclusion from the government of the Irish kingdom in favour of New English Protestants. Added to this was the perception among the new governing class that Old English Catholics could not be trusted with positions of authority. And Pope Pius V's excommunication of Elizabeth must greatly strengthened the view that being Catholic and loyal were incompatible.[43] Despite the protestations of loyalty to Elizabeth by Old English Catholics, the government refused to listen.

To Elizabeth, the threat from Catholicism was real. In England, the Catholic Church had been in upheaval since Henry VIII's divorce from Katharine of Aragon and his declaration of supremacy over the Church. Elizabeth's very existence had been precarious, as Mary, her Catholic half-sister, imprisoned her, and for a while her life was in danger due to Mary's intense suspicion of her. After Mary's death in 1558, Elizabeth became queen but was exposed to several assassination plots by her own Catholic countrymen.[44] Moreover, Elizabeth was

15, p. 52, ll. 1353–6 & see p. 354.   **41** Bradshaw, 'Native reaction to the westward enterprise', pp 72–5. These stanzas describe Aodh as the defender of East Leinster, comparing him to Cú Chulainn, see *Leabhar Branach*, no. 1, ll. 53–60, p. 3. This compares Fiach's leadership of Leinster to that of Cormac Conluingheas who was invited by the men of Ulster to succeed his father, see also no. 28, pp 118–19. O'Byrne, 'Glenmalure', pp 150–79. For the strength of Catholic religious fervour among the Irish of Leinster, see O'Sullivan Beare, pp 18–19.   **42** *CSPI*, 1574–85, no. 66, p. 237; Price, 'Notes', p. 148.   **43** Lennon, 'The Counter-Reformation in Ireland, 1542–1641', pp 77–82.   **44** Starkey, *Elizabeth*, pp 118–307.   **45** Elton, *Reformation*

involved in a battle of intrigue with her cousin, Mary Stuart, queen of Scots. As Elizabeth had remained single and therefore childless, the Scottish queen was poised to claim the English throne upon Elizabeth's death.

However, much of the danger facing Elizabeth originated on the continent. Ever since Martin Luther nailed his theses to the door of the castle church of Wittenberg in October 1517, Europe had been in turmoil over the question of religious doctrine and reform. Inevitably, the ensuing debate became confrontational as secular princes took the side of the established church or that of Luther, resulting in the wars of the Reformation.[45] Consequently, Elizabeth was acutely aware of the possibility of a successful invasion of England, led by Philip II of Spain with the blessing of the papacy. For much of Elizabeth's early reign, Spanish armies were preoccupied in the Netherlands, fighting the Protestant forces of William of Nassau (1533–84) and his allies. But a series of Spanish victories in 1568 saw them reclaim lost ground.[46] An event that traumatized the Protestant psyche was the massacre of Huguenots on St Bartholomew's Day, 23/24 August 1572, perpetuated by French Catholics, with the approval of Charles IX; its effects on the contemporary policies of the English government were considerable. While Elizabeth herself seems to have been largely unmoved by religious sentiment, she was not prepared to lose her kingdom to either real or perceived Catholic dangers. Ireland was now an another arena for the latest round of wars of the Reformation; it had strategic importance as Protestant England's backdoor.

Elizabeth had every reason to be fearful about Catholic intrigues in Ireland. Fiach and Baltinglass were not alone in identifying religion as a unifying force in the struggle against the English. Albeit much later, Aodh O'Neill, 2nd earl of Tyrone, pragmatically used the struggle for religious liberty to fuel the Nine Years War.[47] In contrast, both Fiach and Baltinglass were fully-fledged Counter-Reformation Catholics. Like many of his friends and contemporaries, Baltinglass had been educated at Grey's Inn, one of the most prestigious inns of court in London. On finishing his education, he spent a period during the 1570s living in Rome. Baltinglass was very much representative of his class. From the 1560s, many Old English Catholic families opted to send their sons to universities in Catholic Europe rather than enroll them in English ones. The exposure of these young men to the Catholic Counter-Reformation caused them to be more militant towards the policies of the government on their return to Ireland. Baltinglass was the clearest exponent of this militancy and publicly proclaimed his views. For his trouble, he earned a night in jail, a fine, a sermon, and an enduring feud with the Protestant archbishop of Dublin, Adam Loftus. While Fiach may have lacked the formal education of Baltinglass, he was fully conversant with the great issues of the day, thanks to the tutelage of his

Europe, 1517–59, pp 15, 239–74.   **46** Limm, *The Dutch revolt, 1559–1648*, pp 32, 36–7, 39, 50. **47** Elliot, *The Catholics of Ulster*, p. 59 However, it has to be said Tyrone's personal religious devotion was questionable.

confessors. Fiach's fusion of Catholicism with his considerable anti-English feeling meant that he was fully aware of the struggle between Catholicism and Protestantism on the continent. On 29 October 1580, Dr Nicholas Saunders, the papal legate, in a note to a cardinal, confirmed that Fiach's religious principles were responsible for his joining with Baltinglass. And later, Archbishop James O'Hely of Tuam wrote admiringly of Fiach's fervent support of Spain and the papacy.[48] Baltinglass and Fiach had much in common. In life, their fathers were rivals among the borderlands of west Wicklow, a struggle recorded in the battle roll of Aodh's victories;[49] but since then relations had considerably mellowed between the Fitzeustaces and the O'Byrnes so much so that Viscount Roland complained to the government about the wrongful taking of Aodh's cattle in 1578. Viscount Roland and Aodh died in 1578 and 1579 respectively, leaving Fiach and Baltinglass in full control of their respective dynasties.

Along with Baltinglass, Fiach planned a war to unite both Irish and Old English Catholics against an administration they perceived as unjust. It has been argued that Fiach simply used Baltinglass for his own ends, but this is manifestly not the case. It is clear that the movement of Baltinglass and Fiach to war began sometime after mid-1579. For much of that year Fiach had co-operated with the government and Harrington,[50] though a change in his attitude can be detected after the arrival on the scene of James fitzmaurice Fitzgerald, the swashbuckling cousin of Desmond. In July 1579, James fitzmaurice landed at Dingle with some Spaniards and Dr Saunders, with the intention of fomenting a Catholic crusade. The deaths of Viscount Roland and Aodh ensured that nothing could restrain their sons. However, Fiach's activities did not escape unnoticed, as in early October 1579 Lord Justice Pelham commanded him to control his followers. Pelham's suspicions were further aroused when, a month later, a letter from Desmond was intercepted en route to Glenmalure in which Desmond urged Fiach to join him in a war for the defence of Catholicism.[51]

The interception of this letter alerted the government that something was happening in Fiach's lands. Their unease with these developments is reflected in Harrington's suit for the release of Fiach's pledge, Aodh Dubh O'Byrne of Knockrath, on 3 December 1579.[52] That Aodh Dubh was released at this point is highly significant. All through the lordship of Aodh (Fiach's father), Aodh Dubh had been unswerving in his loyalty to his cousin. However, Aodh Dubh did not have the same intimacy with Fiach: as early as 1575, Kildare allegedly warned Fiach that Aodh Dubh was too friendly with Agarde, then seneschal of O'Byrnes' Country.[53] Maintaining a facade of loyalty, Fiach met Lord Justice

48 Hagan 'Miscellanea Vaticano-Hibernica', p. 246; *Estado* 839, ff 56, 66; Silke, 'The Irish appeal of 1593', pp 364 & 366.   49 *Leabhar Branach*, no. 18, ll. 1657, p. 64.   50 *CSPI, 1574–85* no. 60, p. 168.   51 *Cal. Carew MSS, 1575–88*, no. 187, p. 177, no. 474, p. 304; *The Walsingham letter book*, pp 245, 260; *CSPI, 1574–85*, no. 21 (vii), p. 4. This mentions correspondence between Desmond and Aodh between 1573 and 1574.   52 *Cal. Carew MSS, 1575–88*, no. 192, p. 178.   53 Price, 'Notes', n.15, p. 151.

Pelham in January 1580, as a result of which a nervous Pelham decided to release Fiach's pledges to forestall a possible outbreak of violence; furthermore he also alerted Harrington, Masterson, Sir Peter Carew the younger and Robert Harpoole to be on their guard and to expect trouble.[54] As for Fiach and Baltinglass, their first response to the overtures of the Catholic forces in Munster was a letter in February 1580, declaring their intention to fight 'in the defence of the pope's cause'.[55] In return for their assistance, they demanded the acknowlegement of their lands and titles, which was conceded by Sir John Fitzgerald of Desmond. Once this concession had been extracted, Fiach and Baltinglass honed their plans.

Unforeseen events forced Fiach's hand. In January 1580 Dúnlaing, the O'Byrne overlord, attacked settlers in reprisal for Harrington's brutal behaviour in east Wicklow. The reason why this formerly loyalist lord was in arms was the government's refusal to recognize his traditional rights over O'Byrnes' Country. This violence did not greatly affect Fiach's lordship of Críoch Raghnuill, but it had spread to Wexford by late January 1580.[56] Throughout this upheaval, Fiach studiously avoided conflict, but busied himself, rather, with preparations, attending a marathon three-day meeting during Easter week 1580 at Baltinglass' Monkstown (Co. Dublin) residence. There, under heavy guard, Fiach outlined his plan to an assembled group of clergy and Old English nobility.[57] The apparent intention was to start a war in East Leinster focused upon the Pale and the adjoining English counties, which would tie up government forces. Meantime Fiach's midland allies would link up with some of Desmond's forces and over-throw the plantations of Offaly and Laois, while, to the north of Offaly, the Nugents of Delvin would devastate Meath as well as link with Fiach's allies of southern Ulster.[58] These synchronized attacks, if successful, would leave Dublin and its Pale isolated and vulnerable. What Fiach planned for Dublin is unknown, but it is clear there was a substantial disaffected Catholic population there. Perhaps it was hoped that they would drive the New English out and surrender Dublin to the Catholic army under Baltinglass' leadership. It was later alleged during the course of these meetings, that Christopher Nugent, 14th Baron Delvin, read out a letter from Kildare, a personal friend of Fiach, promising support for war once it began. According to a later statement made by Fiach's second wife Rose O'Toole while being interrogated in prison in January 1581, Kildare's promise had a profound effect upon her husband, for he returned to Ballinacor from Monkstown steeled for war. There is little doubt that Fiach firmly believed that Kildare was fully committed and would join eventually in a war against the New English government.[59]

54 *Cal. Carew MSS, 1575–88*, no. 262, p. 202, no. 274, p. 205.   **55** PRO, SP 63/76/25.   **56** *Cal. Carew MSS, 1575–88*, no. 282, p. 207.   **57** O'Connor, 'The Baltinglass rebellion', pp 80–3.   **58** Ibid., p. 106; *CSPI, 1574–85*, no. 77, p. 238. This source mentions that Baltinglass had the oaths of Toirdhealbhach Luineach O'Neill, Sir Aodh Dubh O'Donnell, the O'Connors of Sligo as well as the O'Rourkes of Leitrim.   **59** O'Connor, 'The Baltinglass rebellion', pp 82–3; PRO, SP 63/93/79, 80–1; see Carey, *Surviving the Tudors*, p. 210.

Throughout April and May, Fiach remained quiet, dispatching messengers to the Leinster Irish to canvass support. Meanwhile large quantities of munitions were smuggled from Dublin into his heartland.[60] Harrington's spies reported a considerable military build-up in the central Wicklow uplands. Mindful of his experience at the hands of Ruaidhrí Óg, Harrington took the initiative by instigating an assassination attempt upon Fiach's life. But it was Masterson's massacre on 10 April 1580 of fifty captured men of the Art Boy Kavanaghs that exploded the East Leinster time-bomb. These men and their leader Domhnall Spainneach MacMurrough-Kavanagh, Fiach's kinsman, enjoyed the protection of Ormond, so Ormond was naturally outraged by Masterson's actions; he demanded that punitive action be taken against the seneschal; the council refused to do any such thing. Although Fiach swore revenge, he still held off until he was ready for war. The first backlash against Masterson came from an unexpected quarter – the senior O'Byrnes. By April, Dúnlaing, the senior O'Byrne overlord, was apparently dead, which left Gerald Odhar O'Byrne of Clone, near Aughrim, as the most powerful lord of O'Byrnes' Country. (Gerald Odhar belonged to the O'Byrnes of Newrath who had been enemies of Fiach's family since the late 1540s.) In late April, Gerald Odhar looted Masterson's lands around Ferns, returning on 30 April 1580 with the surviving Art Boy Kavanaghs to plunder the seneschal's possessions; on the latter occasion these allies returned with their spoils to the safety of the Butler lordship of Arklow (which suggests Ormond's sanction).[61] Harrington now intensified the crisis by killing some of Kildare's kerne near Castledermot, and later bursting into Kildare's house in Dublin, dragging out the earl's protected man, Tibbot O'Toole. Once outside, Harrington carried him off to Newcastle McKynegan where he hanged him without trial:[62] so offended was Kildare by this that he went in pursuit of Harrington, intent on killing him. The council imprisoned Harrington in Dublin Castle and forced him to apologize to the earl,[63] but Harrington's removal from the region seriously weakened the government's ability to combat the Catholic forces. Fiach, realizing how exposed Masterson was, now made up with Gerald Odhar in an unprecedented alliance.[64] This done, Leinster now teetered upon the greatest explosion of violence since the Kildare rebellion forty-six years earlier.

In allying with the gentlemen of O'Byrnes' Country, Fiach gained two important advantages over the forces opposing him. Prior to this unlikely alliance, the senior O'Byrnes long regarded Fiach's house as upstarts. Now this alliance allowed him to pose as the great unifier of the extended O'Byrne dynasty – a dream he particularly cherished; and it also brought to him the not inconsiderable resources of manpower and firepower of the majority of the nobles of O'Byrnes' Country (the only notable exception being Murchadh mac

---

60 Lennon, *Sixteenth century Ire.*, p. 203; idem, *The lords of Dublin in the age of reformation*, pp 152–3.   61 Hore, *Wexford town*, vi, pp 68, 72.   62 *CSPI, 1574–85*, no. 3, p. 221; Carey, *Surviving the Tudors*, p. 201.   63 Hore, *Wexford town*, vi, p. 72; *CSPI, 1574–85*, no.4, p. 221. 64 *CSPI, 1574–85*, no. 1, p. 230.

Edmund of Kiltimon, a personal enemy of Fiach, who remained in government service).[65] By his declared intention to avenge the Art Boy Kavanaghs, Fiach as leader of Leinster now posed as the champion of Irish liberties. He adroitly side-stepped the government, reaping the harvest of bitter disaffection sown by the ill-considered barbarities of Masterson, Harrington and other New English captains in Leinster. Moving with great purpose, he now thundered into north Wexford in pursuit of Masterson, devastating the whole region in June 1580.

On 1 July 1580, Harrington, alarmed by Fiach's actions, wrote to the council, begging to be allowed to march against the gathering Catholic forces in the Wicklow uplands. From his information received, Harrington estimated that Fiach had about 700 men and 60 shot under his command. By some means, Harrington established direct communication with Fiach. Fiach duplicitously replied that he did not intend to harm the queen's loyal subjects and was not a danger to the Pale; artfully, he said that if granted and assured of safe conduct to Dublin, he would present his case before the council.[66] Clearly Fiach was double-dealing, for his actions contradicted his words. On 14 July 1580, Fiach's plans now known to the government, Baltinglass hurried to Glenmalure and told Fiach to begin operations. The government, clearly alarmed by Baltinglass' association with Fiach, dispatched his cousin Sir Nicholas Fitzeustace to Glenmalure to implore the viscount to reconsider. From the safety of Glenmalure both Fiach and Baltinglass haughtily told Sir Nicholas of their intention to fight a war in defence of Catholicism. By 19 July 1580 their forces were attacking the Pale, causing Lord Chancellor Gerrarde to write despairingly to Elizabeth's chief spymaster, Sir Francis Walsingham. Another parley at Kilbolen bridge near Ballymore on 23 July 1580 failed.[67]

Now Harrington's absence told, for Fiach had a virtually free hand to attack at will. Kildare was ordered to bring Fiach to heel.[68] Instead, he hesitated; not so Fiach, who now ravaged the Idrone lands of the Carews in Carlow before turning his attention to east Wicklow, when his first attack was on Harrington's town of Newcastle McKynegan. On 28 July 1580, after firing the town, Fiach's triumphant troops dramatically unfurled the papal colours, parading them throughout the wider region and in attacks on the Pale.[69] The Catholic army in East Leinster were further strengthened in early August by the defections of two of Kildare's captains with their companies of shot as well as by the arrival in Glenmalure of Sir John Fitzgerald of Desmond and Dr Saunders, the papal legate, along with small forces from Munster and the midlands.[70] The arrival of Saunders further cemented the crusading zeal of the Catholic commanders; and

65 These included the powerful Bran mac An Calbhach O'Byrne of Kilnamanagh. For Bran mac An Calbhach, see Nicholls, 'Crioch Branach', p. 29; *CSPI, 1574–85*, no. 46, p. 300 & no. 40 (ii), p. 344. **66** Hore, *Wexford town*, vi, p. 72. **67** *CSPI, 1574–85*, no. 49, p. 235; O'Connor, 'The Baltinglass rebellion', p. 92; *Cal. Carew MSS, 1575–88*, no. 429, p. 280. **68** *Cal. Carew MSS, 1575–88*, no. 483, p. 316. **69** Berleth, *The twilight lords*, p. 147; *Cal. Carew MSS, 1575–88*, no. 483, p. 316. **70** *Cal. Carew MSS, 1575–88*, no. 476, p. 311; ibid., no. 474, pp 303–4; Edwards, 'The MacGiollapádraigs (Fitzpatricks) of Upper Ossory, 1532–1641', p. 348.

throughout August, Fiach and Baltinglass received reinforcements from the O'Tooles, MacMurrough-Kavanaghs, O'Connor Falys, O'Mores, Keatings and Piers Grace in preparation for a major showdown with the government. While Fiach trained these forces for battle, Baltinglass used his considerable powers of persuasion to drum up support, armaments, and supplies from his co-religionists in the coastal towns.[71] News of the outbreak of war between the government and the Catholic army quickly reached the ears of the Spanish ambassador to England, Bernardino de Mendoza, who informed Philip II about it on 7 August 1580. Lorenzo Priuli, the Venetian ambassador to France, was also watching developments in Ireland and, in a July letter, told his master, the doge of Venice, that Elizabeth had dispatched an army of 3,000 to Ireland to deal with Fiach and Baltinglass.[72]

The English army that landed at Dublin on 12 August 1580 was greeted with considerable relief by the beleaguered administration. Its commander and new lord deputy was Sir Arthur Grey de Wilton, a hard-line Calvinist who had never commanded an army in battle. Although Grey possessed great personal courage, both his religious beliefs and his cultural perceptions blinded him to the dangers of Fiach. Like many of his faith, Grey had been deeply disturbed by the St Bartholomew's Day massacre of 1572.[73] Like Fiach and Baltinglass, he was also a devout man who fervently believed in the righteousness of his religion. Both Grey and the Catholic commanders facing him considered themselves to be part of separate crusades to suppress each other's faiths; in this latest war of the Reformation, there was no room for compromise. Grey's assumption of command injected steel into the struggle against the Catholic forces in the Leinster mountains above Dublin. With typical briskness, on 18 August Grey marched his largely inexperienced army out of Dublin to rendezvous with militias under Cosby and Kildare at Naas.[74] Unfortunately for him, Fiach's spies reported every step of Grey's army; so, instead of confronting Grey in the open field, Fiach retreated, luring him deeper into the mountains.

On the morning of 25 August 1580, overruling the vehement protests of Cosby and other senior officers, Grey committed his troops to entering Glenmalure. This proved to be a major error of judgment, for he underestimated the Catholic forces there. For Fiach, the day of reckoning had come, and his agents obtained a promise of defection from the Irish kerne serving with the English army. And in a well-executed ambush in Glenmalure, within half an hour Fiach wiped out about half of Grey's army, inflicting around 1,000 fatalities. If it had not been for the personal heroism of Grey, many more of his troops would have met their end. The victory at Glenmalure, immortalized by Spenser in *The Faerie Queene*, proved intensely satisfying for Fiach, as many of his enemies

---

71 Ibid., no. 443, pp 289–90, no. 444, p. 290, no. 483, p. 316; O'Byrne, 'Glenmalure', pp 163–5. **72** *Cal. S.P. Spanish, 1580–6*, iii, no. 37, p. 44; *C.S.P.V., 1558–80*, vii, no. 811, p. 642. **73** McCabe, 'The fate of Irena: Spenser, and political violence', pp 113–14.   **74** *CSPI, 1574–85*, no. 40, p. 243.

lay scattered among the dead.[75] In particular, he took especial pleasure in the killing of Cosby, the scourge of Ruaidhrí Óg and his wife, Fiach's sister. According to local tradition, he sought out Cosby's body and kept it as a prize of war, burying it in a secret location high in the hills above Glenmalure.[76]

However, his celebrations were brief. Grey's bitter retreat to Dublin left the Catholic army virtually unopposed as it emerged from the mountains, and Fiach's next move was into Carlow, where, with Muircheartach Óg MacMurrough-Kavanagh of Garryhill, he burnt Idrone, capturing Master Wood and Dean Roger Hooker of Leighlinbridge.[77] Fiach then split his forces, sending Sir John of Desmond and Piers Grace across the Barrow into the midlands to raid Ormond's estates, linking up with some of the O'Mores, O'Connor Falys, O'Carrolls, and MacGillapatricks to burn Abbeyleix before attacking the plantation towns of Philipstown and Maryborough.[78] By early September 1580 the O'Connor Falys were raiding throughout Offaly, and the prominent local loyalist Ross MacGeoghegan had been killed.[79] Fiach now sent forces to attack north Kildare and south Dublin, burning a small suburb of Dublin on 10 September as well as Rathmore and Saggart during 16–17 September. These victories, though, were bought at a price, as two of Fiach's brothers and a son were reputedly killed in the fighting.[80] Encouraged by their success, Sir John of Desmond and Robert Fitzgerald burnt Saggart again on 20 September. Fiach and Baltinglass then agreed in late September to divide their forces yet again; on 7 October 1580, Baltinglass and Sir John of Desmond took a large force to Munster to lend support to Desmond and to the mixed force of 600 Spanish and papal troops that had landed at Smerwick Harbour in Kerry during September 1580; meanwhile while Fiach directed operations in Leinster.

In early October Fiach defeated government troops defending Wicklow town and then razed its castle. On 19 October 1580, he descended from the Wicklow uplands with almost 700 men and plundered the Pale towns of Coolmine and Rathcoole. His choice of Rathcoole was particularly significant as many of the families of Harrington's men lived there. Once the town was taken, he ordered all the English put to the sword.[81] Inevitably, the counter-offensive began: in late October 1580 Grey marched his army into Munster to confront Desmond and his allies in Kerry, leaving Kildare to fight Fiach. Marching at breakneck speed, Grey and his army appeared before the fort of Del Oro at Smerwick on 6

75 E. Spenser, 'The Faerie Queene Book V' in *The works of Edmund Spenser* (London, 1995), p. 278. **76** O'Byrne, 'Glenmalure', pp 169–79. **77** Dowling, *Annals*, p. 43. **78** *CSPI, 1574–85*, no. 73, p. 246; ibid., nos 74, 77, 79 pp 246–7; Bradley, 'Early urban development in Co. Laois', p. 267; Edwards, 'The MacGiollapádraigs (Fitzpatricks) of Upper Ossory, 1532–1641', pp 348–9; AFM, 1580. The O'Mores had been disturbed already in 1579, then Conall mac Giollapádraig O'More was killed at Birr. See AFM, 1579. This Conall was pardoned at unknown date in 1579, see *Cal. Fiants Eliz,* no. 3597. **79** Ibid., no. 16, p. 249, no. 22, p. 250. **80** Ibid., no. 25, p. 250, no. 45, p. 253; Nicholls, 'The genealogy of the Byrnes of Ranelagh', fn. 31, p. 110. Nicholls notes the possibility of the news of the killing of Fiach's kinsmen as being a false report. **81** Ibid., no. 22, p. 259, no. 56, p. 263, no. 4, p. 265.

November 1580. Having invested the fort from the landward and seaward sides, Grey's artillery bombarded the trapped garrison. The fort's commander, Sebastiano di San Giuseppe, seeing that no help was forthcoming from Desmond and that his fort could not resist a direct assault, unconditionally surrendered on 8 November 1580. During the negotiations, Grey came to realize that San Giuseppe's force was not authorized by either the pope or Philip II of Spain; therefore, as adventurers, they were outside the rules of war and entitled to no mercy. At the stroke of his pen, Grey, still smarting from the humiliation of Glenmalure, ordered the execution of the entire garrison, bar San Giuseppe and his senior officers – an act that forever besmirched the reputation of Grey in Ireland.

While Grey was in Munster, Kildare began his campaign against Fiach, but, as in July 1580, Kildare's assault lacked Grey's cut. There were many reasons for Kildare's hesitancy to challenge the Catholics in open field. Clearly, he possessed considerable sympathy for them. Strong suspicions were being voiced of Kildare's complicity with them, and it was alleged that he had secured Fiach's promise not to burn his lands.[82] Nevertheless Kildare temporarily laid aside his differences with Harrington to plan a campaign against Fiach. As a matter of policy, they jointly agreed to avoid a direct confrontation and resolved to exploit the hardships of winter upon the Catholic army. Thus, in a co-ordinated pincer movement in early November 1580 Kildare struck into Fiach's country from the west of the mountains, while Harrington raided from the east. Their objective was clear – the economic base that sustained the Catholic forces ensconced in the mountains. The effect of these raids for livestock upon the Catholic army was profound. In January 1581 Grey confirmed the success of these raids, noting 'Baltynglas and Feagh pinched with winter'.[83] Despite Kildare's success against Fiach, Grey was displeased with the progress of the war and was disturbed by the rumours of the earl's encouragement of the Catholic leaders. Undoubtedly the combination of these rumours convinced Grey to relieve Kildare of his post and arrest him and Christopher Nugent, 14th Baron Delvin, in December 1580 on charges of treason.[84]

The tide turned in spring 1581. The arrests of Kildare and Delvin signalled a more aggressive approach by government against Fiach and Baltinglass. The re-establishment of the garrison at Wicklow town drew an unsuccessful assault from Fiach and Baltinglass on 15 January 1581.[85] Although Grey parleyed with Fiach at Baltinglass abbey in early February, he was intent on revenge. Before he left for Munster, he delegated responsibility for this war of attrition to his lieutenants. Because of mounting pressure, both Fiach and Baltinglass suffered personal losses. During January, Fiach's wife, Rose, was captured, and another of his brothers was killed in the attack on Wicklow town. One of Baltinglass' brothers, Thomas, was captured, while another was killed in a skirmish in April 1581.[86] Sir William

---

82 *Cal. Carew MSS, 1575–88*, no. 483, p. 316; O'Byrne, 'Glenmalure', pp 156, 162, 163.
83 *CSPI, 1574–85*, nos 18 & 23, p. 266, see ibid., no. 32, p. 283.   **84** Ibid., no. 275, p. 275.
85 Ibid., no. 10, p. 280.   **86** Ibid., no. 10, p. 291.

Stanley, in the company of Fiach's eventual nemesis, Captain William Russell, even penetrated into Glenmalure and burnt Ballinacor before plundering parts of Críoch Raghnuill. Across the Barrow, English forces steadily gained the upper hand. In April, Captain Mackworth killed 100 O'Mores, while the resistance of the Nugents collapsed and William Nugent fled to Toirdhealbhach Luineach O'Neill during the same month.[87]

Furthermore, the establishment of English garrisons at the castles of Kilcommon near Rathdrum and Castlekevin close to Fiach's heartland effectively began the fencing-in of the Catholic army.[88] To the south of the Wicklow mountains between May and July 1581, the army gained several successes over Fiach's MacMurrough-Kavanagh and O'Toole supporters in East Leinster, particularly after Grey's return to East Leinster in June.[89] The separate submissions of Crimthann MacMurrough of Coolnaleen (Fiach's choice for the kingship of Leinster) and Muircheartach Óg MacMurrough-Kavanagh of Garryhill as well as the Kinsellas, in early July 1581 were serious blows to Fiach's campaign.[90] Even worse, Fiach's staunchest allies, the Art Boy Kavanaghs, were under heavy pressure from Grey's army even within their densely forested heartland of the Blackstairs mountains, so much so that it took a long-distance dash by Fiach that month to prevent their surrender to officials outside Enniscorthy.[91]

The near-capitulation of the MacMurrough-Kavanaghs was a cause of deep concern for Fiach and Baltinglass. While they remained militarily undefeated and continued to strike at outposts along the fringes of the Leinster mountains, Grey's fabian tactics took a heavy toll. At this point Fiach considered his options. Clearly a change of policy was looming when Fiach's brother-in-law, Féilim mac Toirdhealbhach O'Toole of Powerscourt, reapplied for a pardon on 17 July 1581. And, perhaps initially unknown to Baltinglass, Fiach opened negotiations with Harrington about 20 July 1581, petitioning for a pardon. When Fiach delivered his pledges to the government in late August, it was reported that a disbelieving Baltinglass 'wandereth in great astonishment';[92] Grey's offensive seems to have split the Catholic leadership. However, there was more to Fiach's sudden change of strategy. While Fiach may have independently opened communication with Harrington, it is clear that Baltinglass had some inkling of what he was about to do. During the protracted talks for his pardon in July 1581, Fiach refused to accept his pardon unless Baltinglass was included. Baltinglass reluctantly accepted

87 Ibid., no. 6, p. 296, no. 18, p. 297, no. 46, p. 300; Ellis, *Tudor Ireland*, p. 284; Venning, 'The O'Carrolls of Offaly', pp 196–7; these relate how the sons of O'Connor Faly, probably Fiach's allies, killed Sir William Odhar O'Carroll on his return from Dublin, see AFM, 1581. **88** Ibid., no. 405, p. 307. **89** PRO, SP 63/84/23; PRO, SP 63/83/45; PRO, SP 63/84/12. For the pardon of Féilim O'Toole of Powerscourt and his wife Elizabeth and Arthur Dowsdon of Tallaght on 13 May 1581, see *Cal. Fiants Eliz*, no. 3713; More, 'The MacMurrough-Kavanaghs', p. 15. **90** *CSPI, 1574–85* no. 12, p. 310; More, 'The MacMurrough-Kavanaghs', p. 16. In 1582 Crimthann was executed for his part in aiding Baltinglass to escape. **91** PRO, SP 63/84/12; *CSPI, 1574–85* no. 12, p. 310, no. 16 (iv), p. 310; Hore, *Wexford town*, vi, p. 404. **92** *CSPI, 1574–85* no. 23, p. 311, no. 44, p. 313, no. 32, p. 317.

the grim situation,[93] and a plan was formulated whereby Baltinglass would escape to seek help from Spain, while Fiach opened negotiations for a cessation with Grey. This plan was reported to Philip II of Spain. Baltinglass agreed to appoint Fiach commander-in-chief of the Catholic forces in Leinster during his impending absence. To the consternation of many officials, Grey accepted Fiach's petition for a pardon on 31 July 1580; their misery was compounded when it was reported that Fiach showed his contempt for Grey by making a mockery of his pardon.[94] Fiach was not really surrendering: his actions simply protected his lands from further ravages by Grey's army and gained breathing space for the Catholic army.

Even though Grey accepted Fiach's submission, he was sceptical of his sincerity. On 23 August 1581, he authorized Harrington to receive Fiach into mercy on condition that he disband his forces. Five days later Fiach, by attorney, made a formal submission ending his official involvement in the war. However, Grey suspected it to be a ruse by Fiach to postpone a offensive until after the harvest. That said, Grey pressed ahead against Baltinglass, striking at him where he could. As a warning to those still in the field, on 12 August 1581 Grey ordered Stanley to publicly execute prisoners at Arklow.

Baltinglass was clearly protected by Fiach and still had access to the O'Byrne nexus in Leinster. Probably with Fiach's approval, Féilim mac Toirdhealbhach O'Toole of Powerscourt and the O'Connor Falys joined Baltinglass in attacks on the Pale in early October 1581. Generally speaking though, Fiach was co-ordinating the winding-down of the Catholic army, as evidenced by the submissions of Domhnall Spainneach MacMurrough-Kavanagh and James 'Meagh' mac Cétach O'More, Ruaidhrí Óg O'More's first cousin.[95] The petitions of Féilim mac Toirdhealbhach and Conchobhar O'Connor Faly, Ruaidhrí Óg's old ally, for pardons on 10 October 1581 support this perception. Beyond pardon, Baltinglass made his preparations to flee to Spain, which he did with Fiach's help in November. Shortly afterwards Fiach arrested his former subordinate Captain Gerald Fitzgerald on his way to Dublin. Allegedly, Fitzgerald had evidence of Kildare's covert support for the Catholic leaders in Leinster; this prompted several English attempts to rescue him from Fiach's clutches;[96] determined not to allow Fitzgerald disclose his secrets, Fiach hanged him in December. The ruthless dispatch of Fitzgerald enraged several New English officials, and the government briefly considered executing Fiach's pledges. Doubtless Fiach did hang Fitzgerald to protect Kildare, but the exact nature of the earl's relationship with the Catholic forces still remains uncertain. Also on the

93 *Cal. S.P. Spanish, 1580–6*, iii, p. 167.   **94** PRO, SP 63/84/44; *CSPI, 1574–85*, no. 53, p. 314.   **95** *CSPI, 1574–85*, no. 10, p. 322. For the O'Mores in this period, see Carey, 'The end of the gaelic political order', pp 215, 246–8. Féilim mac Toirdhealbhach had been involved in attacks on the Pale from about 15 July. Earlier in May he had been pardoned but had returned to war because of the arrest and execution of his brother on 28 August 1581.   **96** J. Hooker, 'The description of the conquest and inhabitation of Ireland', in *Holinshed's Irish Chronicle* (1587 edn), ii, p. 177; Elrington-Ball, *A history of the County Dublin*, iv, p. 40.

night of 17 December, Féilim mac Toirdhealbhach burnt much of St Patrick's Street in Dublin – a direct slight upon Archbishop Loftus, who owned the destroyed property. However, one of the raiding party was captured, and under interrogation confessed to coming from Glenmalure, thereby implicating Fiach in the actions of his O'Toole brother-in-law. The next day Féilim mac Toirdhealbhach paid dearly for his daring when Captain Edward Denny killed his son, Garret.[97]

Against the background of Grey's witch-hunt in the Pale for Baltinglass' conspirators, Fiach suspended operations and attended to the improvement of his estates.[98] Briefly, Féilim mac Toirdhealbhach continued to fight, but the executions in January 1582 of another of his sons along with two sons of Ruaidhrí Óg convinced him of the benefits of peace. He secured his pardon on 18 March.[99] While Kildare and many Catholic Palesmen lived in fear of the block during the reign of terror, a rare calm descended upon the Leinster mountains, where the remnants of the Catholic army were still hiding, waiting for news from Baltinglass in Spain. By May 1582 it was clear that something was afoot as the O'Connor Falys murdered Captain Mackworth in Offaly as retaliation for his raids, skinning him alive.[100] Significantly, Fiach's troops were also seizing corn from the Pale, and their master abandoned his plans for the development of agriculture on his estates. More seriously, he was active among the O'Connor Falys, arranging the marriage of his sister, the widow of Cathaoir Dubh Kavanagh of Clonmullen, to Tadhg mac Giollapádraig O'Connor Faly early in June 1582. This caused alarm in government as did reports that Fiach had patched up differences between his MacMurrough-Kavanagh allies of Garryhill and those of St Mullins. More dangerous for the government were his alleged assurances to the MacMurrough-Kavanaghs that Baltinglass was planning to return very soon with a Spanish army.[101] Fiach and his cohorts were to be disappointed, for the summer brought no foreign army to renew his Catholic crusade. On 16 September 1582 he, Aodh Dubh O'Byrne and Tadhg mac Giollapádraig made their submissions in Dublin; on 5 November, he and Tadhg came to Dublin along with Muircheartach Óg MacMurrough-Kavanagh of Garryhill, and made formal submissions before the lord justices.[102] But nobody put any faith in the sincerity of their actions.

Very conscious of the dangers posed by Fiach and his allies, the government set about weakening Fiach. Those of Fiach's allies who aided Baltinglass' escape to the continent were now hunted down; these included Crimthann MacMurrough of Coolnaleen, Fiach's candidate for the Leinster kingship (he

---

97 O'Connor, 'The Baltinglass rebellion', pp 169–70; *CSPI, 1574–85* nos 51–2, p. 336. **98** Ibid., p. 180; ALC, 1581. This mentions that eighteen heirs of the foreigners of Meath were executed by the justiciar; Ellis, *Tudor Ireland*, p. 282. **99** ALC, 1582; *CSPI, 1574–85* no. 22, p. 341; *Cal. Fiants Eliz*, no. 3844. **100** *CSPI, 1574–85* no. 89, p. 371; Dowling, *Annals*, p. 44; ALC, 1582. **101** PRO, SP 63/93/14; More, 'The MacMurrough-Kavanaghs', p. 16. **102** PRO, SP 63/95/54. On 23 August 1582 Walter mac Edmund (Walter Boy mac Edmund MacDonell), captain of galloglass, and his family were pardoned at the suit of Fiach, see *Cal. Fiants Eliz*, no.

had been pardoned in July 1581, but was clearly unrepentant and had planned the escape of Baltinglass; he was arrested by Masterson, his bitter enemy, and dispatched to Dublin in October 1582 for trial, and later execution).[103] In the midlands, too, the authorities attempted to destroy Fiach's nexus, finding fertile ground to sow discord among the rival branches of the O'Connor Falys in 1583 in the throes of a succession dispute between Tadhg mac Giollapádraig and his cousin, Conchobhar. Although Tadhg had married Fiach's sister in June 1582, he was less receptive to Fiach after the submission of November that year. Their estrangement subsequently matured into an open blood feud, as evidenced by Tadhg's connivance in plots against Fiach in 1587 and 1588.[104] Why Tadhg became estranged from Fiach remains unknown; but it may have to do with government overtures concerning the O'Connor Faly succession. By mid 1583, Tadhg had assumed a loyalist disposition. By contrast, Conchobhar remained close to his O'Byrne master. The struggle between the two cousins dramatically climaxed on 12 September 1583, when both men travelled to Dublin and laid their grievances before the arbitration of the lords justices. Each accused the other of high treason, thereby playing into the hands of the officials. The result was tragic. Before packed galleries, the pair fought in the courtyard of Dublin Castle until Tadhg beheaded Conchobhar. For his pains, Tadhg was rewarded with a farm and a state pension.[105] Dublin Castle was the only winner.

The loss of these allies further weakened Fiach's support base, but he was protected from any backlash by his strict observance of his submission of November 1582. An uneasy truce lasted right up to 1594, although the authorities took the precaution of authorizing Harrington to maintain Kilcommon castle within striking distance of Glenmalure.[106] The respite gained by this latest submission allowed Fiach time to ponder on why the war of 1580–1 had failed. With the benefit of peace, he now began the repair of his dynasty's position within the Wicklow region. It may have been at this time then he welded himself even closer to the O'Tooles of Castlekevin by marrying his sons Féilim and Réamain to his wife Rose's sisters, Uná and Katharine. Furthermore he and Murchadh mac Edmund O'Byrne of Kiltimon sought to settle their differences, and Fiach's heir, Toirdhealbhach, married Murchadh's daughter, Dorothy. The long peace also allowed him to attend to some personal matters such as his education and appearance. Much of this personal improvement may have been conducted under the guidance of priests who had sought refuge in Glenmalure. We know that the power of these clerical advisers caused rifts among Fiach's retainers.[107]

3961. James mac Cétach O'More alias James Meagh was also pardoned a day earlier, see ibid., no. 3959, p. 171. *CSPI, 1574–85* no. 15, p. 409; *CSPI, 1574–85* nos 12, 14, p. 376, no. 54, p. 399. **103** ALC, 1582; O'Connor, 'The Baltinglass rebellion', p. 168.   **104** Morgan, 'Perrot's poison plot', p. 194.   **105** ALC, 1582; *CSPI, 1574–85* no. 69, p. 468; ibid., no. 20, p. 473; *CSPI, 1586–8*, no. 21, p. 41. For Tadhg mac Giollapádraig's pardon of 4 May 1588, see *Cal Fiants Eliz*, no. 5174.   **106** *Calendar of Irish Council Book, 1581–6*, pp 93 & 166.   **107** Nicholls, 'The genealogy of the Byrnes of Ranelagh', p. 113. Nicholls notes that Toirdhealbhach mac Fiach was married to Dorothy before April 1590; Lambeth Palace Library Carew MSS 612; *Leabhar*

With the exception of Captain John Parker, a veteran of Glenmalure, Fiach completely changed his policy towards government officials.[108] Instead of intransigence, he now presented an amicable face, establishing a degree of rapport with Harrington. Upon the arrival of Sir John Perrot, the reputed half-brother of Queen Elizabeth, as lord deputy in June 1584, Fiach promised to observe the writ of the English courts in Ireland,[109] and delivered a son and an uncle as pledges. His seemingly good intentions were displayed by the holding of the sessions of the southern assize court at Ballinacor in September, and by his purchase of lands in east Wicklow. At these sessions, Fiach presented vociferous complaints against the excesses of the seneschals, particularly Harrington.[110] Nevertheless, in November, he and Harrington arrested and executed some cattle raiders. To Harrington's surprise, Fiach surrendered a son for collusion with the raiders. Fiach's reformation seemed complete when he, as an observer, was the only Leinster lord to attend Perrot's parliament in April 1585;[111] to many of those present, Fiach had embarked upon a transition from warlord to landowner.

Even more illustrative of Fiach's apparent change of heart were his links with the Protestant archbishop of Dublin, Lord Chancellor Adam Loftus. Although on paper Fiach and Loftus were complete opposites, in both political outlook and religion, there had been precedents for individual agreements between O'Byrne lords and the archbishops of Dublin, stretching from the fourteenth century.[112] These centred mainly upon the lost revenues of the former lands of the archbishopric lying within the lordships of the Wicklow Irish; in addition, because Dublin's economy was heavily dependent upon raw materials such as foodstuffs and timber, there were always close trading links between its merchant and upper classes and the O'Byrne and O'Toole lords.[113] Loftus, a Yorkshire man, had been archbishop of Dublin since 1567, and throughout his tenure of this office and that of lord chancellor he used his power for the aggrandisement of himself and his family. What seems to have transpired between Loftus and Fiach was an unwritten agreement dating from about the mid 1580s, concerning the tithes of the archdeaconry of Glendalough. Before this date Loftus had no hope of collecting these monies due to Fiach's dominance over these lands, but by 1586–9 Fiach was allowing officials into this territory to assess the monies due. By August 1592, the archbishop's nephew, another Adam Loftus, was receiving the annual sum of £16. 10s.[114] Without doubt, this situation could not have

Branach, no. 26, pp 108–15.   **108** *CSPI, 1574–85* no. 3, p. 438.   **109** Ibid., no. 1, p. 517, nos 29 & 31, p. 519; PRO, SP 63/111/31.   **110** Ibid., no. 43, p. 521; *Cal. Fiants Eliz*, no. 4510–1, These pardons included Fiach, his mother, Shawe ny Phelim, his wife, Rose, his uncle, Edmund McShane Óg. His sons Toirdhealbhach and Feilim were pardoned on 17 August 1584. See *CSPI, 1574–85* no. 26, p. 531. During this circuit 181 men were arrested 48 of whom were executed; PRO, SP 63/112/261 (i).   **111** *CSPI, 1574–85* no. 90, p. 539, no. 9, p. 540; Price, 'Notes', p. 149; AFM, 1585; PRO, SP 63/124/47.   **112** TCD, MSS E.3.25 (588), ff 202v–204; *Rot. Pat. Hib*, no. 113, p. 238b.   **113** *A roll of the proceeding of the king's council in Ireland*, p. 181; *Ancient records of Dublin*, i, pp 347, 252–3. For the claims of the city of Dublin to lands in the Wicklow mountains see ibid., p. 252; Matthew, pp 192–5.   **114** *Ancient records of Dublin*, ii,

come about without Fiach's consent. But relations between Fiach and Loftus went deeper: in September 1592 Loftus was forced to deny the accusations of Barnaby Riche and Robert Legge that he fostered one of his children in Fiach's country, while in 1594 he was charged with sheltering Fiach's wife Rose in his own house in Dublin. Furthermore, the behaviour of the company of Captain Adam Loftus, the archbishop's own son, during Harrington's defeat near Rathdrum by Fiach's sons on 29 May 1599 was criticized in the subsequent court martials.[115] In return for Fiach's permission to collect the tithes of Glendalough, Loftus may have acted as an advocate for the redress of some of Fiach's grievances as in November 1588.[116]

Others were not convinced of Fiach's reported reformation. But there was more to it than sheer duplicity. In 1585 Butler ambitions and rapacity again focused upon the southern half of Fiach's lordship. And just as his father and grandfather had been drawn into conflict with the Butlers, Fiach too had little choice but to oppose them. Fiach's reformation was really an attempt to obtain government protection. In preparation for their drive into the south of Críoch Raghnuill, the Butlers now exploited the feud between Fiach and Aodh Dubh O'Byrne of Knockrath, one reason for which perhaps Fiach's outraged sense of personal and dynastic loyalty at Aodh Dubh's attempts to establish himself as an independent force. Anyway, Aodh Dubh decided to throw in his lot with the Butlers; and his grievances did not go unheard: on 25 April 1584 Ormond, Elizabeth's cousin, fired a broadside across Fiach's bows by appointing Aodh Dubh as constable of his Arklow lordship.[117]

Spearheading the second prong of Ormond's assault on Fiach were the Butlers of Cloghgrenan. Ormond now encouraged his nephews James and Piers fitzEdmund Butler of Cloghgrenan to establish a land corridor between Arklow and Tullow. Dangerously for Fiach, it bordered his own estates in Shillelagh.[118] The father of these Butlers was Sir Edmund Butler of Cloghgrenan, Fiach's former friend and now partner of his first wife, so there was a personal element in the developing struggle. An alarmed Fiach stepped up his co-operation with Perrot in the hope that he would stop the Butlers. Despite the outbreak of war between England and Spain in August 1585, Fiach chose to remain loyal, but, as an insurance policy, he resumed his negotiations with other Catholic leaders in Ireland. In February 1586, Fiach's son escaped with Art O'Neill from Dublin Castle; and although Fiach swiftly presented another son as a substitute pledge, his role in the escapes was exposed by the capture of his own brother while escorting Art back to Ulster. More concerned by the Butler threat along his southern border, Fiach obtained a safe conduct to present his case at Dublin. By

pp 203, 225, 228; *CSPI, 1588–92*, no. 54, p. 575. In 1604, the archbishopric had £45 from the lands of Glendalough, see *CSPI, 1603–6*, no. 267, p. 170.   **115** *CSPI, 1588–92*, no. 59, p. 585; *CSPI, 1599–1600*, no. 73, p. 52. In June 1599 eight of the servants of Loftus slipped out of his house to join the Catholic forces under the O'Byrnes in the mountains, see ibid., no. 92, p. 67. **116** Ibid., no. 22, p. 75; Price, 'Notes', p. 151.   **117** Price, 'Notes', p. 151; *COD*, vi, no. 7, pp 7–8.   **118** Edwards, 'In Tyrone's shadow', p. 219.

April 1586, Perrot, anxious to keep the peace, ignored Fiach's role in the escapes and petitioned to present him at court. This scheme came to nothing. Yet Fiach continued to surprise, for he presented himself before Perrot clad in fashionable attire in May 1586. This latest protestation of good faith and loyalty earned his pardon.[119] Throughout that summer Fiach continually delighted Perrot, sending in heads of supposed outlaws. More accurately, though, they were the rivals of his nephew and protégé, Uaithne mac Ruaidhrí Óig O'More. A pleased Perrot sang Fiach's praises, believing that he was greatly encouraged by Elizabeth's recent declaration that the Protestants and Catholics of Ireland should be treated equally. Others, such as Sir Henry Wallop, were convinced Fiach was playing Perrot for a fool.[120]

By August 1586, Fiach's border war with Ormond in Shillelagh was clearly beginning to hurt. Despite Fiach's request for aid, Perrot did not stop the Butlers. Disillusioned, Fiach took matters into his own hands and moved quickly to turn the tables on the over-confident Butlers. His first move was decisive – the marrying of his daughter Margaret to Walter Riabhach Fitzgerald, probably during summer 1586. Walter Riabhach was the son of Maurice Fitzgerald, the 11th earl of Kildare's former constable of Shillelagh, and Honora O'Toole of Powerscourt. His disaffection stemmed from Harrington's unwelcome acquisition of Shillelagh during 1578.[121] By 1585 Walter Riabhach's family also found themselves targets of Butler rapine in Shillelagh. Naturally, they needed protection, and they found it in Fiach. In Walter Riabhach and Conall mac Cétach O'More, Fiach discovered his most able lieutenants of the late 1580s; with Butler strength growing in Shillelagh, Fiach unleashed them in August 1586, while he himself turned on the MacMurrough-Kavanagh allies of the Butlers.[122] When asked to explain himself, he declined; but officially he remained at peace.

This tense climate in East Leinster was further heightened by the change in ownership of Idrone in 1585. Ironically, this tension arose because of the death of Idrone's owner, Sir Peter Carew the younger, at Glenmalure on 25 August 1580. Because of Sir Peter's substantial debts, his brother Sir George Carew was compelled to sell Idrone for £2,200 to Dudley Bagenal, second son of Marshal Nicholas Bagenal. In addition, Sir George made the ill-considered appointment of young Bagenal as sub-constable of Leighlinbridge, a decision with disastrous ramifications for relations with the MacMurrough-Kavanaghs. On 30 November 1586, Captain Henry Heron, Bagenal's agent and brother-in-law, murdered

---

119 *Cal. Carew MSS, 1575–88*, no. 612, pp 426–7; see also Morgan, 'Perrot's poison plot', p. 183.
120 Morgan, 'Perrot's poison plot', p.185; *CSPI, 1586–8*, no. 47, p. 64; PRO, SP 63/139/7.
121 *Cal. Fiants Eliz.* no. 5111. They were certainly married before 18 December 1587 as Margaret is included as Margey O'Birne the wife of Walter Riabhach in this pardon; Fitzgerald, 'Walter Reagh Fitzgerald', pp 299–302.   122 *CSPI, 1586–8*, no. 53, p. 137, no. 55, p. 139. Walter Reagh also captured one of Ormond's clients, Edmund Archdeacon, and held him captive for a period, see Fitzgerald, 'Walter Reagh', pp 300–1; This Conall mac Cétach O'More may be the brother of James mac Cétach, the O'More leader who died in June/July 1584, see *CSPI, 1574–85*, no. 1, p. 517.

Muircheartach Óg MacMurrough-Kavanagh of Garryhill, Fiach's cousin and ally. The origin of this latest outrage lay in the recent theft of some of Bagenal's cattle; naturally, the followers of Muircheartach Óg were suspect, and accordingly a posse set off in pursuit; when Heron and his band thundered into Garryhill, the 70-year-old Muircheartach Óg, fearing for his life, hid in nearby forests. When he was dragged before Heron, who demanded the cattle, the old man protested, saying he knew nothing of the animals and even promising to pay for them. This was to no avail. An enraged Heron hacked him down, killing him, an act that shocked even the most hardened officials.[123] Muircheartach Óg had resolved to live out his dotage peaceably (he had recently refused the Leinster kingship as being too dangerous). Unwittingly Heron had sealed Bagenal's fate for Fiach placed his own forces at the disposal of Muircheartach Óg's sons. Thus, on 21 March 1587, Walter Riabhach, with Muircheartach and Donnchadh MacMurrough-Kavanagh, lured Bagenal out of Leighlinbridge, and somewhere in the surrounding countryside Bagenal was killed and horribly mutilated.[124] On Fiach's orders, Walter Riabhach fled in May to Ulster. Even more serious for the government than Fiach's private wars in East Leinster was the report of a Dublin sailor returned from Lisbon in April 1587, according to which Fiach was again intriguing with the Spanish and had offered to take Spanish troops into his country to attack Dublin.[125] Perrot's illusions were shattered. As a result, Perrot and Wallop requested that Elizabeth give them 100 troops for a three-month campaign against Fiach. Once Fiach was removed, Wallop confidently asserted, the MacMurrough-Kavanaghs, O'Connor Falys and O'Mores would collapse.

Throughout the remainder of 1587, Fiach resumed his role of arch-plotter. In December 1587, Walter Riabhach returned from Ulster and submitted to Perrot; he was allowed to enter Dublin, where he was nearly killed by the Bagenals.[126] He had returned at the request of Fiach. According to the later deposition of a double agent, Father Denis O'Roughan, Fiach had dispatched him with a letter to Spain, promising assistance to any proposed Spanish invasion. Two years later, when facing trial for treason in October 1590, Perrot submitted a statement vigorously defending his deputyship between 1584 and 1588. In it, he portrayed Fiach as the greatest supporter of Spain in Ireland; according to Perrot, Fiach, advised by Catholic clergy, refused to answer any summons throughout 1587–8 because he was preparing for a Spanish landing. As a result of that alleged conspiracy, Perrot authorized operations to procure Fiach's death. In this ill-starred adventure he hired Tadhg O'Nolan to lure Fiach and his heir Toirdhealbhach into an ambush laid by Harrington and Sir William Collier. When this failed, O'Nolan offered to poison father and son – a plan which also

123 More, 'The MacMurrough-Kavanaghs', p. 17; see also Nicholls, 'The Kavanaghs' (1982), p. 194.   **124** *CSPI, 1586–8*, no. 111, pp 288–9; see also Morgan, 'Perrot's poison plot', p. 186; Hughes, 'The fall of the Clan Kavanagh', p. 296; ALC, 1587.   **125** Ibid., no. 32, p. 322 & no. 64, pp 338–9.   **126** Fitzgerald, 'Walter Reagh', p. 301; for Walter Riabhach's pardon dated 18 December 1587, see *Cal. Fiants Eliz.* no. 5111.

failed. Arising from Perrot's impending trial, in 1591/2 Lord Deputy Sir William Fitzwilliam granted safe passage for Fiach to attend an interview in Dublin, in which he examined his dealings with Perrot between 1584 and 1588. Fiach came to Dublin and was forthcoming; unfortunately his deposition has not survived.

Perrot's strenuous defence contained much truth: in summer 1588 the government was watching Fiach with increasing trepidation.[127] They had reason to do so, for, throughout the Spanish Armada crisis of those months, Fiach had refused to supply them with troops. Instead, he positioned lookouts on the coast, raised men and bought arms. He dispatched orders from Ballinacor to his bailiffs to requisition provisions throughout Críoch Raghnuill and raid the Pale.[128] In his 1590 deposition, Perrot explained how he peeled away many of Fiach's confederates; in particular, he had exploited rifts between Fiach and his brothers-in-law, Tadhg mac Giollapádraig O'Connor Faly and Féilim mac Toirdhealbhach O'Toole, and he also encouraged Ormond's constable Aodh Dubh to attack Fiach (presumably during June 1588). Perrot's plotting of that time coincided with the re-emergence of Fiach's feud with Harrington. In June 1588, Fiach shrewdly submitted to Perrot's successor as lord deputy, Sir William Fitzwilliam, before retiring to his lordship to await the Spanish landing. By the end of August, Fiach learned that the Armada was scattered.[130] However, he faced a considerable battle to subdue his clients. Perrot's version of 1587/8 is supported by evidence from the State Papers that shows Fiach fighting for survival. By September 1588 Fiach had ridden the storm and gone on the offensive. On 26 September, it was reported that he and his son Toirdhealbhach were gradually re-establishing their suzerainty. During a venomous parley with Féilim mac Toirdhealbhach, Fiach violently clashed with him, forcing O'Toole to flee for his life. Even more worrying for the government were reports of Fiach's ongoing preparations for a Spanish landing. Significantly, there was only one dissenting voice within the government – that of Lord Chancellor Archbishop Loftus, who bizarrely wrote to William Cecil, Lord Burghley, stating that Fiach intended no harm.[131] Loftus' words were at odds with the fact that Fiach was crushing all Irish opposition to him in Wicklow. On Fiach's orders, his son Toirdhealbhach, with Kavanagh help, ruthlessly stamped out Féilim mac Toirdhealbhach O'Toole's rebellion, forcing his recognition of Fiach's overlordship about Christmas that year.[132]

With Féilim's surrender, Fiach began the second phase of his clean-out. Doubtless his experiences of 1586–8 made him more belligerent, as shown by the prolonged presence of minor Irish lords from Longford at Ballinacor, particularly that of Hubert mac Fergus O'Farrell in late 1588 and early 1589.[133] A further indication of Fiach's hostility was indicated by the escape of the

127 *CSPI, 1586–8*, p. 526.   **128** *CSPI, 1588–92*, no. 1, p. 3.   **130** *CSPI, 1588–92*, no. 18, p. 11.
131 Price, 'Notes', p. 151.   **132** *CSPI, 1588–92*, no. 45, p. 66; ibid., no. 46, p. 113.
Toirdhealbhach killed two nephews of Féilim mac Toirdhealbhach during the winter 1588.
See ibid., no. 25, p. 92, no. 46, p. 113.   **133** Ibid., no. 46, p. 113.

O'Byrne and the other hostages from Dublin Castle on 25 February 1589.[134] By March 1589, Fiach was strong enough to attack Aodh Dubh and his Butler patrons. In late March he burnt Knockrath, forcing Aodh Dubh to take up permanent residency in Arklow.[135] And, to add insult to injury, he took into custody Aodh Dubh's wife Margaret O'Byrne, which rubbed salt into the already wounded pride of his rival. In mid-October 1589, before the walls of Arklow, he demanded that Aodh Dubh be handed over to him or his forces would storm the fortress. Aodh Dubh, safe behind Arklow's walls, defied him, forcing Fiach to content himself with burning the surrounding area.[136] Throughout 1590, Fiach remained on the offensive, leading his forces and the Walshes against the Cloghgrenan Butlers and wasting their lands. By August, he had won this latest round.[137] The experience of these years reinforced his position as leader of the Leinster nobility and of southern disaffected Catholics and saw him become noticeably more belligerent towards the English and Protestantism. Notably, the courts of the southern assize were never held again in Ballinacor. Indeed, Ballinacor returned to its more recognizable role as a safe haven for priests and Spanish agents. They now nurtured Fiach's brooding discontent, reinvigorating him as the greatest threat to Anglicization and Protestantism in the southern half of Ireland. From his Glenmalure pulpit, Fiach again preached the doctrine of Catholic nationalism and intrigued with sympathizers throughout the country. This would inevitably lead to war.

---

134 Ibid., no. 41, p. 126.   135 Ibid., no. 58, p. 140, no. 61, p. 140.   136 Ibid., no. 49, pp 255–6.
137 *Acts Privy Council*, xix, pp 410–1.

CHAPTER 11

The end of Gaelic Leinster, 1590–1606

Fiach mac Aodha O'Byrne represented a new development on the Irish political landscape. In 1979 Bradshaw, arguing that Fiach's poem-book projected a distinctly nationalistic perspective, highlighted three dominant themes in it – the right of the Irish to Ireland; the long struggle of the Irish nobility against the English; and the need for Irish unity.[1] These poems cannot be viewed as the sole evidence of Fiach's advocacy of Irish Catholic nationalism. Central to his own and his father's career is the fact that both of them disturbed the traditional order in the course of their rise from obscurity to provincial prominence to country-wide importance. Even at a local level in Wicklow, Fiach presented himself as the great unifier of both his own Gabhal Raghnaill followers and the rest of the O'Byrnes, although it has to be said that his ambitions among the O'Byrnes could cause as much disunity as unity. From 1579 at least, the twin themes of Fiach's career were Catholicism and Irish unity. In Leinster, his influence was widespread, as shown by the election of his clients as provincial kings and by their oaths of loyalty to him. As the joint leader of a Catholic crusade in Leinster between 1580 and 1581, he earned the respect of committed Counter-Reformation Catholics such as Baltinglass and Saunders, and, later, Archbishop James O'Hely of Tuam. Not only did he intrigue with Spanish and papal agents, but he was prepared to act forcefully against the English.

During this period Fiach's confessors also cemented his religious fervour by inculcation of Catholic Counter-Reformation principles. This may have further intellectualized the struggle between Catholicism and Protestantism in Fiach's mind; and the Butler war, along with Perrot's intrigues, finally convinced Fiach to eschew compromise with those whom he regarded as heretics, and to return to his old plan of destroying English and Protestant power in Ireland. The extent of Fiach's reinforced militancy and commitment to Catholicism even shocked his poets: in a poem dedicated to Fiach, Fergal McKeogh commented with alarm on the increasing clerical grip upon his lord. On the other hand, Fiach's militancy proved beneficial to the poets, for he went on a propaganda offensive, portraying himself as the protector of the Irish.[2] The crowing tones emanating

---

1 Bradshaw, 'Native reaction to the westward enterprise', pp 73–5. 2 *Leabhar Branach*, no. 26, pp 108–15; ibid., no. 97, pp 97–102, no. 30, pp 122–8; Bradshaw, 'Native reaction to the westward enterprise', pp 72–7.

from Ballinacor during the early 1590s proclaimed that all the Leinstermen were finished – except for Fiach, the hero of prophecy who would drive the English from Ireland.[3]

Before re-embarking upon his Catholic crusade, Fiach shored up his position in Leinster. Between 1590 and 1592 he remained obdurate, fighting the Butlers as well as terrorizing his Irish neighbours of north Wexford.[4] As usual, the government played right into his hands by meddling among the O'Tooles in 1590 and 1591. This interference effectively drove Féilim mac Toirdhealbhach O'Toole of Powerscourt, Fiach's errant brother-in-law, back into his camp. Féilim's discord was caused by the government's promotion of the claims of his nephew, Art O'Toole. Initially Perrot took Art under his wing – probably to force Féilim to fight Fiach in 1587 and 1588.[5] After Féilim's failure to curb Fiach, Art pressed his claim. Central to the dispute was Féilim mac Toirdhealbhach's appropriation of the lands of his elder brother, Brian, Art's father, upon his death in April 1549. At that time Art was dispatched to the English court for his education before making a career in the English army. Upon his return to Ireland in the mid-1580s, he laid his claim to Powerscourt and found a receptive ear in Perrot. The ensuing trouble along the borders of Dublin Pale convinced Perrot that he had made a mistake, so he tried to have Art assassinated in Dublin about 1587/8 – probably in an attempt to placate Féilim.[6] Undeterred, Art again petitioned Elizabeth for redress of his grievances in June 1591; but, instead, her deputy, Fitzwilliam, appeased Féilim and his O'Byrne master.

Now strengthened, Fiach devoted himself to the Catholic cause. By 1591, his defeat of Grey and his subsequent career had made Fiach a legend among Irish nobility. This status attracted many to Glenmalure to speak with him. Of all the major Irish leaders, Fiach was the only one who remained openly defiant; more importantly, he was also seen to have been relatively successful. Although Fiach was in contact with the Irish nobility of Connacht during the Leinster war of 1580–1,[7] he may have fallen out of touch following the end of the war; but his experiences of 1585–7 apparently prompted the resumption of contact. By 1588 (as we saw), he was receiving minor Irish lords from Longford at Ballinacor.[8] In April 1590 he allied with Feriagh O'Kelly of Roscommon, while Fergus O'Farrell of Annaly once again dispatched his son Hubert to Glenmalure that

3 Ibid., no. 39, pp 147–8, no. 32, pp 130–5; Bradshaw, 'Native reaction to the westward enterprise', pp 72–7; Gerald of Wales notes that according to St Brechan (St Berchan) 'almost all the English of Ireland will be dislodged by a king who will come from the lonely mountains of Patrick [the Wicklow mountains], and on the night of Our Lord's day will overrun a castle in the wooded region of Uí Fáelain': see *Expugnatio*, p. 233. It is unknown whether Fiach's poets had access to the prophecies of Brechan. **4** *Cal. Carew MSS, 1589–1600*, nos 97 & 99, pp 44–5; Hore, *Wexford town*, vi, p. 96. **5** *Acts Privy Council*, xvi, pp 106 & 125; The English privy council instructed Perrot to enforce Art's claims; For Art's earlier pension grants see *CSPI, 1588–1592*, nos 64–74, 401–3. **6** O'Toole, *The history of the Clan O'Toole*, pp 326–8; *CSPI, 1588–1592*, no. 65, pp 401–2. **7** *CSPI, 1574–85*, no. 77, p. 238; *Cal. Carew MSS, 1575–88*, no. 437, p. 282, no. 481, p. 314, no. 483, p. 316. **8** *CSPI, 1588–1592*, no. 25, p. 92, no. 46, p. 113.

month to negotiate a similar alliance. On 10 May Sir Roger Wilbraham, a client of Fitzwilliam, wrote to Burghley about Fiach's links to the O'Rourkes of West Bréifne, proposing that an attack be made upon him.[9] Fiach's interest in this region of Connacht/Ulster was in response to what was happening there.

From the middle of 1580s, the reform of Connacht/Ulster was high on the government's agenda. By 'reform' the government meant the systematic abolition of the near-autonomous power exercised by the Irish lords over their lordships. To facilitate the breaking of these suzerainties, common law and sheriffs were to be introduced, the government's favourite lever being the promotion of the tenurial rights of lesser nobles. Part of this policy was the government's dramatic kidnapping of Aodh, son of Sir Aodh Dubh O'Donnell of Donegal, in September 1587. And after the death of Sir Ross MacMahon of Monaghan in summer 1589, Fitzwilliam refused to recognize his brother and successor, Aodh MacMahon (this eventually led to the latter's trial and execution in late 1590). Following hard upon this was the survey of the MacMahon lordship and its division among its freeholders. This was a devastating attack upon the social structure of an Irish lordship. Effectively, the crown had replaced the lord as the power in his ancestral territory. The O'Rourkes of the Leitrim lordship of West Bréifne were under similar pressure. There the Irish reaction was more forceful, as Sir Brian O'Rourke and his Oxford-educated son, Brian Óg, attacked government forces in April 1589. By spring of the following year West Bréifne had been invaded; this forced father and son into exile in Donegal; after Sir Brian's later extradition from Scotland to execution at London in November 1591, Brian Óg attempted to come to terms with the government. But beyond meeting, advising and allying with the O'Farrells, O'Kellys and O'Rourkes, there is no evidence that Fiach lent them any significant military assistance. However, his interference was deeply worrying, causing Sir Richard Bingham, governor of Connacht, to complain about it on 14 July 1592.[10]

The origin of Fiach's labyrinthine relations with Aodh O'Neill, 2nd earl of Tyrone, remain obscure. It is uncertain whether the two leaders ever actually met, although, if they did, the first time would probably have been during April and May 1585, when (it was recorded) both men attended parliamentary sessions, beginning on 26 April.[11] During these sessions O'Neill, then baron of Dungannon, was conferred with the earldom of Tyrone. Fiach's O'Neill connections were really with Tyrone's rival, Toirdhealbhach Luineach O'Neill (these bonds dated from the Leinster war of 1580–1).[12] Later, in February 1586 as we saw, one of Fiach's sons along with Art O'Neill, Tyrone's enemy, escaped from Dublin Castle, and Fiach's complicity in this was uncovered when his own brother was captured while escorting Art back to Ulster,[13] so Fiach was probably hostile towards Tyrone,

9 Ibid., no. 76, p. 332 & no. 19, p. 341; for Wilbraham see Morgan, *Tyrone's rebellion*, p. 59. **10** *CSPI, 1588–1592*, no. 20, p. 544. **11** AFM, 1585. **12** *Cal. Carew MSS, 1575–88*, no. 437, p. 282, no. 481, p. 314, no. 483, p. 316; Berleth, *The twilight lords*, p. 111. This mentions that a daughter of O'Byrne was the first wife of Conn Bacach O'Neill, first earl of Tyrone. See *Carew MS 635*. **13** Morgan, *Tyrone's rebellion*, pp 100–3; *CSPI, 1586–8*, p. 32.

whom he may have regarded as an outright loyalist; indeed, their actions during the Armada crisis illustrate their differing political views: while Fiach busied himself to aid the Spanish, Tyrone's troops slaughtered 500–600 shipwrecked Armada survivors in Inishowen (though the earl did shelter a number of high-ranking Spanish officers as well as some commoners).[14]

For centuries, Tyrone has remained an enigmatic figure. But the 1993 publication of Hiram Morgan's magisterial *Tyrone's Rebellion* has done much to clarify his career. Described as possessing a 'dissembling manner',[15] Tyrone was a highly calculating sort of a person skilled in the art of masking his intentions. For much of the first thirty years of his life, he played the loyalist because he needed government support to establish himself against Toirdhealbhach Luineach O'Neill and the sons of Seán O'Neill. From 1587, however, Tyrone faced growing government interference within the traditional ambit of his ancestors in Connacht/Ulster – particularly Monaghan. Also, he was fighting the renewed assault of Toirdhealbhach Luineach and the sons of Seán O'Neill who sought to exploit his difficulties. These troubles, combined with the government's behaviour in Monaghan, Donegal and West Bréifne, caused him great concern.

A clear shift in Tyrone's position can be detected in 1589. Outwardly, he manipulated the government behind a visage of loyalty, but behind the scenes he was creating a network of support throughout Ireland and aboard. This date of 1589 is confirmed by Tyrone's letter of 8 October 1596 to Philip II, in which he mentions that he had sought Spanish aid for the previous seven years.[16] This was a complete volte-face, given the actions of his troops in 1588. Tyrone also desired to remove the increasing English presence in Donegal. Crucial to his strategy was the release of Aodh O'Donnell of Donegal, his son-in-law, imprisoned in Dublin Castle since autumn 1587. According to Conn O'Neill's allegations in summer 1590, Tyrone had conspired in a plot to obtain O'Donnell's escape – perhaps in late 1589 or early 1590.[17] Given Fiach's involvement in O'Donnell's escapes of 1591 and 1592, Tyrone had possibly cultivated an alliance with Fiach about 1589–90. His reasons were obvious: by this date Fiach's reputation as the leading Spanish sympathizer in Ireland was well established; moreover, his defence of the Catholic faith had earned him respect throughout Catholic Ireland and on the continent, allowing him access to networks which may have been denied to Tyrone. But what really brought both men together was government meddling in their spheres of influence. Thus, both men began to tailor their plans to obtain the release of O'Donnell – which was crucial to Tyrone's strategy.

According to the accounts given by O'Sullivan Beare and the Four Masters, Fiach planned the escape of O'Donnell from Dublin Castle in January 1591.[18] They tell of how O'Donnell, after breaking his bonds, fled into the snow-capped Wicklow mountains with the English in pursuit. He managed to reach

---

14 Edwards, 'In Tyrone's shadow', pp 220–1; Morgan, *Tyrone's rebellion*, pp 106, 162.   15 Morgan, *Tyrone's rebellion*, p. 217.   16 *Cal. S.P. Spanish*, iv, p. 642.   17 J. Perrot, *The chronicle of Ireland, 1584–1608*, ed. H. Wood (Dublin, 1990), p. 65.   18 O'Sullivan Beare, p. 66; AFM, 1590.

Castlekevin, where Fiach's wife Rose convinced her brother Féilim O'Toole of Castlekevin (who these sources call the master of Castlekevin) to pretend to hold the fugitive prisoner pending Fiach's arrival from Glenmalure. However, heavy snows caused the Avonmore to break its banks, preventing Fiach from crossing. While Fiach was desperately searching for a suitable crossing-point, English troops arrived at Castlekevin and took O'Donnell from Féilim.[19] However, another version, contained in the letter of about 1597 from Art O'Toole to Elizabeth, illustrates the complexity of the political rivalries that still existed between Fiach and the O'Tooles. In it, Art says that Barnaby O'Toole, Féilim's elder brother, was lord of Castlekevin and that Barnaby placed O'Donnell in irons, on arrival in Castlekevin and handed him over to English troops (Barnaby O'Toole was a sometime enemy of Fiach).

If Art's account is true, Barnaby's defiance must have proved seriously embarassing for Fiach.[20] Even so, Fiach and Tyrone orchestrated a second escape of O'Donnell (in the company of Henry and Art O'Neill) on 6 January the following year. There is some evidence originating in Scotland to suggest that Fiach, at Tyrone's wish, may have authorized the murder of Art during the second escape from Dublin to Glenmalure.[21] In April 1595 Robert Bowes, treasurer of Berwick and resident English ambassador in Scotland, received a letter dated 25 March that year from John Auchinross – servant of Lochlainn MacLean of Duart. Its contents were startling. Auchinross told of the enmity of MacLean (a cousin of Art and Henry) towards Tyrone arising from the earl's earlier hanging of their brother, Aodh Gavelach O'Neill, in 1590. Then Auchinross dropped his bombshell, telling of his master's outrage at the killing of Art during the second escape from Dublin. This is in direct contradiction of the account of the second escape contained in the Annals of the Four Masters, in Lughaidh O'Clery's biography of O'Donnell, and in the writings of O'Sullivan Beare – all written during the early decades of the seventeenth century. Instead of murder in the mountains, O'Clery (an O'Donnell partisan) presented the causes of Art's demise from a combination of injuries sustained in a fall and from exposure to the wintry conditions. However, Auchinross' account of Art's death cannot be easily dismissed, as it tends to fit with the prevailing political realities of the time. Moreover, James Fitzgerald (Walter Riabhach's brother) in his deposition of 1595 stated that Aodh O'Donnell in January 1592 swore on a book sealing an alliance with Fiach; he also gave his word to Fiach that he would encourage Tyrone and Aodh Maguire of Fermanagh to swear the same oath.[22] Walter Riabhach, presumably acting as Fiach's envoy, accompanied

19 P. Walsh (ed.), *The life of Aodh Ruadh O'Domhnaill, transcribed from the book of Lughaidh Ó Cléirigh* (1948), p. 17; O'Sullivan Beare, pp 66–8; AFM, 1592. See also MacEiteagain, 'Feagh McHugh and the Ulster princes', pp 197–211. 20 *Calendar of manuscripts of the marquis of Salisbury*, xiv (London, 1923), p. 31. 21 *Calendar of state papers, Scotland, 1593–5*, xi, no. 497, p. 558; Edwards, 'In Tyrone's shadow', pp 222–3. 22 PRO, SP 63/178/53, inclosure vi; O'Brien, 'Feagh McHugh', p. 15; Price, 'Notes', p. 154. After this ceremony O'Donnell was given into the care of Toirdhealbhach Buidhe O'Hagan and was escorted into Meath by a company of

O'Donnell into Ulster – heightening government fears of conspiracy. O'Donnell's homecoming sparked the expulsion of the English, resulting in his stage-managed acclamation as lord of Donegal.[23] Although the English suspected him of collusion, Tyrone managed to stay in the background. But the expulsion of the English from Donegal hastened the slide to war.

Now O'Donnell behaved as Tyrone's frontman, engaging leading Catholic churchmen such as Edmund MacGauran, primate of Ireland, and Archbishop James O'Hely of Tuam in 1592. Crucial to the success of the conspirators was the platform upon which they stood. Although Counter-Reformation Catholicism made little impact upon the ordinary people until the seventeenth century, their devotion to Catholicism and the papacy was genuine. However, among the elite, of whom Fiach was a prime example, the Counter-Catholic Reformation already had profound effects. This class, who stood to lose the most if their regional overlordships were dissolved by the New English tide of common law and sheriffs, used their Catholicism as a unifying weapon to win the support of the Catholic Old English nobility, Spain and the papacy. However, this does not seem to have been Tyrone's idea: the placing of Catholicism as the central plank in the conspiratorial platform smacks of Fiach's influence. It had not been forgotten how he utilized the struggle for religious freedom to such devastating effect during the Leinster war of 1580–1. We find Primate MacGauran, acting as Philip II's eyes, presiding over a conference attended by seven northern bishops in Donegal during December 1592, and three months later dispatching a report to Spain, stating that the Irish would support a Spanish landing. Along with MacGauran's messages, there were two other letters – one from O'Donnell, the other from Aodh Maguire – which also contained the pledges of Brian Óg O'Rourke, the Burkes and the seven bishops. Archbishop O'Hely was delegated as the conspirators' ambassador to the Spanish court and was instructed to present the case for Spanish intervention in Ireland to Philip II.[24]

O'Hely was now convinced of Tyrone's commitment to a war against the English. Another figure impressed him – Fiach. References to his Catholic zeal, his importance to the conspiracy and his interest in a new Catholic crusade appear in the archbishop's report of summer 1593 to Philip. Increasingly, it looks as if Fiach formed the third part of a (now forgotten) triumvirate which also included Tyrone and O'Donnell. Any remaining doubts of Fiach's centrality to the conspiracy are dispelled by O'Donnell's letters to the exiled Viscount Edmund Fitzeustace, brother of the now deceased Baltinglass. According to O'Donnell, if Fitzeustace returned to Leinster, Fiach would exploit his strategic

Fiach's horse under the command of Féilim of Castlekevin and perhaps his brother Barnaby. See MacCarthy, 'The O'Byrnes of Wicklow', p. 34. This also mentions the connivance of certain Catholic Palesmen with O'Donnell and Fiach, namely the Warren family. See AFM, 1590, 1592. These references mention that Féilim visited O'Donnell during his imprisonment and that he and his brother commanded O'Donnell's escort home. Morgan, *Tyrone's rebellion*, p. 132.   **23** Price, 'Notes', p. 153; Morgan, *Tyrone's rebellion*, p. 133.   **24** Morgan, *Tyrone's rebellion*, p. 141.

position upon the Pale's borders to maximum effect.[25] Viscount Edmund, who had sailed with the doomed 1588 Armada, found the idea of returning to Ireland to lead a Catholic crusade immensely attractive, so Fitzeustace dispatched a letter signalling his approval – but his interest ended with his death in Lisbon during autumn 1594.[26] Another piece of evidence highlights the depth of Fiach's involvement: in 1593 a John Slattery confirmed that Fiach was communicating with the exiled Irish Catholic diaspora, (including the Baltinglass and Desmond factions in Spain and Portugal) as well as the Fitzgerald party in Munster.[27]

Outright war with the government moved a step further because of the Fermanagh crisis of late April 1593, when Aodh Maguire was provoked into conflict by the invasion of his lordship by its would-be sheriff, Captain Humphrey Willis. After surviving the initial onslaught, Maguire was succoured by Tyrone and O'Donnell's covert dispatch of reinforcements. In May, Maguire attacked Sligo and burned Bingham's Ballymote base. Hiram Morgan argues that, from this point on, Tyrone was waging a war by proxy with the government.[28] With the whiff of the earl's Spanish conspiracy and his dubious dealings with Maguire on the wind, the government's attention focused more sharply upon Tyrone. Despite its investigation of rumours connecting Tyrone with conspiracy (which led to talks at Dundalk with him about a dilution of his power over the O'Neill patrimony), the earl temporized and avoided arrest. In mid-September, when Maguire was proclaimed a traitor, Tyrone agreed to accompany the English during their forthcoming campaign in Fermanagh, but his confederates supported Maguire both openly and secretly. Fiach sent troops under Feriagh O'Kelly to aid Maguire in September (an indication that he was privy to the earl's designs). After Maguire's defeat by the English and Tyrone at an Erne ford near Belleek, Maguire dispatched O'Kelly to cause trouble in Roscommon to divert English troops from the Fermanagh front. O'Kelly did cause considerable unrest, but he was badly wounded and had to limp back to Wicklow late in November.[29]

With Maguire on the run, the government considered how to implement a settlement of Fermanagh. Plainly, the Monaghan model was the preferred option. In response, Tyrone withdrew his co-operation from the government in the months that followed. His decision was matched by a rise in the activities of Fiach's lieutenants in Leinster. While Fiach disclaimed any involvement, the government was not convinced. (Significantly, Harrington was excused from military service in Meath so that he could check developments in Wicklow.) The tension between Tyrone and the government intensified in the early months of

---

25 Estado 839, ff 56, 66; Silke, 'The Irish appeal of 1593', p. 366.   **26** Silke, 'The Irish appeal of 1593', pp 290, 365–8; see also *CSPI, 1592–6*, no. 62, p. 65. A Fernadino O'Toole was reported as fighting for Spain in France.   **27** *Cal. S.P. Spanish, 1587–1603*, iv, no. 623, pp 611–2. Significantly, Slattery informed his Spanish handlers of the near impregnability of Fiach's heartland of Glenmalure where he said fifteen well armed men could hold out.   **28** Morgan *Tyrone's rebellion*, pp 142–4.   **29** *CSPI, 1588–1592*, no. 2 (7), pp 160, no. 15, 172 and nos 35, 38 pp 190–1.

1594. Suspicions of O'Donnell's complicity with Maguire in the Fermanagh campaign were sent by the council to Elizabeth. She delegated Tyrone to deal with his son-in-law, but in February he refused; nor would he allow Sir Henry Bagenal to pass through western Tyrone to parley with O'Donnell, claiming that Maguire was active in that area. Through their spies the government also discovered that O'Donnell was prepared for war. Tyrone himself was obviously sitting on the fence: he did agree to meet government commissioners for a series of conferences lasting from 8 to 15 March, in the course of which, he slammed government actions in Ulster over the previous decade. An agreement of sorts was concluded on 15 March; the earl promised to prevent his own followers from attacking the Pale, to check any influx of Scottish mercenaries into Ulster, to forestall any disturbances against government forces and to await Elizabeth's decision concerning his grievances.[30] Both sides thought they had prevented the outbreak of open hostilities. Within three days, war was back on the horizon because of events in Leinster.

The events in question were the deaths of Sir Piers Fitzgerald, sheriff of Kildare, and his family during the early hours of 18 March. They had been burned to death during an attack by Fiach's sons and Walter Riabhach upon their Barrowside castle of Ardree near Athy.[31] O'Sullivan Beare offers a reason for this attack: it was made in revenge for a recent Fitzgerald raid upon Walter Riabhach's home in Shillelagh.[32] In subsequent correspondence with the government, Fiach denied any connection with the outrage and offered to banish Walter Riabhach. But it is difficult to see how he was not complicit in the attack. Sir Piers had been a sometime enemy of Fiach (these relations between the pair had settled somewhat over the years); but the attack upon the Fitzgeralds may have been designed to derail Tyrone's negotiations with the government. Although Fiach protested his innocence, Fitzwilliam did not believe him; he was sure that Fiach and Tyrone were preparing to pounce, and he now requested the dispatch of 1,500 troops to Ireland.[33] By March, however, Elizabeth decided on Fitzwilliam's removal as lord deputy, and temporarily replaced him with Sir Robert Gardiner and Sir Richard Bingham, the lord justices, before naming Sir William Russell as lord deputy in April. In Leinster the situation developed. On 3 May it was reported that Fiach's forces were on full alert and that he was fearful of retribution. More importantly, English intelligence discerned that he was considering embarking for Spain, leaving the Leinster leadership to his sons and Walter Riabhach.[34] On 11 May, Fiach wrote again to Fitzwilliam, asking for the swift granting of his pardon. This cut little ice with Fitzwilliam, who recommended to the English privy council that an attack be made on Fiach.[35]

30 Edwards, 'In Tyrone's shadow', p. 226; Morgan, *Tyrone's rebellion*, pp 160, 163–4.   31 *CSPI, 1592–1596*, no. 91 (6), p. 227; PRO, SP 63/175/24.   32 O'Sullivan Beare, p. 75.   33 PRO, SP 63/174/50; *CSPI, 1592–96*, no. 50 (1), p. 245. On 13 June 1595, Lord Deputy Sir William Russell wrote to Burghley, stating that Fiach was not at the burning of Ardree, see ibid., no. 31, p. 329; PRO, SP 63/173/91.   34 PRO, SP 63/174/53; *CSPI, 1592–1596*, no. 53, i, p. 245.   35 *CSPI,*

However, Fiach's resolve was steeled by the arrival in Glenmalure in May of Spanish military advisors with a Jesuit from Brittany. (Significantly Don Juan del Aguila – the Spanish commander at Kinsale in 1601 – had commanded the Spanish troops in Brittany from 1590. There they fought alongside the French Catholic League against the French monarchy.) The arrival of the Spanish caused consternation in the corridors of power. Fiach immediately ordered the manufacture of a large quantity of pikes.[36] Like Tyrone, he was determined to transform the face of battle in Ireland. In Ulster, Tyrone had drilled his traditional levies into a well-disciplined force clad in red coats, proficient with both musket and pike. Fiach appears to have already instituted some form of muster system within his lordship, as evidenced by his mobilization of October.[37] From his considerable experience as a commander, he realized that if he was to be successful his forces would have to best English armies in open country; this meant transforming his forces along the lines pursued by Tyrone. Clearly, Fiach was preparing for conflict with government units stationed close to Dublin and in wider Leinster.[38] The *Leabhar Branach* suggests that Fiach's Spanish cadre took part in a successful attack upon a castle in Leinster. Fiach now held the upper hand; his cash-strapped opponents had not enough troops to stop him, their recourse being to ponder the merits of a timely assassination.[39]

On 1 August Sir William Russell finally arrived in Ireland to replace Fitzwilliam. His task was formidable. Six days after his landing, Tyrone's brother, Cormac, and Maguire defeated an English force on its way to the relief of Enniskillen. The earl himself did not show his hand. He now gambled, declaring his loyalty and submitting before Russell at Dublin on 17 August. In Leinster, the situation was so serious that Elizabeth reintroduced martial law there; mindful of its previous abuse, she entrusted its execution to a seasoned administrator, her cousin Ormond. Martial law was declared on 15 August, and Ormond was instructed to use it only on Fiach's forces.[40] Fiach reacted immediately by dispatching his protégé Uaithne mac Ruaidhrí O'More to raise hell among the midland planters to divert English forces from the Wicklow theatre. It is clear that Fiach had been waiting for the day when Uaithne would return to Laois and assume his late father's lordship. As Uaithne was barely out of his teens, Fiach sent the seasoned Piers Grace to advise the young man. Soon the pair had Laois burning. In October, Fiach again raised the stakes by mobilizing all males between sixteen and sixty within Críoch Raghnuill, and by unleashing men led by a natural son of his (possibly Brian) on the settlers.[41] Government spies,

---

1592–1596, no. 53, p. 245. **36** PRO, SP 63/174/65; *CSPI, 1588–1592*, no. 65, p. 248; ibid., no. 53, vi, p. 299. See also PRO, SP 63/178/53. **37** Morgan, *Tyrone's rebellion*, pp 179–88; PRO, SP 63/177/5, inclosure iii. **38** From English reports, and later evidence, his preparations for war appear to have been meticulous. Passes and forests were plashed, while food, weapons and gunpowder had been also stockpiled in hidden underground stores. See *CSPI, 1592–6*, no. 53, vi, p. 299. **39** *Leabhar Branach*, no. 41, p. 150; *Calendar of the manuscripts of the marquis of Salisbury*, iv (London, 1892), p. 564. **40** *COD, 1584–1603*, iv, no. 97, pp 70–1. **41** Edwards, 'In Tyrone's shadow', p. 228; PRO, SP 63/177/5; *Cal. Carew MSS, 1589–1600*, no. 270, p. 237.

reporting correspondence between Fiach and Tyrone, informed their masters that Fiach had requested reinforcements from Ulster and had met with Brian Óg O'Rourke of Leitrim. Many feared that Fiach's activities heralded the early entry of Tyrone.[42] Deceitfully, on 26 October Fiach offered to submit and asked for a grant of his lands by letters patent, expressing as well a wish to go to England.[43]

In response to Fiach's offers, the government was equally duplicitous. After an exchange of letters, Russell agreed on 1 November that no harm would come to Fiach until Elizabeth's will was known.[44] Russell knew exactly how to fight Fiach, having benefited from his service on Grey's campaign of attrition and encirclement of January to July 1581. Until his forces were in place, however, Russell maintained communications with Fiach.[45] By 6 December Russell had decided upon his course, resolving to attack Fiach as soon as possible. This decision was probably, in part, spurred on by Fiach's correspondence with Tyrone; furthermore he was bolstered by encouragement from several of Fiach's Irish neighbours.[46] On 12 December, Fiach, possibly aware of Russell's resolution, dispatched an apology for not sending in his hostage. Four days later Walter Riabhach also requested that Fiach be pardoned for the sake of peace.[47] Russell was not impressed. Instead, he forced Fiach to raise the stakes. After Christmas, Sir Nicholas White reported that Fiach, accompanied by 160 pikemen, marched threateningly through counties Carlow and Kildare to Saggart and had sent messengers to Ulster for reinforcements. While Fiach paraded his troops along the edge of the mountains, Walter Riabhach and the MacMurrough-Kavanaghs attacked the lands of the Irish loyalist, Art Kinsella.[48] This latest display convinced Russell to act. In 1595, Glenmalure was to revert to the bloody bear-pit that had hosted so much of the Leinster war of 1580–1.

Despite Fiach's public flexing of his muscle, his raising of the stakes fractured his own support base. On 27 December Muircheartach Óg MacMurrough-Kavanagh made terms for himself. Also, one of Fiach's trusted circle was a spy for Sheriff Joshua Mynce of Carlow,[49] and Mynce now encouraged Russell to attack Fiach as early as possible. Russell took the spy's reports seriously and placed Ballinacor's capture as the central tenet of his emerging strategy, striking

This Uaithne is probably the Rory Óg who was burning in Laois during October 1595; Deignan, 'Portlaoise: genesis and development', p. 696; PRO, SP 63/177/5, inclosures ii–iii; *CSPI, 1592–6*, no. 59, p. 277. **42** PRO, SP 63/177/31; *CSPI, 1592–6*, no. 31, p. 285, no. 45, p. 287. **43** PRO, SP 63/177/5; *CSPI, 1592–6*, no. 5, i, p. 281; *Cal. Carew MSS, 1589–1600*, no. 270, p. 224. **44** Russell was the second son of the earl of Bedford and a veteran of the Leinster war of 1580–1. Indeed, he had first hand experience of Fiach. During April 1581, along with Sir William Stanley he had burnt Ballinacor before suffering heavy losses at the hands of its obviously irate owner. See O'Brien, 'Feagh McHugh', p. 16. **45** *Cal. Carew MSS, 1589–1600*, no. 270, p. 224. **46** *CSPI, 1592–6*, no. 1, p. 280; AFM, 1595. **47** PRO, SP 63/177/45, inclosure iv; *CSPI, 1592–6*, no. 45, iii–iv, p. 287. **48** MacCarthy, 'The O'Byrnes of Wicklow', p. 34; Hore, *Wexford town*, vi, pp 422–3. **49** *CSPI, 1592–6*, no. 48, p. 287; MacCarthy, 'The O'Byrnes of Wicklow', pp 79–81; O'Rourke, p. 23. From the previous summer this spy had been providing Russell with invaluable information about Fiach's activities. See PRO, SP 63/177/5, inclosure iv.

at Fiach's heartland during the night of 16 January 1595.[50] Russell got within earshot of Ballinacor undetected and would have captured Fiach but for the noise of a dropped drum; it was heard by Fiach's guards, who warned their master. Although surprised, he led his followers through an escape passage into the surrounding forests, where his forces began firing on the English, pinning them down until the morning before retiring to the upland forests of Dromkitt, near Ballinacor.[51]

With Fiach regrouping in Dromkitt, Russell garrisoned Ballinacor under Captain Henry Street. However, his strike had profound effects upon Fiach's inner circle, as one of his brothers surrendered within days of Ballinacor's fall. The fall of Ballinacor completely changed the situation in the Leinster. No longer had Fiach a secure base from which to direct operations; and, worse, a garrison had been established in his heartland. From Ballinacor, patrols led by Captain Street and Aodh Dubh of Knockrath seriously disrupted Fiach's plans by terrorizing the populace. Just to the north of Ballinacor, the O'Tooles of Castlekevin were also ejected from their residence by another English garrison, while along the coast Newcastle McKynegan, Wicklow and Arklow blocked any possible eastern breakout by Fiach. To the south and west, Fiach was limited by the establishment of government outposts at Clonmore, Rathvilly, Knockloe and Ballymore. Furthermore, Ormond now opened a second front in Shillelagh against Fiach's forces. Fiach tried to regain the initiative by authorizing attacks into the Pale, dispatching men to spy in Dublin.[52] Although Fiach's sons and the Fitzgeralds burnt Crumlin on 30 January and stole the lead roof of its church for ammunition, Russell demonstrated his advantage by attacking them the following day.[53] The speed of Russell's counter-attack shook the resolve of Fiach's lieutenants, leading many of them to submit.

Realizing that Russell was in the ascendant, Tyrone and his confederates met in late January. In a letter to Sir Edward Moore of Mellifont on 2 February, Tyrone conveyed their demand that the offensive against Fiach cease.[54] Meantime Fiach played for time, requesting a parley on 4 February. Russell refused, but authorized Harrington to meet Fiach. The parley on 5/6 February ended as neither side was prepared to back down.[55] On 6 February Sir Geoffrey Fenton,

---

50 The key to Russell's success was his usage of the ground and of the all-important element of surprise. Using the cover of dense woodland and winter darkness, Russell's troops guided by Aodh Dubh drove Fiach out of Ballinacor before the arrival of the Ulster reinforcements. See *CSPI, 1592–96*, no. 10, p. 291, nos 14, 19, p. 292; PRO, SP 63/178/19; MacCarthy, 'The O'Byrnes of Wicklow', p. 81; AFM, 1595. Aodh Dubh may be amongst Fiach's neighbours mentioned in the Four Masters who insisted upon the attack on Ballinacor. According to these annals, Russell stayed in Ballinacor for 10 days before leaving two companies of troops there. **51** AFM, 1595. His most prominent casualty was the Jesuit who was shot dead while standing with Rose, watching the fighting. See MacCarthy, 'The O'Byrnes of Wicklow', p. 82. **52** *Cal. Carew MSS, 1589–1600*, no. 270, pp 225–6. **53** AFM, 1595. **54** PRO, SP 63/178/36 inclosures iii–iv; *CSPI, 1592–6*, no. 36, iii–iv, p. 295. **55** Hore, *Wexford town*, vi, p. 424; *Cal. Carew MSS, 1589–1600*, p. 226.

secretary of the Dublin council, wrote to Burghley, recommending a temporizing course with Fiach. Russell would have none of it and commissioned fresh fortifications at Ballinacor. Now his strategy of hemming in Fiach's forces moved into its second phase. This meant the establishment of secure supply routes from government-held territory through hostile country to the various theatres of operations. Ballinacor was supplied from the south by a line running from Arklow through Avoca, while from the east it was victualled from Wicklow through Glenealy to Rathdrum and onwards to Glenmalure. To the southwest of Ballinacor, another supply route was established through Kilcommon to service the movement of food and munitions from Carlow and Wexford into the central Wicklow highlands.

On 9/10 February, Russell burnt Fiach out of Dromkitt. Fiach appealed to Tyrone, who acted decisively, ordering his brother Art to take the Blackwater fort near Armagh on 16 February. Undismayed, Russell set a reward of £100 on Fiach's head and £140 for his capture. Like a big game hunter, he systematically stalked Fiach's chain of command – particularly the Fitzgeralds.[56] After 20 February, he directed a new offensive into Shillelagh. Walter Riabhach was driven from his house at Cronyhorn near Carnew, and his brother Gerald was captured and tortured. Before he died, he revealed that Fiach had pressed Tyrone for reinforcements. Russell was intent on isolating Fiach from his principal commanders; Walter Riabhach's capture was a priority. Russell knew Fiach and his lieutenants were still dangerous and may have been responsible for the burning of Arklow on 28 February.[57] In late March and early April Fiach changed his tactics, breaking his large force into a series of smaller ones to prevent Russell from forcing a decisive engagement; and it would appear he commuted between his forces to issue instructions, accompanied only by a small bodyguard. However, Fiach suffered a huge setback when Walter Riabhach was betrayed to the English by the O'Tooles of Imaal on 7 April; under torture he revealed Fiach's links with the Spanish and Tyrone, confessing that the earl promised to land a force of 1,000 men at Arklow; and before his execution on 10 April, he confessed that Philip II had consented to sending aid to Tyrone.[58] In Wicklow the noose tightened. On 28 April, Rose O'Toole was captured by Harrington, while after 16 May several members of Fiach's foster family were killed in Glenlorcan near Glendalough.[59] After a trial for treason in Dublin on 27 May, Rose was sentenced to be burned as a witch. Three days later, Fiach was shot in the thigh and stabbed by Captain Street's soldiers. His advancing years, ill health and now these wounds caused Harrington to pen a letter to Russell, declaring that Fiach was no longer a force to be reckoned with.[60]

The actions of the O'Tooles of Imaal and Rose's capture show the pressure that Fiach was under. In the past, these O'Tooles were allied to Fiach, so their

56 *CSPI, 1592–6*, no. 44, p. 297; Hore, *Wexford town*, vi, pp 424, 426.   57 *Cal. Carew MSS, 1589–1600*, no. 270, pp 228–30.   58 Price, 'Notes', pp 157–8; AFM, 1595; MacCarthy, 'The O'Byrnes of Wicklow', pp 34–5.   59 Ibid., p. 159; *Cal. Carew MSS, 1589–1600*, pp 230–1; O'Brien, 'Feagh McHugh', p. 17.   60 *CSPI, 1592–6*, no. 92, p. 319, no. 22, iii, p. 328; PRO, SP

betrayal of Walter Riabhach reflected a movement away from Fiach's cause. (The one major anomaly in Russell's relations with the loyalists was his unexplained arrest of the usually loyal Murchadh mac Edmund O'Byrne of Kiltimon on 21 April.)[61] Rose's capture had the most serious ramifications. Although Fiach was under huge pressure, with his troops even had killed their horses for food, and Fiach's continuing defiance led Russell to suspect that he was being secretly provisioned by sympathizers.[62] To destroy the Catholic leadership, Russell now ruthlessly exploited Rose's death sentence. In a very unclear incident, Rose, while awaiting execution during May/June 1595, became convinced that Toirdhealbhach, Fiach's eldest son, intended to betray his father to Russell. She conveyed a message to Fiach (it was shortly after he was seriously wounded), effectively presenting him with a terrible dilemma: he should give up his son to save his wife – or vice versa.

In late May, Fiach arrested Toirdhealbhach in spite of his son's denials. He authorized his foster-sister to open negotiations with Harrington, offering to put in Uaithne mac Ruaidhrí O'More as a pledge.[63] On 1 June, however, Harrington informed Russell that Fiach was prepared to hand over Toirdhealbhach and Maurice Fitzgerald, Walter Riabhach's brother. Fiach's decision seemed so reprehensible that it earned even Russell's rebuke. On 7 June, Fiach wrote asking for a pardon for himself, Rose and his followers, promising to deliver Toirdhealbhach and Fitzgerald. He sent his son and Fitzgerald to Dublin to virtual death sentences on 18 June. There, government officials tried to bargain with Toirdhealbhach to kill his father, which he refused to do. He was accordingly executed on 18 July.[64] Following her stepson's death, Rose was quietly released and returned to her husband. Toirdhealbhach's fate, combined with Tyrone's entry into the war in May 1595, alleviated the pressure on Fiach. In response to Tyrone's capture of Monaghan and his defeat of a relieving English force on 27 May, Russell was forced to take pressure off Wicklow and was obliged to divert troops to fight Tyrone. In late June, Fiach, his followers and lands were granted protection and Russell's offensive all but ceased.[65] Peace had come at a terrible cost to Fiach personally.

Fiach's military position improved when divisions emerged between Russell, a client of the earl of Essex, and Sir John Norris, an ally of Burghley. Norris, who arrived in Ireland during May 1595, saw Tyrone as the main danger. Accordingly, he advised Burghley and the English privy council to give less importance to Russell's campaign and give priority to one against Tyrone.[66] By August, Russell

63/181/7.   **61** On April 12 Dúnlaing mac Brian Kavanagh of Tincurry sent in the heads of Fiach's supporters. Donnio Spannio was also in service as was Aodh Dubh O'Byrne that April, see *Cal. Carew MSS, 1589–1600*, no. 270, p. 229. Dúnlaing mac Brian was married to Fiach's cousin, the daughter of Muircheartach Óg Kavanagh of Garryhill (*d.*30 November 1587), Nicholls, 'The Kavanaghs', (1978), p. 575.   **62** MacCarthy, 'The O'Byrnes of Wicklow', p. 84; *CSPI, 1592–96*, no 7, i, p. 336; Hore, *Wexford town*, vi, p. 426.   **63** *CSPI, 1592–6*, no. 31, i, p. 329.   **64** Ibid., no. 41, p. 330; Hore, *Wexford town*, vi, p. 435; *Cal. Carew MSS, 1589–1600*, no. 270, p. 234; PRO, SP 63/181/7, inclosure (i); O'Sullivan Beare, pp 76–7.   **65** Edwards, 'In Tyrone's shadow', p. 234; *CSPI, 1592–6*, no. 10, p. 339.   **66** Ibid., pp 234–6.

and Norris were campaigning against Tyrone (this allowed Fiach to reorganize). Tyrone had the best of the fighting, forcing negotiations in October. On 25 September, after more lengthy talks with Fiach, Harrington emerged with a deal. Fiach professed repentance, declaring himself anxious to be received into the queen's mercy. As a sign of good faith, he delivered a hostage and was duly granted two months' further protection.[67] On a more local level, his position continued to improve as a serious dispute broke out between a local English commander, Captain Thomas Lee, and Harrington. Also, on 25 September Harrington angrily complained to Burghley that Lee had killed Cétach O'Toole and maimed his brother, Diarmait (both had helped in the capture of Walter Riabhach).[68] On 9 November, Fiach, under Harrington's protection, submitted on his knees before Russell in Dublin, obtaining a further protection of three months.[69]

However, the government remained uneasy. Fiach and Rose's movements were closely monitored in case of further plots with Tyrone. No doubt this apprehension was magnified by the capture of Piers O'Cullen, a priest, in Drogheda before he could take ship for Spain. On his person were letters from Tyrone and O'Donnell to Philip II, Prince Carlos and Don Juan del Aguila, in which the confederates protested that they were fighting for the Catholic faith, offered the Irish crown to Philip II and asked for the dispatch of a Spanish expeditionary force to aid their campaign. Naturally, these letters focused attention back upon Fiach. Government unease was captured in a letter from Sir Henry Wallop, a Wexford planter, dated 17 November to Sir John Puckering, lord keeper of the English great seal, urging the renewal of the offensive against Fiach. Early in 1596 Tyrone and O'Donnell again demanded Fiach's pardon, while he himself maintained his mask of loyalty. To highlight his repentance, he sent in pledges and also asked Russell to rein in his commanders.[70] In April, he petitioned Burghley to expedite his pardon and asked for a grant by letters patent of his estates as well as the return of Ballinacor. Most disconcerting of all for the government was the fact that Fiach's letter to Burghley was loaded with a barely disguised threat of a return to war if these demands were not met.[71] In reality, his forces already had become active again. While Fiach remained outwardly loyal, he orchestrated events like a puppet master – authorizing his sons and the O'Mores, Graces, Kavanaghs, O'Farrells and Butlers to burn throughout the midlands that spring. In Laois, Uaithne mac Ruaidhrí immediately teamed up with some MacGillapatricks to exploit the relatively weak position of the planters, settling old scores with the Cosbys at Stradbally bridge on 19 May.

In late April, Tyrone was outwardly engaged in negotiations with the government to conclude a lasting peace. Behind the scenes, though, he resumed contact with the Spanish, with messengers flitting between Madrid and Dungannon

---

67 Hore, *Wexford town*, vi, p. 431.   **68** *CSPI, 1592–6*, no. 52, p. 397; *Cal. Carew MSS, 1589–1600*, no. 237, p. 237.   **69** Ibid., no. 14, p. 432; PRO, SP 63/184/14.   **70** *Cal. Carew MSS, 1589–1600*, p. 127; Hore, *Wexford town*, vi, pp 432–3; *CSPI, 1592–6*, nos 88–92, p. 481.   **71** PRO, SP 63/188/37. See also Fiach's letter of 29 February 1596 to Russell in PRO, SP 63/186/92.

between March and May. Ominously, Spanish shipping was spotted off the Kerry coast, and three separate Spanish diplomatic missions met with Tyrone and O'Donnell at Lifford in Donegal during late May and early June. The ships had been sent by Philip II to ascertain the commitment of the confederates in preparation for a Spanish landing. During the course of talks with Captain Alonso Cobos in May, Tyrone agreed to reject the emerging peace with Elizabeth's government. Finally, Tyrone and O'Donnell again requested Philip to send an army to Ireland before petitioning the king to appoint his nephew, Archduke Albert, governor of the Spanish Netherlands, as their sovereign prince.

Fiach's activities during June indicate that he was aware of Tyrone's plans. The government, who knew of Tyrone's intrigues, was obviously concerned and replenished the ammunition stores of the Ballinacor garrison, whereupon Fiach drew the sons of his old rival Sir Edmund Butler of Cloghgrenan into the conspiracy. It was reported in May that James Butler of Cloghgrenan intended to marry Doireann O'More, Fiach's niece.[72] The decision by Piers and James Butler of Cloghgrenan to become involved in Fiach's plot was an act of sheer political opportunism: their motivation had to do with their exclusion from the contest to succeed their uncle as the next earl of Ormond. The question of Ormond's successor had been a moot point since the death in 1590 of his only son James Butler, Lord Thurles. As the early 1590s progressed, James and Piers steadily became disaffected with the earl's inability to procure the repeal of the act of attainder of 1570 passed upon their father. By forming an alliance with Fiach in 1596, the brothers hoped to pressurize the government to repeal the act of attainder and reinstate them as heirs to the Butler earldom.

Fiach was naturally suspicious of their intentions. While he pondered how to make them demonstrate their commitment to the Catholic cause, his preparations for war gathered pace. Catholic activities in north Carlow and Wexford increased, while raids were launched into Kildare for horses.[73] Soon afterwards, Fiach launched a campaign of intimidation against neighbouring Irish loyalists. On 13 June, Fiach wrote to Thomas Butler, 10th earl of Ormond, ordering him to cease his interference with the lands of his mother in Cosha. Reporting this, Ormond informed Russell that Fiach was openly plotting with the MacMurrough-Kavanaghs. Fiach also wrote on 21 June to Sir Thomas Colclough of Tintern, Co. Wexford, demanding he desist from raiding south Wicklow and from attacking St Mullins in Carlow.[74] Two days later, Colclough complained to the government that Fiach was intimidating the loyal Donnchadh Riabhach MacMurrough-Kavanagh, and, worse still, assembling troops in the forests north of Mount Leinster known as the Briskillo. According to Colclough's informant, Féilim mac Fiach held a major conference there with Gerald mac Muircheartach MacMurrough-Kavanagh of Garryhill and Uaithne mac Ruaidhrí O'More. Colclough's letters voiced suspicions that the Keatings, Viscount Edmund Butler of Mountgarret

72 PRO, SP 63/189/46, inclosure xi.   **73** Edwards, 'In Tyrone's shadow', p. 237.   **74** *CSPI, 1596–7*, no. 15, viii & ix, pp 29–30; Hore, *Wexford town*, vi, p. 435.

(another potential successor of Ormond) and the Cloghgrenan Butlers were also implicated. Four days later, Colclough again highlighted the emerging danger in East Leinster, reporting that Uaithne mac Ruaidhrí had crossed the Barrow at Carlow early on 25 June to rendezvous with the Butlers and the MacMurrough-Kavanaghs. According to Colclough, Piers Butler of Cloghgrenan had sworn oaths binding himself to Domhnall Spainneach MacMurrough-Kavanagh, king of Leinster, and the two had travelled to an evening conference with Fiach in the Coolattin forests.[75] Apparently this build-up caused the defection of several Irish loyalists of Wexford to Fiach.[76] These developments were profoundly worrying for the New English administration in Dublin and for the planters of the midlands. Any lingering doubts of a Catholic military build-up in Leinster were dispelled when Uaithne mac Ruaidhrí again appeared in Wicklow in early July to take instruction about the same time as messengers from Tyrone and MacMahon arrived at Fiach's camp. Elsewhere, Sir Edward Moore of Mellifont noted that Fiach's messenger was in the earl's retinue at a conference later that month, while Tyrone and O'Donnell were making preparations to dispatch 200 troops to augment Fiach's forces.[77]

In this game, Fiach had the edge on Russell. Russell's ability to check him was further hindered because his army was under strength throughout Leinster. Moreover, Fiach outmanoeuvred him again by concluding a secret peace with Norris to last until Christmas, thereby winning the latest round of this phoney war. Government frustration erupted in late July. Then Captain Thomas Lee, perhaps urged by Russell, tried to capture or kill Fiach at a parley. As Fiach arrived, the English cavalry charged, but he again escaped.[78] In spite of this provocation, Fiach bided his time. On 22 July the English privy council told Russell that Elizabeth was resolved to grant Fiach his pardon and that all activities cease forthwith. Four days later, Harrington wrote to the council, at Fiach's request, protesting Fiach's loyalty and enquiring as to when letters patent to his estates would be issued.[79]

For Ormond, Fiach's alliance with the earl's nephews of Cloghgrenan was extremely worrying, not to say embarrassing.[80] Fiach was bent on having them irreversibly committed to his cause; that is to say, he was beyond redemption in the eyes of the law. On 3 August 1596 Fiach and the Butlers formalized their alliance in a solemn covenant on Barnacashel Hill in Shillelagh – a commitment that was copperfastened by Piers Butler's assault on the government outpost of Knockloe in Shillelagh and doubly so by James Butler's marriage to Doireann

75 *CSPI, 1592–6*, no. 44, xii, p. 543, no. 47, ii, p. 544. In 1596 Uaithne is recorded as warring throughout Laois and as having killed Alexander Cosby, see AFM, 1596. For Domhnall Spainneach, read Nicholls, 'The Kavanaghs' (1979), p. 732; Hore, *Wexford town*, vi, p. 434. **76** *CSPI, 1592–6*, no. 47, ii, p. 544; See also More, 'The MacMurrough-Kavanaghs', pp 19–20. **77** Hore, *Wexford town*, vi, pp 434–5; *CSPI, 1596–7*, no. 23, p. 36, no. 26, p. 37, no. 34, p. 41, no. 37, p. 45. **78** *CSPI, 1596–7*, no. 16, pp 81–82, see also no. 45, p. 53; Edwards, 'In Tyrone's shadow', p. 238. **79** Ibid., no. 42, p. 48; *Acts Privy Council*, xxvi, p. 45. **80** Price, 'Notes', p. 162.

O'More – probably later that month.[81] Ironically, on 3 August the English privy council granted Fiach his pardon and ordered Ballinacor and his lands to be returned.[82] But the activities of Fiach's lieutenants throughout Leinster infuriated Russell, who could find no grounds to take action against Fiach. On 13 August, Captain Tutcher Parkins, commander of the Ballinacor garrison, urgently dispatched a letter to Russell, informing him that James Butler of Cloghgrenan, Uaithne mac Ruaidhrí and the MacMurrough-Kavanaghs had arrived at Fiach's camp a day earlier.[83] Indeed, Uaithne mac Ruaidhrí's presence with Fiach was an act of brilliant manipulation. On 7 August Uaithne had agreed to a truce of eight days with government forces in Laois – which freed him for the Wicklow campaign. Later, Parkins was to tell that James Butler attacked the fort of Ballinacor and executed six of the garrison. Once again Fiach's hand was detected, for Parkins alleged that Fiach had demanded that Butler hang the six.[84] Subsequently, Parkins was proved correct: Fiach and Uaithne did make the hanging of the soldiers a precondition for the Butler brothers' access to the Catholic inner circle of command. When asked to explain the attacks on the fort, Fiach blamed it on strangers. At midnight on Monday, 16 August, the Ballinacor garrison was attacked again by the Butlers. Fiach's craft earned even Russell's grudging admiration: in a letter of 15 August, he famously commented to Burghley that Fiach had greater ability than Tyrone. Fiach now readied himself for the final push on the fort. A letter was dispatched on 17 August, informing Tyrone that he was ready to take the fort at this junction and requesting Tyrone to allow O'Donnell release a company of Connacht shot to serve as his personal bodyguard. In the letter Fiach absolved himself of provoking Lee's attack upon him during July, blaming the captain's treachery for the affair. On its way to Ulster, this letter was intercepted by Lee, who copied it for Russell before sending it on its way to Tyrone.[85]

Tyrone had been encouraging Fiach to recapture Ballinacor to coincide with the expected arrival of the Spanish.[86] Fiach was to open a second front against the English in preparation for the landing. On 3 September it was reported that the Butler brothers were behaving rebelliously near Carnew.[87] Fiach's manipulative skills now shone: he convinced a sergeant and others of the Ballinacor garrison to betray the fort;[88] aided by this treachery Fiach retook Ballinacor on 9 September. According to the statement of Sergeant-Major John Chichester, Fiach commanded the forces that took Ballinacor. His son Réamain was also implicated, having ambushed garrison troops before the attack. After an obstinate defence,

---

81 *CSPI, 1596–7*, no. 7, ix, pp 72–3; Hore, *Wexford town*, vi, p. 436.   82 *Cal. Carew MSS, 1589–1600*, no. 247, pp 181–2.   83 *CSPI, 1596–7*, no. 11, ii, p. 80.   84 Ibid., no. 7 (x) , p. 74; Hore, *Wexford town*, vi, p. 436.   85 *CSPI, 1592–96*, pp 81–2; *Cal. Carew MSS, 1589–1600*, p. 182; Edwards, 'In Tyrone's shadow', p. 238.   86 *CSPI, 1596–7*, no. 10, p. 103.   87 Hore, *Wexford town*, vi, p. 436; Later on 13 October 1596, Ormond was commissioned to make war on Uaithne O'More, the Butler brothers and their cousin, Walter Butler – the natural son of Viscount Mountgarret. See *Cal. Fiants Eliz*, no. 6020.   88 Price, 'Notes', pp 163–4; *Cal. Carew MSS, 1589–1600*, no. 270, p. 248.

Fiach spared the garrison. When Parkins was brought before him, Fiach acted as if he was going to behead him before telling him that he would keep his word.[89] A sergeant was set free to inform Russell that the price of Parkins' release was the cancelling of undertakings made by Rose to avoid execution. Fiach then turned on Lee and burned his lands at Newtown in Carlow.[90] However, his daring gamble doomed him, for the Spanish fleet was wrecked by storms on 13 October.[91] Believing that the Spanish were on their way, Fiach pushed his advantage as far as he could. In a campaign with Barnaby O'Toole and Domhnall Spainneach he threatened to besiege Castlekevin and burnt throughout much of east Wicklow and south Dublin, encouraging some Catholic Palesmen to join him. Further afield, his lieutenants even attacked Meath.[92] Russell had no doubts that Tyrone was behind Fiach's attack on Ballinacor, noting that the earl's messenger had been with Fiach shortly before his capture of the fort. The lord deputy's letters of 10 and 17 September leave no illusions that Tyrone and Fiach timed their move to coincide with the arrival of the Spanish fleet off Ireland.[93]

Fiach's plans were further hindered by the military incompetence of Piers and James Butler of Cloghgrenan. Their rebellion against Ormond was designed to throw his earldom into chaos and keep the government off balance, allowing Fiach to press his advantage in East Leinster. However, Ormond in September moved decisively, seizing his rebellious nephews' castles at Cloghgrenan and Tullow. In October he dealt a further blow to them, arresting their father Sir Edmund and Viscount Mountgarret. With Ormond re-establishing his control over Kilkenny and Carlow, Russell was free to focus on Fiach. Russell established his headquarters in the now fortified church of Rathdrum to prevent Fiach from attacking O'Byrnes' Country and raiding the Pale. Russell's reappearance in Wicklow signalled a war to the death with Fiach, which began with major clashes between the rival armies at Greenan Ford beside Ballinacor on 24 September.[94] Fiach's tactics clearly demonstrate that he had learned from the experience of the last war. Russell's capture of Ballinacor in January 1595 had forced Fiach into a mainly defensive war; now Fiach was determined to prevent Russell from establishing a foothold in Glenmalure. This set the tone of the conflict. Throughout the winter, Russell attempted to break into Glenmalure, while Fiach battled to keep him out. Furthermore, the government's efforts were actively supported by the loyalist gentlemen of O'Byrnes' Country and those of Co. Wexford and Co. Dublin. In the meantime Tyrone had opened negotiations

89 MacCarthy, 'The O'Byrnes of Wicklow', p. 235; *Cal. Carew MSS, 1589–1600*, no. 270, p. 248. 90 O'Brien, 'Feagh McHugh', p. 17; Hore, *Wexford town*, vi, pp 436–7. 91 Edwards, 'In Tyrone's shadow', p. 241; *Cal. Carew MSS, 1589–1600*, no. 270, p. 253. 92 *CSPI, 1596–7*, no. 20, vi, p. 111, nos 6–7, p. 137, no. 15, p. 139. See ibid., no. 48, p. 129, no. 27, p. 167; AFM, 1596. 93 Ibid., no. 20, p. 110, see also ibid., no. 10, p. 103. 94 He also made an example of the treacherous sergeant and some other soldiers by executing them. See *Cal. Carew MSS, 1589–1600*, no. 270, p. 249; *CSPI, 1596–7*, no. 32, p. 117. One of Fiach's brothers was killed in the fighting between 24 September and 14 October, see Hore, *Wexford town*, vi, p. 439.

with Norris. According to his letter dated 12 September to Fiach, Tyrone claimed that he had obtained Norris' agreement to a peace lasting sixteen days that included Fiach.[95] If so, Russell disregarded it and pursued a scorched earth policy in Wicklow that winter. In response, Fiach's troops vigorously guarded Glenmalure, fighting fierce engagements with Lee's soldiers at Greenan Ford on 3 and 23 October and 10 November. Significantly, the bitterness of the combat forced Russell to come to Lee's rescue during all three melées.[96] In spite of Fiach's strenuous defence of Glenmalure, Russell had gained his foothold by mid-November, and once this foothold was consolidated, the war began to go badly for Fiach. On 4 November, Russell executed the foster-brother of Féilim mac Fiach O'Byrne before putting the natural son of Fiach to death twelve days later.[97] Russell's pressure caused Fiach to create diversions throughout Leinster, appealing with the Butler brothers that month to uncommitted Irish Catholic nobles to fight for their faith.[98]

With Russell in the ascendancy, Fiach wasn't safe anywhere and was nearly captured with Rose in the early hours of a November morning.[99] But the misery caused by the war convinced many to call for its cessation. Sir Geoffrey Fenton, secretary of the Dublin council, wrote to Sir Robert Cecil on 25 November, telling them that famine was widespread and that the war against Fiach should cease. According to a letter dated 22 November from Loftus and Bishop Thomas Jones of Meath to Burghley (the father of Sir Robert Cecil), Fiach was never included in the peace concluded by Tyrone and Norris. In the face of Russell's adamant refusal to admit Fiach to protection, Tyrone hovered with a force of several thousand near Dundalk and threatened to enter the Pale to draw the heat out of the offensive against Fiach.[100] Despite Tyrone's posturing, Russell held his nerve and informed the earl on 30 November that Fiach would continue to be persecuted 'according his deserts'.[101] On 2 December, Tyrone refused to accept Russell's interpretation of his peace with Norris, telling Fiach to make terms and saying that his confederates would not make peace until Fiach had his pardon. Two days later Tyrone again wrote to Russell, instructing him to halt his Wicklow campaign.[102] On 8 December, Norris warned Cecil that Tyrone's forces were on the Pale borders and that the earl had proclaimed he would to go to war unless Fiach was pardoned. Tyrone's concern for Fiach was well-justified, for, on 11 December, Ormond told Russell that his nephews were preparing to make their flight to Ulster.[103]

Fiach now changed his tactics in dealing with Russell's troops at Greenan. He attempted to isolate them from the main body of Russell's campaign army by cutting their supply lines.[104] Later that month it was noted that the government

---

95 *CSPI, 1596–7*, no. 16, p. 142; ibid., no. 32, i, p. 118. **96** Ibid, no. 3, p. 156; *Cal. Carew MSS, 1589–1600*, no. 270, pp 250–2. **97** *Cal. Carew MSS, 1589–1600*, no. 270, p. 252. **98** *CSPI, 1596–7*, no.7, v, p. 159. **99** Ibid., no. 3, p. 156. **100** Ibid., no. 37, p. 175, no. 2, p. 180; see also ibid., no. 27, p. 167. **101** *Cal. Carew MSS, 1589–1600*, no. 254, p. 185. **102** Ibid., no. 255, p. 185; see also no. 256, p. 186. **103** *CSPI, 1596–7*, no. 10, p. 184; see also ibid., no. 31, iv, p. 192. **104** Confirming this strategic shift were his attacks upon their lifelines – the supply trains.

offensive slowed as Russell was encountering considerable difficulties in sup-
plying his troops in the central highlands. Broadly speaking, though, the military
situation was bleak for Fiach. To the south of Glenmalure, Chichester and
Ormond inflicted serious reverses upon the MacMurrough-Kavanaghs and Piers
Butler of Cloghgrenan in the Briskillo, while Lee enjoyed a minor victory over
Fiach himself late in December. On 27 December a confident Russell wrote to
Cecil, advising that the campaign should be pursued until the bitter end. But yet
Fiach grimly hung on, forcing Norris to entertain the pleas of Tyrone for his
pardon.[105]

The war continued into 1597. Even though Fiach's army suffered considerable
losses, he still offered stout resistance. In January, Tyrone now moved a step closer
to outright war with the English by sending Captain Richard Tyrrell, his
lieutenant, into the midlands.[106] There he linked up with Uaithne mac Ruaidhrí,
but was wounded in a skirmish. In spite of this, Uaithne ensured that Tyrell was
able to meet Piers Butler of Cloghgrenan, who had travelled from the Briskillo
to be guided to Tyrone by Fiach's troops under Féilim Riabhach O'Connor.
Soon afterwards, Tyrone's negotiations with Norris bore fruit, in a peace that
seemingly included Fiach. On 5 January, the earl wrote to Fiach, telling him of
the news and instructing him to respect a cessation.[107] Russell was no respecter
of this truce and continued fighting. The natural death of Barnaby O'Toole,
which took place on 17 January in Glenmalure, deprived Fiach of yet another of
his lieutenants,[108] and may have prompted him to swiftly shore up his alliance
with the O'Tooles of Castlekevin by arranging the marriage of his daughter
Margaret, Walter Riabhach's widow, to Barnaby's brother Féilim.[109] On 24
January, Secretary Sir Geoffrey Fenton championed the Pale's desire for peace
and questioned the purpose of Fiach's continued prosecution.[110] Strikingly,
Fenton mentioned that Fiach's military position had improved and that he had
actually derived encouragement from Russell's inability to finish him off. On 8
February, Fiach wrote to Norris, enquiring whether he was privy to Tyrone's
peace.[111] If Fiach had his doubts about where he stood in it, Norris confirmed
them. On receipt of Fiach's request, Norris dispatched a letter to Cecil, telling
him of Fiach's desire to be admitted to the peace. In spite of the increasing
hardships suffered by the English army in the Leinster mountains, Norris
recommended the general prosecution of Tyrone and Fiach; and in a letter to
Burghley the next day, Russell also rejected Fiach's application.[112]

Although his attack of 14 December ultimately failed and cost the lives of Muiris Dubh
Kavanagh, his nephew and secretary, his plan had some success in alleviating pressure. See *Cal.
Carew MSS, 1589–1600*, no. 270, p. 253; *CSPI, 1596–7*, no. 27, pp 169–70, see also no. 34, p. 173.
105 *CSPI, 1596–7*, no. 31, vi, p. 192; no. 13, viii, p. 207; see also ibid., no. 10, p. 184, no. 13, i, p.
186.   **106** Ibid., no. 7, i, p. 240; see also ibid., no. 13, vii, p. 206.   **107** Ibid., no. 13, x, p. 207; see
also ibid., no. 65, i, p. 226.   **108** O'Toole, *The history of the Clan O'Toole*, p. 370. Captain
Thomas Lee was granted the custody of Barnaby's lands and the wardship of Fiach, Barnaby's
heir, probably in May 1597, see *Cal. Fiants Eliz*, no. 6105.   **109** On 13 July 1601 Féilim of
Castlekevin, Margey Birne, his wife, and Rose Basnett, his mother, were pardoned, see *Cal.
Fiants Eliz*, no. 6560.   **110** *CSPI, 1596–7*, no. 46, p. 219.   **111** Ibid., no. 71, p. 228.   **112** Ibid.,

With his back firmly against the wall, Fiach displayed remarkable leadership, and shared the hardships of his men. But he continued to believe in the Spanish. Sir Edward Moore of Mellifont reported that Muircheartach O'Toole, Fiach's emissary to Philip II, was in Dungannon, having returned to Ireland through Scotland from Spain with Philip's credentials. Meanwhile the mood for peace among the Dubliners increased when an ammunition train exploded on 13 March, destroying some streets.[113] The strain was also showing among Fiach's ranks: Piers Butler of Cloghgrenan asked protection of Sir William Harpoole, constable of Carlow castle, on the same day. Yet Fiach defiantly held out. And as war weariness set in all round, Russell became increasingly desperate to kill his adversary. Another of his secret operations to assassinate Fiach was apparently bungled on 14/15 March.[114] Yet while Russell was steadily drawing the net in, Fiach still used his considerable guile to try and effect a ceasefire. According to two pieces of disputed evidence, both Harrington and Harpoole were negotiating with Fiach unknown to Russell. Significantly, Rose, Fiach's premier envoy, figured in both sets of allegations. The first piece of evidence emerged within weeks of Fiach's death and the second some thirteen years later. During summer 1597, Lee accused Harrington of holding several secret audiences with Rose during the height of Russell's offensive.[115] According to the second piece of evidence, which surfaced in March 1610, Donnchadh O'Brien, 4th earl of Thomond, also accused Sir William Harpoole of harbouring Rose during Russell's last campaign.[116] While this evidence cannot be taken as wholly trustworthy, it is possible that Fiach was communicating with Harrington and Harpoole. Also, he may have sent his wife away from the war zone to safety as the military situation became desperate. By late March the writing was on the wall. Confirming this fact, Féilim mac Toirdhealbhach O'Toole of Powerscourt, Fiach's brother-in-law and erstwhile ally, was in service.[117] Fiach's precarious position was further exacerbated by the killings of the sons of Aodh Geangach O'Byrne of Clonmore as well as James Butler of Cloghgrenan by Lee during March.[118] According to a spy's report of 24 March, Tyrone was now seriously worried.[119] In April Tyrone threatened to send a force to Wicklow and met with Norris before telling Fiach to send Rose to attend the talks on 17 April. On 30 April 1597, Norris advised Cecil of Tyrone's request that Fiach be pardoned.[120]

This came too late for Fiach. It is clear that he was still in Glenmalure, fighting the English as well as commuting between his forces throughout East

no. 96, p. 234 and no. 99, p. 235.   **113** Ibid., no. 102, p. 236; *Cal. Carew MSS, 1589–1600*, no. 270, pp 256–7.   **114** Price, 'Notes', p. 169.   **115** *CSPI, 1596–7*, no. 70, p. 304.   **116** *CSPI, 1608–10*, no. 651, p. 401; Cosby, 'The English settlers in Queen's County, 1570–1603', p. 287.   **117** *Cal. Carew MSS, 1589–1600*, no. 270, p. 257.   **118** Ibid., no. 270, pp 256–8; Cathaoir Ruadh Kavanagh, brother to Fiach's first wife, was also captured in the Briskillo during March 1597. He was probably later executed by Russell's forces, see also Nicholls, 'The Kavanaghs', (1981), p. 193.   **119** Tyrone reputedly said: 'if wars continued, he would make Feagh McHugh's glynns more hot for the lord deputy then they were for Lord Grey'. See *CSPI, 1596–7*, no. 37, p. 249.   **120** *CSPI, 1596–7*, no. 111, ii, p. 272 and no. 128, p. 278.

Leinster. His decision to remain there was not his undoing: treachery was. His whereabouts were disclosed to Russell by a disgruntled relative – possibly the spy of Sheriff Joshua Mynce of Carlow. In the small hours of Sunday, 8 May 1597, Russell's forces, guided by the traitor, captured and killed Fiach.[121] Fiach's death hastened the advance of English government in Leinster and throughout the country. The reactions to Fiach's end were mixed. Russell, of course, made the most of it. His diarist recorded on 8 May that 'his carcass was brought to Dublin, to the great comfort and joy of all that province'.[122] On 9 May he recorded that 'the people of the country met him with great joy and gladness, and, as their manner is, bestowed many blessings on him [Russell] for performing so good a deed'. The same day that Fiach's head arrived in Dublin, Loftus and the council announced to the English privy council 'that ancient and cankered traitor' had been killed.[123] Secretary Fenton's letter to Cecil about the death of Fiach shows palpable relief, exclaiming, 'they (the Spanish) built more for their purpose upon Feagh than upon Tyrone himself'.[124] On the other hand, Sir Edward Stanley, in a letter dated 12 May to Cecil, wrote that the hearts of the people 'are so hardened, that few of them rejoice at any good service done'. There are also extant eyewitness accounts of the McKeogh poets of Wicklow who saw the grizzly display of Fiach's butchered corpse along the walls of Dublin Castle; Domhnall McKeogh's lament was particularly heartfelt, wishing for blindness after viewing the horrible sight.[125]

From the grave, Fiach still cast a long shadow in Leinster and Ireland. Undoubtedly, such was the effect of his memory that Féilim and Réamain, who held their father's religious beliefs continued to resist the New English conquest of Leinster. Militarily, though, the situation in Leinster was grim, but Fiach's remaining confederates were galvanized by the manner of Fiach's death and the exhibition of his remains at Dublin. On a wider scale, though, Fiach's end was a huge setback to Tyrone. The untenable military situation in Leinster perhaps spurred Tyrone to encourage Domhnall Spainneach MacMurrough-Kavanagh and the sons of Fiach to withdraw into the safety of Ulster. They were joined on their trip northward by Uaithne mac Ruaidhrí and his elder half-brother, Brian Riabhach O'More, further proof of the crisis besetting the Catholic leadership of Leinster.[126] The escape of Féilim mac Fiach caused irritation at court, spurring Cecil to predict: 'his son be still out, his youth will better his father's age'.[127] Others were not so fortunate. After the refusal of Sir William Harpoole to grant protection to Piers Butler of Cloghgrenan, the latter escaped from the increasingly desperate situation in Wicklow to the midlands. From there he tried to proceed northward along the Shannon to the security offered by Tyrone.

---

121 AFM, 1597; *Cal. Carew MSS, 1589–1600*, no. 270, pp 258–9. The O'Mores were fighting in West Leinster on 4 May 1597, see *Cal. Fiants Eliz*, no. 6077.   122 Ibid, no. 270, p. 259.
123 *CSPI, 1596–7*, no. 22, p. 286.   124 Ibid, no. 25, p. 287.   125 *Leabhar Branach*, no. 42, pp 151–3. See also the poem of Domhnall's probable son, Donnchadh mac Domhnaill, no. 44, pp 155–8.   126 *CSPI, 1596–7*, no. 115, p. 322 & no. 106, p. 388 see especially no. 30, i, p. 345; *CSPI, 1598–99*, no. 112, p. 213.   127 Ibid., no. 60, p. 300.

Ormond, eager to remove the stain of rebellion from his family, ensured Piers never made it to Tyrone. The earl hunted Piers down, capturing the fugitive before having him publicly beheaded at Thurles in late May.

The rise of Brian Riabhach O'More to the forefront of the leadership of the Leinster Catholics in arms was an unexpected event arising from the death of Fiach. Brian Riabhach was a natural son of Ruaidhrí Óg O'More from an affair with a woman of the O'Carrolls of Ely. Ruaidhrí Óg had never acknowledged Brian Riabhach as his son – which may mean that his dalliance with Brian Riabhach's mother was conducted behind the back of her husband, a leading O'More vassal. According to Sir Charles O'Carroll of Ely, Brian Riabhach's life took a dramatic twist in 1589, when his mother told him that Ruaidhrí Óg was his real father. This had a major affect upon the young man, transforming him from an vassal (one of the mac Lochlainn branch of the O'Mores of Laois) into one of the most prominent claimants to the O'More leadership. Brian Riabhach's emergence as a major force in Laois politics must have irked his half-brother Uaithne and his O'Byrne mentors. Brian Riabhach may have also felt aggrieved over the favouring of the claims of Uaithne (his junior), considering that, as recognized sons of Ruaidhrí Óg, they had an equal claim to the lordship. By the early 1590s, Brian Riabhach, through his determination to become a force in the midlands, had come to the attention of the English. In 1592 he went to London probably en route to join the Spanish forces in the Netherlands. In Cheapside in London, he encountered his enemy – Sir Charles. O'Carroll immediately went to the authorities and had him arrested and thrown in jail. It is unknown how long Brian Riabhach remained imprisoned, but he may have secured his release by promising service against Fiach and Uaithne. In July 1594 a John Byrd conveyed Brian Riabhach's offers to Sir Robert Cecil, saying that O'More would deliver the head of Fiach and O'Byrne's secret correspondence with Tyrone.[128]

Brian Riabhach did not keep his promise to attack Fiach and Uaithne, but, on the other hand, he did not actively support or oppose the activities of Fiach and his nephew. His relations with Fiach were, in fact, as the latter urged him in November 1596 to fight for his Catholic faith. In spite of a rapidly deteriorating military situation in the midlands for the Catholics, Brian Riabhach and Uaithne were clearly at loggerheads in Laois. On 13 May 1597 Brian Riabhach complained to Tyrone that 'he had only the few men that Ony O'More, chief of the O'Mores and son of the late Rory Oge, had in his country. All others that gave their consent to O'Neill, would no more help him than hang themselves.'[129] When Brian Riabhach arrived in Ulster, Tyrone placed him, Féilim mac Fiach O'Byrne and Murchadh MacMurrough-Kavanagh in charge of the fort on the Ulster Blackwater. They did not exactly cover themselves in glory, losing the fort to English forces that July. However, Tyrone was impressed with Brian

---

128 *Calender of manuscripts of the marquis of Salisbury*, iv, pp 285, 354, 564.   129 *CSPI, 1596–7*, no. 33, p. 289.

Riabhach's capabilities, and in August dispatched him with Réamain O'Byrne and 1,000 men to Wicklow. It was only in late September that Tyrone consented to send the rest of the Leinster émigrés home to continue Fiach's war. Their first target was the midland plantations and Co. Kildare before passing into the mountains of East Leinster. On 18 October Archbishop Loftus reported that they, with 800 of Tyrone's belated reinforcements under Brian Riabhach, had burned towns within six miles of Dublin before attacking the English of Wexford.[130] While Brian Riabhach continued to attack the English in East Leinster before raiding Upper Ossory, Uaithne mac Ruaidhrí and his brother Edmund Carrach O'More were dispatched to Laois to attack the plantations. There they won a major engagement on 7 December against Warham St Leger, the governor of Laois.[131]

Despite Tyrone's truce of December 1597 with the English, fighting continued in the midlands, although in East Leinster it seems to have largely ceased. In fact, Féilim O'Byrne in January 1598 agreed to respect Tyrone's truce, gaining his pardon in May,[132] but in the midlands the O'Mores were eager to prolong the war in order to destroy the plantations. Uaithne mac Ruaidhrí in early 1598 travelled northward to Ulster to confer with Tyrone to ask for more troops to complete the task. During Easter 1598, Brian Riabhach also pushed into north Tipperary, spending the holiday in the O'Meagher lordship of Ikerrin. There he was attacked by James fitzEdward Butler without the consent of Ormond. The Butler forces were defeated by the Catholic forces and captured their leader; within a week, though, Brian Riabhach handed his captive into the custody of Ormond. In May Uaithne mac Ruaidhrí combined forces with Brian Riabhach to spoil parts of Ossory and Kilkenny before penerating Wexford to attack the forces of the Dublin government. On 19 May the Catholic forces enjoyed a major success against the combined forces of Sir Henry Wallop and Captain Richard Masterson. This victory was quickly followed up by a sustained campaign against the English of Wexford throughout much of June – particularly against the settlers living near the town of Enniscorthy. However, Brian Riabhach's own end was not long in coming. At Camagh near Ballyfin in Laois on 6 July he was mortally wounded while resisting Ormond's troops, and died on 10 July.[133] This left Uaithne mac Ruaidhrí as the principal Catholic

---

130 Ibid., no. 30, i, p. 345; see also ibid., no. 22, p. 423, see also no. 7, p. 414; For Féilim's pardon of 28 May, see *Cal. Fiants Eliz*, no. 6232. Interestingly this pardon includes Cathaoir, Domhnall, Toirdhealbhach – the sons of Aodh Dubh. In June there was considerable disturbances between Ormond the Catholic forces in the midlands. In a major battle with Ormond's forces, Brian O'More was killed. AFM, 1598.   **131** AFM, 1597; O'Sullivan Beare, p. 97.   **132** *CSPI, 1598–9*, no. 39, p. 47; AFM, 1598; *Cal. Fiants Eliz*, nos 6216, 6217. For a fresh commission of martial law on 25 March 1598 to Charles Montague and Gerald Byrne for O'Byrnes' Country and a similar commission on 29 March for Kildare to James Fitzgerald, its sheriff. *CSPI, 1598–9*, no. 72, p. 180 & no. 1, p. 218 & no. 135, p. 305; The tension in Leinster is evident by the grant of martial law to Robert Bowen on 17 June 1598. See *Cal. Fiants Eliz*, no. 6240.   **133** AFM, 1598; O'Sullivan Beare, pp 104–5.

commander in the midlands and in Leinster. Flushed with the success of his victory over Sir Henry Bagenal at the Yellow Ford on 14 August, Tyrone ordered Uaithne, Réamain Burke and Tyrrell to extend the war into Munster. Before Uaithne departed for the campaign in Munster, he took the precaution of securing the Catholic position in the midlands, by seizing the castles of Strabally and Ballybrittas, Co. Laois, and Croaghan, Co. Offaly. In late September he then transferred the midland command to his brother Edmund Carrach O'More, appointing the latter his lieutenant. During the Munster campaign in October, Uaithne and his allies devastated the province from north Tipperary to Kilmallock in Co. Limerick, installing James fitzThomas Fitzgerald as earl of Desmond before returning to Leinster. Central to Uaithne's strategy was his determination to take the fort of Maryborough; this he attempted this through direct assaults and by ambushing its supply trains, mauling Ormond's relief column at Blackford in late 1598.[134]

By late 1598, war was back on the agenda of the Irish of East Leinster. In October, Féilim mac Fiach O'Byrne held a conference with other Catholic leaders, principally Domhnall Spainneach and Viscount Mountgarret, before returning to war in 1599. Uaithne mac Ruaidhrí thrived in these circumstances, enjoying spectacular success: on 17 May, along with Tyrrell and Mountgarret's sons, he inflicted an embarrassing reverse in a pass near Maryborough upon the army of Robert Devereux, earl of Essex, and the new lord deputy. In spite of this success, they were unable to prevent Essex from placing a strong garrison the next day in Mountgarret's castle at Ballyragget, Co. Kilkenny. Eleven days later, however, Uaithne mac Ruaidhrí joined Féilim O'Byrne to annihilate the column of Sir Henry Harrington in Wicklow. However, the effect of these successes was blunted somewhat by Essex's battering of the assembled Catholic forces of Leinster on 29 June outside Arklow.[135]

In spite of Essex's victory, Catholic resistance in Leinster continued into 1600. On 9 April, Uaithne mac Ruaidhrí earned a fortuitous and unexpected success, capturing Ormond at Corrandhu near Ballyragget. On that occasion, Uaithne with the Jesuit, Father James Archer, attended a parley with the earl and several English officials, during which Ormond became abusive and threatened to harm Archer. Uaithne's supporters, fearing that Ormond was about to draw his sword on the priest, surrounded the earl and apprehended him before driving off his troops. Uaithne then spirited Ormond into Laois before lodging him in the MacGillapatrick castle of Gortnaclea, where Archer tried for three weeks to convince the earl to return to the Catholic faith of his ancestors and to join Tyrone. Either at the end of April or at the beginning of May, Uaithne transferred Ormond back into Laois and onwards to the O'Dempsey fortress of Ballybrittas. It was reported that Tyrone wrote to Uaithne, asking him to deliver

134 AFM, 1598; O'Sullivan Beare, p. 122.   **135** *CSPI, 1598–9*, no. 144, p. 333; see also *CSPI, 1599–1600*, no. 74, p. 53, no. 75, pp 58–60; AFM, 1599, 1600; *Cal. Carew MSS, 1589–1600*, no. 305, pp 310–2; O'Sullivan Beare, p. 124.

Ormond to him. Uaithne refused – which indicate a considerable independence in mind and in his military command. Ormond remained in Ballybrittas castle until terms were arranged on 12 June for his release.[136] On 16 June Uaithne released Ormond for a ransom of £3,000 and 17 hostages. Despite this success, 1600 was the decisive year of the war in Leinster. Essex was replaced as lord deputy by Charles Blount, Lord Mountjoy; unlike the somewhat erratic Essex, Mountjoy was systematic in his approach to the war in Leinster. There was heavy fighting throughout the summer,[137] and the increase in pressure on the Leinster Catholics was dramatic. On 11 August, Mountjoy and his army hunted down Uaithne mac Ruaidhrí O'More and his brother Fiach. They were finally cornered near Vicarstown Co. Offaly, Uaithne mac Ruaidhrí receiving two fatal gunshot wounds. Before he died that night, he appointed Uaithne mac Seáain O'More as his successor and urged him to continue to fight for the Catholic cause. The dying man, fearful that his head fall into English hands and be displayed as a trophy, ordered his followers to remove it from his dead corpse and bury it secretly.[138] The loss of Uaithne mac Ruaidhrí, the most talented Irish commander in Leinster, was a disaster for the Catholic forces in the province; it demoralized their leaders, undermining their will to fight on. Accordingly the last king of Leinster (Domhnall Spainneach MacMurrough-Kavanagh) sur-rendered on 24 August to Mountjoy near Cashel. Mountjoy's troops made short work of Uaithne mac Seáain O'More, pressing him so fiercely that he fled from Laois into Munster to an uncertain fate. Uaithne mac Ruaidhrí's brothers Réamain and Edmund Carrach O'More fought on into 1601, but the desertion of most of their followers rendered their position impossible; Réamainn's surrender during 1601 effectively ended resistance in the midlands.[139]

The death of Uaithne mac Ruaidhrí O'More and the surrender of Domhnall Spainneach convinced Féilim O'Byrne to seek a truce. In September, Ormond met him and agreed to grant him his personal protection.[140] Mountjoy, however, was determined to take the fight into the Leinster mountains. In a campaign reminiscent of those of Grey and Russell, Mountjoy went for the kill, seizing Ballinacor from Féilim, in a surprise night-time attack, on 6 December. Although inclement weather and the flooding of the Avonmore prevented Mountjoy from finishing off Féilim, the war was effectively over by late January

---

136 *CSPI, 1600–1600*, no. 148, i & ii, p. 127; Carrigan, *History … Ossory*, ii, pp 103–4; AFM, 1600.   **137** AFM, 1600. On 19 March a commission of martial law was granted to Henry Davells, sheriff of Carlow, see *Cal. Fiants Eliz*, no. 6375. For cracks in Féilim's forces see the pardon on 13 June of his McDonnell commander, Walter McEdmund of Booley boye Co. Dublin see ibid., no. 6406. See other pardons: 7 July, no. 6408, Gerald McMortagh Kavanagh; 12 September, no. 6432, William McHubert O'Byrne; 13 Sept, no. 6433 Walter Boye Roche of Newton Co. Wexford; no. 6447, Brian mac Donnchadh Kavanagh of Ballyloghan Carlow. **138** HMC, *De L'Isle and Dudley MSS*, ii (London, 1934), p. 483; *Cal. Carew MSS, 1589–1600*, no. 442, p. 432.   **139** *CSPI, 1600–1600*, no. 15, p. 422; Hamilton, 'Fiach MacAodha Uí Bhroin and Domhnall Spainneach Caomhanach', p. 113; O'Sullivan Beare, pp 132, 176.   **140** Ibid., no. 55, p. 449, no. 92, p. 472.

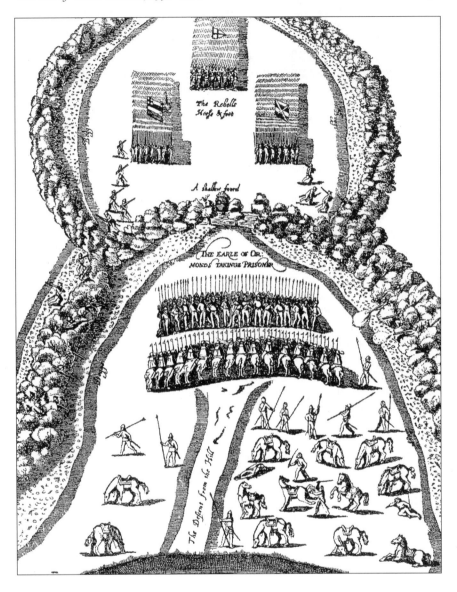

The Rebells
Horse & foot

A shallow foord

THE EARLE OF OR:
MONDS TAKINGE PRISONER

The Descent from the Hill

6 The capture of the earl of Ormond by Uaithne mac Ruaidhrí, 1600 (from *Pacata Hibernia*, 1633)

1601. Finding themselves virtually alone, Féilim and his brother Réamain surrendered in March before the Dublin council, to be followed by Féilim O'Toole of Castlekevin.[141] The government was inclined to mercy; this change in policy was designed to finally pacify the formerly disaffected Catholic Leinster aristocracy and to detach them from Tyrone. On 15 May, Domhnall Spainneach was granted his pardon, while the O'Byrne brothers along with the O'Tooles of Castlekevin were pardoned in July.[142]

Féilim and Domhnall Spainneach resolved to become loyal subjects of Elizabeth. This momentous decision finally ended the war that Fiach had started in Leinster, and it was confirmed by their refusal, despite Tyrone's urgent request, to attack government forces after Don Juan del Aguila's expeditionary force landed in September 1601 at Kinsale. No doubt Féilim was determined to avoid the fate of Féilim mac Toirdhealbhach O'Toole of Powerscourt who was murdered by the Wingfields, planters, on 14 May 1603 (they would later receive a grant of the dead man's estates).[143] And so, both men embarked upon the transition from warlord to landowner, declaring their loyalty to James I. Féilim, in particular, was intent upon preserving Fiach's lordship by incorporating himself into the new order; he received a grant of his estates from James on 25 March 1604, and entered into negotiations in October 1605 with the government for the inclusion of his lordship within the proposed county of Wicklow. This led to a prolonged dispute over territory with his brother Réamain, but they settled their differences satisfactorily by March 1606. Their consent allowed the establishment that year of the last of the Irish counties – Co. Wicklow.[144] The shiring of the Wicklow nobility's estates, combined with the Cosby victory over the O'Mores at Aughnahilly that year finally stilled the heartbeat of Gaelic Leinster.

For the O'Mores and their vassals the fruits of defeat were unbearably bitter, as many of them were forcibly transplanted in June 1609 from their Laois homeland to Tarbert, Co. Kerry.[145] Others would not suffer the ignominy of transplantation; instead, an unnamed brother of Uaithne mac Ruaidhrí O'More led them into exile and into the service of Archduke Albert, governor of the Spanish Netherlands. By 1616, the O'Mores in Kerry had tired of their exile and

141 *CSPI, 1600–1*, no. 82, p. 89, no. 15, p. 152, no. 105, p. 240; *Cal. Carew MSS, 1601–1603*, **142** *Cal. Fiants Eliz*, no. 6517 Domhnall's pardon also included Muircheartach mac Gerald Kavanagh of Clonmullen, Edmund mac Brian Kavanagh and Eleanor, Domhnall's wife and also Edmund's sister. Eleanor was also Fiach's niece and therefore Féilim's first cousin. Significantly this pardon also includes Donal O'Cahan, Toirdhealbhach O'Neyle and fourteen O'Dorchys. These must have been troops sent by Tyrone at some point. Earlier Richard Butler son and heir of Mountgarret was also pardoned on 28 March, see ibid., no. 6484. For the O'Toole pardon on 13 July, see no. 6560. For Féilim's pardon, see no. 6577.   **143** *CSPI, 1601–3*, p. 381; *Cal. Inquisitions* J 1 11/18, p. 326; O'Toole, *The history of the Clan O'Toole*, pp 411–12, 426.   **144** *CSPI, 1603–6*, no. 567, p. 342, no. 661, p. 416.   **145** Cosby, 'English settlers in Queen's County, 1570–1603', p. 284; Dunlop, 'The plantation of Leix and Offaly', pp 91–3; *CSPI, 1615–25*, no. 239, p. 121.

were returning to their Laois homeland, to the trepidation of the planters. Although Gaelic Leinster was dead, the age-old issues of land, law and culture (and now religion and parliamentary representation) remained deeply contentious matters. In fact, the struggle between the Catholics and Protestants of Ireland had been merely postponed. These issues would dominate Irish politics over the coming decades, leaving the deepest of divisions and the most enduring scars. In November 1641 the tension finally snapped. On snowy November nights, many of the Irish nobility (most of them verging on bankruptcy) rose up with their retainers throughout much of Leinster against the New English settlers and expelled them from their plantations. The later deposition of the Wicklow planter Thomas Trowte reveals how some of the O'Byrnes stormed his house at Rathdrum and threw him out into a blizzard. As he fled for his life over the snow-capped mountains of Wicklow to the safety of Dublin, the cries of the Irish nobles rang in his ears, proclaiming (he reported) 'that the land was theirs and all that thereon was'.

Appendix

1 Donnchadh MacMurrough (*sl.*1115), king of Leinster (*r.*1110–15)
2 Diarmait MacMurrough (*d.*1117), king of Leinster (*r.*1115–17)
3 Énna MacMurrough (*d.*1126), king of Leinster (*r.*1117–26)
4 Diarmait MacMurrough (*d.*1171), king of Leinster (*r.*1127–66 (*dep.*) 1167–71).
5 Murchadh MacMurrough (*sl.*1172), king of Uí Cheinnselaig (*r.*1166–7 (*dep.*), 1171–2)
6 Domhnall Kavanagh (*sl.*1175), king of Leinster (*r.*1171–5)
7 Muircheartach MacMurrough (*d.*1193), king of Uí Cheinnselaig (*r.*1172–93).
8 Muircheartach MacMurrough (*sl.*1282), king of Leinster (*r. c.*1265–82). (His brother Art mentioned as king of Leinster in 1276)
9 Muiris MacMurrough (*d. c.*1314), king of Leinster (*r. c.*1290–1314).
10 Domhnall Riabhach MacMurrough (*d.*1317), king of Leinster (*r.*1314–17).
11 Unnamed figure (*sl.*1323), king of Leinster, (*r. c.*1317–23)
12 Domhnall mac Airt MacMurrough (*d. c.*1338), king of Leinster (*r. c.*1323–38).
13 Domhnall Óg MacMurrough (*sl.*1347), king of Leinster (*r. c.*1338–47).
14 Muircheartach MacMurrough (*ex.*1354), king of Leinster (*r.*1347–54).
15 Art MacMurrough (*d.*1362), king of Leinster (*r.*1354–62).
16 Diarmait Láimhdhearg MacMurrough (*ex.*1369), king of Leinster (*r.* 1362–9).
17 Donnchadh MacMurrough (*sl.*1375), king of Leinster (*r.*1369–75).
18 Art MacMurrough (*d.* 1414), king of Uí Cheinnselaig (*r.* 1375-79).
19 Art Mór MacMurrough, (*d.* 1416/17), king of Leinster (*r.* 1375–1416/7).
20 Donnchadh MacMurrough (*d.*1478), king of Leinster (*r. c.* 1416/7–57).
21 Domhnall Riabhach Kavanagh (*d.* 1476), king of Leinster (*r. c.* 1457–76).
22 Murchadh Ballach MacMurrough (*d.* 1511/12), king of Leinster (*r.* 1476–1511/2).
23 Art Buidhe MacMurrough (*d.* 1517), king of Leinster (*r.* 1511/2–17).
24 Gerald MacMurrough (*d.* 1523), king of Leinster (*r.* 1517–23).
25 Muiris MacMurrough (*d.* 1531), king of Leinster (*r.* 1523–31).
26 Cathaoir MacInnycross MacMurrough (*d. c.* 1544), king of Leinster (*r.* 1532–44).
27 Muircheartach MacMurrough (*d.*1547), leader of the MacMurroughs (*r. c.* 1544–7).
28 Cathaoir mac Airt MacMurrough-Kavanagh (*d.* 1554), captain of the MacMurroughs (*r.* 1547–52), baron of Ballyanne (1554).
29 Murchadh MacMurrough (*ex.*1557), leader of the MacMurroughs, baron of Coolnaleen.
30 Brian mac Cathaoir Kavanagh (*d.* 1578), most powerful of his nation.
31 Crimthann MacMurrough, (*ex.* 1582), claimant to Leinster kingship.
32 Muircheartach Óg MacMurrough-Kavanagh (*sl.* 1586)
33 Domhnall Spainneach Kavanagh (*d.* 1632), king of Leinster (*r. c.*1590–1632).

246 Appendix

TWELVE GENEALOGIES

1 The MacMurrough-Kavanagh kings of Leinster, *c*.1126–1430
1a The family of Donnchadh MacMurrough, *c*.1430–1630
1b The family of Gerald MacMurrough, *c*.1430–1645
2 The senior O'Byrnes, *c*.1260–1600
2a The O'Byrnes of Críoch Raghnuill, *c*.1170–1579
2b The O'Byrne house of Ballinacor, *c*.1490–1652
3 The O'Toole over-kings of Fercullen and Imaal, *c*.1295–1652
4 The O'More kings of Laois, *c*.1280–1601
5 The O'Connor Faly kings of Offaly *c*.1050–1590
6 The MacGillapatrick kings and barons of Ossory/Upper Ossory *c*.1160–1613
7 The O'Carroll kings of Ely, *c*.1200–1581
8 The O'Connor kings of Connacht, *c*.1050–1316
8a The family of Ruaidhrí O'Connor, *c*.1156–1273
8b The family of Cathal O'Connor, *c*.1200–1316
9 The lords of Leinster, *c*.1171–1330
10 The Fitzgeralds of Kildare, *c*.1270–1600
11 The Butlers of Ormond, *c*.1300–1614
12 The monarchs of England, *c*.1171–1625

Outline Genealogy 1: The MacMurrough-Kavanagh
kings of Leinster, *c*.1126–1430

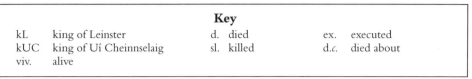

Key

kL	king of Leinster	d.	died	ex.	executed
kUC	king of Uí Cheinnselaig	sl.	killed	*d.c.*	died about
viv.	alive				

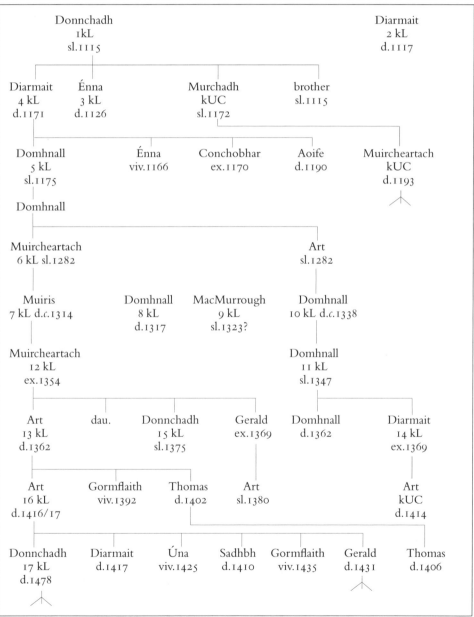

Outline Genealogy 1a: The family of Donnchadh
MacMurrough, *c.*1430–1630

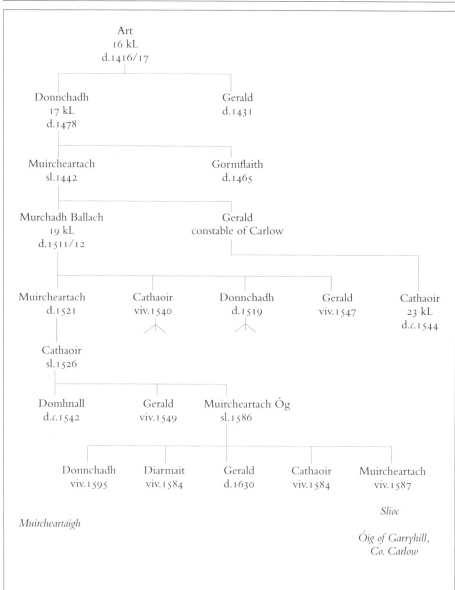

Key					
kL	king of Leinster	viv.	alive	sl.	killed
kUC	king of Uí Cheinnselaig	d.	died	ex.	executed

Art
16 kL
d.1416/17

Donnchadh
17 kL
d.1478

Gerald
d.1431

Muircheartach
sl.1442

Gormflaith
d.1465

Murchadh Ballach
19 kL
d.1511/12

Gerald
constable of Carlow

Muircheartach
d.1521

Cathaoir
viv.1540

Donnchadh
d.1519

Gerald
viv.1547

Cathaoir
23 kL
d.*c.*1544

Cathaoir
sl.1526

Domhnall
d.*c.*1542

Gerald
viv.1549

Muircheartach Óg
sl.1586

Donnchadh
viv.1595

Diarmait
viv.1584

Gerald
d.1630

Cathaoir
viv.1584

Muircheartach
viv.1587

Slioc

Muircheartaigh

Óig of Garryhill,
Co. Carlow

Outline Genealogy 1b: The family of Gerald
MacMurrough-Kavanagh *c.*1430–1645

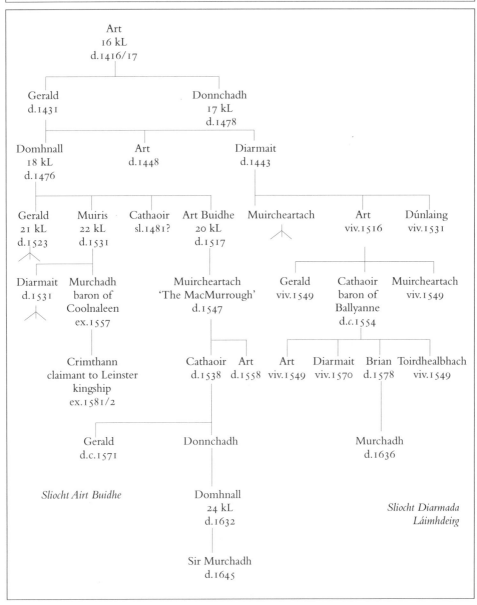

Key

kL	king of Leinster	viv.	alive	sl.	killed
kUC	king of Uí Cheinnselaig	d.	died	ex.	executed

Art
16 kL
d.1416/17

Gerald
d.1431

Donnchadh
17 kL
d.1478

Domhnall
18 kL
d.1476

Art
d.1448

Diarmait
d.1443

Gerald
21 kL
d.1523

Muiris
22 kL
d.1531

Cathaoir
sl.1481?

Art Buidhe
20 kL
d.1517

Muircheartach

Art
viv.1516

Dúnlaing
viv.1531

Diarmait
d.1531

Murchadh
baron of
Coolnaleen
ex.1557

Muircheartach
'The MacMurrough'
d.1547

Gerald
viv.1549

Cathaoir
baron of
Ballyanne
d.*c.*1554

Muircheartach
viv.1549

Crimthann
claimant to Leinster
kingship
ex.1581/2

Cathaoir
d.1538

Art
d.1558

Art
viv.1549

Diarmait
viv.1570

Brian
d.1578

Toirdhealbhach
viv.1549

Gerald
d.*c.*1571

Donnchadh

Murchadh
d.1636

Sliocht Airt Buidhe

Domhnall
24 kL
d.1632

*Sliocht Diarmada
Láimhdeirg*

Sir Murchadh
d.1645

Outline Genealogy 2: The senior O'Byrnes, *c.*1260–1600

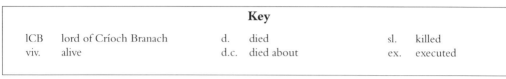

Key

| lCB | lord of Críoch Branach | d. | died | sl. | killed |
| viv. | alive | d.c. | died about | ex. | executed |

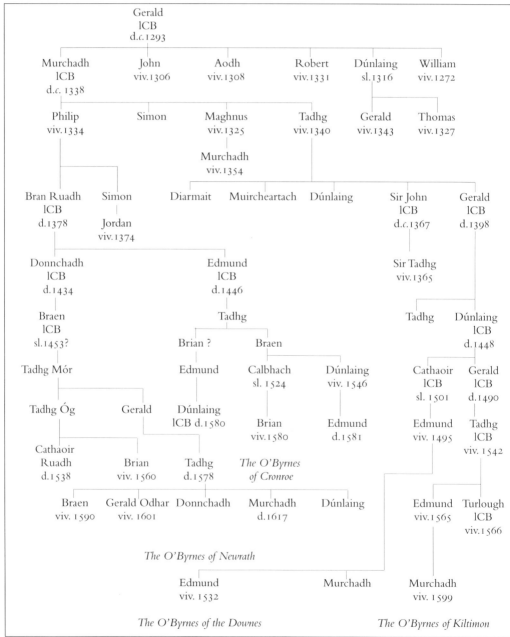

Gerald
lCB
d.*c.*1293

Murchadh lCB d.*c.*1338 — John viv.1306 — Aodh viv.1308 — Robert viv.1331 — Dúnlaing sl.1316 — William viv.1272

Philip viv.1334 — Simon — Maghnus viv.1325 — Tadhg viv.1340 — Gerald viv.1343 — Thomas viv.1327

Murchadh viv.1354

Bran Ruadh lCB d.1378 — Simon — Diarmait — Muircheartach — Dúnlaing — Sir John lCB d.*c.*1367 — Gerald lCB d.1398

Jordan viv.1374

Donnchadh lCB d.1434 — Edmund lCB d.1446 — Sir Tadhg viv.1365

Braen lCB sl.1453? — Tadhg — Tadhg — Dúnlaing lCB d.1448

Brian ? — Braen — Cathaoir lCB sl.1501 — Gerald lCB d.1490

Tadhg Mór — Edmund — Calbhach sl.1524 — Dúnlaing viv.1546 — Edmund viv.1495 — Tadhg lCB viv.1542

Tadhg Óg — Gerald — Dúnlaing lCB d.1580 — Brian viv.1580 — Edmund d.1581

Cathaoir Ruadh d.1538 — Brian viv.1560 — Tadhg d.1578 — *The O'Byrnes of Cronroe*

Braen viv.1590 — Gerald Odhar viv.1601 — Donnchadh — Murchadh d.1617 — Dúnlaing — Edmund viv.1565 — Turlough lCB viv.1566

The O'Byrnes of Newrath

Edmund viv.1532 — Murchadh — Murchadh viv.1599

The O'Byrnes of the Downes   *The O'Byrnes of Kiltimon*

Outline Genealogy 2a: The O'Byrnes of Críoch Raghnuill, *c.*1170–1597

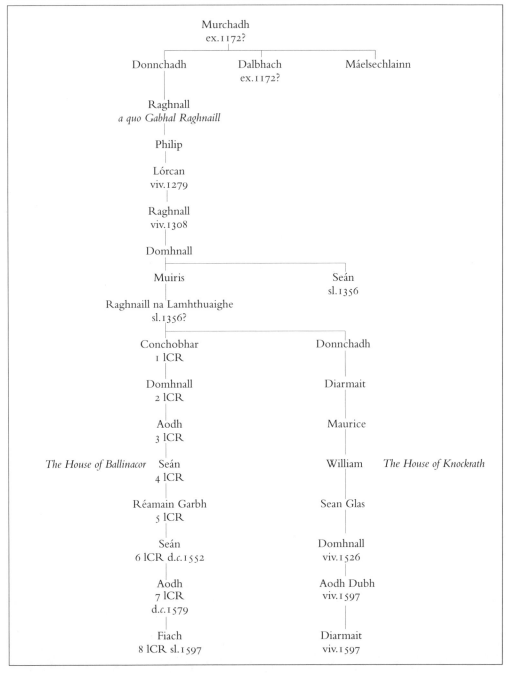

	Key	
lCR	lord of Críoch Raghnuill	d.c. died about
viv.	alive	sl. killed
d.	died	ex. executed

Murchadh
ex.1172?

Donnchadh — Dalbhach ex.1172? — Máelsechlainn

Raghnall
a quo Gabhal Raghnaill

Philip

Lórcan
viv.1279

Raghnall
viv.1308

Domhnall

Muiris — Seán sl.1356

Raghnaill na Lamhthuaighe
sl.1356?

Conchobhar 1 lCR — Donnchadh

Domhnall 2 lCR — Diarmait

Aodh 3 lCR — Maurice

The House of Ballinacor Seán 4 lCR — William *The House of Knockrath*

Réamain Garbh 5 lCR — Sean Glas

Seán 6 lCR d.*c.*1552 — Domhnall viv.1526

Aodh 7 lCR d.*c.*1579 — Aodh Dubh viv.1597

Fiach 8 lCR sl.1597 — Diarmait viv.1597

Outline Genealogy 2b: The O'Byrne house of Ballinacor, *c.*1490–1652

Réamain Garbh
5 lCR
viv.1490

Seán
6 lCR
d.*c.*1552

Réamain

Fiach

Aodh
7 lCR
d.1579

Réamain

Réamain Óg
sl.1596

Pádraig
viv.1549

dau.

Edmund
viv.1601

Gerald
viv.1601

Feílim
viv.1584

Gerald
viv.1573

Murchadh
viv.1601

Dúnlaing
viv.1601

An Calbhach
viv.1601

Aodh
viv.1601

Fiach
8 lCR
sl.1597

Cathaoir
viv.1601

James
sl.1580?

Conall
viv.1606

Séan
sl.1577

Art
viv.1597

son
viv.1581

son
sl.1572

Margaret
sl.1577

Elizabeth
viv.1608

Honora
viv.1573

dau.
viv.158?

Uaithne
viv.1606

Fiach
viv.1606

Réamain

Edmund

Seán
viv.1616

Brian
viv.1616

Féilim
9 lCR
d.1631

Toirdheabhach
ex.1595

Brian
ex.1596

son
sl.1581

Mary
viv.1600

Margaret
viv.1601

Réamain
viv.1642

dau.   dau.

Fiach
viv.1646

Féilim
viv.1641

John
viv.1641

Katherine
viv.1642

Brian
10 lCR
viv.1652

Gerald
viv.1630

Aodh
viv.1652

Fiach
viv.1642

Colla
viv.1642

Toirdhealbhach
viv.1642

Art
viv.1642

James
viv.1642

Cathaoir
ex.1652

Rose

Grainne
viv.1628

Eleanor

Sadhbh

Aodh

Art

Seán
viv.1652

Muircheartach
viv.1631

Cathaoir Óg

Outline Genealogy 3: The O'Toole over-kings of Fercullen and Imaal, *c.*1295–1652

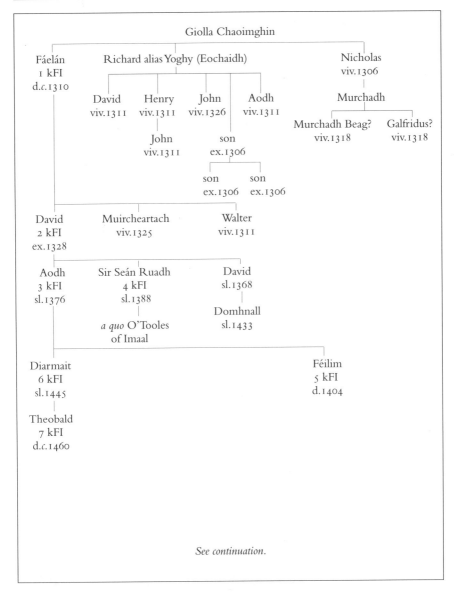

Key			
kFI	king of Fercullen and Imaal	d.*c.*	died about
viv.	alive	sl.	killed
d.	died	ex.	executed

Giolla Chaoimghin

Fáelán
1 kFI
d.*c.*1310

Richard alias Yoghy (Eochaidh)

Nicholas
viv.1306

David
viv.1311

Henry
viv.1311

John
viv.1326

Aodh
viv.1311

Murchadh

John
viv.1311

son
ex.1306

Murchadh Beag?
viv.1318

Galfridus?
viv.1318

son
ex.1306

son
ex.1306

David
2 kFI
ex.1328

Muircheartach
viv.1325

Walter
viv.1311

Aodh
3 kFI
sl.1376

Sir Seán Ruadh
4 kFI
sl.1388

a quo O'Tooles
of Imaal

David
sl.1368

Domhnall
sl.1433

Diarmait
6 kFI
sl.1445

Féilim
5 kFI
d.1404

Theobald
7 kFI
d.*c.*1460

See continuation.

Outline Genealogy 3 (continuation)

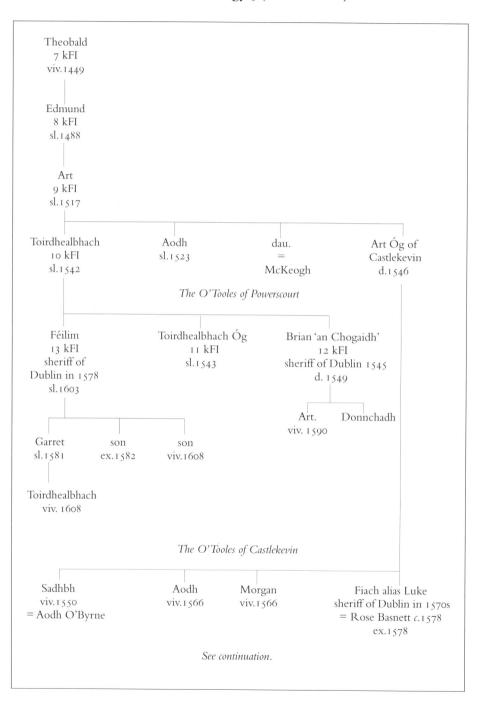

Theobald
7 kFI
viv. 1449

Edmund
8 kFI
sl. 1488

Art
9 kFI
sl. 1517

Toirdhealbhach   Aodh   dau.   Art Óg of
10 kFI   sl. 1523   =   Castlekevin
sl. 1542   McKeogh   d. 1546

The O'Tooles of Powerscourt

Féilim   Toirdhealbhach Óg   Brian 'an Chogaidh'
13 kFI   11 kFI   12 kFI
sheriff of   sl. 1543   sheriff of Dublin 1545
Dublin in 1578   d. 1549
sl. 1603

                                                   Art.   Donnchadh
                                                   viv. 1590

Garret   son   son
sl. 1581   ex. 1582   viv. 1608

Toirdhealbhach
viv. 1608

The O'Tooles of Castlekevin

Sadhbh   Aodh   Morgan   Fiach alias Luke
viv. 1550   viv. 1566   viv. 1566   sheriff of Dublin in 1570s
= Aodh O'Byrne   = Rose Basnett *c.* 1578
                                                   ex. 1578

See continuation.

Outline Genealogy 3: (continuation)

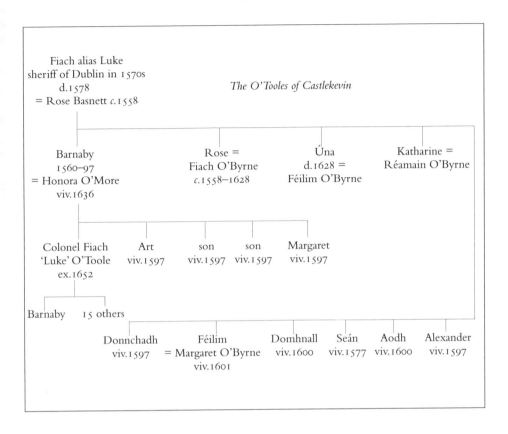

Fiach alias Luke
sheriff of Dublin in 1570s
d.1578
= Rose Basnett *c.*1558

The O'Tooles of Castlekevin

Barnaby
1560–97
= Honora O'More
viv.1636

Rose =
Fiach O'Byrne
*c.*1558–1628

Úna
d.1628 =
Féilim O'Byrne

Katharine =
Réamain O'Byrne

Colonel Fiach
'Luke' O'Toole
ex.1652

Art
viv.1597

son
viv.1597

son
viv.1597

Margaret
viv.1597

Barnaby   15 others

Donnchadh
viv.1597

Féilim
= Margaret O'Byrne
viv.1601

Domhnall
viv.1600

Seán
viv.1577

Aodh
viv.1600

Alexander
viv.1597

Outline Genealogy 4: The O'More kings of Laois, *c.*1280–1601

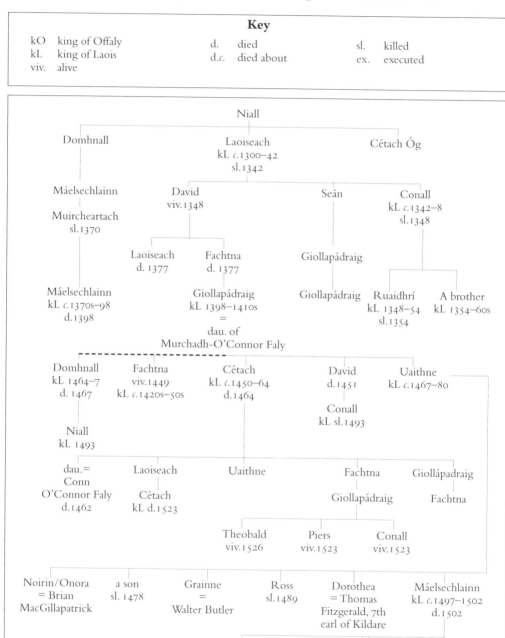

See continuation.

Outline Genealogy 4: (continuation)

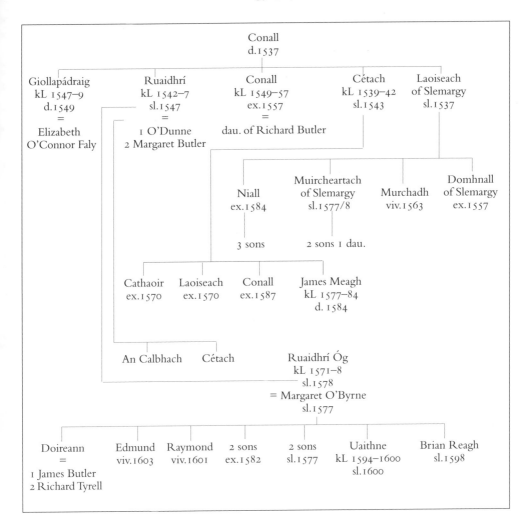

Outline Genealogy 5: The O'Connor Faly kings of Offaly, *c.*1050–1590

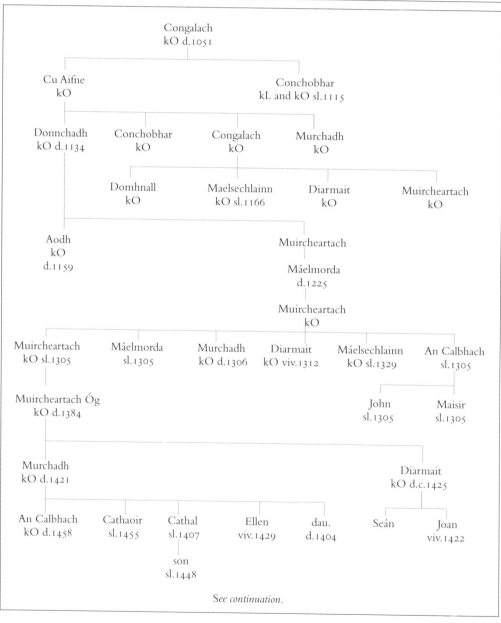

See continuation.

Outline Genealogy 5: (continuation)

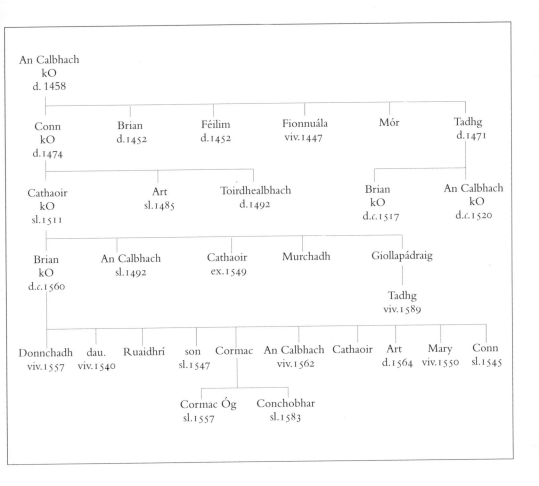

Outline Genealogy 6: The MacGillapatrick kings and barons of Ossory/Upper Ossory, *c.*1160–1613

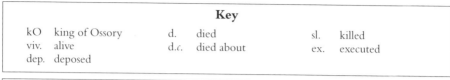

Key

kO	king of Ossory	d.	died	sl.	killed
viv.	alive	d.*c.*	died about	ex.	executed
dep.	deposed				

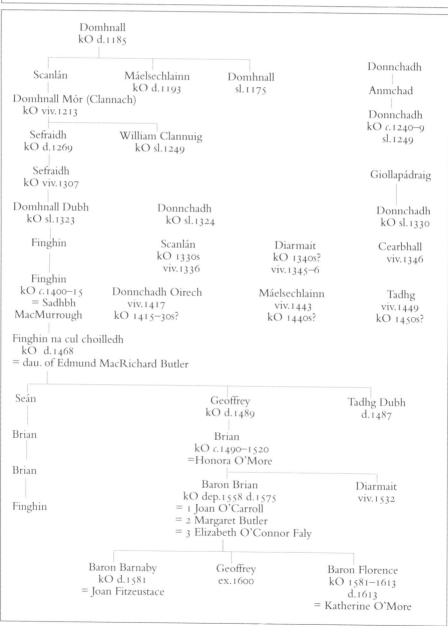

Outline Genealogy 7: The O'Carroll kings of Ely, *c.*1200–1581

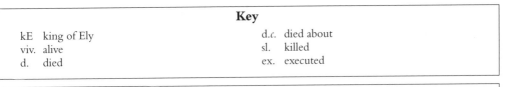

Key

kE king of Ely	d.*c.* died about
viv. alive	sl. killed
d. died	ex. executed

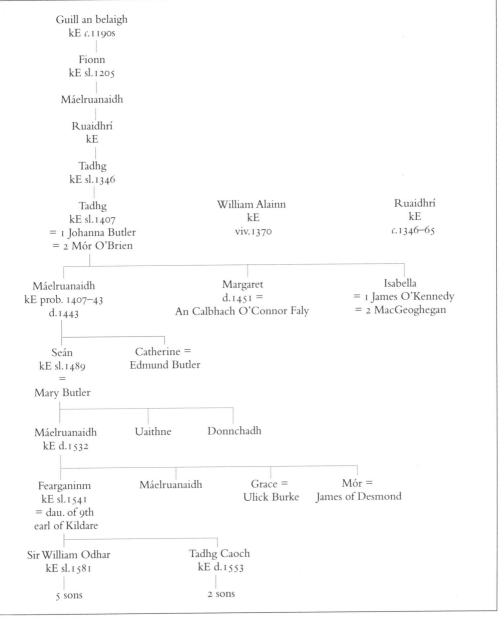

Outline Genealogy 8: The O'Connor kings of Connacht, *c.*1050–1316

Key			
kC	king of Connacht	=	married
hkI	high-king of Ireland	d.	died
tC	tanaiste of Connacht	sl.	killed
NC	North Connacht	ex.	executed
viv.	alive	dep.	deposed

Aodh
kC sl.1067

Ruaidhrí
kC d.1118

Cathal
kC sl.1082

Tadhg
sl.1062

Aodh
kC sl.1093

Domhnall
kC
dep.1106 d.1119

Niall
sl.1093

Tadhg
d.1096

Toirdhealbhach
hkI
d.1156

Aodh
bld.1136

Conchobhar
sl.1143

Brian
sl.1181

Maghnus
sl.1181

Máelsechlainn
sl.1154

Brian
d.1184

Muircheartach
tC d.1210

Domhnall
lord of NC
d.1176

Cathal
kC
d.1224

Ruaid
hkI
d.119

Máelsechlainn
sl.1181

Muircheartach
sl.1181

Muiredhach
sl.1181

Aodh
sl.1198

Mathghamhain
sl.1207

Donnchadh
sl.1185

Aindrias

Tadhg

Donnchadh

Tuathal
d.1244

Maghnus
d.1244

Conchobhar
sl.1245

Brian

Domhnall
sl.1307

Tadhg
sl.1247

Tadhg

Domhnall

Maghnus tC
sl.1316

Cathal kC
sl.1324

Brian
sl.1249

Donnchadh
d.1249

Diarmait
sl.1248

Domhnall
d.1274

The O'Connors of Sligo

Mathghamhain
viv.1248

Tuathal

Máelsechlainn
sl.1246

Maghnus
kC d.1293

Cathal
kC sl.1293

Tadhg
sl.1248

Tadhg
sl.1251

Ruaidhrí
kC sl.1316

Aodh
kC sl.1310

Clan Muircheartach Muimhnech O'Connors

Outline Genealogy 8a: The family of Ruaidhrí O'Connor, *c.*1156–1273

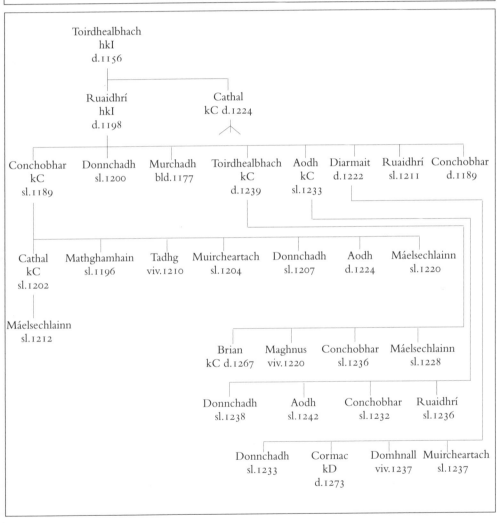

Key

kC	king of Connacht	=	married
hkI	high-king of Ireland	d.	died
kD	king of Donegal	sl.	killed
viv.	alive	ex.	executed

Outline Genealogy 8b: The family of Cathal O'Connor, *c.*1200–1316

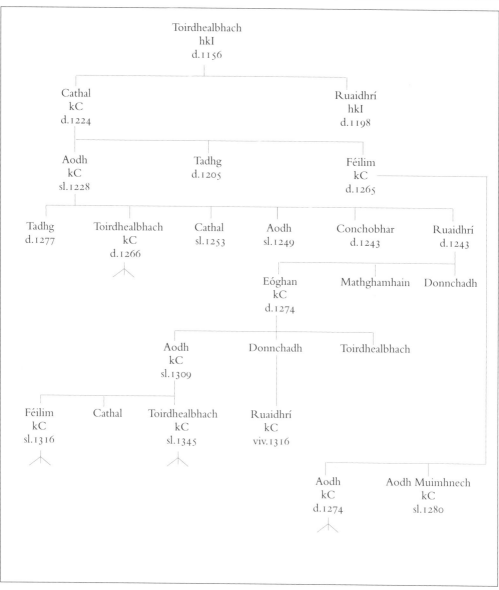

Key

kC	king of Connacht	d.	died
hkI	high-king of Ireland	sl.	killed
viv.	alive	ex.	executed
=	married		

Toirdhealbhach
hkI
d.1156

Cathal
kC
d.1224

Ruaidhrí
hkI
d.1198

Aodh
kC
sl.1228

Tadhg
d.1205

Féilim
kC
d.1265

Tadhg
d.1277

Toirdhealbhach
kC
d.1266

Cathal
sl.1253

Aodh
sl.1249

Conchobhar
d.1243

Ruaidhrí
d.1243

Eóghan
kC
d.1274

Mathghamhain

Donnchadh

Aodh
kC
sl.1309

Donnchadh

Toirdhealbhach

Féilim
kC
sl.1316

Cathal

Toirdhealbhach
kC
sl.1345

Ruaidhrí
kC
viv.1316

Aodh
kC
d.1274

Aodh Muimhnech
kC
sl.1280

Outline Genealogy 9: The lords of Leinster, c.1171–1330

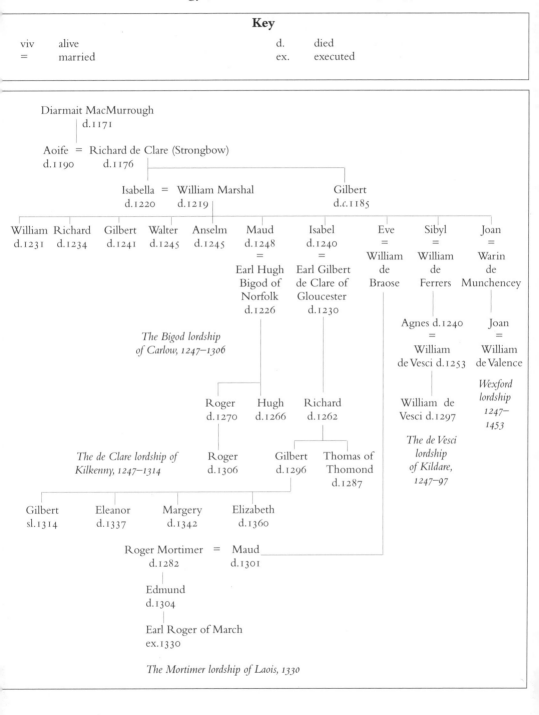

Key			
viv	alive	d.	died
=	married	ex.	executed

Outline Genealogy 10: The Fitzgeralds of Kildare, *c.*1270–1600

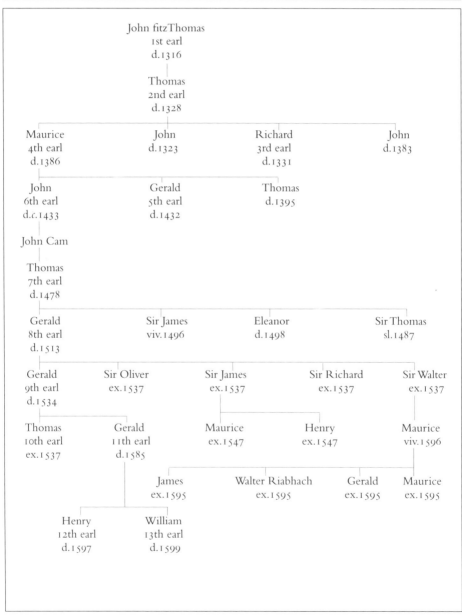

Key

earl	earl of Kildare		d.	died
viv.	alive		sl.	killed
=	married		ex.	executed

John fitzThomas
1st earl
d.1316

Thomas
2nd earl
d.1328

Maurice
4th earl
d.1386

John
d.1323

Richard
3rd earl
d.1331

John
d.1383

John
6th earl
d.*c.*1433

Gerald
5th earl
d.1432

Thomas
d.1395

John Cam

Thomas
7th earl
d.1478

Gerald
8th earl
d.1513

Sir James
viv.1496

Eleanor
d.1498

Sir Thomas
sl.1487

Gerald
9th earl
d.1534

Sir Oliver
ex.1537

Sir James
ex.1537

Sir Richard
ex.1537

Sir Walter
ex.1537

Thomas
10th earl
ex.1537

Gerald
11th earl
d.1585

Maurice
ex.1547

Henry
ex.1547

Maurice
viv.1596

James
ex.1595

Walter Riabhach
ex.1595

Gerald
ex.1595

Maurice
ex.1595

Henry
12th earl
d.1597

William
13th earl
d.1599

Outline Genealogy 11: The Butlers of Ormond, *c*.1300–1614

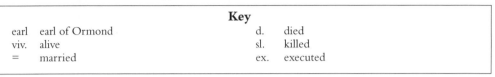

Key

earl	earl of Ormond	d.	died
viv.	alive	sl.	killed
=	married	ex.	executed

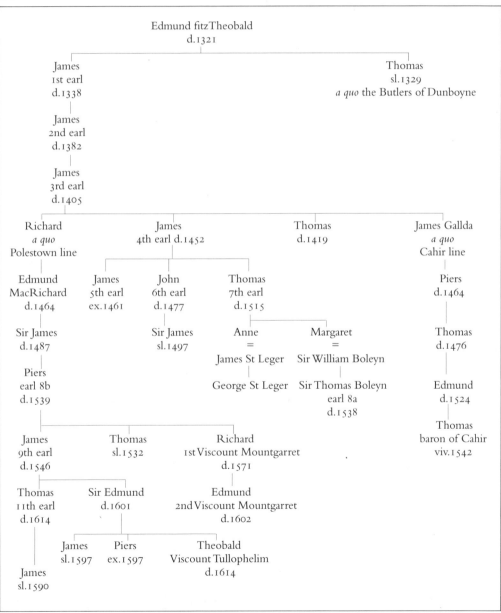

Edmund fitzTheobald
d.1321

James
1st earl
d.1338

Thomas
sl.1329
a quo the Butlers of Dunboyne

James
2nd earl
d.1382

James
3rd earl
d.1405

Richard
a quo
Polestown line

James
4th earl d.1452

Thomas
d.1419

James Gallda
a quo
Cahir line

Edmund
MacRichard
d.1464

James
5th earl
ex.1461

John
6th earl
d.1477

Thomas
7th earl
d.1515

Piers
d.1464

Sir James
d.1487

Sir James
sl.1497

Anne
=
James St Leger

Margaret
=
Sir William Boleyn

Thomas
d.1476

Piers
earl 8b
d.1539

George St Leger

Sir Thomas Boleyn
earl 8a
d.1538

Edmund
d.1524

Thomas
baron of Cahir
viv.1542

James
9th earl
d.1546

Thomas
sl.1532

Richard
1st Viscount Mountgarret
d.1571

Thomas
11th earl
d.1614

Sir Edmund
d.1601

Edmund
2nd Viscount Mountgarret
d.1602

James
sl.1597

Piers
ex.1597

Theobald
Viscount Tullophelim
d.1614

James
sl.1590

Outline Genealogy 12: The monarchs of England, 1171–1625

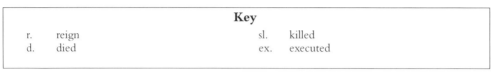

Key			
r.	reign	sl.	killed
d.	died	ex.	executed

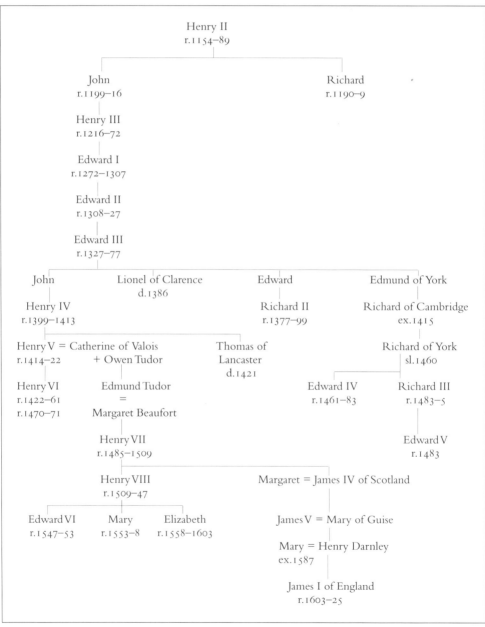

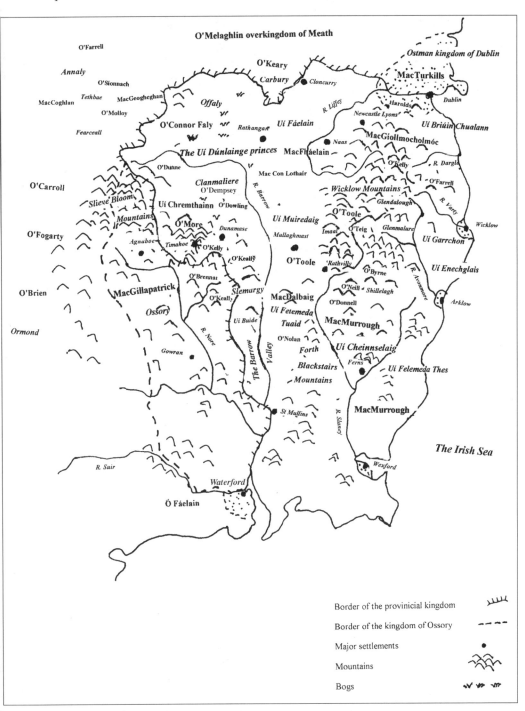

Map 1. The kingdom of Leinster, *c.*1165

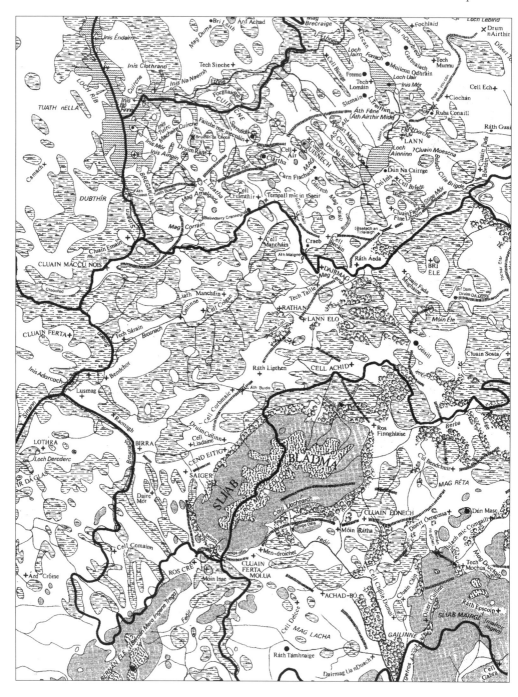

Map 2. Topographical map of North-Western Leinster (after A.P. Smyth)

Map 3. Leinster, *c.*1470

Bibliography

MANUSCRIPT PRIMARY SOURCES

Archivo General de Simancas
Estado, legajos 176, 431, 596, 839 and 2604.
Archivum Parochiale de Rathdrum
Liber II. The will of Phelim McFeagh O'Byrne (1630).
British Library
BL Egerton Ms 1782
Dublin, National Archives of Ireland
NA, RC 7/13 (iv), pp 22–4; NA, PRO 7/13 c.15–18.
Dublin, National Library of Ireland
Genealogia Joannis Byrne, Armigeri apud Burdigalam in Galliarum Regna, NLI MSS 162, reel
    no. 971, pp 128–9.
Lansdowne MSS 159, fols 12–13.
Lane-Poole Papers, NLI MS 5378
The Papers of Sir William Betham, NLI (GO) MSS 191, pp 57–8.
NLI, G 992 sff 256–66; NLI, MS 8008 (ii).
Dublin, Royal Irish Academy
Leabhar Donn, RIA MSS 1233 (23/Q/10), leaves 43–4.
RIA, MSS 24 H.17; RIA, 2 (23/F/16), p. 113; RIA, 1 (23/D/14), p. 62.
Dublin, Trinity College
TCD, MSS F.3.25 (588), ff 202v–204; TCD, MSS E.3.18 (581), fol. 54; TCD, MSS 811;
    TCD, MSS 9827/1-5.
Dublin University College
McFirbis' Genealogies, UCD, microfilm no. 473, p. 475.
London, Lambeth Palace Library
Carew Papers
MSS 612 and 635.
London, Public Record Office
PRO E101/239/24; PRO E101/248/15
SP 61. State papers Ireland, Edward VI.
SP 62. State papers Ireland, Philip and Mary.
SP 63. State papers Ireland, Elizabeth.
Oxford, Bodleian Library
Carte MS 55. Papers of Sir William Fitzwilliam, 1561-75.

PRINTED PRIMARY SOURCES

A census of Ireland circa 1659, ed. S. Pender (Dublin, 1939).

Account roll of the priory of the Holy Trinity, Dublin, 1337–1346, ed. J. Mills (Dublin, 1891).

Acts of the privy council of England, 1542–1631, 46 vols. (London 1890–1964).

Account of Thomas de Chaddisworth, custodee of the temporalties of the archbishop of Dublin from 1221 to 1256 (*recte 1271–9*), ed. W. Betham, *PRIA*, 5 (1850–3).

An account of military expenditure in Leinster, 1308, ed. P. Connolly, *Anal. Hib.*, 30 (1982).

Annala Connacht: the Annals of Connacht, A.D. 1224–1544, ed. A.M. Freeman (Dublin, 1944).

Annala rioghachta Eireann: Annals of the kingdom of Ireland by the Four Masters, ed. J. O'Donovan, 7 vols. (Dublin, 1990).

Annala Uladh: Annals of Ulster ... 431 to 1541, eds W.M. Hennessy [and B. MacCarthy] 2 vols. (London, 1871).

Annales Monastici, ed. H. Luard, iv (London, 1869).

Ancient Irish histories: the chronicle of Ireland, ed. Meredith Hanmer (Dublin, 1809).

A roll of the proceedings of the king's council in Ireland for a portion of the sixteenth year of the reign of Richard the second, A.D. 1392–3, ed. J. Graves (London, 1877).

Caithreim Thoirdhealbhaigh [by J. MacRory MacGrath], trans. by S.H. O'Grady (London, 1929).

Calendar of Archbishop Alen's register, c. 1172–1534; prepared and edited from the original in the registry of the united dioceses of Dublin and Glendalough and Kildare, ed. C. McNeill; index by L. Price (RSAI, Dublin, 1950).

Calendar of ancient records of Dublin, ed. J. Gilbert 19 vols. (Dublin, 1899–1944).

Calendar of Irish patent rolls of James I: facsimile of the Irish record commissioners' calendar prepared prior to 1830, with foreword by M.C. Griffith (Dublin, 1966).

Calendar of manuscripts of the marquis of Salisbury, iv (London, 1892).

Calendar of state papers, relating to Ireland, 26 vols. (1860–1910).

Calendar of state papers, Scotland and Mary, Queen of Scotland, 1547–1603, 13 vols. (Edinburgh and Glasgow, 1898–1969).

Calendar of state papers, Venice 1558–80, iii, ed. R. Brown and G. Cavendish Bentinck (London, 1890).

Calendar of the Carew manuscripts preserved in the archiepiscopal library at Lambeth, ed. J.S. Brewer and W. Bullen. 6 vols. (London, 1867–73).

Calendar of the close rolls ... 1272–1509, 47 vols. (London, 1909–74).

Calendar of documents relating to Ireland ... 1171–[1307], ed. H.S. Sweetman and G.F. Handcock. 5 vols. (London, 1875–76).

Calendar of entries in the papal registers relating to Great Britain and Ireland (London, 1893–).

Calendar of inquistions, ed. M.C. Griffith (Dublin, 1991).

Calendar of Ormond deeds, 1172–1603, ed. E. Curtis. 6 vols. (Dublin, 1932–43).

Calendar of the fine rolls ... 1272–[1509], 22 vols. (London, 1911–62).

Calendar of the Gormanston register circa 1175–1397, ed. J. Mills and M.J. McEnery (Dublin, 1916).

Calendar of the justicary rolls ... of Ireland ... Edward I, 1295–1305, ed. J. Mills, 2 vols. (Dublin, 1905–14).

Calendar of the justicary rolls of Ireland: I to VII years of Edward II, ed. H. Wood and A.E. Langan; revised by M.C. Griffith (Dublin, 1956).

Calendar of the patent rolls, 1232–1509 (London, 1891–1971).

Calendar of the patent and close rolls of chancery of Ireland, i, ed. J. Morrin (Dublin, 1861).

Calendar of the patent and close rolls of chancery in Ireland, Henry VIII to 18th Elizabeth, ed. J. Morrin (Dublin, 1863).

Calendar of the Salisbury manuscripts, ii. (London, 1888).

Calendar of the Salisbury manuscripts, iv and vi (London, 1892).

Calendar of various chancery rolls (London, 1912).

Calendarium inquisitionum post mortem sive excaetarum, ed. J. Cayley & J. Bayley, iv (London, 1873–7).

Chartularies of St Mary's abbey, Dublin; with the register of its house at Dunbrody, and annals of Ireland, ed. J.T. Gilbert, 2 vols. (London, 1884).

Chronicum Scotorum: a chronicle of Irish affairs … to 1135, and supplement … 1141–1150, ed. J.T. Gilbert, 2 vols. (London, 1884–6).

The civil survey, A.D. 1654–56, ed. R.C. Simington, 10 vols. (Dublin, 1931–61).

Cogadh Gaedheal re Galliabh, ed. J. Todd (Dublin, 1866).

Crede mihi: the most ancient register book of the archbishops of Dublin, ed. J.T. Gilbert (Dublin, 1887).

Crown surveys of the lands, 1540–41, with the Kildare rental, ed. G. MacNiocaill (Dublin, 1992).

Documents on the affairs of Ireland before the king's council, ed. G.O. Sayles (Dublin, 1979).

Extents of Irish monastic possessions 1540–1, ed. N. White (Dublin, 1943).

The fasti of St Patrick's Dublin, ed. H.J. Lawlor (Dundalk, 1930).

Foedera, conventiones, litterae et cuiuscunque generis acta inter reges Angliae, ed. T. Rymer, 3rd. ed. reprinted, 10 vols. (Farnborough, 1967).

HMC, *Haliday MSS: Irish privy council, 1556–1571* (London, 1897).

Irish historical documents, 1171–1922, ed. E. Curtis and R.B. McDowell (London, 1968).

Liber Primus Kilkenniensis, ed. J. Otway-Ruthven (Kilkenny, 1961).

Original letters illustrative of English history, ed. Sir H. Ellis, First series (London, 1824).

Original letters illustrative of English history, ed. Sir H. Ellis, Second series (London, 1827).

Original letters illustrative of English history, ed. Sir H. Ellis, Second series (London, 1969).

The annals of Clonmacnoise, being annals of Ireland from the earliest period A.D. 1408, trans. Connell Mageoghagan, ed. D. Murphy (Dublin, 1896).

The annals of Loch Cé: a chronicle of Irish affairs, 1014–1590, ed. W. Hennessy (Dublin, 1951).

The annals of Inisfallen, ed. S. MacAirt (Dublin, 1951).

The annals of Ireland by Friar John Clyn and Thady Dowling, together with the annals of Ross, ed. R. Butler (Dublin, 1849).

'The annals of Ireland, from the year 1443 to 1468', trans. J. O'Donovan, *Miscellany of the Irish Archaeological Society* (Dublin, 1846).

The annals of Tigernach, ed. W. Stokes, 2 vols. (Felinfach, 1993).

The Book of Leinster, formerly Lebar na Nuachongbala, ed. R.I. Best, O. Bergin, M.A. O'Brien, and A. O'Sullivan, 6 vols. (Dublin Institute for Advanced Studies, 1954–83).

The O Doyne manuscript, ed. K.W. Nicholls (Dublin, 1983).

The Sidney state papers, 1565–70, ed. T. O'Laidhin (Dublin, 1962).

The Walsingham letter book, May 1578–Dec 1579, (eds.) J. Hogan and N. McNeill (Dublin, 1959).

20th Deputy Keeper's Report (Dublin, 1888).

35th Deputy Keeper's Report (Dublin, 1903).

38th Deputy Keeper's Report (Dublin, 1906).

39th Deputy Keeper's Report (Dublin, 1907).

42th Deputy Keeper's Report (Dublin, 1911).

Froissart's chronicles, ed. and trans. J. Joliffe (London, 1967).

Giraldus Cambrensis, *Expugnatio Hibernica: the conquest of Ireland,* ed. A.B. Scott and F.X. Martin (Dublin, 1978).

Giraldus Cambrensis, *The history and topography of Ireland,* ed. J.J. O'Meara (Mountrath, 1982).

Grace, Jacobus, *Annales Hiberniae,* ed. R. Butler (Dublin, 1842).

Historic and municipal documents of Ireland, 1172–1320, ed. J.T. Gilbert (London, 1870).

Holinshed's Irish chronicle: the historie of Irelande from the first inhabitation thereof, unto the year 1509: collected by Raphael Holinshed, and continued till the year 1547 by Richarde Stanyhurst, ed. L. Miller and E. Power (Dublin, 1979).

Inquisitionum cancellariae hiberniae repertorium, i (London, 1828).

Letters and papers illustrative of the reigns of Richard III and Henry VII, ed. J. Gairdner, 2 vols. (London, 1861–3).

Letters and papers, foreign and domestic, Henry VIII, 21 vols. (London, 1862–1932).

Letters and state papers, Spanish, iii, ed. M. Hume (London, 1896).

Letters and state papers, Spanish, iv, ed. M. Hume (London, 1899).

Miscellaneous Irish annals (A.D. 1114–1437), ed. S. Ó hÍnnse (Dublin, 1947).

Perrot's chronicle of Ireland, 1584–1608, ed. H. Wood (Dublin, 1890).

The chronicle of Ireland printed in Ancient Irish histories: the works of Spencer, Campion, Hanmer and Marleborough, ed. J. Ware (Dublin, 1809).

The chronicles and memorials of Great Britain and Ireland during the middle ages, ed. F.C. Hingeston (London, 1858).

'The enrolled account of Alexander Bicknor, treasurer of Ireland, 1308–14', ed. J. Lydon, *Anal. Hib.,* 2 (1931).

The Irish chartularies of Lanthony Prima and Secunda, ed. E. Brooks (Dublin, 1954).

The Irish pipe roll of 14 John, 1211–12, ed. O. Davies and D. Quinn, *UJA.,* 3rd ser., iv, supp. (July, 1941).

The O'Clery book of Genealogies, ed. S. Pender, *Anal. Hib.,* 18 (1951).

The proceedings and ordinances of the privy council 12 Henry IV to 10 Henry V, ed. H. Nicholas (London, 1834).

The proceedings and ordinances of the privy council, vii, ed. H. Nicholas (London, 1837).

The register of the abbey of St Thomas Dublin, ed. J. Gilbert (London, 1889).

The register of wills and inventories of the diocese of Dublin in the time of Archbishop Tregury and Walton, 1457–83, ed. H.F. Berry (Dublin, 1898).

The red book of the earls of Kildare, ed. G. MacNiocaill (Dublin, 1964).

The red book of Ormond, ed. N.B. White (Dublin, 1932).

The register of John Swayne, ed. D.A. Chart (Belfast, 1935).

Topographical poems by Seaán Mór Ó Dubhagain and Giolla na Naomh Ó Huidhrin, ed. J. Carney (Dublin, 1943).

Reports on the manuscripts of Lord de L'Isle & Dudley, ed. C. Kingsford, ii (London, 1934).

Rotulorum patentium et clausorum cancellarie Hiberniae calendarium, ed. E. Tresham (Dublin, 1828).

Sheedy, M. (ed.), *Pontifica hibernica: medieval chancery documents concerning Ireland, 640–1261,* 2 vols. (Dublin, 1962–3).

State papers, Henry VIII, 11 vols. (London, 1830–32).

Statutes and ordinances and acts of the parliament of Ireland: King John to Henry V, ed. H.F. Berry (Dublin, 1907).

Statutes rolls of the parliament of Ireland, reign of King Henry IV, ed. H.F. Berry (Dublin, 1907).
Statutes rolls of the parliament of Ireland, 1st to 12th year of the reign of King Edward IV, ed. H.F. Berry (Dublin, 1910).
Statutes rolls of the parliament of Ireland, 12th and 13th to the 21st and 22nd years of the reign of King Henry IV, ed. H. F. Berry (Dublin, 1914).

SELECTED SECONDARY WORKS

Allmand, C., *The reign of King Henry VI, the exercise of royal authority, 1422–6* (London, 1981).
——, *Lancastrian Normandy, 1415–50* (Oxford, 1983).
——, *Henry V* (London, 1992).
Andrews, J., 'Ireland in maps: a bibliographical postscript', *Ir. Geography*, iv, no. 4 (1962).
Arian, *The campaigns of Alexander* (London, 1971).
Ball, F.E., *A history of the County Dublin*, 6 vols. (Dublin, 1995).
Bartlett, T. and Jeffrey, K. (ed.) *Military history of Ireland* (Cambridge, 1996).
Bartlett, R. and McKay, A. (ed.), *Medieval frontier societies* (Oxford, 1989).
Bartlett, R., *Gerald of Wales* (Oxford, 1982).
——, 'Colonial aristocracies of the high middle ages' in Bartlett and McKay (ed.), *Medieval frontier societies.*
——, *The making of Europe* (London, 1993).
Barry, J., 'The Norman invasion of Ireland: a new approach', *Journal of the Cork Historical and Archaeological Society*, lxxv (1970).
Barry, T., *The archaeology of medieval Ireland* (Cambridge, 1987).
Barry, T., Frame, R. and Simms, K. (ed.), *Colony and frontier in medieval Ireland* (London, 1995).
Becker, P., 'An analysis of the Dublin guild merchant roll, c.1190–1265', MPhil thesis, University of Dublin 1995.
Beresford, D., 'The Butlers in England and Ireland, 1405–1515', PhD thesis, University of Dublin, 1998.
Berleth, R., *The twilight lords* (London, 1978).
Berenger, J., *A history of the Habsburg empire, 1273–1700* (London, 1994).
Bernard, J., 'Richard Talbot, archbishop and chancellor, 1418–1449', *PRIA,* 35 (1919/20).
Bhreathnach, E., 'Kings, the kingship of Ireland and the regnal poems of *laidshenchas Laigen*: a reflection of the dynastic politics in Leinster, 650–1150', in A.P. Smyth (ed.), *Seánchas: studies in early and medieval Irish archaeology, history and literature in honour of Francis J. Byrne* (Dublin, 2000).
Blake-Butler, T., 'Henry VIII's Irish army list', *Ir. Geneal.*, 1 (1937).
——, 'The barony of Dunboyne', *Ir. Geneal.*, 2, no. 3 (October, 1945).
——, 'The barony of Dunboyne', *Ir. Geneal.*, 2, no. 4 (October, 1946).
Bingham, C., *James V, 1512–42* (London, 1971).
Bradley, J. (ed.), *Settlement and society in medieval Ireland* (Kilkenny, 1988).
Bradley, J., 'Early urban development in Co. Laois', in Lane and Nolan (ed.), *Laois: history and society.*
Bradshaw, B., 'Native reaction to the westward enterprise: a case-study in Gaelic ideology', in K.R. Andrews, et al. (ed.), *The westward enterprise* (Liverpool, 1979).

——, 'Manus the magnificent: O'Donnell as renaissance prince', in Cosgrove and MacCartney (ed.), *Studies in Irish history* (Dublin, 1979).

——, *The Irish constitutional revolution of the sixteenth century* (Cambridge, 1979).

Brady, C., 'The government of Ireland', 2 vols, PhD thesis, University of Dublin, 1980.

Brady, C. and Gillespie, R. (ed.), *Natives and newcomers* (Dublin, 1968).

Brady, C., 'Court, castle and country: the framework of government in Tudor Ireland', in Brady and Gillespie (ed.), *Natives and newcomers*.

——, 'Thomas Butler, tenth earl of Ormond (1531–1614) and reform in Tudor Ireland', in C. Brady (ed.), *Worsted in the game*.

—— (ed.), *Worsted in the game: losers in Irish history* (Dublin, 1989).

——, *The chief governors: The rise and fall of reform government in Tudor Ireland 1536–1588* (Cambridge, 1994).

——, *Shane O'Neill* (Dundalk, 1996).

——, *A viceroy's vindication?* (Cork, 2002).

Brogan, F., 'Into the valley of death', *Irish Times*, 11 August 1982.

Bryan, D., *Gerald Fitzgerald, the great earl of Kildare (1456–1513)* (Dublin, 1933).

Burry, J., 'The pattern of medieval settlement in the barony of Nethercross, Co. Dublin', MLitt thesis, University of Dublin, 1995.

Butler, G., 'The battle of Piltown', *Ir. Sword*, 6 (1963/4).

Butler and Bernard, 'The charters of the abbey of Duiske', *PRIA* 35 (C) (1919–20).

Byrne, F.J., *The rise of the Ui Neill and the high-kingship of Ireland* (O'Donnell Lecture) (NUI, 1969).

——, *Kings and high-kings* (London, 1987; new ed., Dublin, 2001).

——, 'The trembling sod: Ireland in 1169', in A. Cosgrove (ed.), *NHI,* ii (Oxford, 1987).

Cantwell, I., 'Climate, change and the Gaelic annals' (unpublished paper).

——, 'Glendalough, Castlekevin, and the O'Tooles' (unpublished paper).

——, 'The O'Toole Genealogy' (unpublished paper).

——, 'The O'Tooles of north Wicklow' (unpublished paper).

Carey, V., 'Massacre at Mullaghmast', *IHS*, 31 (1999)

——, 'The end of the Gaelic political order: the O'More lordship of Laois, 1536–1603', in Lane and Nolan (ed.), *Laois: history and society*.

——, *Surviving the Tudors: the 'wizard' earl of Kildare and English rule in Ireland, 1537–1586* (Dublin, 2002).

Carrigan, W., *History and antiquities of the diocese of Ossory*, 4 vols. (Dublin, 1905).

Cavanagh, S., 'Licentious barbarism: Spenser's view of the Irish and the Faerie Queene', *Irish University Review*, xxvi, no. 2 (1996).

Clarke, M., 'The abbey, Wicklow', *JRSAI*, 123 (1943).

——, 'The Black Castle', *JRSAI*, 124 (1944).

Colfer, W., 'Anglo-Norman Settlement in Co. Wexford', in Whelan and Nolan (ed.), *Wexford: history and society*.

——, *Arrogant trepass: Anglo-Norman Wexford 1169–1400* (Enniscorthy, 2002).

Colfer, W., 'Anglo-Norman settlement in medieval Shelburne, 1169–1307', MLitt thesis, University of Dublin, 1986.

Connolly, P., 'Lionel of Clarence, 1361–6', PhD thesis, University of Dublin, 1977.

Conway, A., *Henry VII's relations with Scotland and Ireland, 1485–98* (New York, 1972).

Cosby, I., 'The English settlers in Queen's County', in Nolan and Lane (ed.), *Laois: history and society*.

Cosgrove, A., 'The execution of the earl of Desmond, 1468', *Kerry Arch. Soc. Jn.*, 7 (1975).

——, *Late medieval Ireland, 1370–1541* (Dublin, 1981).

——, 'Ireland beyond the Pale 1399–1460', in A. Cosgrove (ed.), *NHI*, ii (Oxford, 1987).

——, 'England and Ireland 1399–1447', in A. Cosgrove (ed.), *NHI*, ii (Oxford, 1987).

——, 'The emergence of the Pale 1339–1447', in A. Cosgrove (ed.) *NHI*, ii (Oxford, 1987).

Cunningham, G., *The Anglo-Norman advance into the south–west midlands of Ireland, 1185–1221* (Roscrea, 1987).

Curtis, E., 'The clan system among the English settlers in Ireland', *EHR*, 25 (1910).

——, 'The FitzRerys, Welsh lords of Cloghran, Co. Dublin', *Louth Arch. Soc. Jn.*, 5, no. 1 (1921).

——, *A history of medieval Ireland* (Dublin, 1927).

——, *Richard II in Ireland 1394–5 and the submissions of the Irish chiefs* (Oxford, 1927).

——, 'Unpublished letters from Richard II in Ireland 1394–99', *PRIA*, 37 (1927).

——, Richard, duke of York as viceroy of Ireland 1447–1460; with unpublished materiels for his relations with the native chiefs, *JRSAI*, 112 (1932).

——, 'Janico Dartas, Richard II's 'Gascon Squire': his career in Ireland 1394–1426', *JRSAI*, 113 (1933).

——, 'The barons of Norragh, Co. Kildare, 1171–1660', *JRSAI*, 65 (1935).

——, 'Some medieval seals out of the Ormond archives', *JRSAI*, 66, part 1 (1936).

——, *A history of medieval Ireland from 1086–1513* (London, 1938).

Davies, N., *Europe: a history* (London, 1997).

Davies, R., *Domination and conquest* (Cambridge, 1999).

D'arcy McGee, T., *A memoir of the life and conquests of Art MacMurrough* (1847).

Deignan, M., 'Portlaoise: Genesis and development', in Lane and Nolan (ed.), *Laois: history and society*.

Dobbs, M., 'The Ban-shenchas', *Revue Celtique*, xlviii (1931–32).

Donnelly, N., 'Incumbents of Killadreenan and the archdeacons of Glendalough in the fifteenth century with extracts from the Roman archives', *JRSAI*, 23 (1893).

Donovan, B., 'Tudor rule in Gaelic Leinster and the rise of Feagh McHugh O'Byrne', in C. O'Brien (ed.) *Feagh McHugh O'Byrne*.

Duffy, S., 'Ireland and the Irish sea region, 1014–1318', PhD thesis, University of Dublin, 1993.

Duffy, S., 'The Bruce brothers and the Irish Sea world, 1306–29', *Cambridge Medieval Studies*, 21 (Summer 1991).

——, 'Irishmen and Islesmen in the kingdoms of Dublin and Man, 1052–1171', *Eriu*, 43 (1992).

——, 'The first Ulster plantation', in Barry, et al. (ed.), *Colony and frontier in medieval Ireland*.

——, 'King John's expedition to Ireland, 1210: the evidence reconsidered', *IHS*, 30, no. 117 (May, 1996).

——, 'The problem of degeneracy', in J. Lydon (ed.), *Law and disorder in thirteenth-century Ireland*.

——, *Ireland in the middle ages* (Dublin, 1997).

Dunlop, R., 'The plantations of Leix and Offaly', *EHR*, 6 (1891).

——, 'Feagh McHugh O'Byrne', in S. Lee (ed.), *A dictionary of national dictionary*, xvi (London, 1909).

Eagar, B., 'The Cambro-Normans and the lordship of Leinster', in J. Bradley (ed.), *Settlement and society in medieval Ireland*.

Edwards, D., 'The death of the ninth earl of Ormond', *Butler Soc. Jn.*, iii (1986–87).

——, 'The Butler Revolt of 1569', *IHS*, 28, no. iii (May, 1993).

——, 'In Tyrone's shadow: Feagh McHugh, forgotten leader of the Nine Years War', in C. O'Brien (ed.), *Feagh McHugh O'Byrne*.

——, 'The MacGillapatricks (Fitzpatricks) of Upper Ossory, 1532–1641', in Lane and Nolan (ed.) *Laois: history and society*.

Elliot, M., *The Catholics of Ulster* (London, 2000).

Ellis, S., 'Parliaments and great councils, 1483–99: addenda et corrigenda', *Anal. Hib.*, 29 (1980).

——, *Tudor Ireland* (New York, 1992).

——, *Tudor frontiers and noble power; the making of the British state* (Oxford, 1995).

Elton, G., *Reformation Europe, 1517–59* (London, 1971).

Empey, C., 'The Butler lordship in Ireland, 1185–1515', PhD thesis, University of Dublin, 1970.

Empey, C., 'The cantreds of medieval Tipperary', *N. Munster Antiq. Jn.*, 13 (1970).

——, 'The cantreds of the mediaeval county of Kilkenny', *JRSAI*, 101, part 2 (1971).

——, 'Tipperary in the medieval period, 1185–1500' in W. Nolan (ed.), *Tipperary: history and society* (Dublin, 1985).

——, 'County Kilkenny in the medieval period', in Nolan and Whelan (ed.), *Kilkenny: history and society*.

——, 'From rags to riches: Piers Butler, 8th earl of Ormond, 1515–39', *Butler Soc. Jn.*, 2 (1984).

Etchingham, C., 'Evidence of Scandinavian settlement in Wicklow', in Hannigan and Nolan (ed.) *Wicklow: history and society*.

Firth, C.H (ed.), *The memoirs of Edmund Ludlow, lieutenant-general of the horse in the army of the commonwealth of England, 1625–72*, 2 vols. (Oxford, 1891).

Fitzgerald, W., 'Walter Reagh Fitzgerald, a noted outlaw of the sixteenth century', *JRSAI*, 28, part 2 (1898).

——, 'The manor and castle of Powerscourt Co. Wicklow in the sixteenth century, formerly a possession of the earls of Kildare', *Kildare Arch. Soc. Jn.*, vi (1909–11).

——, 'Historical notes on the O'Mores and their territory of Leix to the end of the sixteenth century', *Kildare. Arch Soc. Jn.*, vi (1909–11).

Fitzpatrick. L., 'Margaret an Einigh O'Cearbhaill – the best of the women of the Gaedhil', *Kildare. Arch. Soc. Jn.*, xviii (1992–3).

Fitzsimons F., 'The O'Connor Faly lordship, 1520–1570', in Nolan and O'Neill (ed.), *Offaly: history and society*.

Flanagan, M., 'MacDalbaig, a Leinster chieftain', *JRSAI*, 111 (1981).

——, 'Henry II and the kingdom of Uí Fáeláin', in J. Bradley (ed.), *Settlement and society in medieval Ireland*.

——, *Irish society, Anglo-Norman settlers, Angevin kingship* (Oxford, 1989).

——, 'Historia Gruffud vab Kenan and the origins of Balrothery Co. Dublin', *Cambrian Medieval Celtic Studies*, 28 (1994).

Flower, R., 'Manuscripts of Irish interest in the British Museum', *Anal. Hib.*, 2 (1931).

——, 'The Kilkenny chronicle in Cotton MS', *Anal. Hib.*, 2 (1932).

Ford, A., 'The Protestant Reformation in Ireland', in Brady and Gillespie (ed.), *Natives and newcomers*.

Frame, R., 'The Dublin government and Gaelic Ireland, 1272–1361', PhD thesis, University of Dublin, 1971.

Frame, R., *English lordship in Ireland, 1318–61* (Oxford, 1982).

——, 'War and peace in the medieval lordship of Ireland', in J. Lydon (ed.), *The English in medieval Ireland* (Dublin, 1984).

——, *The political development of the British Isles* (Oxford, 1990).

——, 'Military service in the lordship of Ireland', in Bartlett and McKay (ed.), *Medieval frontier societies* (Oxford, 1989).

——, 'Two kings in Leinster: the crown and the MicMhurchadha in the fourteenth century', in Barry, et al. (ed.), *Colony and frontier in medieval Ireland*.

——, 'The defence of the English lordship, 1250–1450', in Barlett and Jeffrey (ed.), *A military history of Ireland*.

——, *Ireland and Britain, 1170–1450* (London, 1998).

——, 'The justiciar and the murder of the MacMurroughs in 1282', in R. Frame (ed.), *Ireland and Britain, 1170–1450* (London, 1998).

——, 'English officials and Irish chiefs in the fourteenth century', in R. Frame (ed.), *Ireland and Britain, 1170–1450* (London, 1998).

Fraser, A., *Mary, queen of Scots* (London, 1970).

Gilbert, J., *A history of the city of Dublin*, i (Dublin, 1854).

——, *A history of the Irish Confederation and the war in Ireland*, i (Dublin, 1882).

Glasscock, R., *Moated sites and deserted boroughs and villages: two neglected aspects of Anglo–Norman settlement in Ireland*. Belfast (1970).

——, 'Land and people c.1300', in A. Cosgrove (ed.), *NHI*, ii (Oxford, 1987).

Grant, N., *The Campbells of Argyll* (London, 1975).

Graves, J. and Hore, H.F. (ed.), *The social state of southern and eastern counties in the sixteenth century* (Dublin, 1870).

Graves, J., 'Original documents of the MacMurroughs', *JRSAI*, 6 (1883/4).

Graham, B., 'Medieval settlements in Co. Meath', *Riocht na Midhe*, 5, no. 4 (1974).

Griffith, M., 'The council in Ireland 1399–1452', BLitt thesis, University of Oxford, no date given. Preserved in the postgraduate library of the Medieval History Department of Trinity College.

Griffith, M., 'The Talbot-Ormond struggle for control of the Anglo-Irish government 1414–1447', *IHS*, ii (1941).

Griffiths, R., *The reign of Henry VI, the exercise of royal authority 1422–1461* (London, 1961).

Gimble, I., *The Harrington family* (London, 1957).

Gwynn, A., 'The diocese of Limerick in the twelfth century', *N. Munster Antiq Jn*, v, nos 2–3 (1946–7).

——, 'Edward I and the proposed purchase of English common law for the Irish c.1276–80', *Transactions of the Royal Historical Society*, 5th Series, x (1960).

——, *The Irish church in the eleventh and twelfth centuries* (Dublin, 1992).

Hadfield A. and Maley, W. (ed.), E. Spenser, *A view of the state of Ireland* (Oxford, 1997).

Hagan, J. (ed.), 'Miscellanea Vaticano-Hibernica', *Archivum Hibernicum*, 7 (1918–21).

Hamilton, G., 'Fiacha MacAodha Uí Bhroin and Domhnall Spainneach Caomhanach', *JRSAI*, 5, 6th Series (1915).

Hand, G., *English law in Ireland 1290–1324* (Cambridge, 1967).

Hannigan, K. and Nolan, W. (ed.), *Wicklow: history and society* (Dublin, 1994).

Harrison, S., 'The lordship of Arklow, c.800–1461'. BA thesis, University of Dublin, 1993.

Hayes-McCoy, G., 'Strategy and tactics in Irish warfare, 1593–1601', *IHS*, 2, no. 7 (March, 1941).

Holton, K., 'Medieval Cloncurry', *Riocht na Midhe*, 9, no.3 (1997).

Hore, H (ed.), 'The rental book of Gerald Fitzgerald, ninth earl of Kildare, begun 1518', *JRSAI*, 4, (1864).

Hore, P., *The history of the town and county of Wexford* (London, 1900).

——, *The history of the town and county of Wexford* (London, 1911).

Hughes, J., 'The fall of the Clan Kavanagh', *JRSAI*, 11, part 2 (1873).

Johnston, D., 'Richard II and the submissions of Gaelic Ireland', *IHS*, 22 no. 85 (1980).

——, 'The interim years: Richard II and Ireland, 1395–1399', in J. Lydon (ed.), *England and Ireland in the middle ages* (Dublin, 1981).

Johnson, P., *Duke Richard of York, 1411–1460* (Oxford, 1988).

Joynt, M (ed.), 'Echtra Mac Echach Mugmedoin', *Eriu*, 4 (1907–10).

Kelleher, J., 'Mac Anmchaid Lebroir', *Eriu*, 42 (Dublin, 1991).

Knecht, R., *Renaissance warrior & prince: the reign of Francis I* (Cambridge, 1994).

Lane, P. and Nolan, W. (ed.), *Laois: history and society* (Dublin, 1999).

Lawlor, H., 'Calendar of the Liber Ruber of the diocese of Ossory', *PRIA*, 27 (C) (1908).

Leask, H., 'A cenotaph of Strongbow's daughter at New Ross, Co. Wexford', *JRSAI*, 78, part 1 (1948).

Le Fanu, T., 'The royal forest of Glencree', *JRSAI*, 23 (1893).

Lennon, C., 'The counter reformation in Ireland, 1542–1641', in Brady and Gillespie (ed.), *Natives and newcomers*.

——, *The lords of Dublin in the age of reformation* (Dublin, 1989).

——, *Sixteenth century Ireland: the incomplete conquest* (Dublin, 1995).

Limm, P., *The Dutch revolt, 1559–1648* (London, 1997).

Lodge, J., *The peerage of Ireland, or a genealogical history of the present nobility of the kingdom*, 4 vols. (Dublin, 1754).

Long, H., 'Three settlements of Gaelic Wicklow 1169–1600', in Hannigan and Nolan (ed.), *Wicklow: history and society*.

Lydon, J., 'The hobelar: an Irish contribution to mediaeval warfare', *Ir. Sword*, ii (1954–6).

——, *The lordship of Ireland* (Dublin, 1972; new edition, Dublin 2003).

——, 'Richard II's expeditions to Ireland', *JRSAI*, 93 (1963).

——, 'The expansion and consolidation of the colony, 1215–54', in A. Cosgrove (ed.), *NHI*, ii (Oxford, 1987).

——, 'The years of crisis, 1254–1315', in A. Cosgrove (ed.), *NHI*, ii (Oxford, 1993).

——, 'A land of war', in A. Cosgrove (ed.), *NHI*, ii (Oxford, 1993).

——, 'Medieval Wicklow, a land of war', in Hannigan and Nolan (ed.), *Wicklow: history and society*.

—— (ed.), *Law and disorder in thirteenth-century Ireland* (Dublin, 1997).

——, *The making of Ireland* (London, 1998).

Lynch, M., *Scotland, a new history*, (London, 1992).

Lyons, M., 'Manorial administration and the manorial economy in Ireland c.1200–1377', PhD thesis, University of Dublin, 1984.

Lyons, M., *Gearoid Óg Fitzgerald* (Dundalk, 1998).

MacAirt, S., (ed.), *An Leabhar Branach* (Dublin, 1944).

MacCarthy, B., 'The riddle of Rose O'Toole', in S. Pender (ed.), *Feilscribhinn Torna* (Cork, 1947).

MacCarthy, E., 'The O'Byrnes of Wicklow', in *Duffy's Hibernian Magazine* (July, 1860).

MacEiteagain, D., 'The renaissance and the Great Ó Domhnaill, prince of Tír Chonaill 1505–1537', MA thesis, University College Dublin, 1994.

MacFarlane, L., *William Elphinstone and the kingdom of Scotland, 1431–1514* (Aberdeen, 1995).

MacNeill, E., *Celtic Ireland* (Dublin, 1981).

MacShamhráin, A., 'The Uí Muiredaig and the abbacy of Glendalough in the eleventh to thirteenth centuries', *Cambridge Medieval Celtic Studies*, 25 (1993).

——, *Church and polity in pre-Norman Ireland: the case of Glendalough* (Maynooth, 1996).

Martin, F., 'Diarmait MacMurchadha and the coming of the Anglo-Normans', in A. Cosgrove (ed.), *NHI*, ii (Oxford, 1987).

——, 'Murder in a monastery, 1379', in G. MacNiocaill and P. Wallace (ed.), *Keimelia* (Galway, 1988).

——, 'Allies and an overlord, 1169–72, in A. Cosgrove (ed.) *NHI*, ii (Oxford, 1993).

——, 'Overlord becomes feudal lord, 1172–85', in A. Cosgrove (ed.), *NHI*, ii (Oxford, 1993).

——, 'John, lord of Ireland, 1185–1216', in A. Cosgrove (ed.) *NHI*, ii (Oxford, 1993).

Matthew, E., 'The governing of the Lancastrian lordship of Ireland in the time of James Butler, fourth earl of Ormond *c*.1420–52', PhD thesis, University of Durham 1994.

McCabe, R., 'The fate of Irena: Spenser and political violence', in P. Coughlan (ed.), *Spenser and Ireland: an interdisciplinary perspective* (Cork, 1989).

McCorristine, L., *The revolt of Silken Thomas: a challenge to Henry VIII* (Dublin, 1987).

McGovern, A., 'Church and polity in pre-Norman Ireland: the case of Glendalough', PhD thesis, University of Dublin, 1994.

McKenna, E., 'Political role for women in medieval Ireland', in C. Meek and K. Simms (ed.), *The fragility of her sex* (Dublin, 1996).

McNeill, T., *Castles in Ireland* (Routledge, 1997).

Meenan, R., 'Deserted medieval villages of Westmeath', MLitt thesis, University of Dublin, 1985.

Miller, H., *Henry VIII and the English nobility* (London, 1986).

Millet, B., *The Irish Franciscans, 1651–1656* (Rome, 1964).

——, 'The friars minor in Co. Wicklow Ireland (1260–1982), *Archivum Franciscanum Historicum*, 77 (1984).

Mills, J., 'Accounts of the earl of Norfolk's estates in Ireland, 1279–1294', *JRSAI*, 22., part.1 (1892).

——, 'The Norman settlement in Leinster – the cantreds near Dublin', *JRSAI*, 24, (1894).

Moore, D., *English action, Irish reactions: the MacMurrough-Kavanaghs, 1530s–1630,* Maynooth Historical Series, no. 4 (1987).

Morgan. H., 'Extradition and treason-trial of a Gaelic lord: the case of Brian O'Rourke', *Ir. Jurist*, xxii (1987).

——, 'Tom Lee: the posing peacemaker', B. Bradshaw, A. Hadfield and W. Maley (ed.), *Representing Ireland: literature and the origins of conflict, 1534–1660* (Cambridge, 1993).

——, *Tyrone's Rebellion* (London, 1999).

——, 'Perrot's poison plot', in C. O'Brien (ed.), *Feagh McHugh O'Byrne.*

Murray, J., 'Archbishop Alen, Tudor reform and the Kildare rebellion', *PRIA*, 89 (C) (1989).

Murtagh, D., 'The Anglo-Norman earthworks of Kildare, 1169–1350', PhD thesis, University of Dublin, 1993.

Ní Bhrolchain, M., 'The Prose Banshenchas', PhD thesis, University College Galway, 1981.

Nic Ghiollamhaith, A., 'Kings and vassals in later medieval Ireland: the Uí Bhriain and the MicConmara in the fourteenth century', in Barry, et al. (ed.), *Colony and frontier in medieval Ireland.*

Nicholls, K.W, 'Miscellanea counties Carlow and Wicklow', *Dinnseánchas* 4/2 (Dublin, 1970).

——, 'Rectory, vicarage and parish in western Irish diocese', *JRSAI*, 101 (1971).

——, *Gaelic and gaelicised Ireland* (Dublin, 1972).

——, 'The Kavanaghs 1400–1700', *Ir. Geneal.*, 5, nos 4 (1977) and 6 (1979); 6, nos 2 (1981).

——, 'Anglo-French Ireland and after', *Peritia*, 1 (1982).

——, 'Late medieval Irish annals', *Peritia*, 2 (1983).

——, 'Land of the Leinstermen', *Peritia*, 3 (1984).

——, 'Medieval Irish dynasties: three topographical notes', *Peritia*, 5 (1986).

——, 'Gaelic society and economy', in A. Cosgrove (ed.), *NHI*, ii (Oxford, 1987).

——, 'The lordship of the Byrnes' Country and the rise of the house of Ballinacor', given as part of the Feagh McHugh O'Byrne Quartercentenary lecture programme before the members of Rathdrum Historical Society on 9 September 1996.

——, 'Crioch Branach: the O'Byrnes and their country', in C. O'Brien (ed.), *Feagh McHugh O'Byrne*.

——, 'The genealogy of the O'Byrnes of Ranelagh', in C. O'Brien (ed.), *Feagh McHugh O'Byrne*.

——, 'The O'Byrne sept of Knockrath', in C. O'Brien (ed.), *Feagh McHugh O'Byrne*.

——, 'Some O'Byrne genealogical charts', in C. O'Brien (ed.), *Feagh McHugh O'Byrne*.

Nicholson, R., 'An Irish expedition to Scotland in 1335', *IHS*, 13, no. 51 (March, 1963).

Nicholson, R., *Scotland: the later middle ages* (Edinburgh, 1974).

Nolan, W. and O'Neill, T. (ed.), *Offaly: history and Society* (Dublin, 1998).

O'Brien, C., 'The Byrnes of Ballymanus', in Hannigan and Nolan (ed.), *Wicklow: history and society*.

—— (ed.), *Feagh McHugh O'Byrne*.

——, 'The Byrnes of Ballymanus and the Gabhal Raghnaill connection', in C. O'Brien (ed.), *Feagh McHugh O'Byrne*.

——, 'Feagh McHugh O'Byrne: firebrand of the Wicklow Mountains', *History Ireland*, 8, no. 1 (Spring, 2000).

O'Byrne, [—], *Historical reminiscences of the O'Byrnes, O'Tooles, O'Kavanaghs and other Irish chieftains* (London, 1843).

O'Byrne, E., 'The origins of the Uí Bhroin of Wicklow and their lordship to 1434', MPhil thesis, University of Dublin, 1996.

——, 'War, politics and the Irish of Leinster – 1156–1606', 2 vols, PhD thesis, University of Dublin, 2001.

——, 'The rise of the Gabhal Raghnaill', in C. O'Brien (ed.), *Feagh McHugh O'Byrne*.

——, 'The battle of Glenmalure, 25 August 1580', in C. O'Brien (ed.), *Feagh McHugh O'Byrne*.

——, 'The trend in warfare in Gaelic Leinster', *Ir. Sword*, 22, no. 88 (2000).

Ó Cléirigh, C., 'John fitzThomas, fifth lord of Offaly and first earl of Kildare, 1287–1316', PhD thesis, University of Dublin, 1996.

Ó Cléirigh, C., 'The O'Connor Faly lordship of Offaly, 1395–1513', *JRSAI*, 96 (1996).

——, 'The problems of defence: a regional case-study', in J. Lydon (ed.), *Law and disorder in thirteenth-century Ireland*.

——, 'The impact of the Anglo-Normans in Laois', in Lane and Nolan (ed.), *Laois: history and society*.

O'Connor, E., 'The rebellion of James Eustace, Viscount Baltinglass III', MA thesis, University of Maynooth, 1989.

O'Conor, K., *The archaeology of medieval rural settlement in Ireland* (RIA, Dublin, 1998).

——, 'Anglo-Norman castles in Co. Laois', in Lane and Nolan (ed.), *Laois: history and society*.

Ó Corrain, D., 'The career of Diarmait mac Máel na mbo', part 1, *Old Wexford Soc. Jn.*, 3 (1970–1); part 2, idem, 4 (1972–3).

——, 'Irish regnal succession: a reappraisal', *Studia Hibernica*, 11 (1971).

——, *Ireland before the Normans* (Dublin, 1972).

——, The Uí Cheinnselaig kingdom of Leinster, 1072–1126', part 1, *Old Wexford Soc. Jn.*, 5 (1974–75); idem, part 2, idem, 6 (1976–7).

Ó Cuiv, B., 'A fragment of the Irish annals', *Celticia*, 14 (1981).

——, 'A poem composed for Cathal Cróibhdhearg O'Conchobhair', *Eriu*, 34 (1983).

——, 'Personal names as an indicator of relations between native Irish and settlers in the Viking period', J. Bradley (ed.), *Settlement and society in medieval Ireland*.

O'Donovan, J., *The tribes and territories of ancient Ossory* (Dublin, 1851).

O'Dwyer, B., *The conspiracy of Mellifont, 1216–1231* (Dublin, 1970).

Ó Floinn, R., 'Clonmacnoise: art and patronage in the early medieval period', in C. Burke (ed.), *From the Isles of the North* (1990).

O'Hart. J., *Irish pedigrees*, i (Boston, 1989).

O'Loan, J., 'The manor of Cloncurry Co. Kildare and the feudal system of land in Ireland', *Dep. Agric. Jn.*, 58 (1961).

Orpen, G.H, *Ireland under the Normans*, 4 vols (Oxford, 1911 and 1920).

——, *The song of Dermot and the earl* (Oxford, 1892).

O'Rourke, B., 'English policy: the response of the junior O'Byrnes of Gabhal Raghnaill, 1530–1620s' MA thesis, University of Maynooth, 1992.

O'Sullivan Beare, P., *Ireland under Elizabeth*, ed. M. Byrne (Dublin, 1903).

O'Toole, P., *History of the Clan O'Toole and the Leinster septs* (Dublin, 1890).

Otway-Ruthven, A.J, 'The request of the Irish for English law, 1277–80', *IHS*, 6, no. 24 (1949).

——, 'The native Irish and English law in medieval Ireland', *IHS*, 7, no. 25 (March, 1950).

——, 'The medieval county of Kildare', *IHS*, 11, no. 49 (March, 1959)

——, 'Knight's fees in Kildare, Leix and Offaly', *JRSAI*, 91 (1961).

——, 'The character of Norman settlement in Ireland', *Historical Studies*, 5 (London, 1965).

——, 'Ireland in the 1350s: Sir Thomas de Rokeby and his successors', *JRSAI*, 97, part 1 (1967).

——, 'The partition of the De Verdon lands in Ireland in 1332', *PRIA*, 66 (C) (1968).

——, *A new history of medieval Ireland* (New York, 1993).

Palmer, W., *The problem of Ireland in Tudor foreign policy, 1485–1603* (London, 1994).

Parker, C., 'The internal frontier: defence and settlement in late medieval Ireland', in Barry, et al. (ed.), *Colony and frontier in medieval Ireland*.

Perros, H., 'Crossing the Shannon frontier: Connacht and the Anglo-Normans', in Barry, et al. (ed.), *Colony and frontier in medieval Ireland*.

Philips, J.R.S, 'Irish remonstrance of 1317: an international perspective', *IHS*, 27, no. 106 (Nov. 1990).

Price, L., 'Armed forces of Irish chiefs in the early sixteenth century', *JRSAI*, 62 (1932).

——, 'Notes on Feagh MacHugh O'Byrne', *Kildare Arch. Soc. Jn.*, 11 (1932).

——, 'The Byrnes' Country in Co. Wicklow in the sixteenth century', *JRSAI*, 63 (1933) and 66 (1936).

——, 'The case of Phelim McFeagh and the lands of Ranelagh', *JRSAI*, 73 (1943).

——, 'Placename study as applied to history', *JRSAI*, 79 (1949).

——, 'Powerscourt and the territory of Fercullen', *JRSAI*, 83 (1953),

——, *Placenames of Co. Wicklow* (Dublin, 1980).

Quinn, D., 'Anglo-Irish local government, 1485–1534', *IHS*, 1 no.7 (September, 1939).

——, 'The bills and statutes of the Irish parliaments of Henry VII and Henry VIII', *Anal. Hib.*, 10 (1941).

——, 'The early interpretation of Poynings' law, 1494–1534', *IHS*, 2, no.7 (March 1941).

——, 'Henry VIII and Ireland', *IHS*, 12, no. 48 (September, 1961).

——, 'Historical revision, Henry VIII and Ireland, 1509–34', *IHS*, 12, no. 48 (September, 1961).

——, 'Aristocratic automony, 1460–94', in A. Cosgrove (ed.), *NHI*, ii (Oxford, 1987).

——, 'The hegemony of the earls of Kildare, 1494–1520', in A. Cosgrove (ed.), *NHI*, ii (Oxford, 1987).

——, 'The re-emergence of English policy as a major factor in Irish affairs, 1520–34', in A. Cosgrove (ed.), *NHI*, ii (Oxford, 1987).

——, 'Irish Ireland and English Ireland', in A. Cosgrove (ed.), *NHI*, ii (Oxford, 1987).

Ridley, J., *Henry VIII* (London, 1984).

Ronan, M., 'Ancient churches of the deanery of Wicklow', *JRSAI*, 58 (1928).

——, 'Killadreenan and Newcastle', *JRSAI*, 63 (1933).

Sasso, C., *The Desmond rebellions, 1569–1573 and 1579–1583* (London, 1984).

Scarisbruck, J., *Henry VIII* (London, 1997).

Senior, M., *The life and times of Richard II* (London, 1981).

Seymour, St John., 'The coarb in the medieval Irish church', *PRIA*, 41 (C) (1932–34).

Sheehan, A., 'Irish towns in a period of change 1558–1625', in Brady and Gillespie (ed.), *Natives and newcomers.*

Silke, J., 'The Irish appeal of 1593 to Spain: some light on the genesis of the Nine Years War', *Ir. Ecclesiastical Record*, 5th Series, xcii (1959).

Simms, K., 'Gaelic lordships in Ulster in the later middle Ages', PhD thesis, 2 vols, University of Dublin, 1976.

Simms, K., 'Warfare in the medieval Gaelic lordships', *IHS*, 12, no. 47 (1975).

——, 'The legal position of Irishwomen in the later middle ages', *Ir. Jurist*, 10 (1975).

——, 'Guesting and feasting in Gaelic Ireland', *JRSAI*, 108 (1978).

——, *From kings to warlords* (London, 1987).

——, 'Frontiers in the Irish church – regional and cultural', in Barry, et al. (ed.), *Colony and frontier in medieval Ireland.*

——, 'Late medieval Donegal', in W. Nolan, L. Ronayne and M. Dunlevy (ed.), *Donegal: history and society* (Dublin, 1995).

——, 'Gaelic warfare in the middle ages', in Bartlett and Jeffrey (ed.), *Military history of Ireland.*

Simpson, L., 'Anglo-Irish settlement in Uí Briúin Chualann 1169–1350', in Hannigan and Nolan (ed.), *Wicklow: history and society.*

Smyth, A., *Celtic Leinster: towards a historical geography of early Irish civilisation* (Dublin, 1982).

—— 'Kings, saints and sagas', in Hannigan and Nolan (ed.), *Wicklow: history and society.*

Spenser, E., *The works of Edmund Spenser* (London, 1995).

Starkey, D., *Elizabeth* (London, 2000).

Strickland, G., 'Irish soldiers in the service of Henry VIII', *JRSAI*, 103 (1923).

Sun Tzu, *The art of war* (London, 1981).

Thornley I., (ed.), *England under the Yorkists* (London, 1920).

Todd, M., *The northern barbarians* (London, 1975).

Valkenburg, G., 'A study in diplomacy: Gerald, eleventh earl of Kildare (1525–1585)', *Kildare Arch. Soc. Jn.*, 14 (1968).

Venning, T., 'The O'Carrolls of Offaly: their relations with the Dublin authorities in the sixteenth century', in Nolan and O'Neill (ed.), *Offaly: history and society*.

Vowell, J., *The life and the times of Sir Peter Carew* (London, 1887).

Walsh, P., *Gleanings from Irish manuscripts* (Dublin, 1933).

Walton, H., 'The English of Connacht', PhD thesis, University of Dublin, 1980.

——, (ed.), *The life of Aodh Ruadh O'Donnell*, trans from the book of Lughaidh Ó Cléirigh, part 1 (ITS, 1948).

Waters, K., 'The Anglo-Irish gentry of Meath', MPhil thesis, University of Dublin, 1999.

Watt, J., *The church and the two nations in mediaeval Ireland* (Cambridge, 1970).

——, 'Gaelic polity and cultural identity', in A. Cosgrove (ed.), *NHI*, ii (Oxford, 1987).

——, 'The Anglo-Irish colony under strain, 1327–99', in A. Cosgrove (ed.), *NHI*, ii (Oxford, 1987).

Webb, J., 'The deposition of Richard II', *Archaeologia*, 20 (1824).

Whelan, K. and Nolan, W. (ed.), *Wexford: history and society* (Dublin, 1987).

Wormald, J., 'Taming the magnates', in K.J. Stringer (ed.), *Essays on the nobility of Scotland* (Edinburgh, 1985).

——, *Lords and men* (London, 1985).

Index